Social Indicators

TECHNOLOGY, SPACE, AND SOCIETY

Series Prepared by the American Academy of Arts and Sciences

GENERAL EDITORS:

Raymond A. Bauer, Harvard Graduate School of
Business Administration
Edward E. Furash, Arthur D. Little, Inc.

Social Indicators, edited by Raymond A. Bauer

*The Railroad and the Space Program: An Exploration in
Historical Analogy,* edited by Bruce Mazlish

Social Indicators

Edited by **RAYMOND A. BAUER**

THE M.I.T. PRESS
Massachusetts Institute of Technology
Cambridge, Massachusetts, and London, England

To Alice Bauer

whose long concern over social statistics,
good and bad, inspired this volume

Foreword

In this, the second volume of the series prepared by the American Academy of Arts and Sciences for the National Aeronautics and Space Administration on the impact of the space program on American society, Raymond Bauer and his colleagues examine an issue of major importance in a society increasingly dominated by rapid technological change — the need to anticipate the consequences of that change. As Professor Bauer points out in his essay, any massive technological effort, such as the space program, has effects far beyond those that were originally intended; effects that reach into every corner of our society and that cannot be anticipated with any precision or, in many instances, even at all by the agency or organization that sets them in motion. Yet, along with this increased rate of change through science and technology, there is a growing demand for more effective techniques to anticipate the results of change and for planning mechanisms that will take into account the widest possible spectrum of effects. The space program is not, of course, the unique or the sole agent of technological change in American society; NASA, however, is a pioneer among government agencies in its sensitivity to the wide-ranging nature of its effects on society and in its awareness of the need to develop methods for anticipating these effects and — if possible — bringing them under some degree of conscious control.

The substance of this volume deals with the problems and difficulties of anticipating the secondary effects of the space program; it also proposes a means by which our society can assess where we are now and where we have been, and provides a basis of anticipation — rather than prediction — of where we are going in a number of areas critical to our national welfare. The proposal for social indicators advanced by Bertram Gross and Albert Biderman suggests that our highly developed national system of economic indicators, which allows us to measure the state of our economy in considerable detail, needs to be supplemented by an equivalent set of indicators that will provide us with information on the state of our society in those areas not usually subject to quantitative measurement or within the professional domain of the economist. As Professor Bauer remarks, in many of the areas "in which social critics pass judgment, and in which policies are made, there are no yardsticks by which to know if things are getting better or worse." Such measures of social performance are all the more important in a "postindustrial" society, one in which the satisfaction of human interests and values has at least as high a priority as the pursuit of economic goals. The development of a system of social indicators and accounting is a subject of real interest to the Johnson administration; NASA, with its far-sighted concern with what it is setting in motion on earth as well as on the moon, deserves commendation for its contribution to the discussion.

We are indebted to NASA for providing the support for this study under Grant NSg-253-62 and for the independence of scholarly inquiry which allowed us to challenge accepted notions and to range into many areas which are not related to the primary mission of NASA.

EARL P. STEVENSON
Chairman, Committee on Space
American Academy of Arts and Sciences

Preface
A Historial Note on Social Indicators

Although initiated as part of an effort to appraise the social impact of outer space exploration, the focus of this volume is nothing less than "the entire set of social indicators used in our society."[1]

If I were not myself a contributor to this volume, I should be tempted to herald it as a major contribution to man's efforts to find out where he has been, where he is, and where he is going.

In my role as commentator on the entire volume, however, it is more appropriate to point out its historic roots, thereby emphasizing continuity as well as discontinuity.

First, this volume is a continuation of the great information-gathering tradition of Western civilization, particularly of the United States.

Second, it is a symptom of a widespread rebellion against what has been called the "economic philistinism" of the U.S. government's present statistical establishment.

Third, as with all proposals that involve going beyond established practices, the book will inevitably produce misunderstandings among both supporters and adversaries.

Finally, from a still broader viewpoint, it may be regarded as a humanist effort to develop more open spaces (not merely on the moon or beyond) in the minds of people on this planet.

The significance of these points is partially suggested by the fact that the ideas generated by its production have already moved more rapidly than the processes of final drafting and printing. Some of the basic proposals and viewpoints contained in it are already being considered by the President and Vice-President of the United States and by national leaders in France, India, Canada, and England. Drafts of various chapters have been carefully studied by officials of the United Nations, and previews have appeared in popular articles. As a result, new research efforts have already been stimulated in both government and academe.

[1] Raymond A. Bauer, Chapter 1.

Let me now touch briefly upon each of the four points mentioned above.

The Bible, the Constitution, and "Economic Indicators"

In the long history of Western civilization progress is repeatedly associated with efforts to obtain new kinds of information. Thus, in the Old Testament, Joseph's forecast of the seven fat years and the seven lean years was based upon an interpretation of Pharaoh's dream. Yet, it led to a careful measurement of all the lands in Egypt, so that the corn produced by one-fifth of the land could be stored in Joseph's "ever-normal granary."[2] Shortly after the Hebrews left Egypt, the Lord commanded Moses to take the first recorded census. A major purpose was to count "all that were able to go forth to war."[3] Another purpose was to determine the basis of taxation. As governments grew in size and scope, census operations became increasingly significant. We learn from the New Testament that Mary and Joseph went to Bethlehem for enumeration purposes. Because all the inns were filled with people waiting to be counted, they had to stay overnight in a stable.

During the Middle Ages, as Biderman points out in Chapter 2, the Latin phrase *ratio status* (the predecessor of the word "statistics") was used to refer to the factual study of politics and government. With the Renaissance and the Enlightenment, the idea of number was freed from the classical Euclidean confines of spatial boundaries and directly perceived magnitudes. Descartes and Leibniz opened up new worlds of points, functions, transformations, the infinitesimal calculus, and infinity. Western civilization entered an era in which time was measured out by mechanical clocks[4] but in which the prime symbol was pure and limitless space. Western political leaders and intellectuals started the endless process of collecting information on the "states of nations." As Biderman points out, the term *statistic* was first coined in German to refer to "the political science of the several countries." It first appeared in English in a 1770 translation from the German.

In the United States, the Founding Fathers — led by enthusiasts of the Enlightenment — wrote a constitution that was, in the words

---

[2] *Genesis*, XLI.

[3] *Numbers*, I.

[4] As one contemplates the long history of tower clocks and pocket watches in Europe one cannot help but wonder whether modernization (which seems to require a certain approach to temporal indicators) would not be advanced in the villages of Asia and Africa by a combined program of watchtowers and wristwatches.

of the French statistician Moreau de Jonnes, "without parallel in
all history." The reference was to the provisions for a decennial
census in Article I, Section 2. As Moreau de Jonnes pointed out
in wonderment, this was a phenomenon of "a people who instituted
the statistics of the country on the very day when they founded
their government and regulated by the same instrument the census
of inhabitants, their civil and political rights and the destinies of
the nation."[5] It is also interesting to note that James Madison and
Thomas Jefferson both took quick steps to have the constitutional
mandate extended through legislative interpretation. Madison was
"successful in 1790 in getting Congress to break down the 'Free
White Male' population into '16 years and over' and '16 years and
younger' — a category not required for the Constitutional enumeration, but certainly valuable for a new nation ready to start about
its business." Jefferson went still further. In 1800, as President of
the American Philosophical Society, he asked Congress for a further
breakdown of population "by age, by native-born and foreign-born,
by occupation (including 'paupers')." But, as often happens with
Presidents and intellectuals who breed ideas before their time,
Jefferson was turned down. His proposed breakdowns were not
included in a federal census until twenty years later.[6]

But Moreau de Jonnes, interested primarily in the *production* of
statistics, did not notice the Constitutional provision that touches
upon their *distribution* as well. Article II, Section 3, provides that
the President "shall from time to time give to the Congress information of the state of the Union." The framers of the Constitution
hereby recognized the informational function of government, one
that has until recently been neglected by political scientists. They
sensed the power — for good or evil — of the Presidency as a
disseminator of information. They saw the political significance of
information being made available to Congress rather than being
carefully guarded by executive officials.

As Biderman points out, Presidents have tended to include more
and more statistical information in their State of the Union messages. But these messages themselves are no longer single documents. They are part of a remarkably sophisticated and rapidly
evolving information system operating at the pinnacle of government. The State of the Union message is now closely integrated
with two back-up messages: the *Budget Messages*, started under

---

[5] Quoted in Ben J. Wattenberg, *This U.S.A.* (New York: Doubleday & Company, Inc., 1965), pp. 13–14.
[6] Ibid., pp. 15–16.

the Budget and Accounting Act of 1921, and the *Economic Report,* set up by the Employment Act of 1946. This trio is followed by a long series of fact-packed Presidential messages and reports, including the annual *Manpower Report* (under the Manpower Development and Training Act of 1962). Then there are scores of annual reports of the cabinet departments and independent agencies. These contain an almost unbelievable wealth of detailed data. Finally, there is the modern version of the farmers' almanac, *The Statistical Abstract of the United States.*

Although there are elements of *disorder* in this vast output of information, the most impressing thing about it is the *order* established by "one of the great social inventions of the modern world," national economic accounting. As I explain in Chapter 3, national economic accounting plays important roles, both analytical and social, in modern society. During the twenty-year period from 1946 to 1966 these roles have increased in significance. This increase is best illustrated by the importance of the *Economic Report of the President,* with the accompanying detailed report of the Council of Economic Advisers. Structured around the national income accounts, this report finds its way to the desks of the major elites of the country. Thus, in 1965, in addition to the free copies sent to members of Congress, government officials, the press, and depositary libraries, the Superintendent of Documents sold more than fifty thousand copies of the *Economic Report,* and this figure has risen every year. In addition, the Council's monthly *Economic Indicators,* a carefully organized set of thirty-seven charts with tables, has become the basis whereby people "in the know" keep their fingers on the pulse of the economy.

From "Economy" to "Society"

The Great Society looks beyond the prospects of abundance to the problems of abundance. . . . Everywhere there is growth and movement, activity and change. But where is the place for man? . . . The task of the Great Society is to ensure our people the environment, the capacities, and the social structures which will give them a meaningful chance to pursue their individual happiness. . . . Thus the Great Society is concerned not with how much, but how good — not with the quantity of our goods but the quality of our lives.[7]

As suggested in Chapter 3, President Johnson's "Great Society" program is responsive to the new political situation created by the

[7] Richard N. Goodwin, address to visiting foreign students at the District of Columbia Armory, July 20, 1965.

transformation of an advanced industrial society into the world's first example of "postindustrialism."

Yet during the initial processes of transformation, it is interesting to note, both the President and his key advisers are forced to rely upon concepts and data that have decreasing relevance to the new national goals. If we examine the President's major policy documents, particularly the *Economic Report* and the *Budget Message*, we find practically no information whatsoever on "social structures." We find that the major indicators deal not with how good but how much, not with the quality of our lives but rather with the quantity of goods and dollars. This continuation of "economic Philistinism" is exacerbated by the increasing emphasis upon "cost-benefit analysis" (often used as a way of releasing resources for Great Society programs), operating on the premise that any meaningful benefits from government programs can be expressed in dollars and cents.

Fortunately, there has long been a tradition of trying to obtain information on the society as a whole, not merely on that part of society called the "economy." One of the first efforts along these lines was made by President Hoover's Research Committee on Social Trends, whose influential report, *Recent Social Trends in the United States*, was published in 1943. Considerable influence in this direction was also exercised by the expert committee appointed by the Social Science Research Council and the American Statistical Association. During the subsequent quarter century, great progress was made in carrying out the proposals not only of this expert committee but of a host of specialized committees subsequently established under the Budget Bureau's office of statistical standards. Under the pressure of complex economic problems associated with prewar depression, wartime mobilization, and postwar reconversion, most of the new statistical indicators turned out to be economic in character. This, of course, is what made it possible to produce increasingly sophisticated economic reports and economic indicators. These developments unquestionably contributed — although to an extent that cannot be statistically measured — to the avoidance of the widely anticipated postwar depression and the subsequent "miracle" of sustained economic growth in the 1960's.

A major broadening step was undertaken at the beginning of the Kennedy administration when Wilbur J. Cohen (now Undersecretary of Health, Education and Welfare) initiated the annual HEW *Trends* and the monthly HEW *Indicators*. These valuable publications are becoming increasingly comprehensive, intensive, and sophisticated. They may one day parallel the *Economic Report* and *Economic Indicators*. Indeed, a new Presidential mandate to move more rapidly in this direction has recently been announced:

Through the programs entrusted to its care, the Department of Health, Education and Welfare exercises continuing concern for the social well-being of all our people. Already, as I have indicated in this message, it has become possible to set ambitious goals for the future.

To improve our ability to chart our progress, I have asked the Secretary to establish within his office the resources to develop the necessary social statistics and indicators to supplement those prepared by the Bureau of Labor Statistics and the Council of Economic Advisers. With these yardsticks, we can better measure the distance we have come and plan for the way ahead.[8]

In still broader terms President Johnson has instituted a new "Planning-Programing-Budgeting System" requiring every government agency to relate carefully selected information on the cost of inputs to outputs of service (including financial aid, advice, and regulation) provided by government and private programs, and appraise them in terms of the resulting benefits provided, directly or indirectly, to various beneficiaries. The new interest in information on direct and indirect benefits (and disbenefits) to different groups or beneficiaries is already leading to a search for better social indicators.

A call for more ambitious government action has been issued by the National Commission on Technology, Automation and Economic Progress. The Commission's final report points out that our ability to chart social change has lagged seriously behind our ability to measure economic change. Without reservations the members of the Commission called unanimously for some system of social accounts that would broaden our concept of costs and benefits and put economic accounting into a larger framework. Specific emphasis was placed on the measurement of the utilization of human resources in four areas:

1. The measurement of social costs and net returns of innovations.

2. The measurement of social ills (e.g., crime, family disruption).

[8] President Lyndon B. Johnson, Message to the Congress on domestic health and education, March 1, 1966.

3. The creation of "performance budgets" in areas of defined social needs (e.g., housing, education, and welfare).

4. Indicators of economic opportunity and social mobility.[9]

Outside of government all sorts of pioneering ventures are beginning to get under way. At the Russell Sage Foundation, Eleanor Sheldon and Wilbert Moore are fashioning new techniques for "monitoring social change" in selected fields. Syracuse University's Maxwell School, in cooperation with the Newhouse Communications Center, will bring out next year a special volume of *The Annals* of the American Academy of Political and Social Science on "Social Goals and Indicators for a Great Society." This volume will deal with such vital subjects as the reduction of poverty, freedom from discrimination, social and political participation, civil liberties and the administration of justice, art and culture, employment and leisure, learning and education, health and well-being, the production of knowledge, the natural environment, the urban environment, and the mass media.

The present volume, however, is the first occasion on which the entire field has been surveyed and a comprehensive set of proposals, based upon careful analysis, has been developed. It may well be expected to contribute not only to the acceleration of the developments referred to but to periodic reviews of progress made toward the development and use of social indicators.

Inevitable Misunderstandings

Because the subject is complex and the treatment somewhat sophisticated, the contents of this volume are bound to be misunderstood. In fact, each author surely expects the misunderstandings to grow in direct proportion to the progress made in developing social indicators; nonetheless, there is some merit in warning against the most obvious ones.

The first misunderstanding is the idea that in advocating *social* indicators, the authors are depreciating the value of *economic* indicators. Yet the distinction between *economic* and *social* — while having many uses — cannot be carried too far. Although economic information deals completely with nothing, it tends to touch everything, often significantly. There are few social ends to which scarce economic resources do not need to be allocated. Moreover, creative economists are among the most effective opponents of "economic

[9] Report of National Commission on Technology, Automation and Economic Progress (Washington, D. C.: Government Printing Office, January 1966).

Philistinism." They have repeatedly ventured beyond the more narrow confines of traditional economic analysis and have developed new economic measures in such traditionally *social* fields as income distribution, education, and health. Still more important, as stated in a penetrating U.N. report, *Methods of Determining Social Allocations*, rational policy decisions require "the development of a comprehensive set of criteria that will take account of both economic and social considerations, not by forcing the one kind into the mould of the other, but by integrating them at a higher level of abstraction."[10] Indeed, "social accounting" may well be regarded as referring to this very integration at a higher level of abstraction. In this context "social" may be taken to mean "societal" or "pertaining to the social system." Social accounting then refers to an ordered set of relevant indicators, without particular reference to how they may have been traditionally labeled.

Second, some people will get the impression that the authors of the volume are attacking the use of statistics. After all, considerable attention is given to the inaccuracy of much statistical data, built-in distortions, widespread misinterpretations, and increasing manipulability. Almost every chapter is based upon the well-supported premise that we now live in an era in which it is scarcely worth while to lie without statistics. Yet the skepticism pervading the volume is also based upon the premise that better information on the quality of life requires improvements in both the quantity and the quality of statistics. The emphasis is placed upon the need for a greater variety of regularly collected data and special *ad hoc* inquiries and for significant improvements in the way in which data are collected, processed, interpreted, and used. Indeed, it is recognized that at the present state of the art, the first efforts to collect new kinds of data will be seriously defective. Here the conclusion seems to be that rather than do nothing it is preferable to start out with bad data, warn everyone about the defects and limitations, and aim at gradual 'improvement through use."

Third, still more people may get the impression that in asking for social indicators the authors are guilty of the "fallacy of misplaced concreteness" and are trying to extend the modern "numbers game" to areas still untouched by the manipulations of statisticians. Others may feel that if the viewpoint of the book were widely adopted,

---

[10] Report of the Secretary-General to the Sixteenth Session of the Social Commission, Economic and Social Council, *Methods of Determining Social Allocation* (March 31, 1965), p. 10.

a second-order consequence — whether the authors foresee it or not — would be to "dehumanize" life by reducing more and more of human values to "cold statistics." So far as the book's intent is concerned, this would be a clear-cut example of misunderstanding. Social indicators may be "soft" as well as "hard," qualitative as well as quantitative, ordinal as well as cardinal quantities, but whether statistical or not, they are not necessarily "cold." No matter what we do, all of them — as suggested by Biderman in Chapter 2 — will be used by human beings in the heat of human combat as vindicators, indictors, and certifiers. Nor is it at all clear that "dehumanization" would necessarily be promoted if our information on culture and the enjoyment of human rights became as good as that on cows and corporate profits.

As one of the authors, however, I must confess that in favoring greater awareness of second-order consequences, we have not fully explored the second-order consequences of such awareness. Perhaps *we* are the ones who misunderstand. But to throw more light on this question, we need something more than personal expressions of humanistic intent, deferential obeisance to something called "human values," and routinized attacks on the tendencies toward dehumanization in modern society. We need more efforts to understand our society, efforts based upon the collection and interpretation of whatever information may be relevant. This, of course, is exactly what we are advocating. The view that "dehumanization" would be the result of a system of social indicators is in itself a second-order consequence of the program that we are advocating. If not a misunderstanding, it is a prophetic warning, a warning that — by alerting us to dangers in the situation — may hopefully serve as a self-defeating prophecy.

From Limited to Broader Agendas

The economist, Kenneth E. Boulding, has recently issued the following warning:

There seems to be a fundamental disposition in mankind to limit agenda, often quite arbitrarily, perhaps because of our fears of information overload. We all suffer in some degree from agoraphobia, that is, the *fear of open spaces*, especially *open spaces* in the mind. As a result, we all tend to retreat into the cosy closed spaces of limited agendas and responsibilities, into tribalism, nationalism, and religious and political sectarianism and dogmatism. . . . It is our attempt to defend ourselves against information overload which forces us into malevolence, prisoners' dilemmas, arms races, price wars, class wars, schisms, feuds and divorces. . . .[11]

It is interesting to note that Boulding warns particularly that "the quantification of value functions into value indices, whether this is money or whether it is more subtle and complicated measures of payoff, introduces elements of ethical danger into the decision-making process, simply because the clarity and apparent objectivity of quantitatively measurable subordinate goals can easily lead to a failure to bear in mind that they are subordinate." He illustrates the point by referring to profit-and-loss bookkeeping, which can lead businessmen to neglect "such things, for instance, as morale, loyalty, legitimacy, and intimacy and complexity of personal relations."

Boulding's conclusion is that we need a widening of agendas, an opening up of our minds to a greater variety of information. This means combating information overload not by narrowing our sphere of attention but by improving our capacity to handle a larger variety of information. "It may be," Boulding speculates, "that the horizons of the power of ethical ideas may be substantially extended by the development of improved methods of information processing by the individual and by the organization."[12]

In my judgment, this volume supports the speculation. Indeed, the kinds of social indicators called for in it require an abandonment of the Ptolemaic perspective with which people see the world rotating around ourselves. They demand a kind of Copernican revolution through which we may better "regard our decisions as involving the total social system, and not only that part of it which revolves around our own persons."[13] It may well be that during the coming decades, as man at last escapes the confines of the earth and explores the solar system, he will at the same time discover and explore as yet unknown vistas in the human mind.

BERTRAM M. GROSS

[11] Kenneth E. Boulding, "The Ethics of Rational Decision," *Management Science, 12* (February 1966), 161–169.
[12] Ibid., p. 167.
[13] Ibid., p. 168.

Contents

1

Detection and Anticipation of Impact:
The Nature of the Task

Raymond A. Bauer

Introduction

This volume as a whole is devoted to the topic of social indicators — statistics, statistical series, and all other forms of evidence —
that enable us to assess where we stand and are going with respect
to our values and goals, and to evaluate specific programs and determine their impact. Our interest in this topic originated with the
widespread concerns and speculations expressed over the actual or
potential wide-ranging impact on our society of the program of
space exploration. If such concerns are to be taken seriously, presumably we shall want to detect and measure such effects. This
leaves us with an important question: how? That is, what yardsticks
are there or should there be for carrying out this task?

The use of evidence for social criticism is wrought with flaws,
which the public and most critics themselves are not fully aware of
and which seem to cause them little concern. Serious users of social
statistics, however, are acutely aware of large gaps in our data, and
of defects or limitations in much of the information that is available.
The writers of the various sections of this book have devoted themselves to an examination of the current state of such evidence, to
proposals for improvement in our information systems, and to a
critical examination of how information might be used to evaluate
the impacts of a federal program, such as space exploration.

Though our interest originated with the problem of detecting the
impact of the space program, the problem of measuring the impact
of a single program could not be dealt with except in the context
of the entire set of social indicators used in our society. There are
several reasons for this, but perhaps one will suffice to justify the
choice. Since there is no consensus on how wide ranging the ramifications of space exploration may be in their effect on our lives,

clearly the information system used to make such an evaluation must be broad enough to answer this question insomuch as it is important to us.

There could be two criteria for constructing such a general information system. One could be to build it to measure those effects that have specifically been postulated as stemming from the space program. I have just indicated our reasons for not following that course. Since the extent of these effects is itself the subject of debate, the system of indicators must be broader than the range of effects postulated if only to determine what the range is. The other could be to take as a point of departure those values, goals, and features of the society that we consider important in assessing the state and direction of the society. While such a general system could conceivably miss certain specific impacts of space exploration, it would nevertheless reflect those that we regard as important. At the same time, a more general system has the advantage of serving a multiplicity of purposes. A single, narrow-focus program could not economically bear the costs of a broad information system. Furthermore, a single-purpose program also has vital defects for making many of the comparisons that ought to be made. These considerations will be expanded on later.

This chapter is in itself but an introduction to the rest of this volume. Within this framework, I shall discuss the general problem of the secondary consequences of a program such as space exploration and the use of information for program evaluation, and introduce and comment on the contributions of the other authors.

Space Exploration and Social Indicators

The work of the American Academy's Committee on Space was premised on the following consideration:

> In the conduct of human affairs, our actions inevitably have second-order consequences. These consequences are, in many instances, more important than our original action.[1]

Ramifications of Technical Innovation

It has long been observed that innovations, particularly technical innovations, have consequences that ramify well beyond what was intended or anticipated. One of the more popular examples is the

---

[1] *Space Efforts and Society: A Statement of Mission and Work*, a document of The Committee on Space Efforts and Society of the American Academy of Arts and Sciences (Boston, January 1963), p. 9.

introduction of the automobile as a means of transportation. It has changed our leisure life and (allegedly) our sexual mores and practices; spawned suburban living; changed our patterns of home ownership and retail distribution; introduced the use of road building as a source of patronage; decimated the railroads; and introduced a new holiday pastime of counting death tolls. None of these events, insofar as we know, was intended, few were anticipated, and not all are desired.

The exploration of space is one of the most massive technological efforts ever deliberately undertaken. It is natural that both NASA and the society at large should be actively concerned with the wide range of impacts, both favorable and unfavorable, that may result from this program.

We are not, of course, the first persons to draw attention to the wide range of potential secondary impacts. The Brookings report of 1961[2] contained two hundred pages devoted almost entirely to informed speculation; occasionally a dozen or more potential implications were enumerated on a given page. I have tried to give a brief sampler of the sorts of impacts about which there have been speculation. They include changes in man's conception of himself and of God; almost incredible consequences of vastly expanded communications via satellite communications systems (for example, one school of thought suggests that the available TV channels would increase so much that conferences would be held with people in their offices or homes employing a conference TV network); improved short- and long-range weather forecasting; moment-to-moment surveillance of military installations throughout the world, including virtually immediate detection of hostile missile launchings; contact with beings higher, lower, or sideways from us, *or*, if there is no contact, speculation and concern over the possibility of contact; drain on our economy and military strength, *or*, stimulus to our economy and military strength; competition with the Russians, cooperation with the Russians, *or* some combination of the two; drain on skilled and scientific manpower, *or* stimulus to the development of skilled and scientific manpower; changes in attitudes toward education and toward stupidity; revolutions in medicine via new knowledge, via telemetry, new substances, and use of computers for diagnostic purposes; revolutions in data processing and retrieval (partially by using communications satellites to facili-

[2] Donald N. Michael, *Proposed Studies on the Implications of Peaceful Space Activities for Human Affairs*, a document prepared for the Brookings Institution (Washington, D. C., 1961).

tate central storage); stimulation of our system of higher education, *or* disruption of our system of higher education.

As I have indicated, technical changes have proved historically to be particularly explosive sources of second-order social, economic, and political changes that were never envisioned. This arises largely because at the beginning technical developments tend to be viewed in a rather restricted context. They are seen as an answer to an agreed problem, and tend to be judged in terms of their adequacy in solving that problem. Probably the most dramatic example of this in modern times has been the development of potent insecticides, which were only later found to have profound effects on the ecological cycles of man and beast. Similarly, there is the instance of the innocuous substitution of detergents for soap. It was scarcely anticipated that detergents would disrupt the plumbing systems of tall apartment buildings, causing waste to back up into sinks, tubs, and toilet bowls; or that streams would be contaminated to the point of destroying their fish life.

True, the phenomenon of the far-ranging consequences of technical change is recognized in principle. But in practice, as a *given* technical change is considered, it is not customary to anticipate second-order consequences. An action is often labeled "technical" to offer reassurance as to its limited implications. The very phrase "purely technical" is used to convey the notion that an action does *not* have widespread ramifications. Because a technical development is both seen and judged as an answer to a rather specific problem, there is, I contend, a strong bias against being concerned over, trying to anticipate, or even thinking about its possible wider consequences.

Furthermore, the second-order consequences, if any, of introducing a technical innovation are inevitably a matter of speculation. At best, they can be anticipated with less than certainty, and usually with considerably less probability. The solution to the technical problem, by contrast, tends to be relatively unequivocal. Detergents either dissolve grease or they do not; DDT either kills flies or it does not. Granting that the evidence for even the immediate solution of technical problems is often less than perfect, it is usually considerably firmer than the evidence for second-order consequences — in the event that those consequences are even contemplated. In addition, the yardsticks for measuring technical performance are usually more clean cut than those for evaluating the larger social ramifications.

We can see both of those factors — the greater certainty of identifying the technical results and the greater precision in measuring them — in the current social concern over the secondary consequences of automation. The ability of a given system of automation to do a job can be assessed quite cleanly, as can the increase in efficiency it produces. Against this, we have the uncertain effect on over-all employment in the economy at large, and the absence of an agreed metric for putting a value either on over-all or on structural unemployment. On what metric do we compare a given level of unemployment among unskilled, young, Negro men with a given rate of increase in productivity? How do we project such a comparison into the future, how far into the future, and on what assumptions?

Finally, technical innovations are usually seen as advances in technology in general, and therefore they are identified with progress. In a civilization that places a high value on science and technology, and places almost a supreme value on progress, it is no wonder that concern for the consequences of technological change is frequently met with the rejoinder "But you can't stand in the way of progress!" An additional culturally popular argument is that while innovation has always been greeted with doubts, Western civilization has continued to make material progress.

Obviously, there has been no absolute inhibition against our thinking about the second-order consequences of technical innovation. True, some of the most active thinking has been done by those persons who were immediately adversely affected — workers displaced by machines, homeowners displaced by highway construction, and scholars made obsolete by advances in knowledge.

It is probably accurate to say that the two groups mainly concerned with the second-order impact of technological developments have been those persons adversely affected and the scholars who studied the wide ramifications of past changes as a matter of history. It would, of course, be fatuous to assert that the introduction of technical change has gone unchallenged in Western civilization. I am only contending that there is a systematic bias against concern over second-order consequences of technical innovations.

However, this is a changing phenomenon. The reasons behind the change are many, and to some extent interrelated. It has been said that the development of nuclear weapons systems has destroyed Western faith in the inevitability of progress. Probably it is premature to make such a global judgment. But it does seem tenable to argue that the specter of nuclear war has undermined any disposition to accept technological progress as "a good thing," and has heightened the feeling that man must, at least to some extent, act to control his over-all destiny. Furthermore, the realization that even our enemies may have a common interest with us in the management of certain destructive technology may be the final step in the now almost platitudinous view of an increasingly complex and interrelated world in which any one development may have widespread consequences.

Possibly increasing affluence is in itself a facilitation of the change. Urban renewal programs increasingly include provision for aid to persons displaced by the program. Provision is made for retraining and relocating workers made unemployed by new technology. Plans are being made for repairing the ecological damage done by our use of insecticides. It cannot be said that in the past we were not or could not have been aware of such secondary problems. Nor is it enough to say that we have an increased sense of social responsibility. This increased responsibility has been expressed and listened to as it became clearer that we have the capacity to deal constructively with the second-order consequences of our actions.

At the same time, a single but widespread technological development, automation, has stimulated what may be unprecedented concern over its second-order consequences. One might well speculate on why this trend in technology has generated such apparently unparalleled interest in advance of its full impact. (For example, International Business Machines gave Harvard University $5 million to study the topic.) However, regardless of the reasons for this concern, it in turn seems to have created an environment in which further consideration of the second-order consequences of other developments is encouraged.

But perhaps at the core of the change is a revised notion of social planning, and of planning in general. And this revised view of planning stems from a new conception of social systems, and of systems in general. Interestingly, this revised model of how systems work was in itself generated out of modern science and technology.[3]

While modern technology has provided us with a new model for planning our affairs that I shall discuss shortly, the Soviet Union has done mankind the unintended service of demonstrating the bankruptcy of what has long been the prevailing notion of how man might plan and control his affairs.[4] The Soviet system of planning

[3] For a discussion of the impact of the cybernetic model on modern culture, see Harvey Brooks, "Scientific Concepts and Culture Change," *Daedalus*, 94 (Winter 1965), 63–83.

[4] For earlier and more complete statements of this position see Raymond A.

and action, as it developed under Stalin, was designed explicitly to play down the importance of second-order consequences. Specific goals were established and pursued until the accumulated difficulties that resulted piled up to the extent that some of them in turn became priority items. Any feedback of adverse consequences was dampened, again until they could no longer be ignored. As long as there was a surplus of certain resources — for instance, manpower — this approach could be used to achieve certain specific objectives, such as expansion of heavy industry. This system was also crucially dependent on the use of coercion.

But it has apparently become obvious to the post-Stalin leaders of the U.S.S.R. that, even with the use of extreme coercion, a mechanistic formula for planning and action is inoperable over the long haul. It is calculated to generate problems at least as rapidly as it solves them. Basically (and explicitly) it is founded on a simplistic social model stemming from the assumption that too great a concern for second-order consequences of one's actions inhibits one's ability to pursue primary goals. While this is a viewpoint that has an element of validity, is has been carried too far in the Soviet model of planning and action. More recently, the Soviet leaders have given indications of backing off somewhat from the idea that *rigid* forward planning is practicable. This softening of viewpoint indicates a degree of Soviet concern to anticipate and deal with consequences beyond the U.S.S.R.'s primary objectives.

At the opposite pole from the Soviet position of tight, centralized, rather long-range planning is the historic British doctrine of "muddling through." In a sense this doctrine appears to be the antithesis of planning. But note that the doctrine of muddling through is based on elaborate concern for second-order consequences of actions. It assumes that social systems and processes are very complex phenomena, and that it is impossible to determine in advance exactly what results will be created by one's actions or what difficulties will be encountered. However, the doctrine of muddling through has a contemporary look in its sensitivity to feedback from the environment, and its disposition to change tactics when the data fed back suggest that the results produced differ from those intended.

Today, the dichotomy between "planning" and "not planning" has

---

Bauer, "The implications of the succession crisis in the Soviet Union for East-West relations," *Social Problems, 1* (October 1953); and Raymond A. Bauer, Clyde Kluckhohn, and Alex Inkeles, *How the Soviet System Works* (Cambridge, Mass.: Harvard University Press, 1956), Chapters 4 and 5.

disappeared. It has disappeared in part because of strictly pragmatic considerations in that there is a consensus that certain aspects
of both national and private affairs simply must be planned ahead.
The dichotomy has also atrophied because no reasonable man acquainted with the Soviet experience would advocate the sort of total
planning that once appeared to have attractions to some people.
But the distinction between planning and not planning is most
fundamentally undermined by the dynamic model of guidance that
has come explicitly or implicitly from modern technology. The concept of cybernetics, a term coined by Norbert Wiener from the
Greek word for "steersman," is based on the notion that error is an
inherent aspect of natural, physical, and social systems. One can set
goals and make plans, but the cybernetic model demands an active
information system with sensors to determine the consequences of
actions. In addition, it demands provision for feeding this information back to decision centers and readiness to change one's behavior
in response to signals of errors being committed. Thus a sophisticated approach to planning shares some of the characteristic features of "muddling through," which has long been regarded as the
extreme of "not planning."

By and large, sensible men avoid worrying over things about
which they can do nothing. It is in this sense that I have indicated
there is an element of validity in Soviet concern that consideration
of second-order consequences would inhibit the will to pursue primary objectives. However, the greater affluence of our society, our
better comprehension of the complexity of social processes, and the
new model of planning all suggest that a wider sensitivity to a fuller
range of the consequence of one's actions is both desirable and
necessary.

This brings me to the point of this book. If our view of the planning and guiding of large-scale programs, such as the exploration of
space, demands a sensitivity to a wide range of the impacts of a
given program, this assumes that such impacts can be detected and
measured. The issue we shall raise is that of the sort of information
that would be required for a reasonably complete program evaluation, the extent to which such information is available, why it is or
is not available, how it is used, and what might be done to improve
the system.

NASA and Second-Order Consequences

Because the work of the Space Committee of the American Academy has been concerned with the second-order consequences of
space exploration, and because this volume deals with the avail-

ability or nonavailability of evidence with which to measure such impacts of the space program, various assumptions may be made by the reader as to what we think NASA should or could do about such impacts. It is therefore preferable that we make our own views clear.

The primary objectives of the space program have been set, changed, and adjusted by the country's political leadership. Regardless of how the mission of NASA, or any other agency involved in space exploration, may be defined or redefined, the program will be a massive and complex one. While much has been made of the technological aspects of the space program, the management problems may be even more formidable. Few organizations have been faced with the management of rapid growth similar to that of NASA. The obvious parallels are military organizations in wartime. But the comparison is inaccurate to start with, since peacetime military organizations are manned, trained, and organized to expand themselves into a structure that is a large version of the original core. NASA began with a core of the NACA (National Advisory Committee for Aeronautics), but had rapidly to transform itself into a new type of organization, adding new programs as it went along, and managing a web of external and internal relationships of a complex and changing nature.

In short, I wish to stress the fact that the achievement of the primary goals that have been set for NASA is in itself a very difficult job. While, anyone might, in some context, feel free to quarrel with these primary goals, we take them in this context as one of the given elements in the situation. As long as these primary goals remain unchanged, it is relatively untenable simultaneously to question the attainability of the goals, challenge the cost of the program, and demand that NASA pay serious attention to a wide range of the second-order consequences. There is a limit both to the number of problems to which a management can pay attention and the extent to which finite resources can be stretched.

Because of its drama, size, and symbolic embodiment of advanced technology, the space program has caught much public attention, and secondary consequences of the most remote sort are attributed to it. It was not unusual, for example, that a young suburban mother, in commenting on new methods of teaching mathematics in the primary schools, said, "I have a feeling it all stems from Sputnik."[5] Our own research traces the social organization of families in space-impacted communities, the demand for technical man-

[5] "New Math — a 'Tiger,'" *The Christian Science Monitor*, February 19, 1965.

power, religious beliefs, and the attitudes of businessmen, to mention a partial list. Friends and foes of the space program have commented on the diffusion or lack of diffusion of space technology to the civilian economy, the location of NASA installations, the allocation of NASA contracts, the program's effects on the educational system, the supply of scientists and technology, and so on. I have already given a brief sampler of the impacts that have been inferred.

It should be noted that many additional topics could be added to this list, and that, in one way or another, the Space Agency has already been responsive to such issues. And it should further be noted that the administrators of the NASA program have indicated on many occasions not only their cognizance of the program's many impacts beyond its primary mission, but their anxiousness for these secondary consequences to be as beneficial as possible. This was the motive, in fact, for awarding a grant to the American Academy of Arts and Sciences to study the social impact of space exploration.

At several points in our work, we consider what a total system of feedback to NASA might involve. In this volume in particular we do not face up to the practical problem of *which* of the impacts of the space program should be measured. Rather, we consider what a total information system would look like. This is not with the presumption that the present or any future administrator would contemplate such a total system. If practical decisions of selection have to be made — and they must — it is, on the whole, useful to know from what array the choices are being made.

It is characteristic of both organizations and organisms that they can respond to only a portion of the signals they get from the environment. Hopefully, the selection will be both practical and wise.

NASA has been charged with a broad primary mission — the exploration of space — with numerous related subsidiary missions. Manifestly, the administrator of NASA must give priority to feedback that affects the Agency's ability to carry out its primary mission. Since ability to execute the primary mission is affected by a wide range of concerns — including support in the various publics, Congress, and in the other branches of the administration — the impacts that bear on the primary mission are in themselves wide ranging. These extend to those actual or presumed effects that may take place in the educational system, the displacement of local businesses in land taking, and others that generate reactions bringing pressure on NASA and Congress. With these issues in mind, even a casual reading of the newspapers will reveal that NASA is already aware of, and having to deal with, a considerable number of second-order consequences of its primary mission.

What is important about the current feedback to NASA is that it comes almost entirely from groups representing organized interests. Generally speaking, an agency needs to take little direct initiative in order to *receive* such feedback — though responding may, indeed, take much energy. The difficulty with such feedback, however, is that it ordinarily comes when some interest is seen as hurt. The prudent administrator is ordinarily concerned with avoiding those occurrences. He seeks information that "feeds forward" — that is, lets him anticipate and avoid or reduce such difficulties. There are various devices for accomplishing this. One is to announce plans publicly and far enough in advance so that the various interests may express themselves.

However, even under the best of circumstances, certain consequences will not be anticipated well in advance. The highest priority in building a deliberate feedback system in the environment must be given to *the earliest possible detection or anticipation of impacts that bear on the primary mission.* In this way opportunities can be capitalized on maximally, and difficulties nipped in the bud.

The reader who grasps the full implication of what I have proposed may bridle at the idea. It implies, for example, that if the location of a new NASA installation affects two groups of citizens, only one of which is organized and vocal and can affect the progress of the NASA program, this group should get first attention. But this is no more than to say that the administrator of the space program is what he is; while, as I suggested above, any one of us may not agree with NASA's primary mission, the administrator has specifically been charged with this mission and is responsible for it.

To say that the primary mission of NASA must be given priority is probably a tautology, but it is also a necessary reminder that the administrator of any program cannot be equally responsible for *all* the second-order effects on the society. The responsible administrator will, of course, be concerned with those impacts of his actions that have no substantial repercussions on his program. He will not gratuitously undermine a local school system, even though he has no stake in either its success or failure. Nor will he be indifferent to the fate of unorganized groups that can neither help nor hinder him.

Not only is it true in general that the responsible administrator will be concerned with consequences that extend beyond those which have practical significance for his own program, but NASA itself has been specifically enjoined to conduct its program so as to maximize its beneficial effect on other national goals and programs.[6] But this concern with other aspects of the society must be tempered with administrative judgment, just as we do not expect the Commissioner of Education to assume the same degree of responsibility for the space program as he does for education.

Even if NASA had the most complete feedback system possible and the organization were aware of an exceedingly wide range of its actions, it would be a matter of judgment — difficult, but necessary — as to what range of considerations it could respond to without ceasing to be fundamentally the *Space* Agency.

Furthermore, the extent of the information system itself must be a matter of sober judgment. There are two important criteria of constraint. The first is that there is a limit to the amount of information that any single organization can process. Once that limit is exceeded, the organization will be less, rather than more, responsive to its environment, since it will be paralyzed with the burden of handling the information and incapable of acting effectively. The second constraint is that if an organization is known to go to the trouble of making itself aware of a problem, it generates the expectation that it will do something about it. Any information system that is explicitly identified with a given program ought to be constructed and operated in such a way that it does not create the impression that it is concerned with issues clearly beyond its capacity to handle.

Why these caveats? First, because we are, in this volume, considering the nature of a full set of social indicators for assessing the state of a society, as well as evaluating specific programs. This circumstance could easily lead the reader to assume that we are advocating something in the nature of a total societal information system for a single program, such as space exploration. This is not so. Second, in indicating why a total information system is neither desirable nor feasible (perhaps not even conceivable), I have tried to indicate the sort of criteria that should, and presumably would, be used both in extending such a system and in deciding on its limits. In doing this, I have hoped to attain an additional objective, and that is to communicate *why* NASA and the space program cannot be held responsible for all the affairs of the society. Any exten-

[6] Section 102(c) of the National Aeronautics and Space Act of 1958 specifies that space activities be conducted to contribute to related national activities.

sion of NASA's concern beyond social impacts that affect its primary mission in one way or another is laudable. On the other hand, what I have been saying is equally an injunction to various publics that they have a responsibility to exercise restraint in the demands they put on the space program for their own interests.

To oppose the space program per se is a legitimate position. However, to expect it to solve all our problems or not create *any* is untenable.

The Public and Second-Order Consequences

The foregoing section was involved with the range of concerns that the public might reasonably expect NASA to attend to. The responsibilities of NASA and the public are, of course, not identical. Earlier in this chapter I mentioned that the thrust of this volume is toward an over-all societal information system of social indicators. Such social trend statistics as will be discussed would, of course, always be available to administrators concerned with space exploration, and might or might not be incorporated systematically into its own information system.

However, it is assumed that interest in the social impact of programs, such as that of space exploration, is not limited to the persons directly responsible for carrying the programs out. Most of this volume is devoted to the consideration of a broad system of social indicators, generally available and presumably to be used by a wide range of parties concerned with evaluation of such programs.

This distinction between the responsibilities of the program directors and those of the public and public officials is essential for understanding that we must also think in terms of two information systems — one general and one specific — to the program to be evaluated. Not all of the elements of a general system will be pertinent to every specific program, nor will the needs of a specific program be served completely by a general system of social indicators. Parallel to this is the circumstance that all parties will not want to use the same criteria in evaluating a given program. The more general sort of system we shall discuss later makes it possible for various parties to use a fairly wide range of criteria. Thus if a given individual has some model of the economic system in which the space program is seen as affecting the flow of money in and out of the country, he will want to look at this statistic, even though few others would. He will then be free to express his conclusions as to this particular impact and its significance.

Impacts, Indicators, and Inferences

There is a topic of central importance that is related to the subject of this volume, but which is not fully dealt with here. This is the difficult question of how one actually relates a given activity to the secondary effects that it presumably produces. We shall argue for better data as to the state of the society, but the existence of such data will not automatically establish the causal connection between a program, such as space exploration, and the phenomenon that has been observed. The weakness of social criticism and program evaluation, as practiced in the press and popular magazine writing, lies not only in the inadequacy of the data, but in the casualness of the inferences which are drawn. One suburban housewife, mentioned previously, who guessed that the "new math" in the primary schools must be due to Sputnik, offers a good example of the casualness of such inferences.

To begin with, it is probable that certain effects of the space program can never be distinguished in any event from the effects of other developments in society. In many respects the program for space exploration is part and parcel of widespread developments in technology. To some extent these developments might be regarded as stimulated by the space program, but actually the military missile program already had given the impetus to miniaturization and strict standards of quality that are so often associated with the areospace program. We could count the number of technologists of a certain sort hired by the areospace industry in a given year. But if we knew the increase in enrollment in engineering institutes during a given period, we would have a difficult time assessing what proportion of this interest should be attributed to the space program. We might survey the student population, but their answers could provide only a crude estimate. On the primary- and secondary-school levels, a certain proportion of children get discouraged because they come to believe that they have no hope for worthwhile employment unless they receive a technical education of a very high level. How can one say what proportion of this is attributable to the space program? Here, even the student's own reports would have to be treated with extreme skepticism since the influences that bring about such a situation will be so complex and subtle that a youngster is not likely even to be aware of them. If a teacher enjoins him with the necessity to get good grades, how can the *child* estimate what portion of the teacher's behavior stems from the space program, automation, computers, or far more diffuse influences?

The fact that in some instances we cannot distinguish the impact of space exploration from other developments in the society is no cause for despair. There are certain respects in which the space program (let alone its impact) is itself not distinguishable from other events, nor could one expect it to be. The mobility of families of technologists who are associated directly with the space program is scarcely distinguishable from the mobility of families as a result of the demand for technologists in other parts of industry. In instances such as this, we can tell *which* families moved because of the space program, but we cannot regard this as a phenomenon distinctive to the space program, nor can we say, in all probability, that these same families would not have moved if it were not for the space program.

Problems of this sort will be dealt with at various points in other volumes of this series. Here, I wish only to make the general point that the existence of good data on certain changes in the society will not necessarily make it possible to isolate the effect of a specific program. This is because some attributes of a given program cannot properly be construed as distinctive of that program. Rather, they are part of some larger set of events. Thus, in our study of the role of technicians in the space age, we make no over-all attempt to separate the impact of the space program, except as it symbolizes and dramatizes advanced technology.

In other instances the identification of an impact may be possible, but the measure of its magnitude impossible. It is possible to trace the transfer of specific items of aerospace technology into the civilian economy. More often, however, the aerospace technology is transformed as it is transferred. In such instances it is somewhat difficult to *conceive* how relative values could be assigned both to the original invention and to the reinvention that transformed it. More difficult will be the estimate of the contribution of aerospace technology to the over-all economy, or even to large segments of the economy. It would even be much more difficult, perhaps impossible, to estimate the total diffusion of aerospace technology into the civilian economy. A conservative estimate is possible in the sense that every instance that can be located provides a minimum estimate. However, it is probable that even the most diligent search would underestimate the magnitude of the phenomenon. Erroneous reporting of adoptions that did not originate in the aerospace industry would be identified and rejected. However, attempts to uncover errors of underreporting — that is, failure to mention an item that was adopted — would be incredibly difficult.

I have referred so far in this chapter to the inherent difficulties of assessing causal relations and impacts that apply when an honest effort is made. What is much more dangerous, however, is the prevalent practice of irresponsible inference that I have already mentioned. The reader might attempt to recall the number of explanations offered as to the reason why the Soviet Union put a satellite into orbit before we did. Some explanations were, on the surface, preposterous. For example, the state of our secondary schools in 1957 could not by any stretch of responsible thinking be held responsible for the lag of our space program. Nor was this lag due to the general moral fiber of our society. Rather, it was due to specific decisions that might have gone one way or the other if different judgments had prevailed back in the late 1940's when the Soviet leaders first began their all-out space program.

In the third chapter of this volume Bertrand Gross proposes an elaborate set of social indicators. If such a set of indicators had been in effect back in those days, it would have been extremely rare that the state of any one of the indices could have revealed the exact cause of our space lag. However, it could have alerted us to a state of affairs in which we were interested, and stimulated the additional data gathering and analysis that would have uncovered the causal relation between it and some other event or institution of the society.

Examples of how such social indicators can properly be employed will be found in various examples of the use of economic indicators in assessing the state of the economy. An "interesting" change in the indicator series does not by itself reveal what caused it. Though economists are scarcely ever in complete agreement on causes or prognoses, statements are ordinarily bolstered by evidence of direct linkage of the change in the indicator to the supposed causal event.

The major point to be made is that the establishment of a series of social indicators, such as those that will be discussed in this volume, does not make the job of program evaluation automatic. More often than not, a statistical series will be but one element in the web of evidence whereby the impact of a program, such as space exploration, is evaluated — but it is a vital element.

Anticipation and Action

Up to this point, I have discussed the use of social indicators as measures of impact, and the problem of inferring causal relations between a given program, such as space exploration, and the social phenomena that are observed. This can, at best, tell us what has happened. But a data system for assessing the consequences of a program would scarcely be justified if it were only to satisfy our sense of historical curiosity. It is a useful guide to action only if it improves our understanding of what the future is likely to be. The effectiveness of actions increases as one can anticipate the conditions with which one will have to cope, and the possible consequences of actions under varying circumstances.

The problem of foreseeing the future is, of course, as difficult and unsolved as any with which man is confronted.[7] Yet it is a problem which is inescapable. Therefore, a possible solution must be attempted — no matter how poor the result. I will make no pretext of offering an over-all scheme for doing this. However, at this point, I would like to spell out some of the notions that have guided the work of the Committee on Space in their thinking about a systematic approach to understanding the social impact of space exploration.

The word *anticipation* of the future has been used deliberately in lieu of the more popular term *prediction*. This is because of an attempt to avoid certain prevailing errors in thinking about the future as a guide to action. For example, *prediction* ordinarily is thought of as identifying that future state of affairs which is considered to be the most probable of all the conceivable outcomes. However, a program of action must contemplate more possible states of affairs than solely that one which appears to be the most probable. It must take into consideration a whole range of events which are reasonably probable and reasonably important. For this reason, we prefer the broader concept of *anticipation* to that of *prediction*, which has come to imply concern with the single most probable future event among all those that are possible.

I have mentioned two aspects of future events that are of significance — the probability of their occurrence and their importance in the event they do occur.[8] There is a prevailing tendency to confuse these two aspects in writings on public policy problems.[9] Events that might prove important, particularly if they hold prom-

---

[7] I recognize that the issues dealt with here are identical to those involved in the economists' model of decision making which traditionally *assumed* perfect knowledge of the future. In successive elaborations of this model, economists have attempted to deal with risk and uncertainty. Here, I postulate only that risk and uncertainty exist, and that in *some way* they will be dealt with.

[8] The point of view expressed here is a reflection of the approach of statistical decision theory. The best expression of this is found in Robert Schlaifer, *Probability and Statistics for Business Decisions* (New York: McGraw-Hill Book Company, 1960).

[9] For a more detailed discussion of the prevalence and importance of this error see Raymond A. Bauer, "Accuracy of Perception in International Relations," *Teachers College Record*, 64 (January 1963), 291–299.

ise of being unpleasant, are often set forth as virtually certain to occur even though they may be quite improbable.

In practice it is often the proper strategy to act on the basis of some highly important possible occurrence, even if it is not the most probable outcome. For example, even though the probability of the guidance system failing on a given manned space flight might be only one in twenty, it would be foolish indeed not to provide a backup guidance system.

However, difficulty in planning rational action is frequently created by the tacit assumption that the most disastrous outcome is the most probable or, even worse, treated as certain. Thus, preparing against the possibility of a sneak enemy attack is one thing. But taking literally the statement "You know the Communists will attack us as soon as they have the chance" is quite another thing. Assigning a probability of certainty to this possible serious event creates a bias against exploring other possibilities.

This particular issue is of real importance in popular writing on the social impact of technological change. For example, many of the purported "predictions" of the consequences of automation are of this order. Closely analyzed, this writing is a warning of what *might* happen, and accordingly of that consequence which we should be prepared to avoid. However, it is usually couched in the form of a statement of what *will* happen.

Both prevailing practices — concentrating on the single most probable future state and treating a highly important outcome as though it were certain to occur — have a common consequence of restricting the range of future states that are anticipated and taken into consideration in setting policy.

The devices that one uses to anticipate future possible consequences of a large undertaking, such as the space program, can be quite varied of course, and there is unlikely to be a great deal of consensus on *how* one should go about this. In our study of the history of the early period of the railroads in America,[10] we undertook an illustrative exercise in looking at historical analogies as one among the many possible devices of anticipation that might be used. Regardless of the devices employed, however, all will involve some general models of the nature of society and of social processes. They are essentially projections into the future of existing knowledge of where we are, and where we have been.

The role of social indicators is not only to record where we are

[10] Cf. Bruce Mazlish, ed., *The Railroad and the Space Program: An Exploration in Historical Analogy* (Cambridge, Mass.: The M.I.T. Press, 1966).

and where we have been but to provide a basis for anticipation of future states and for a continuing reassessment of the relative probability of the various conditions that have been taken into account in planning. For example, in 1960 a survey was made of the attitudes of businessmen toward the space program.[11] These attitudes were found to be highly favorable. But, in view of the lack of information about the space program that was reflected in the survey, one had to consider the possibility that these attitudes were highly unstable and might not guarantee continuing support for the program. However, when this study was repeated in 1963,[12] the businessmen in our study showed much greater knowledge of the program, and only slightly less enthusiasm. The probability of continued support thus seems to have increased.

While the example cited above depended on *ad hoc* studies, it is illustrative of the manner in which continuing statistical series may be employed.

Summarizing the points of importance made in this section, we see that the purpose of social indicators is not primarily to record historical events but to provide the basis of planning for future policies. Such planning should not be based on the assumption of the single most probable outcome, nor should it confuse the probability with the seriousness of the outcome. Rather, it should take into account the range of important consequences that can be anticipated, and both their probability and importance should also be considered. Data series then become the basis for reassessment of these anticipations.

An Approach to the Problem of Social Indicators

Any highly visible social event tends to become the focus of critical comment, whether this comment be favorable or unfavorable. As the single most obvious symbol of the vast technological revolution that is occurring in Western society, the space program is certain to be given the credit for economic prosperity, or the blame for economic failure; the credit for an increase in education, or the blame for juvenile delinquency. Such statements will be made, and

[11] Raymond A. Bauer, "Executives Probe Space," *Harvard Business Review*, 38 (September–October 1960).

[12] Edward E. Furash, "Businessmen Review the Space Effort," *Harvard Business Review*, 41 (September–October 1963). This article is also to be included in a further volume in the series *Technology, Space, and Society*, with the tentative title, *Social Change: Space Impact on Communities and Social Groups*, Robert N. Rapaport, ed.

they will affect national policy. In fact they have already been made, and have affected policy.

The development of the railroads in the nineteenth century served as such a symbol of the major forces in the society. In the studies of the railroad as a historical analogy to space exploration, carried out under the direction of Bruce Mazlish,[13] we found that the magnitude and nature of this relationship has not been properly evaluated even after a century of historical writing. Plausible assertions then were taken for fact, policies set on the basis of such assertions, and both the assertions and the policies based on them were slow to be re-examined.

It is now, of course, commonplace to talk about the increased pace of social developments and the increased interrelationship of events. Things not only happen faster but they have wider ramifications. Hence, there is need for better and more rapid information for the setting of policy. And, as a corollary, it is vital to know the quality of the information that is used.

The basic assumption of this volume will not be a surprise to most experienced users of social statistics. It is this. *For many of the important topics on which social critics blithely pass judgment, and on which policies are made, there are no yardsticks by which to know if things are getting better or worse.*

The import of what we have to say extends well beyond the evaluation of the space program. It provides a background against which space exploration or any other major societal event might be evaluated. The immediate effect should be to develop a more responsible use of evidence in social criticism. The more important, far-reaching effect is to lay the groundwork for the type of information system that is needed for the proper evaluation of large-scale social enterprises.

We have taken literally the notion that NASA or some comparable agency will seriously intend to establish a system of feedback in the society for detecting the full range of consequences of its actions, and for guiding future actions. Whether NASA or any other institution intends so bold and broad a program at this moment is not factually important. Certainly the very proposition that the social impact of space exploration be studied implies that the social impact can be detected and measured, as well as evaluated and responded to. For this reason it has seemed vital to explore the full dimensions of the information system that such assumptions imply.

[13] Mazlish, *op. cit.*

Such an information system would include the following:

1. Regular trend series of social indicators, whereby comparisons from time to time and across societies could be made.

2. Special mechanisms for gathering data on new developments falling outside those regular trends series, and gathering it rapidly enough so that the phenomena had not disappeared or so much time had passed that the information was useless.

3. Some means of reporting this information back with appropriate speed, in appropriate form, to the appropriate agency.

The four major chapters of this volume are directed at assessing the present state of the art, and exploring what would be required in the form of an improved informational system.

The task was broken into four units:

1. Albert Biderman looks at the existing social indicators from the point of view of their relationship to those national goals which have been set forth, the ways in which such statistical series originate, and the multiple uses to which they are put.

With a recognition of the fact that much of social criticism is based on an unwarranted complacency about the evidence available, one of Biderman's objectives is to convince the reader that the problem is indeed a serious one, and that we are not concerned with trivial "technical niceties."

Having established the fact that there is indeed a problem, rather than hurrying to an immediate prescription for the curing of the ill, he makes an intensive sociological analysis of the existing state of affairs. He asks, for example, how do statistical series come into being under present practice? What uses are made and what justifications can be invoked in favor of present practice? What constraints are there on how we might set up an ideal set of social indicators for evaluating the state of the society? More frontally, what can we learn from the existing state of affairs that should give us sober pause in prescribing an ideal set of social indicators?

2. Gross accepts the challenge of Biderman's analysis and sets forth in a broad scheme what such an ideal system of social statistics would look like. He takes modern national economic accounting as his point of departure, extending it to a wide concept of social accounting.

3. Biderman, in the second of his contributions, discusses the need for stand-by research facilities to collect data on events falling outside regular statistical series. Because of the novel nature of the

space program, not only is the occurrence of unanticipated events especially likely, but it is especially critical that there be facilities for their study.

Biderman reviews experience in gathering data on such novel, unanticipated events. He also reviews the existing facilities in this and other countries that might be mobilized into such an over-all facility.

4. Rosenthal and Weiss turn to the final problem of what to do with the new information providing that it might become available. We phrase this in terms of the sort of feedback system a given organization might want to set up, and the consequences, both favorable and unfavorable, of reporting back data on the full range of impact of the organization's actions.

Thus, we have tried to envisage what such an information system might look like, how it might be used, and the advantages and disadvantages that might be associated with it.

The remainder of this introductory essay may be considered as an extended commentary both on the nature of the task, and on the approach of my associates to that task. The reader should be warned that I will take the liberty of going beyond summarization and evaluation. He may expect (hopefully adequately identified) quotation, paraphrase, summary, additional examples, critique, and comments — all intended to be relevant to the over-all effort.

Social Indicators and Goals (Biderman)

Annually the President of the United States delivers a message on "The State of the Nation." This concern of societies with "How are we doing?" has existed for centuries. The word "statistics," which is derived etymologically from the Latin *ratio status*, could well be translated as "state of the nation." For several hundred years the primary concern of men who called themselves statisticians was to set up a system of social indicators by which to judge the performance of the society with respect to its norms, values, and goals.

Such schemes as were proposed were based on the values and judgment of the individual scholar making the proposal. The fact that over a period of several centuries no such comprehensive fact-gathering system was inaugurated in a major country may mean any one or a combination of several things: the entire idea is worthless; it may be worthwhile, but has been judged as uneconomical or technically unfeasible; or, while it is feasible from a narrowly conceived technical point of view, there may be social or political factors that inhibit its implementation. But perhaps we overstate matters, since certain trend series of social indicators do exist. Therefore, a proper question might be, why have some series been developed while others have not? Similarly, since the absense of adequate data has in no way inhibited social criticism, one might well ask what evidence has in fact been used, and for what purposes?

With such questions demanding an answer, Biderman eschews making still one more prescriptive statement of what is needed. Instead, he takes a hard look at the actual availability and use of social statistics in areas of public policy.

We may pose a simple problem:

Consider a journalist, a congressman, or a citizen who wishes to examine a ready source of statistical information on the status or progress of the nation with respect to its goals. Wanting the information in a concise and comprehensive form, he is most likely to turn to the *Statistical Abstract of the United States* (U.S. Bureau of the Census, 1962), and its companion historical volume, *Historical Statistics of the United States* (U.S. Bureau of the Census, 1960).

Suppose then that our curious seeker wants to see how we have performed with respect to the goals set by the President's Commission on National Goals in 1960. This is both the most renowned and the most recent of such major proclamations.

In Table 1.1, reproduced here from Biderman's study, we find a comparison of 81 domestic goals identified by the President's Commission with the availability of data in the two major statistical series. These goals are grouped into 11 goal areas. Thus, there are 6 specific goals concerned with the status of "the individual," 3 concerned with "equality," and so on. It will be noted that data of any kind bearing on these goals were found in these statistical series in only 59 per cent of the instances (48 goals out of 81).

The reader may feel that 59 per cent is a *good* performance considering that only *two* statistical series were consulted. But, if the other two major series, *Economic Indicators* and *Health, Education and Welfare Trends*,[14] are also consulted, the picture scarcely

[14] U.S. Department of Health, Education and Welfare, *Economic Indicators*, and *Health, Education and Welfare Trends* (Washington, D.C.: U.S. Government Printing Office, 1962).

changes at all. Furthermore, Biderman did not specify that the statistics he found be *adequate* measures of the goals but only that they be relevant, that is, in the ball park. As we turn later to the question of adequacy, it will be seen that the criterion of relevancy

TABLE 1.1

AVAILABILITY OF INDICATORS RELEVANT TO NATIONAL GOALS FORMULATED BY PRESIDENT'S COMMISSION*

Goal Areas	Number of Specific Goals	Number of Goals to Which Some Indicator Is Relevant	Number of Goals to Which No Indicator Is Relevant
The individual	6	3	3
Equality	3	2	1
Democratic process	11	5	6
Education	5	5	0
Arts and sciences	8	2	5
Democratic economy	9	5	5
Economic growth	9	9	0
Technological change	5	1	4
Agriculture	5	4	1
Living conditions	10	2	8
Health and welfare	10	10	0
Total	81	48	33

* In *Statistical Abstract of the United States*, or *Historical Statistics of the United States*.

is very loose indeed. It is, therefore, conservative to say that in 4 out of 10 goals in the list of the President's Commission, we would not even find data to wonder about.

Events take on a more ordered appearance if we compare the goal statements of 1960 with those made by a commission appointed by President Hoover in 1933. For those goal statements made in 1933, which were also restated in 1960, there were indicators for 73 per cent, while indicators were available for only 25 per cent of the *new* goals that appeared in the 1960 statement but not in the 1933 statement.

We may deduce from this a rough model that data will be gathered only where there is reasonable consensus on three issues: the problem is important; there is some information which, if available, would be useful; and the relevant phenomena can be measured. We might further conjecture that identifying something as a "national goal" either reflects or produces a consensus that it is important, and thus stimulates efforts to identify relevant information and attempts to measure it. If this model is approximately correct, the comparison of the 1933 and 1960 goal statements against available indicators suggests that it has taken about one generation for the process just described to take place.

If we may set aside for a moment the discussion of the process of lag in statistical indicators, it will be profitable to look at the present implications of such a lag, regardless of the mechanisms by which it occurs.

This lag is especially marked in statistical series that have implications for the evaluation of the space program, and for massive technological innovation in general. The President's Commission posed 5 goals in the areas of technological change, and 8 in the area of the arts and sciences (mostly science). There is only one trend statistic in this series that bears on technological changes. And despite the fact that recent Presidential State of the Union speeches have stressed the role of science, the regular series have data to cover only 1 of the 8 goals set forth.

Other topics of current concern, such as the democratic process, equality of opportunity, and the status of the individual are also notably weak in statistical indicators.

While there is a lag, and the lag is an important issue to which we shall return, there is no lack of concern with statistics or with social trends in the United States. Social criticism and commentary are rampant, and the citation of some sort of statistical number is a "good" thing and is resorted to by critics and commentators alike to substantiate their viewpoints where possible. Biderman notes the pervasive belief in the magic of numbers, especially the notion that things that can be counted are more important. The minimum statement of the nature of number magic is that things that have been counted attract more concern than things that cannot or have not been counted.

Concern with quantification, including the development of really adequate statistics, has increased over time. Strong evidence of this is the development of the system of "economic indicators" in recent decades. Biderman's analysis of the Presidential State of the Union messages over time reflects an increasing citation of quantitative data, averaging 3 per message in the earliest times, and rising to an average of 11 since World War II, with an even more rapid increase in the most recent two decades.

There is little doubt that the statistical series collected by the U.S. government (or by anyone else for that matter) reflect those areas of concern that have occupied the minds of the American people, though with some lag in time. But they reflect these interests unevenly, since the probability of a given statistical series being developed is also affected by

The articulateness and power of the group whose interest is involved.

The susceptibility of the phenomenon to being measured.

The extent to which the phenomenon is socially visible.

The preferences and skills of the agency personnel who gather the statistics.

Statistics are gathered not out of a general sense of curiosity, but rather because it is presumed that they will be guides to planning and action. The census originated as the basis for apportioning representation in the House of Representatives. Economic indicators were set up for guidance of fiscal and other economic policies. Presumably private parties and organizations use such statistics in the same way. In any event, statistical data and projections are regularly reported in business columns and journals, and articles are written on the use of these data for business planning. In point of fact, however, our knowledge is meager of how, and to what extent, advantage is taken of such statistics as guides to private action.

What we do know, however, is that statistics are used *to persuade other persons* to take actions and adopt policies. We probably know more about this function than about the exercise of the supposed primary function. In all likelihood this is because the use of statistics for persuasion is a public event, and thereby readily observable. And it is here that a major difficulty manifests itself in the state and use of social statistics.

The man who uses statistics for the purpose of persuading someone else to adopt a particular policy or particular action is already convinced of the correctness of his position. This dulls his sense of vigilance concerning the technical correctness of the statistics he uses, and turns his attention more to their persuasive power. In the absence of any hard data, he treats the phenomenon as self-evident, which leads to the utterance of persuasive statements as, for example, "The well-known tendency for us to become a nation of conformists . . ." or, "The general decline in the level of our secondary schools. . . ." Often an articulate spokesman for a certain position will make a sweeping statement that is taken as being representative of a large segment of the relevant public. Much of

the controversy over the space program has consisted of such selective citation, pro and con, by articulate spokesmen.

But, the best evidence of all to use — if it favors a selective position — is a government statistic. Biderman cites Sibley to this
effect:

Statistics published in the chaste and solemn 8 pt. and 6 pt. of the Government Printing Office possess a persuasive quality to which even the
most rigorous academic discipline does not produce a complete immunity.

Biderman poses the issue of the dual use of statistics in terms of
two functions: knowledge and certification. The use of statistics for
certification not only tests the ingenuity of the user of the statistics
in achieving his goal of certification, but in some instances actually
results in poorer data being gathered — sometimes at a higher cost.
For example, a complete census has, by custom, come to be regarded as firmer evidence than a sample survey. Yet, most persons
familiar with the technical problems of both a census and a sample
survey know that in many instances a sample survey can give *more
accurate* information, in addition to being quicker and less costly.
Despite this, in hearings on the program of the Bureau of Census
those parties interested in using findings of the Bureau for certification — for instance, state officials concerned with problems of
legislative reapportionment — plumbed for a complete census in a
situation in which this procedure would produce *less* knowledge.

When the goal is certification or persuasion, knowledge suffers in
many ways. We have argued that concern for the persuasive power
of the statistic dulls the critical faculty. If this were a matter of
technical nicety we would drop the whole subject. The problem,
however, is that major evaluations of trends in our society have
been made, most probably erroneously, because the problems of
trend statistics have been ignored.

It is my guess (Biderman is less brash than I have been and
should not share the blame) that this is most true with respect to
evidence of social malignancy. Virtually every trend series pertaining to social problems has a built-in inflationary bias that would
make it look as though things were "getting worse," unless the trend
for improvement were very strong. That is to say, I am making an
educated guess that the inflationary bias is strong enough to offset
any reasonable expectation for improvement.

Some of the problems are technical in the narrowest sense. This
can be seen most clearly in data on mental illness. The inflation be-

gins with the phenomenon itself, in that some disorders that previously would have been considered to be physical diseases are now regarded as mental illness. To this has been added the expansion of the category of illness itself. What once was regarded as "odd behavior," or "bad behavior," is now recognized as a manifestation of disease. The inflation extends itself to the reporting system, where improvements in the system of reporting mental illness exaggerate the apparent rate of increase even beyond the factors just mentioned. Finally, mental illness has become socially acceptable to the extent that doctors will now record cases that previously they would have disguised under more polite labels.

The professional user of such statistics will not forgive me if I do not add a "miscellaneous" category and include such facts as these:

1. Hospital admissions for mental illness are a function of available hospital beds. (It is doubtful that anyone knows what the effect is here, since the proportion of actual beds to the population has gone down, while the turnover of patients has increased. Hence, the number of *available* beds may have increased, decreased, or remained about constant.)

2. As the population has become urbanized, the availability of relatives or servants to take care of the "odd" person has decreased, the size of the housing unit decreased, and, therefore, it has become less tolerable to keep such people at home. Hence, they are more likely to become a statistic in the indices of mental illness.

Many series contain many biases, some of which work in opposite directions. To the best of my knowledge, no one has introduced any serious notion that there might be an element of downward bias in statistics on mental illness.

But error is compounded. When indices of malignancy do go down, the reporting does not necessarily follow the data. Despite evidence to the contrary, there is a prevailing belief that "there is nothing to be lost" by reporting the most pessimistic version of what is happening. The clearest case of this is the reporting of automobile traffic fatalities.[15] The average citizen, listening to and reading about the cataclysmic holiday weekends, would conclude that driving has become increasingly dangerous, especially on holiday weekends. The figures invariably cited are uncorrected for volume of traffic. (By this criterion holiday weekends are probably somewhat safer than ordinary days.) Over-all figures on annual fatalities

[15] The data cited here are from "Traffic Accident Facts," *Traffic Safety* (Chicago, Ill.: The National Safety Council, August 1964).

are usually uncorrected for increase in population. (By this criterion the rate has remained about constant. In 1939 they were 24.7 fatalities per 100,000, and in 1964, 23.1.) They are also uncorrected for automobile miles traveled. (By this criterion, fatalities are less than *one third* of what they were about three decades ago. The 1923–1927 average was 18.2 per 100 million miles. The 1963 figure was 5.51.)

In short, traffic safety has improved remarkably.

The custodians and reporters of the data know this. They tend to attribute the improvement solely to highway engineering, and, generally, they believe that motorists will drive safely only if they are scared. Therefore, out of conscience they have decided to report the data in a selective fashion that reinforces the image of a society going to hell in a handbasket. (In defense of these gentlemen, it should be recorded that they continue the Casandra-like forecasts of holiday fatalities against their will. They are exposed to thinly disguised blackmail from the news media who promise to get "other estimates" if the National Safety Council will not supply them. The National Safety Council fears that the "other estimates" will be less responsible than their own and, hence, goes along with the game.)

A series of pieces of psychological research has suggested very strongly that scaring people can backfire.[16] In fact some of this research is specific to driving safety and indicates that persons most concerned with the dangerousness of driving are least likely to take safety precautions. Thus, an apparently "conservative" policy of reporting statistics in the most pessimistic form may, in fact, be causing deaths by preventing a more effective program of driver safety education.

In fairness to men concerned with traffic safety it should be reported that they themselves have encouraged discussion of this issue, and voluntarily exposed themselves to the data critical of their position. Many of them are even willing to concede privately that it might be better to admit that people drive when they have been drinking, and try to teach people to adopt different driving strategies when they have been drinking. But they fear an adverse public reaction if they adopt anything except a policy of maximizing the fear associated with driving, and especially driving while

[16] For a review of these findings see Raymond A. Bauer and Donald F. Cox, "Rational versus Emotional Communications: A New Approach," in Leon Arons and Mark A. May, eds., *Television and Human Behavior* (New York: Appleton-Century-Crofts, 1963), pp. 140–154.

drinking. (It should be added that isolated local experiments have reinforced this fear of public reaction.)

Hence, we have three factors inflating the reporting of social malignancies:

1. Built-in inflationary biases in the series themselves.

2. A "conservative" tendency of officials to report the worst, either because they believe no harm can result, or because their jobs depend on a belief that a serious and growing problem exists.

3. A tendency for some segments of the public to become morally indignant if by any stretch of the imagination data are reported in a fashion such as to "condone immoral behavior."

We shall return to the technical problems of error and bias in statistical series in connection with the discussion of Gross's piece. Here, however, we want to sound a "first alert." Since Biderman chooses as his example the known and probable errors in the sacrosanct *Uniform Crime Reports*, I have deliberately chosen two other series to accentuate the generality of the problem.

But even in this brief review, I cannot resist using the *Uniform Crime Reports* to make several quick points. They bear on the magnitude of errors that may exist in such series, the extent to which the data, as regularly reported in the press, contain obvious evidence of these errors that go unnoticed by the press, and finally, the way in which a favorable development in the society may be interpreted as an unfavorable development if one does not know what lies behind the data. The first two points can actually be substantiated by a news story[17] in which the annual "increase" in crime was ritually reported. The last paragraph of the dispatch from Washington read as follows:

Nevada was the state with the highest reported crime rate — 2,990 serious offenses for every 100,000 persons. Mississippi had the lowest reported rate — 393 crimes for every 100,000.

Only one journalist, to our knowledge, noticed anything odd about these data. A writer for *Time* magazine commented on the sole fact that Mississippi had the lowest reported crime rate. He attributed this to the fact that crimes by whites against Negroes (and probably Negroes against Negroes, for that matter) were not reported in Mississippi. However, no one raised the obvious question as to what interpretation to put on a series of data that asked

[17] *The New York Times*, July 21, 1964.

the readers to believe that crime in Nevada was 7.6 times as rampant as crime in Mississippi!

Nor did anyone question the increase in "serious" crimes, even in areas such as Boston, where this increase was reported as due to a rise in automobile thefts. True, stealing an automobile for a joy ride is a theft. And it is also true that virtually every automobile is worth more than the $50 that is the cut-off point for a serious theft. But in the decades during which the crime-reporting series has been in existence, the nature of car thefts has changed drastically from highly organized efforts to steal, disguise, transport, and resell automobiles to what are predominantly thefts attributed to teenagers for joy riding. Thefts such as these should not be condoned, but neither should they be equated with the thefts of yesteryear.

Thus, there are first of all reporting problems, which as they are corrected build a certain upward bias in the system.

But, second, there are definitional problems. Definitional difficulties could bias a series, in principle, in either direction. However, the definition of a serious crime in the *Uniform Crime Reports* has one important *upward* bias that not only distorts the series but produces an unfavorable interpretation of a favorable aspect of the society.

The category of serious crimes is strongly weighted toward thefts of automobiles and other items estimated to be worth over $50. The more affluent the society becomes, the more automobiles and non-stationary articles over $50 there will be to steal. The low rate of serious crimes in Mississippi may be due more to the poverty of the state than to poor crime reporting. Similarly, as the society becomes more affluent, more people carry insurance on their personal property. And the theft of an insured object is more likely to be reported than the theft of an uninsured object. Hence, if the tendency of the population to commit larceny were to remain constant, and the reporting system remained constant, the index of serious crimes would still increase *because the standard of living was increasing*. Like many existing series of statistics, the index of serious crimes could be evaluated either negatively or positively, depending on what further knowledge revealed of the various elements that accounted for its rise.

Biderman's exhaustive analysis of the difficulties and ambiguities of the index of serious crimes goes well beyond what I have hinted at here. Suffice to say that I do not overstate the case.

What do mental disease, driving safety, and crime have to do with the space program? First of all, it should be said that we have used these three problems as examples of an apparent general tendency of indicators, which purport to represent defects of the society, to have an upward bias. This should mean that any institution or program which is being evaluated is up against the difficulty of "pessimistic" statistical data in this apparently upward bias of the indicators.

However, without stretching the imagination too much, it is easy to anticipate a direct consequence for the space program if one were to do a thorough comparative study of communities associated with and not associated with the aerospace industry. The simple facts of greater prosperity and mobility in the aerospace communities could well produce the following pessimistic evaluations:

1. An apparent increase in mental illness (a) due to better medical care and, hence, better psychiatric diagnoses, (b) as a result of mobility, or (c) because there are fewer family or neighborhood facilities for taking care of people at home.

2. An apparent increase in reckless driving — probably concentrated among the young, unless accident rates are adjusted for automobile miles traveled, and from the probably greater proportion of youngsters in the more prosperous aerospace communities.

3. An apparent increase in serious crime — as a result of more objects worth $50 or more such valuables being available in the community.

We do not say this as a prophylactic apologia for the space program, but as a general indication of the need not only for more statistical series but especially for more sophistication in the use of those statistics which are presently available.

Apart from the potential problems created by the difficulties of pessimistic indicators, the space program has also the special difficulty that for a variety of reasons it is likely to be underrepresented in the existing statistical series. That is to say, there will be fewer indicators, whether "good" or "bad," than for many other programs. Biderman lists several reasons for this:

1. The over-all novelty of the space program militates against its being represented in the existing statistical series. Aside from the built-in lag in the present mechanisms for developing social indicators, we have seen specifically that factors associated with technological change and the state of the sciences are, in fact, among the poorest represented of our national goal areas.

2. Our indicators, on the one hand, are well-equipped for recording the allocation of public goods — that is, how much does it cost?

— to such a program as space exploration. On the other hand, we are not only not equipped with measures of public benefits, but ill-equipped even to think about the value to be put on them. What value is to be put on the national prestige that accrues from the space program? Traditionally, economists have measured the value of goods and services that private individuals have acquired for themselves in terms of the amount of money they are willing to pay for such goods and services. The tendency has been to use the same convention with respect to the generation of public goods and services; that is, to talk about their value in terms of their cost.

There is some immediate conceptual difficulty in talking about the value of public goods in terms of the cost of acquiring them. The major characteristic of public goods and services is that if one person enjoys them, another person is not deprived of them. Thus, if an investment of $1 billion in space exploration produces for each citizen a given increment in satisfaction via national prestige, it follows that the total public value will increase with the number of citizens of the country. Therefore, the value of $1 billion invested in space exploration cannot be equated with the value of $1 billion invested in automobiles. The latter value is not dependent on the size of the population, but the former is.

As Gross points out in his essay, it is necessary to get some direct measures, however crude they may be, of publicly distributed benefits rather than to use their cost as an indication of their value. But, worse still, the use of cost to estimate the benefits of a public program causes us uniformly to concentrate on the cost *as a cost*, while deflecting our attention away from the benefits.

3. Statistics consist of the counting of many like units. But the space program is geared to creating many unlike units. To quote Biderman:

Indeed, counts are irrelevant to indicating the scope, success, nature, and value of many of the systems involved, or to answer almost any other significant question about them. NASA programs most frequently involve the production of fairly unique, large, costly, complex, and highly integrated systems, rather than the quantity manufactured of large numbers of like or similar units.

He concludes his passage on the following whimsical note:

A spherical trigonometry accuracy measure would assuredly be most unusual in a rundown of where we stand as a nation, yet such a figure might gauge the success of a major national effort much more accurately than the counts of satellites and their weights that currently appear.

Biderman's contribution leaves little doubt that we must scrap any blithe assumption that we are well equipped to measure anything like a full range of social effects. In addition, tracing the effects of a novel large-scale program, such as that of space exploration, is considerably more difficult than that of tracing the effects of more orthodox activities.

But, beyond this, Biderman analyzes the factors that go into the decision as to which series will be developed, the biases in the series themselves, and their selective use. Biderman's conclusion is that the only practical objective we can set for ourselves is to take the existing series and sources of bias as a point of departure, and seek to improve the existing system, but at an accelerated rate. He obviously takes a dim view of the possibility of introducing any master plan of social accounting as a unified package. This reservation comes from his exploration of the social and political forces that have shaped the existing system. His consequent conclusion is that one has to move with deliberation to offset forces that presumably would be mobilized, either in opposition to any single master plan or to capitalize on such selected aspects of it as to throw it strongly out of proportion.

But his attitude toward the vagaries of the social processes that shape our statistics is by no means completely negative. (Nor is mine.) His contention is that it is only by a hard analytical look at the role of statistics in our society, and a cold understanding of *why* they take the form they do, as opposed to some ideal scheme, can we proceed to a better system. It is pretty clear that many prescriptions have been written for the wrong illness. Both Biderman and I would argue that many "ideal" schemes of social reform — whether it be statistics or any other problem — have failed not because of the fault of the society, but because they were not relevant to the ills they were designed to cure.

Hence, he poses a challenge for the sort of grand scheme that Gross develops, and he passes the baton to Gross with the statement that it is fortunate to have two contrasting approaches to the task.

But Biderman's concern for the difficulty of introducing an overall system of social accounting relatively rapidly does not depend on, as some readers might assume, inherent pessimism about the possibility of measuring some of the newer, "softer" phenomena that would be added to existing series:

Social scientists generally agree that the "objectivity" of data regarding a particular problem does not result from anything intrinsic to the phenomena in question, but rather it stems from the state of development of our ways of making and expressing observations of it.

A statement that 35 per cent of a national sample of U.S. adults, drawn by a specified means, answered "yes" to a question is as objective, and probably at least as accurate, as most so-called "hard" data on demography or economics. The difficulty lies, as we shall see in greater detail in discussing Gross's work, in the inferences we make from such objective data. We are seldom interested in the information for its own sake, but rather in the fact that it is taken to represent some more abstract phenomenon about which we are, in fact, interested. There is a big difference between the following two statements: "35 per cent of U.S. adults said yes to the question, 'Should we take a larger part in world affairs?' "; and "35 per cent of U.S. adults are internationalists." Obviously a question about U.S. participation in international affairs is relevant to what we think about when we refer to some sort of concept of "internationalism," but the two are by no means identical.

However, making such a "measurement of internationalism," into "hard" data is not dependent solely on improvement in the techniques of measurement. Such data get "harder" as the analyst acquires experience with them. He learns how to relate them, and how to combine them with other data. He learns what inferences are safe to make in one context, but not in another. (For example, during times of tension an increase in the desire "to take part in world affairs" may mean an increase in hostility toward other countries; in times of peace it may mean an increase in friendliness.)

While this simple example may stretch the matter somewhat, the fact is that the hardness is as much a function of one's familiarity with it as it is a function of the precision of measurement or the nature of the phenomenon. An expenditure of $2,500 on consumption goods and services may mean an infinite variety of things — from a garage filled with breakfast cereal to a trip to Hawaii. However, we have learned the sorts of inferences we may make from such a figure in various contexts, and we feel confident in doing so. As a matter of fact, with familiar data we run into a contrary danger of overconfidence, forgetting that the observations themselves are not the concepts that they have been chosen to represent.

It should be remembered that if a phenomenon is measured, and the measure is available, the phenomenon is more likely to be taken into consideration in the formation of policy. This, in turn, leads to the circumstance that those parties who think a phenomenon should not enter into consideration first attack its use, then contend that it cannot be measured, and if it is measured, attack the measurement. Biderman makes note of this in his chapter:

Attacks on the validity of indicators regarding a phenomenon are a recurrently convenient political device to prevent the policy apparatus from taking account of that phenomenon.

The State of the Nation: Social Systems Accounting (Gross)

Bertram Gross, who has long experience in the development of economic indicators and in the study and execution of economic planning in a number of countries, undertakes the sort of systematic exploration that is a response to the challenge of Biderman's study. Despite the prodigious intellectual effort that Gross has put into the development of a scheme for a system of social accounting, he concludes with the following appraisal:

The ideas set forth in this chapter provide little more than an initial staking out of the territory upon which vast debates must take place.

If his evaluation is correct, it is not because of the limitations of his own contribution but because of the vastness of the task.

It was the existence and success of the set of economic indicators on which planning and policies of both government and industry are based that alerted the Committee on Space to the acute absence of such indicators in most of the other areas of American life. Gross, too, takes the existing economic series as a point of departure for considering the requirements of a broader system of social accounting.

For all of Gross's enthusiasm for the systems of economic accounting that have been adopted in most modern countries, he shows that the defects of the economic indicators in doing their own intended job demand that the system should be expanded.

It is sobering to note that even in areas of statistical reporting that ought to be regarded as "mature," and which have proved their usefulness, writers raise alarms over serious errors of the most ordinary sort. Particular reference is made to the recent volume of Morgenstern, *Accuracy of Economic Observations*.[18] Gross cites Morgenstern as identifying

. . . three principal sources of error in national income statistics: (1) inadequate basic data, (2) the fitting of the data to the concepts, and (3)

[18] Oskar Morgenstern, *Accuracy of Economic Observations* (Princeton, N.J.: Princeton University Press, 1963), pp. 242–282.

the use of interpolation and imputation to fill gaps. The weighted margin of error for such estimates has been estimated as ranging from 10% to 20%. Yet, most of the collection agencies do not make — or else refuse to release — estimates of margins of error. The behavior of economists and statisticians in exaggerating the quality of national income data would in itself be a revealing subject of social — even statistical — research.

Considering the known propensity of economists to confine their counting to things most readily susceptible to being counted — money, other physical objects, and occasionally people — the persistence of these difficulties in the field of economic statistics gives a hint of the further difficulties to be encountered as one moves toward handling what are usually called "qualitative" variables.

But beyond technical errors, which are generally understood and can with diligence be handled, it is apparent that the things the economic indicators now measure do not tell the economists all they want to know.

"Investment," for example, has traditionally been calculated in hard goods. Yet, writers have pointed to obvious instances of "hidden investment" — hidden only because the ordinary accounting scheme ignores them. Such hidden investments are (1) investments of money and manpower in persons, including education and health expenditures that are traditionally classified as consumption outlays, and (2) intangible investment by business and government in research and development, training, and improved methods.

Similarly, goods and services are reported in terms of their monetary value. But economists, such as Wiles, contend that the quality of such goods and services improves more rapidly than does their cost. Hence, there is a tendency to underestimate the trend in improvement in the quality of the supply of goods and services. Wiles proposes that the proper measure is not the cost of such goods and services but their utility to the people who enjoy them. Since measurement of utility is more difficult at the present time than is measurement of monetary cost, this argument of Wiles poses for the first time a question that recurs throughout Gross's essay:

Is it better to have a crude measure of the variable you are really interested in, or a precise measure of a variable which is only an approximation of what you are interested in?

As Gross observes, if these difficulties are to be met, collectors and analysts of economic data "will be deserting the area of data on directly observable transactions in monetary terms."

From this, Gross moves to the conclusion that

... the effort to squeeze all relevant information on action under national planning into an improved system of economic accounts would be tortuous. It would seem much more fruitful to build a broader system of national social accounts that, while not limited to calculations in monetary aggregates, would nonetheless include — and capitalize on — the basic concepts of national economic planning.

By taking the system of economic indicators and their difficulties as a point of departure, Gross establishes a position that may escape the reader. It could be argued that since we have a system of economic indicators based on "good hard data," we would be wise to stay away from the terrifying task of measuring such "softer" phenomena as are involved in a system of *social* indicators. However, it is now clear that the existing set of economic indicators, while useful, has misleading biases in it. These biases arise from the fact of the statistics being confined to those phenomena with which economists have traditionally felt comfortable.

In short, if we are to accept as legitimate the present purposes of the system of economic indicators, we must (1) continue to be misled; or (2) make crude judgmental adjustments; or (3) make a serious attempt at gathering the data that will correct the biases that have already been identified. Since the second choice is only a poor way of doing the third, we are essentially faced with the decision between living with the biases or getting seriously involved in measuring "softer" variables.

It would seem, therefore, that the acknowledged problems of the system of economic indicators suggest quite strongly that we must extend our measurements to other phenomena. The only reasonable question seems to be: How far and how fast? By explicating the full dimensions of a system of social indicators, as he has indicated, Gross stakes out the battleground on which these issues will be resolved.

Here I would like to comment on the relationship of this chapter to that of Gross. There are essentially two types of essays. One, such as this, is selective, concentrating on main themes, and hopefully catering to the reader's interests. The other, the sort of exposition that Gross undertakes, develops a logically exhaustive system. It must perforce explore avenue after avenue, mapping out the minor as well as the major avenues with equal responsibility. This latter type is more demanding of both writer and reader. It is my hope that this portion of the introduction will serve to orient the reader toward the main points and the significance of Gross's work, and thereby enrich the value that he can derive from it.

Much of the terminology that Gross uses is of a sufficient level of abstraction that to repeat it in summary fashion is to do it a disservice. What I hope to convey is the intention and utility of Gross's scheme rather than to summarize it. If I were to report that he says a social system is "characterized by internal and external relations of both conflict and cooperation," the reader is well entitled to say, "So what?" Without having Gross's full exposition of the implications of this highly general statement, the reader has every reason to be confused as to why the statement was made. Only Gross's own *full* exposition of the implications can convey the utility of such characterizations. Hence, my decision to comment without formal summarization.

The basic question is, "What is to be measured?" This question can be answered only if a more fundamental question is asked and answered, "For what purpose?"

We must note that the criteria for evaluating a program of educational reform, a program for stimulating an increase in the productive efficiency of industry, or a program for combating poverty will be different. The criteria for evaluating a broad program, such as the exploration of space, will have to be more wide ranging than those for evaluating some of the narrower programs. But even the space program is narrow relative to the range of programs that one may want to evaluate. It becomes clear on a moderate amount of reflection that any system of social indicators will have to be of *general* utility.

Furthermore, since the study of trends has a time dimension, the designer of such a system should look forward — not confine himself to present problems but try to anticipate the types of data that will be of interest in the future. In an important sense we shall never know many of the effects of space explorations since there are no baseline data on them starting before the beginning of the space program. Thus, the lag of about one generation in the establishment of statistical series is more significant than we have hinted, *if we are to evaluate new programs* from their outset. Therefore, this consideration is another factor forcing us to think in terms of indicators of a fairly high degree of generality — certainly somewhat broader than dictated by our present active concerns.

On the other hand, no system of social indicators designed for general utility will ever be ideal for studying any one program. Thus it is probable that no general set of indicators on the status of education and science would be designed to trace the peculiar confusion of the distinction between science and engineering, which seems to be a by-product of the space programs. The system to be developed must be a reasonable compromise for the range of phenomena that one can anticipate as being of importance.

The natural correlate of the requirement that the indicators be applicable to a reasonably wide range of problems is that the system of indicators be thought of in terms of a fairly generalized model of a social system, using some set of categories broader than a simple description of the institutions of the society in which it is to be applied. Thus, if an inventory is to be kept of the state of political affairs, a provision should be made for comparison of the political system of the country involved with that of other countries.

Perhaps the issue can be made more clear if we take a look at one of the difficulties of a set of economic indicators that have been designed to evaluate events in an industrialized economy. Generally, the volume of consumption goods can be approximated adequately from the total of retail sales or, if the data are gathered from the consumers themselves, the data can be aggregated in money terms. But what is to be done in a society where, as Gross points out, people make their own clothes, weapons, and household goods, either for their own use or for barter? Data on the supply of such goods cannot be gathered from retail outlets. If they are gathered from the consumer, what money value should be put on them? Since, in fact, they would fall outside the systems of economic indicators now in use, could we be led to the conclusion that the natives go unclad?

The reader will probably have noted that I have used the question-begging expression that the system of social accounting to be devised must cover a "reasonably wide range of problems," and must apply to a "reasonably wide range of social systems." How large is reasonable? This is precisely the sort of issue that will have to be fought over in the arena that Gross has staked out. The only point that I want to establish firmly here is that any reporting system — designed for an optimal description of a limited set of issues of concern to one society at one period of time — will certainly make comparisons among societies or across time periods difficult, and probably impossible.

Gross meets the specification that a system of social accounting be designed to evaluate a wide range of programs with the following statement of the performance criteria for evaluating the system as a whole:

The performance of any social system consists of activities (1) to satisfy the interests of various "interesteds" by (2) producing various kinds, qualities, and quantities of output, (3) investing in the system's capacity for future output, (4) using inputs efficiently, (5) acquiring inputs, and (6) doing all this in a manner that conforms with various codes of behavior and (7) varying conceptions of technical and administrative (or guidance) rationality.

These seven criteria are the major performance vectors that he proposes to measure. The fourth item, "investing in the system's capacity," is a key to Gross's approach, since he regards a social system as being composed of both a *performance vector* and a *structural variable*. The structural variable is of importance in that it is the basis for estimating *the future capacity of the system to perform*.

The virtue of an explicit provision for the assessment of the structure of the system can be seen if we examine the consequences of the widespread myth that business organizations function better than other organizations because they are judged by their performance. The harmful aspect of this myth is that "performance" is often taken to mean profitability over some reasonably short length of time. It is quite possible to cannibalize an organization — either deliberately or inadvertently — for a fairly long period of time while having a good performance record. It is a standard practice of some managements, in bad years, to cut budgetary expenses that would normally improve the long-range profit capacity of the firm — research, promotion, management development — in order to show a good earnings ratio in the current year. The addition of an inventory of what Gross calls the structure of the system would give a better picture than a mere measurement of performance.

In recent years a considerable number of writers, usually those concerned with human relations, have asserted that managers should be judged by more criteria than their ability to make a profit over a given period of time. None of these proposals, to my knowledge, has included a comprehensive statement of the structural variables to be measured.

Of course, in addition to providing an estimate of future capacity, the structure of the system at a given point in time may, in itself, be regarded as desirable or undesirable. Thus, there are people who regard a concentration of power in the hands of the federal government as a bad thing per se, or regard the current small nuclear family, consisting only of parents and children, as undesirable compared to the old-fashioned extended family, which included several generations and extended out to first and even second cousins and in-laws. It is possible to argue that the person who reacts in this way is actually concerned with present or future performance —

that is, he is worried about what "big government" will or will not do at some point in the future. However, I think it is more accurate to say that people have come to regard some institutional forms as preferable to others, and they do this without any real evaluation of the effects of these institutional forms. Consequently, as Gross well recognizes, the distinction between performance and structure is not always easy to hold. Nor is it crystal clear that social values should be regarded as a structural feature of the system, as Gross has them, or as an output of the system. They are, of course, legitimately considered as either, depending on the context in which one is thinking of them.

However, it is in considering the existing structure of the system as the basis for future performance that Gross's broader concept makes its great contribution. This approach produces a quite simple solution, in principle, to certain current problems. For example: education, in national economic accounting, is regarded as an item of consumption, and hence government funds going to support of education are "costs." It is well recognized, however, that a better-educated populace is a more productive one, and that *some* portion of the cost of education should be considered as a "capital investment" in the system's capacity. But it is not clear what proportion should be so considered.

Therefore, as part of the assessment of the structure of the system, Gross would take a regular inventory of resources, including human resources. Thus, that change in the economic capacity of the work force, over a given time period, directly attributed to formal education can be considered as the investment portion of the educational bill.

The problem of what is to be considered a cost and what is to be considered a capital investment is a vexing one in both business and government. In business, accounting systems reflect an increase in physical resources (raw material, plant, equipment) though no monetary value is placed on decreases or increases in other aspects of the system that affect its future capacity. Yet, there is no obvious reason why the balance sheet of Company A should look better than that of Company B simply because Company A invested its money in equipment, while Company B invested a like sum in training its management to be more effective. Similarly, an evaluation of the space program ought to reflect a change in the level of competence of its personnel as a result either of NASA's training programs or of on-the-job experience.

Obviously, there are severe measurement problems if one is to take literally the notion that the capability of the work force be assessed in such a way as to convert it into monetary units. As Gross and others have pointed out, in many instances only crude guesstimates can be made. At the very least, a system of *social* accounting, whether applied to a nation or any other organization, has the initial virtue of *legitimizing* variables that are not included in the current systems of economic accounting. This fact, in itself, might bring about rather rapid policy changes. There is a strong tendency for the managers of any system to improve the performance of the system on those variables that are regularly measured. Even a crude, approximate measure would reinforce the manager's judgment on the importance of what are now known as "qualitative" variables.

As I affirmed in my closing remarks on Biderman's first chapter, the picture for measurement of so-called qualitative variables is by no means so bleak as many persons think. We may take, as an example, Gross's proposal for continuing trend studies of the social values of the population. By values we mean those things that the people want, are willing to commit resources to and work for, and for which they have some sense of priority.

One way or another, an assessment of the values of the population is always done. It may be via the intuitive judgment of an experienced political, labor, or social leader. Or more formally, as in recent times, it may be via public opinion polls, which have even in some instances given us good trend data on people's attitudes toward a variety of institutions and issues. Furash's study of two-year trends in businessmen's attitudes toward the space program gave changed perspective to journalistic estimates of what was occurring.

The possibility of making such measures, and with reasonable accuracy, is well established. (The matter of what inferences are to be drawn from such data is a question to be considered separately.) However, the vast majority of public opinion polls suffer from a common defect. Namely, they are too topically oriented and seldom provide meaningful comparisons among groups or across periods of time. Nor do they offer a systematic coverage of the range of social values that seem relevant for assessing the state of a society.

Gross proposes two value systems — one developed by Talcott Parsons, and the other by Clyde and Florence Kluckhohn and their coworkers. These schemes have the virtue of having a wide coverage of basic values, and of being designed specifically to represent what their authors regard as the key values for assessing the state of a society. The Kluckhohn scheme has the additional virtue of having been applied in a considerable number of countries and, by now, with a variety of instruments. It would be my contention that it would be very hard to get complete consensus on *any* system of values that was proposed. Nevertheless, the two systems proposed by Gross have enough to be said for them that they ought to be considered seriously.

Doing such value studies on a continuing basis with an appropriate sample would be technically feasible, and not outrageously expensive. It could also throw some quick light on some perplexing problems — including the social impact of space exploration.

Some of the dimensions that are involved in these value systems have a good deal of practical import. Take Parsons' "pattern variable" that is labeled "affectivity-affective neutrality." What this refers to is that people vary in their disposition toward immediate gratification (affectivity), as compared with deferring gratification in order to work for some longer-range goal (affective neutrality). The distribution of people on this dimension appears to be crucial for problems of economic development.

Parsons' pattern variable also seems to have important implications for our understanding of the role of the Negro in American society, as well as the effect of the space program and similar technological programs on the educational prospects of Negro youths. For the American Negro, who has acquired the values of the American society but is disadvantaged in pursuing them, the issue of whether to indulge in momentary gratification or defer gratification for the longer haul is a crucial one.

A series of studies, summarized in Bauer, Cunningham, and Wortzel, indicate that the Negro community is much more sharply divided on this issue than is the white community.[19] In a wide variety of behavior the "strivers" (those who defer gratification) are markedly different from the "nonstrivers" (those who apparently do not defer gratification). The strivers are the Negroes who are working their way from the fringe into the mainstream of American life.

Should not the space program and similar large technological programs raise the level of aspiration of Negro youths and move a higher proportion into the striving group? The studies the Space Committee has done on the future of technicians in the occupa-

[19] Raymond A. Bauer, Scott M. Cunningham, and Lawrence H. Wortzel, "The Marketing Dilemma of Negroes," *Journal of Marketing*, 29 (July 1965), 1–5.

tional structure indicate that this may not be so. There is a tendency for many Negro youths to look at the educational requirements for jobs of the future with despair and to lower, rather than raise, their aspirations. There is evidence that the expectations of what will be required in the way of an education have been raised by space exploration and related programs to the point where these expectations are actually producing some school dropouts. We do not know, however, what the incidence of this phenomenon is. But it is readily amenable to quantitative study.

As Gross has said in his chapter, and I have said earlier in this one, most of the so-called qualitative variables that would go into a system of social accounting are currently measurable. But, as I have suggested, there is a separate problem of what inferences may be drawn from such measurements. The problems of scientific inference are, of course, vast, and no pretense could be made of dealing with the full range of them here. However, we can deal with one order of problem that is distinctive to a system of social indicators.

The key problem of a system of social indicators, as Gross spells out in a brief but brilliant passage, is that we can never measure the variables that interest us directly, but we must select surrogates that stand in the place of such variables. Thus, we may be interested in whether or not a person is "ambitious." But we cannot observe ambition per se. We can ask a person questions and listen to his answers, or we can observe how hard he will work, and for what rewards. From such observations we can then make an inference that he is or is not ambitious.

In Chart 1.1, which has been reproduced with minor adaptations from Gross, we see what happens as we proceed from a grand ab-

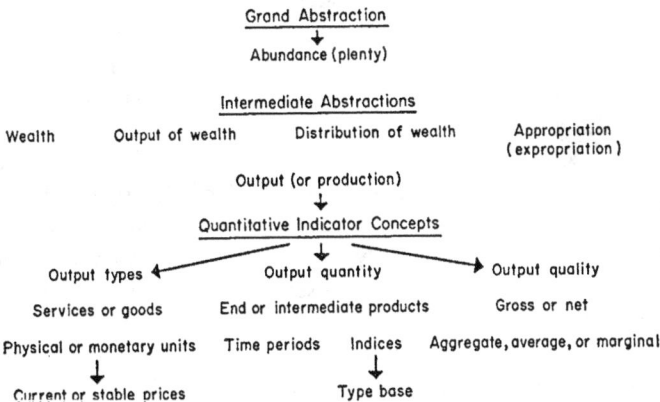

Grand Abstraction
↓
Abundance (plenty)

Intermediate Abstractions

Wealth   Output of wealth   Distribution of wealth   Appropriation (expropriation)

Output (or production)
↓
Quantitative Indicator Concepts
↓
Output types ←   Output quantity   → Output quality

Services or goods   End or intermediate products   Gross or net

Physical or monetary units   Time periods   Indices   Aggregate, average, or marginal
↓   ↓
Current or stable prices   Type base

Chart 1.1.   *The relationships of concepts to observation (adapted from Gross).*

straction, such as "abundance" which is often found in statements of national goals, down to some event or object that can actually be observed, recorded, and communicated. Abundance may mean different things: the nation's total wealth, the rate at which it is adding to its wealth (output), the equitableness of the distribution of wealth, or the rate at which the nation is spending. If we decide to interpret abundance as meaning the output of wealth, we then have to decide in what terms we should measure output. Shall we measure only the quantity of output, or also the types and quality of output? If we decide to measure only quantity, then we must choose between using physical or monetary units. Since there is no ready common denominator of physical units, we shall probably choose to measure the quantity of output in money, and probably in both current and stable prices. This is substantially the GNP (which is computed in both current and stable dollars).

But now we are in a better position to see what the GNP is *not*. For example, it does not tell us the wealth of the nation, although we can make some guesses as to the range of wealth, since it takes an economy of reasonable size to turn out a large GNP. It does not tell us how much was added to the nation's total wealth, since it does not take into account the depreciation of assets during the given time period. (Again, assumptions about depreciation can be and are made.)

There are two points I am trying to make.

The first is that problems of inference are not limited to the measurement of "soft" or social variables. If we begin with any data based on evidence that can be observed directly — that is, the production of goods and exchange of money — these data bear an imperfect relationship to the concepts we are seriously interested in. We often treat the surrogate as though it were identical with the concept that it is supposed to represent, forgetting the inferences we have made and thereby creating a spurious aura of hardness about the data.

The second point is the reverse of the first. If we take a concept such as abundance, or a high standard of living, by the time we have reduced it to a level of abstraction on which we can make observations, we have usually made many choices among surrogates. And the surrogate we have chosen and the way we summarize it may give us a different impression of what is going on than other possible surrogates. We found in Biderman's chapter that for many national goals, as set forth by the President's Commission, there are *no* indicators. From all this we must conclude that to proceed from the existing goal statements to the development of indicators is not going to be a simple process of setting up statistical series in a one-to-one relationship to national goals. Before the establishment of such series is undertaken, some consensus must be reached as to which observations will stand as surrogates for the goal. In addition, probably more than one surrogate will be required in order to give perspective on the selective bias of any individual surrogate.

The impact of Gross's essay, therefore, is not to make the establishment of a national system of social accounting seem simple and within easy reach. The positive features of his attempt are that he does set forth *one* explicit approach, with subschemes of variables, for the assessment of both the structure and capacity of the system, and of its performance. Probably equally valuable is his critique of the problems of measurement, both in the narrower existing system of economic indicators and more generally, since it makes clear that there are no easy consoling reasons for staying within the bounds of the existing system. Neither is the current system adequate for its own purposes, nor are most of the measurement problems qualitatively different from those which would be encountered in a broader system of national accounting.

What Gross has not attempted, and the attentive economist will quickly note this, is to handle the most sticky problem of welfare economics, namely the *value* to be put on the various elements in the system he proposes. For example, if one estimates the future performance capacity of the social system, the value put on that capacity will vary according to the time perspective of the person making the evaluation. Thus Furash[20] found that younger businessmen were more enthusiastic about the space program — which has a long-range payoff — than were older businessmen. Similarly, different evaluations will be made of a given degree of equity or inequity in the distribution of wealth. Such estimates of the value of a given state of affairs will depend on the point of view of the observer. Poorer people have generally been more enthusiastic about equal distribution of wealth than have rich people. Gross proposes only that the data be made available for the persons who wish to, and should, make such evaluations. The ultimate value that the society places on the state of affairs will be a result of the ensuing public debate. This is no different from the situation that exists today with respect to our system of economic indicators. Such indicators provide the data from which varying economists make varying diag-

---

[20] Furash, *op. cit.*

noses and prescribe varying cures. The job of evaluation is not internal to the system of indicators. The indicators are designed to make the evaluation possible.

Gross makes no attempt to undertake the job of suggesting how we can start moving from where we are to the sort of over-all scheme he proposes. This was neither his task nor that of any one of the authors. It is hoped that the juxtaposition of Biderman's first piece, with its analysis of the present state of affairs, to Gross's version of where one might go would serve as a stimulus to readers of this volume to begin to think about this thorny problem.

Anticipatory Studies and Stand-by Research Capabilities (Biderman)

Let us suppose that a thoroughgoing system of social accounting were set up. Even then the evaluation of any large-scale social problem would require additional information that will not fall within any established statistical series. Needless to say, the less perfect our system of social accounting, the greater will be the need for other types of information.

The nature of statistical series is that they monitor an ongoing stream of events, and that in most instances a national system of such statistical series would be shaped to serve a range of the society's interests. This means that there are several sorts of information that will not fall in such a series.

The first of these pertains to phenomena that could reasonably fit into a series but, because of the narrowness of their implication, would not be included. The reasons for not including indicators with narrow implications are economy and avoidance of a glut of information. Biderman's earlier suggestion of "a spherical trigonometry accuracy measure" would be an example of such an indicator. Phenomena of this sort present the same sorts of problems as those discussed in the preceding two chapters. Presumably the response to the lack of this kind of information will be a function of the importance attached to it. A formal series may be established; intermittent formal readings may be taken; or agency personnel may keep an informal tab on what transpires.

There are, however, two types of data that do not fit into trend series, but that may be of considerable importance in evaluating a program. These pertain to unique events that do not fall into a meaningful and useful category, or events that in varying degrees cannot be anticipated. Events in these two overlapping categories are especially important in the evaluation of the space program, because as a novel, large, complex activity the latter generates many novel events, and presumably produces — and will continue to produce — effects that can only vaguely be anticipated.

The problem of gathering such data, Biderman points out, is not so much a research problem as an *institutional* one. The launching of our first satellite, as well as the probability that the U.S.S.R. would beat us to this achievement, was foreseen in the early fifties. Social scientists made the case for gathering base-line data before the event, but they did not have the institutional support. Most specifically, they could not get funds. Futhermore, they themselves were not organized to take advantage of the situation.

The reasons for the current lack of institutional support for gathering research data for program evaluation are several. In the first instance, many of the persons involved are not convinced of the utility of such information and, as a matter of fact, regard it as diversionary (not concerned with important issues) or threatening (causes unwanted problems). This consideration cannot be offset by argument but only by the demonstration of the usefulness of such information over a period of time. Hence, it will not be the subject of further comment here or in Biderman's chapter.

In many respects, however, there has not been an adequate exposition of the difficulties and the possibilities of *ad hoc* research for program evaluation. Biderman's contribution is the exposition of these difficulties and possibilities, and the kind of arrangements they demand, rather than any argument in favor of how useful the information might be. In this connection it will be noticed that *institutional problems* are not limited to lack of support from existing institutions, but also include the absence of the proper institutional arrangements for conducting the research.

The phrase "too little and too late," especially too late, applies to much research done on expectations of, behavior during, and reactions to important events. It is typical that after something happens (e.g., TV becomes an important medium), it is recognized as important. There is then a lag while researchers organize themselves and apply for funds, and still another lag before funds are available. By this time, researchers are put in the hindsight position of having to question people retrospectively as to whether they had expected the event to happen, how they felt about it when it was only a project ("What did you think it was going to be like?"), what they did while the event was happening ("How did you happen to buy a TV set?"), and what effects the event has had on them ("Tell me, are you doing anything different now?").

Enough studies have been made before, during, and after such events to establish that there are characteristic difficulties with retrospective methods. Such studies indicate that we should avoid purely retrospective research wherever possible. But, since it will never be completely possible to avoid the retrospective method, the existing before-during-after studies provide guidance in compensating for the bias of retrospective methods.

Traditionally the natural and the social sciences have striven for measures of the state of affairs both before and after some event (such as an experiment). Where the researcher is working within a well-developed theoretical framework, he can be fairly confident of the inferences that he makes about the processes that occur if there is a change in the state of affairs. Important social events are so complex, however, that inferences as to just what happened to produce the observed change can be made with less than desirable confidence. Hence, we have stressed the importance of studying the event *during* its occurrence, if possible.

The classic before-during-after research in the social sciences has been the panel studies of Presidential elections. In these panel studies, the same individuals are studied over a period of months. There are certain methodological problems in studying the same individual over and over, but the biases produced in this way can be compensated for by introducing new waves of fresh respondents. However, certain phenomena, such as the pattern of switching from one belief or one type of behavior to another, can be observed *only* if the same individuals are studied over a time period. This virtue of the panel design also accounts for its popularity among marketing researchers, who want to understand how an individual shifts from product to product or brand to brand over a period of time.

Research of this sort obviously involves a considerable commitment of all types of resources — money, men, and time. Hence, it is no surprise that such before-during-after research is likely to be done only if there is agreement on the importance of the topic to be studied and of the data that will be forthcoming. However, Biderman calls our attention to another dimension of the issue that is vital but has seldom been made explicit: namely, that research involving a measure before the happening occurs is likely to be made only on events that are virtually certain to occur at a highly predictable time. Elections and the buying of consumer goods are such highly predictable events.

But there are many highly important events — an opportunity to negotiate further arms control measures with the Soviets, discovery of a cancer cure, the time and location of a tornado, a space shot producing sensational findings — that are in varying degrees un-predictable. And people are reluctant to commit money and effort to studying something that might not happen.

Furthermore, as Biderman points out, it is not always clear what aspects of the event will prove of greatest interest. The coincidence of nuclear test ban negotiations with the Soviet Union and the Sino-Soviet rift could have been anticipated only vaguely. The first development to merit the label "cancer cure" will almost certainly be limited to certain types of cancer, and have some unpredictable degree of effectiveness and safety. The same is true of other important events. Typically, when a researcher says that he does not know what is important about the phenomenon he proposes to study, he is often accused of "going on a fishing expedition."

But are things as black and white as all this? It is highly predictable that in a given year there will be a certain number of tornados and other such natural disasters. True, we do not know exactly when and where they will occur, but we can do better than rely on mere chance even for these questions. Experts on international affairs knew that the test ban treaty was increasing in probability, as was the Sino-Soviet rift. Tornadoes occur more frequently in certain seasons and certain regions. Just as the occurrence of such events is not completely unpredictable, so the range of aspects of the event that may be of interest is not definite. Furthermore, if something that was entirely unanticipated occurs in connection with an event, careful advance planning can improve one's chances of studying it effectively despite its element of surprise.

The majority of the events and types of events of most importance to our society are not as neatly scheduled as national elections. The question is, then, how can one execute or approximate the before-during-after research design on such semipredictable events. It is to precisely this question that Biderman has addressed himself:

The problem considered by the present chapter is that of gaining the advantages of *before-during-after* observations when various degrees of uncertainty exist regarding when, where, or whether an important event will occur, or what specific import the event may have. To distinguish the subject of this discussion from the usual *before-after* study, the term "anticipatory studies" can be used for those proposed here.

The basic purposes of the proposed stand-by capability will be to avoid "missed boats" in future programs of research on reactions to space events, and to substitute the presumed more valuable techniques of immediate observation for the current overuse of retroactive methods. . . .

Happily, there are successful examples on which to draw in order to improve our ideas of what such a stand-by facility should be and do.

There is reassurance in one study in which Biderman took part. It was concerned with the predicted mass retirement of military officers in 1961 — the year in which officers commissioned in 1941 would have accumulated twenty years' service. Preliminary work was done on officers' plans for, and attitudes toward, retirement. The expected mass retirement did not occur because of the Berlin crisis that kept most of those officers in active service. It turned out, however, that the nonoccurrence of the event was of just as much interest as the occurrence would have been. The base-line data that had been gathered beforehand proved valuable in studying officers' reactions to the fact that they could *not* retire.

It would seem that the same principle holds for a wide variety of events in which one might be interested. For example, if it is generally believed that a certain event — such as the discovery of life in outer space — is highly likely to occur, then it will be equally important to find out how people will react if life is not discovered. This insight of Biderman's is a powerful counterargument to the frequently expressed notion that certain events are not worth re-searching "because they are not going to happen anyway." The latter argument was frequently encountered by us in planning the work of the American Academy Space Committee. Our rejoinder was that if people *thought* such an event as the discovery of life was likely to occur, then their expectations — whether right or wrong — were a legitimate object of study. Biderman's example indicates that the anticipated probability of an event *occurring* should not be considered as a criterion of research importance with-out considering the degree of interest that would be aroused by its not happening. If its nonoccurrence would be of equal interest, then it is certain that base-line data would prove valuable.

The range of studies that he cites indicates quite persuasively that many events of interest can be anticipated with much greater reliance than has been assumed. Nevertheless, there will be occa-sions when a study must be completely impromptu. Who could have anticipated that an Orson Welles radio broadcast of the later thir-ties would panic large groups of people with the belief that we were being invaded from Mars?

Such completely unexpected events demand, above all, *rapid funding*. Neither Biderman nor I have made a tabulation of how frequent such events are. One could readily do a content analysis of some source, such as the index to *The New York Times* over a ten-year period, and estimate the relative frequency of occurrence of major social events of an unpredictable nature. If the number proved to be reasonably large, there would be an argument for the establishment of a separate funding source that could act with great speed to finance impromptu research.

Lest the reader think that the number would, indeed, be infinitesimally small, I would remind him of the assassination of President Kennedy. Commercial institutions, notably the TV networks, were able to fund research rapidly in order to guide their own programing policies. This research has not been published, nor is it at all certain that it covered topics that the public or responsible officials would be interested in. In the meantime independent scholars, whose interests were broad, found it very difficult to get "instant money," even though they were well-established social scientists who had no difficulty funding research with a longer lead time.

It will be remembered that our goal is to approximate as much as possible the before-during-after design, even where research is completely impromptu. The earlier one can begin the research, the more chance one has of capturing elements of the "during," and even elements of the "before." Certain events — the recovery phase of a disaster, for example — are of sufficient duration that one can begin research on them before they are over. As for recovery of elements of the state of affairs that existed before the event, the advantage of getting in early is that the healing process takes time. This is particularly true if one is dealing with an individual or a community. The individual located and questioned shortly after an unexpected event may be in a state of shock, muttering, "I just couldn't believe it would happen." Several days later, however, he may have rationalized the event, and may say in effect, "It really didn't surprise me at all." Similarly, a disrupted community will erase the traces of the past as it rebuilds.

Our main concern is not with the totally unexpected event, but rather with those events that fall in between the totally unexpected and the virtually certain. It is this intermediate class of events that requires and warrants explicit institutional arrangements with a good deal of preplanning.

The best example of a program of this sort was the research work of the National Opinion Research Center (NORC) under the sponsorship of the Army Chemical Center. The intent was to study public responses to natural disasters that were analogous to the sorts of disasters for which the Army Chemical Center had to plan. By specifying things NORC personnel wanted to learn, the types of persons and behavior to be observed, and developing a detailed day-by-day plan for the work to be carried out at the scene of the disaster, they were able to move onto the scene and observe what transpired while it was actually going on. A key consideration was the instant releasing of a core of NORC personnel from routine duties on receiving the news of a relevant disaster. This special group moved quickly into the field with preassigned research and administrative tasks, among which was the on-the-spot emergency recruitment of additional research personnel.

Since the natural disasters that might be studied vary in their origin (wind, fire, water, earthquake, disease) as well as the type of community in which they occur (small towns, cities, different regions of the country, even other countries), it is obvious that no single research design will be adequate for all situations. But extensive preplanning, plus the ready availability of a core of stand-by researchers, make rapid improvisation to suit many cases possible.

With the NORC model in mind, as well as drawing on other experiences, Biderman presents an illustrative program of stand-by research on events springing out of space exploration. The program that he envisions is useful in two ways: (1) it spells out in detail what would be required in order to have a base-line measure and move into the field with utmost rapidity to observe reactions while they are still taking place; (2) it offers the opportunity for a reasonably priced pilot exercise in assessing the problems and possibilities of a long-range arrangement for stand-by research.

I shall not attempt to capture the details of the plan as proposed by Biderman, although the meticulousness with which it is spelled out is one of its salient features.

Briefly, what is proposed is that competent persons agree on a limited range of space-associated events of sufficient probability so that at least one is highly likely to occur within the next twelve to eighteen months. (It is interesting to note that in his first draft, written early in the history of our project, he chose as one of his likely-to-occur illustrations the "Tiros contribution to avoiding impact of a weather disaster." This event has since occurred.)

Once such a list of possible events had been agreed on, the researchers would gather base-line data on the expectations and attitudes of relevant publics. Biderman proposes three groups of publics. One would be highly involved with the space program — NASA staff members, employees of a large space contractor, and so forth. The other two groups would be a cross-sectional sample of

Americans, and a comparative sample of citizens from one or more other countries. The cost of studying such national samples would be reduced by piggybacking on the work of regular polling organizations.

On the basis of the specific base-line data, plus such generalized expert knowledge as was available, hypotheses would be developed, and research instruments — questionnaires, sample plans, and the like — would be designed to the extent that existing knowledge permitted. Work plans would be developed for the redesign of research instruments to fit specific situations as they occurred. A core of stand-by professionals in this and other countries would be recruited — two requirements of which would be that they commit themselves to be available when an event occurred, and that they keep themselves currently informed on the state of the work plans and instruments.

Biderman's guess as to the cost of such a pilot activity is in the neighborhood of $75,000, but it could possibly go higher.

The question raised by Biderman's chapter is not that of whether such *ad hoc* studies of space-related events should be done, but how they should be done, and by whom. Such events will inevitably be studied; journalists will evaluate their significance and impact; and social scientists will do retrospective studies, with results that might be much improved. Biderman gives the reader some basis on which to judge what might be done in the way of improving our understanding of such events, and whether or not the cost and effort are warranted.

This summary, of necessity, glosses over many details, and since this is a topic on which details are important, it does Biderman a disservice. The reader will discover that he presents a considerable number of alternatives for reducing cost and effort: joint funding, continuing study of a limited number of small communities, cooperation with complementary activity, and so on.

But in closing my commentary on this chapter, I should perhaps raise again the central point of its existence. Any program of reasonable size and duration will eventually (probably very soon) find itself in need of *ad hoc* information concerning phenomena that do not fit into any ongoing information system. At a minimum, assumptions will be made (perhaps only implicitly) as to what the information is. Sometimes deliberate research will be done. The findings will vary in quality. Biderman has specified some of the important factors that cause a variation in quality under existing practice. In particular he has indicated some ways of reducing the loss in quality by taking a more systematic approach to research on events which, while they are not highly predictable, may be of very real importance.

Problems of Organizational Feedback Processes (Rosenthal and Weiss)

The word "feedback" wended its way out of technology terminology and into the general vocabulary with the publication of Norbert Wiener's *Cybernetics*[21] almost two decades ago. It underscores the basic notion that error is inherent in man's conduct of his affairs, and that he can correct the discrepancy between what he intended and what he achieved only if he can know the nature and magnitude of the discrepancy. The concept has the added advantage of reassuring us that even physical and electronic systems designed by engineers require a mechanism (feedback) to detect and correct their errors.

The fact that sophisticated physical and electronic systems have a device for correcting errors built in as an integral part of their design has, no doubt, accelerated the belief that it is a good thing to know about our errors and mend our ways. In fact, the image of the "adaptive organization" adjusting rapidly to signals from its environment has become so pervasive that it is relatively rare to find a balanced discussion of the circumstances under which feedback is useful, the manner in which it should be integrated into an organization, and the limitations of its usefulness. These are the questions to which Rosenthal and Weiss direct their attention.

Importance of Feedback

If the consequences of organizational action were perfectly predictable there would be no need for feedback. This is virtually a redundancy, since if knowledge were identical before and after the event, and we knew it would be so, knowledge gathered after the event would contain no information.

If only one course of action were open to an organization, knowledge of the consequences of that action would serve only to satisfy curiosity. That is to say, if an organization *had* to act, and it had no choice of alternative actions, it could not, by definition, change that action regardless of what was known of the consequences.

[21] Norbert Wiener, *Cybernetics: or Control and Communication in the Animal and the Machine* (Cambridge, Mass. and New York: The M.I.T. Press and John Wiley & Sons, Inc., 2nd ed., 1961).

Finally, if an organization were immune to any reaction to the consequences of what it did — that is, if it could do just what it wanted without any advantage or disadvantage — it would have no self-interest in feedback. Only some form of altruism (or curiosity) could prompt an interest in the results of its actions.

It is highly doubtful that, even in limiting conditions, there are situations in which the consequences of an action are perfectly predictable, there are absolutely no alternatives, or the actor is completely immune. But, organizations and programs do vary markedly in the extent to which the consequences of their actions are predictable, in the extent to which they have choices of alternatives, and the extent to which they are not immune from the repercussions of their actions. To the extent that an organization or program deviates from this "ideal state," feedback is increasingly important. On the whole, the space program — by virtue of its size and complexity, the range of its consequences, and the publics it impinges on — presents a situation that seems to call for a maximum of feedback.

Consequences of action may be difficult to predict for one or both of the following two conditions:

1. Performance may be unreliable, a circumstance that is of peculiar importance to the space program because of its unusually high requirements for reliability in new and complex systems. When an element of a space shot fails, an elaborate electronic monitoring system feeds back the information that makes it possible either to correct the error or to avoid it in the future.

2. The range of secondary and tertiary consequences may be great. This is especially true of the social consequences of the space program which, because of the magnitude and variety of here-on-earth activities, touch on the interests of a great number of groups.

The difficulty of charting the full scope of such possible consequences, let alone of detecting and measuring them, is testified to by the American Academy of Arts and Science's project itself. It came into existence because of NASA's concern with the problem, and its contribution has been as much to document the complexity of the task as to give even partial solutions to it.

To say the conduct of the space program is characterized by many alternatives of methods, time schedules, and subgoals, is not to say that these would all be equally attractive to the officials responsible for executing the program. But, because the program is far from immune to the reactions of various publics, great attention must often be paid to a wide range of possible actions. The selection of the site for the NASA Electronics Center, now apparently firmly committed to Boston, is an excellent example. Presentations by delegations from many cities had to be reviewed, almost certainly from a larger number of cities than would have been warranted on purely technical grounds.

It would be gratuitous to expand on the range of choices open for space officials, or on the lack of immunity of the program to reactions to actual or imputed consequences.

The Representation of Interests

We have seen that the probability of a given social phenomenon being represented in some statistical series is a function of the articulateness and power of the groups whose interests are affected. The same circumstance affects any system of feedback of the social consequences of the space program. Certain reactions will be communicated to NASA spontaneously. Such spontaneous communications will come from two sources.

The first is those persons or groups who are in some sort of contractual relationship with NASA. If NASA personnel policies are unsatisfactory, the Agency will have difficulty in hiring and retaining the persons it wants. If, on the other hand, NASA's employment conditions are more than competitive, there will be an excess of applicants, and it may be possible to adjust policies to effect economies. Similarly, business firms contracting with NASA will make their pleasure and displeasure felt in the most drastic sense by whether they will or will not accept contracts, or in the more moderate sense by communicating the substance of their pleasure and displeasure. Note that such persons and groups need not be organized in order to feed their reactions back to NASA.

The second source of spontaneous reactions comes from groups that are not in a contractual relationship but that are well enough organized to make their feelings heard. Prominent among such groups have been scientific, technical, and educational associations, local communities, certainly Congress, and so on. Such spontaneous feedback is most likely to occur when the group affected is already organized. In other instances groups are organized to express interests. Thus, a community group may be assembled to present the case for locating a NASA installation in that community. Or, if a NASA installation is to be built in the community, a committee may be organized to represent the persons and organizations that may be displaced by land taking. All such groups share with parties in a contractual relationship with NASA the characteristic that feedback from them will occur spontaneously. However, parties in a noncontractual relationship are more effective generally only if they are organized and work in concert.

This does not mean that feedback will be adequate or appropriate. It may be too slow. A group may be irretrievably alienated before it expresses its grievances. Or information may be blocked in the system. A contracting officer, for example, may be reluctant to relay the complaints of contracting firms because he can hope to straighten things out by himself. Or information may be widely dispersed and never have the proper impact. Thus, a given difficulty may occur with low intensity in many places — that is, every contracting officer receives a few complaints about a given policy — so that no one person sees the problem as sufficiently important to warrant action, yet, in the aggregate, the problem may be important. Similarly, some aspect of personnel policy may be of marginal importance in holding or not holding many persons in the program, yet because it does not appear decisive in any one instance this fact may never be reported centrally.

Note that we have already entered into consideration of the fact that feedback is not only *to* the organization but *within* the organization. We shall return to this issue later.

Up to this point, I have argued that if certain interests are affected, feedback will occur spontaneously. This does not mean that this spontaneous feedback will be adequate to the organization's needs. This question must be considered separately.

But what of those interests that do not get represented spontaneously? This will generally occur when the persons involved are not organized and cannot organize themselves, are too powerless or inarticulate to make their voices heard, or do not realize that they are being affected. Or a group may realize it is affected, but it may not occur to the members that they should express their interest. Ironically, the last of these circumstances is likely to occur among the friends of the organization; those who are receiving its benefits but take them for granted. It is rare for an employee or contracting company to write to his Congressman about the pleasures of working for or doing business with an agency, unless that agency or its program is already under fire.

An example of feedback from a group that ordinarily would not be collectively articulate is Furash's previously mentioned survey of the subscribers to the *Harvard Business Review*.[22] This revealed a

[22] Furash, *op. cit.*

surprising degree of support for the space program. It is obvious that the space program or any similar program or activity has a positive interest in deliberately eliciting *favorable* feedback where it would not occur spontaneously. However, when one taps interests that do not speak for themselves, good news cannot always be expected. All one knows is that there *may* be some interest affected, and that the nature of the effect will not be known until it is investigated.

Yet, it seems to be the essence of the idea of building a system of feedback into the society that it be designed to represent interests that will not represent themselves. This is especially pertinent where the effects are not likely to be perceived by the persons affected. Thus, acting as the symbol of the entire aerospace effort and advanced technology, the space program may well contribute to improvements in our system of secondary education and to raising the level of aspiration of the average middle-class youth. The students and their parents are unlikely to see the full range of these benefits as being influenced by the space program. But, on the other hand, by contributing to the acceleration of technological innovation, the space program is probably also contributing to the upgrading of job requirements. This, in turn, increases the rate at which jobs for unskilled workers are disappearing and thus contributes to the rate of unemployment among Negro youths.

The dilemma of a feedback system representing interests that do not represent themselves is that, to a large degree, it involves assuming responsibility for the interests of groups of persons or institutions that are unlikely either to help or hinder. This, in a measure, is what lies behind the ambivalence of policy makers toward public opinion polls on policy issues. In general, such surveys of the broad public call attention to the wishes of people who are not much interested in the issue. The existence of such data forces the public official to take into consideration the interests of a segment of the population that is not likely to help or hinder him in any active fashion and that, in the absence of pooled information, could conveniently be ignored. Thus, feedback may be not only unappreciated but downright inconvenient.

In summarizing the issue of the use of feedback to represent various groups, we have seen that certain interests — those which are in a contractual relationship to the agency and those which are powerful and articulate — will express themselves spontaneously. In these instances the function of the feedback system is to ensure that these expressions of interest will be evoked, transmitted, and processed in such a fashion that they can be acted on appropriately.

Of more interest and difficulty is the functioning of the feedback system to detect those effects that would not be reported spontaneously. This I have labeled as the representation of those interests that cannot represent themselves. There is a certain amount of self-interest in locating beneficial effects that have previously gone undetected. The identification of these beneficial effects can serve to build support for the program involved.

The difficulty arises with the detection of undesirable effects. With a group that is powerful and vocal, there is a selfish interest in early detection of undesirable consequences of the group's actions. This makes it possible to cut off difficulties before they reach a troublesome dimension. However, when the group is unlikely to speak up for itself, the agency or program that uncovers the difficulties of this group assumes on itself the responsibility for correcting a problem when it will get no direct benefit from this remedial action.

From the standpoint of the society as a whole, there can be little doubt about the merits of representing the unrepresented. However, the nature of the responsibility should be broadly understood so that the agency and program are not burdened far beyond their capacity. It should be remembered, as I commented earlier, that each program has its primary objectives and cannot be expected to assume equal responsibility for all the interests of the society.

Feedback and the Organization

The ancient practice of killing the bearer of bad news has come to epitomize barbaric injustice. But the dynamics of this practice persist in any social system of feedback. Good news is greeted with more enthusiasm than is bad news. And this causes characteristic problems for the organization into which information is fed. From the standpoint of the flow of information itself, it may be blocked or facilitated, filtered, distorted, or exaggerated; and the organization may react too little or too much.

The plight of the ancient messenger is found in what Rosenthal and Weiss identify as "boundary roles," which embrace all the positions in the organization that involve contact with the environment. These roles include the top positions — all officials who "represent" the organization; staff and line jobs — those that involve processing information about the environment; contact positions — such as sales, contracts, personnel, purchasing, switchboard, and secretarial.

It should be pointed out that such positions are a source of strain because they involve not only introducing both good and bad news into the organization but also mediation between the organization and the environment. Every person in such a boundary role — from the top executive to the secretary manning the telephone — must, to some extent, deal with the problems of persons and institutions external to the organization. This, of course, produces much of the information concerning the consequences of organizational action. At the same time, the person who expresses the point of view of someone outside the organization tends to be perceived (sometimes correctly) as partially identifying himself with outside persons and institutions.

Since only a few boundary roles — that is, the top positions in the organization — involve direct power to implement actions suggested by information from the environment, the power of most such positions lies in the information itself and in what the possessor of such information does with it. Also, since the organization itself is divided into subunits, this boundary situation repeats itself many times within the organization. (Despite any pious platitudes to the contrary, there are inevitable conflicts of interest between units within any organization.)

The resultant complications for the flow in information are familiar. Rosenthal and Weiss spell out most of the recurrent patterns that occur in organizations. Here it is sufficient to note that impedances and distortions of the flow of information are inevitable, and that the management of a feedback system must take them into account. It should be further noted, however, that such practices are not in all instances bad. They may serve to preserve the morale of the total organization or of one of its subunits, to prevent the overreaction of an anxious executive, to give time to correct some defect before its becomes a source of embarrassment, and so forth.

The issue of the flow of information within the organization is of prime importance for purposes of administration. However, it cannot be ignored when we think of the feedback of information from the environment to the relevant decision centers in the organization. The reason for this is dual.

First, much information about the environment is generated spontaneously out of the daily activities of persons in boundary roles. Specifically, people in these boundary roles are the main, and probably the sole, source of spontaneous feedback from people and organizations with contractual relations. The flow of this information to various points will be a function of the characteristics of the organization. It is well known to students of the topic that such a flow can be highly selective. For example, salesmen are more likely to notice when a competitor has cut his prices than when he raises them. (A cut in prices is a threat to the salesman's competitive position.) Similarly, government contracting officers are almost certain to be more sensitive to developments that cause difficulties than to new opportunities, assuming the developments are of about equal magnitude. Difficulties must be handled, but this is not true of opportunities. However, executives do not always show an appropriate sensitivity to this selective flow.

Second, even with respect to a formally organized feedback system, there is a minimum of one or two organizational layers between the relevant decision points and the entrance of the information into the organization. Suppose we envisage a staff function that both monitors a system of social indicators and commissions or carries out *ad hoc* research of the sort outlined in the several chapters on which we have commented. Suppose further that this function is reported directly to the chief executive. Any information, even though it may be pleasing to the organization as a whole, may well be unpleasant to one or more subunits in the organization. Unless the chief executive succeeds in creating a proper environment, there will be significant distortions even in this system, since the persons carrying out the function will be sensitive to the reactions of those groups in the organization who will be made unhappy.

Information functions similar to what we have been talking about (though not nearly so complete) have been set up in business organizations. They operate well only to the extent that the top officer in the firm is committed to them and understands them. Where he does not, he reacts inappropriately to information that comes to him, permits the function to become a center of organizational strife, and eventually to collapse into disuse. To make such information useful to the organization, he will have to become acquainted with the nature of the feedback system and the organizational problems associated with it, and commit his own power and prestige to keeping it from becoming eroded.

The Nature of the Task: Conclusions

We have addressed ourselves in a literal fashion to the proposition that NASA or some similar institution would want to build a feedback system into the environment in order to detect a fuller range of the consequences of its actions so as to improve the beneficial aspects of these consequences. The fact that many modern corporations do continuing studies of their public image, their relationship to communities, and so on — and this practice is paralleled in whole or in part by government agencies — indicates that we are dealing with something not beyond the range of plausibility.

What is distinctive about our effort is the attempt to consider what a relatively "complete" system would look like, and what it would have to consider. Depending on the reader's predispositions, he may, at times, think we have been naïve, for one of two contrasting reasons: either we have not gone into enough detail or we have been hopelessly utopian. The first person who objects that we have been superficial will be one who believes in the value and feasibility of such a system of social indicators. The second will be skeptical — probably quite skeptical. I would have no necessary quarrel with either position, since our objective has not been to support any concrete proposal but to spell out the considerations that should be taken into account and to give some idea of the options available. In the spirit of Gross's closing passage, we have tried only to stake out the ground on which the issues should be fought over.

Our most optimistic expectation is that the present collection of studies will serve as a stimulus to other scholars to pursue the topic of social indicators more vigorously. As we have indicated at various points, this was an active, in fact the central, issue during the early period of statistics. In recent years voices have been raised from time to time, and there is little doubt that latent interest exists. However, there has been no effort to develop a system of non-economic statistics comparable with that of the economic indicators. Much of what we have to say is not, in itself, new. (Some, we hope, is!) What we have striven for is a reasonably up-to-date statement covering what we envision as the full range of issues that would have to be faced.

One distinctive device has been used, and that is to take the idea that an organization, such as NASA, might want to establish a system of feedback from the environment. This is a realistic and reasonable way of approaching the problem of social indicators, since they make sense only if conceived of as part of an information system that might guide the activities of organizations.

It is conceivable that we might have incorporated into the discussion more of the substance of the problems of the space program. Our experience has made us wary of this. It is very difficult to get deeply into any substantive discussion without becoming engaged in the controversy over the substance itself. As I have noted, we found that the very proposal to study people's expectation of finding life on other planets usually evoked the response that since there was no life on other planets, there was no point in studying people's expectations. In fact, most of the issues of interest are ones on which people have such fixed opinions that a substantial part of them want no feedback. I should be explicit and state that we are not talking about people associated with the space program per se, but about most of the intellectual and official community. On the whole, therefore, I believe it is not expedient to compromise a general discussion on which there can be broad agreement with gratuitous involvement in specific issues.

I might, however, venture a direct opinion as to whether or not NASA *should* establish an elaborate system of feedback into the environment. It is my personal judgment that *at this stage* of the development of the space program any system *much* more elaborate than the present information-gathering activities of NASA would be ill advised. The pursuit of the primary goals of the space program absorbs so much organizational energy that any concern much beyond that currently devoted to second-order consequences would be virtually impossible. Furthermore, the space program and the Agency itself are in such a stage of rapid transition that a high portion of the signals from the environment would refer to historical events rather than to conditions about which something can be done.

However, this is not to say that an agency, such as NASA, that is a leader in technological innovation should not also be a leader in social policy. In fact, a major contribution of the program in the present and near future may be that it stimulates and supports such self-examining ventures as this project of the American Academy. By expressing frank concern for the secondary consequences of its program, NASA has set an example that may be more broadly adopted. And it may be that some older agency, with a more stable program, may venture to build up its information system to more elaborate dimensions.

The proper policy for any agency, whether it be NASA or another, would be one that any prudent administrator would pursue, namely to extend the system gradually, testing it as it was extended. There are two reasons for this gradualism. The first is the need to experiment with the type of information to be gathered and the circumstances under which proper inferences may be made. The second is the necessity of testing the organization's capacity to respond to the information. Both considerations suggest that the extension of the feedback system should begin with *ad hoc* research rather than concentrate on representation in regular data series.

Regular data series are ordinarily preceded by a certain amount of *ad hoc* gathering that tests the possibility of gathering such data in useful form. For example, NASA might begin by experimenting with various ways of assessing the capacities of its personnel and the effect of its own training programs on these capacities. The technology for such experimentation is continuous with much that is presently in use, and the effort therefore feasible. Such studies would move us toward more meaningful measures of the educational level and productive capacity of the labor force. Similarly, continuous study of a few NASA-affiliated communities would help in identification of the major variables of interest in evaluating the social impact of the program on such communities and the best means of measuring these variables. (Obviously, our own efforts, reported by Dodd,[23] are a first step in this direction.)

Such *ad hoc* efforts should not only serve to identify the variables of interest and to develop techniques of measurement. They should also test the utility of the information that is generated. Such information must be of more than academic interest. Even when they themselves have requested it, administrators require a shakedown period in which to get familiar with new information and its use, to assure themselves of its being more helpful than harmful, and to learn the form in which it is most helpful.

Connected with the exploration of the utility of specific data is the organization's over-all capacity to utilize them. This is particularly true with respect to feedback concerning interests not directly involved with the program's primary goals. This is to a large extent a gratuitous acceptance of the wider responsibilities of the total society. To the extent that the assumption of any one such responsibility overtaxes the agency's capabilities, it is highly desirable that the process be reversible and that the agency be able to extricate itself from the responsibility. Hence, the need to explore the extension of the feedback system in a gradual and reversible fashion.

In the meantime, there is reason to hope for some more immediate, though less tangible, benefits from this set of studies. In the writing of them, we have had rather constantly in mind the current state of social criticism and the various misconceptions associated with it. To the extent that scholars, journalists, and public officials

---

[23] Peter Dodd, "Social Change in the Space-Centered Community," to appear in Rapaport, ed., *op. cit.*

have a more realistic understanding of the state of social statistics, and the sorts of information that are needed (and potentially available) for many of the conclusions that are drawn in a cavalier manner, we hope that this criticism may be more responsible.

Any project as novel and visible as the space program is bound to be the subject of much critical evaluation. As such, it is also bound to benefit as the critical evaluations become more realistic. This is not to say that we are selectively concerned with protecting NASA from unwarranted negative criticisms. A program can be seriously crippled by excessive enthusiasm that raises unrealistic expectations or draws attention away from real difficulties. It is in everybody's interest that both the criticism and the expectations of the space program be realistic.

2

Social Indicators and Goals[1]

Albert D. Biderman

"Let us sit on this log by the roadside," says I, "and forget the
inhumanity and ribaldry of the poets. It is in the glorious columns
of ascertained facts and legalized measures that beauty is to be
found. . . ."
"Go on, Mr. Pratt," says Mrs. Sampson. "Them ideas is so original
and soothing. I think statistics are just as lovely as they can be."

O. HENRY, *The Handbook of Hymen,*
as quoted in frontispiece to
M. G. KENDALL and A. STUART,
The Advanced Theory of Statistics

Introduction

Space efforts on the scale currently envisioned will almost surely
produce major changes in our society. The prospect of such effects
has provoked a singular degree of public soul-searching. There is
extensive discussion of the great variety of consequences the national space effort may have on the nation — direct effects and indirect ones; good effects and bad; intended effects and unintended
ones; "spin-offs," "spill-overs," and "feedbacks"; first-order effects
and second-order ones. Many of the disputes concerning the appropriate size and directional emphasis of the program involve differing viewpoints regarding its possible ramifications as well as
differing outlooks on what constitute worthy national purposes.
That the space effort should be approached with self-conscious attention to its many ramifications for the entire society, however, is
rarely questioned.

This self-conscious soul-searching constitutes a departure from
the way in which the nation carries out most of its business. We
are not wont to trace out myriads of possible second-order effects
of social activities, even those of major scope. We tend to feel that

[1] This chapter enlarges on a briefer, earlier paper prepared for the Committee on Space, "National Goals and Statistical Indicators," August 30, 1963.

we are more likely to reach an over-all balance for the good by letting things "work themselves out" rather than by dealing with the effects of one institution on others through explicit planning. A number of factors — novelty, scale, and concentration being important among them — make people more dubious about relying on a "natural harmony" in the case of the space program.

The heightened concern with the program's possible second-order effects may thus itself be one of the important social consequences of the space effort.

Indicators and Sociological Inquiry

The virtue of raising questions about social effects depends on how readily and validly we can answer them and take these answers into account in planning. The material in this essay has been prepared as a part of a broader effort to assess our national ability to consider the social consequences of space programs in providing guidance for their direction. It focuses on the usefulness for such purposes of regularly collected and reported data regarding the society as a whole. My interest is in quantitative data that serve as indexes to socially important conditions of the society: "social indicators." (Except where specifically noted, I shall restrict the term indicators to refer to quantitative statements.) My primary concern is in the relatively neglected areas of noneconomic "social" statistics. However, for reasons of system, comparison, and the lack of clearcut separations of the economic sphere from the remainder of the social system, I shall make continual reference throughout to economic as well as other social indicators.

Since current interest in the topic of social indicators, as represented in the work of the American Academy's Space Committee, arises from a broad, soul-searching concern with the social ramifications of the space program, it is appropriate here to subject social indicators to the same kind of examination. The production and use of social indicators, such as the space program, are organized social activities that have potentially broad impact on the entire life of the society. Here too, a wide range of choices exists among objectives, allocations, methods, and rationales. Here too, we can rely on a laissez-faire attitude, make attempts at broad-scale, rational planning of the activities of social appraisal, or we may settle on various possible points in between.

It is proposed here that social indicators be assessed sociologically. Statistical data about a society are themselves institutional products. They are products of major and usually costly social undertakings; of elaborate institutions. As such, they are influenced and constrained by the principles that pertain to all complex institutions in the society, including some that also shape the phenomena they measure. In addition, they are shaped by some social and cultural factors peculiar to those institutions and their components that have the production of social statistics as a major function.

The social activities that figure in the production and dissemination of social statistics do not exist in isolation from the remainder of the social, economic, or political worlds. Therefore, I take the position that attempts to use social indicators to direct social change will greatly profit by our subjecting social statistics to the same kinds of detached, sociological scrutiny that we give other institutional products.

Demands for Rational Planning

In an article regarding the attitude of businessmen toward the space program, Bauer concluded that the "space race" provided a way in which businessmen could support an economic pump-priming activity of government that "in another garb would be fixed by these same men as dangerously radical."[2] It can be added that it also opens the back door to demands for social planning which are at least equivalently "dangerously radical."

Mannheim saw that the extension of the scale and density of programed social activities generates inevitable demands for new forms for their rational direction.[3] He believed, however, that the forms of social knowledge that were appropriate to a largely laissez-faire socioeconomic order became unsuited to broadly planned areas of social activity. New forms of knowledge and a new form of rationality, he attempted to show, were required to avoid a "partial rationalization" of social enterprise that might be as destructive to society and as distasteful to the democratic temper as no planning at all. He distinguished the "functional rationality" most characteristic of the recent past from the "substantial rationality" which he felt should guide human affairs in the modern world. Functional rationality involved the organization of a series of actions to achieve some given (and isolated) goal. Substantial rationality involved the intelligent insight into the interrelations of

---

[2] See Raymond A. Bauer, "Keynes via the Back Door," *The Journal of Social Issues, XVII* (1961), 50–55.

[3] Karl Mannheim, *Man and Society in an Age of Reconstruction* (New York: Harcourt, Brace and Company, 1948).

events (and goals) in a given situation. The issue Mannheim posed is very much like that with which we are here confronted. A large-scale program, such as that of space exploration, can be rationally coordinated to achieve a limited range of goals. But this partial rationalization may produce drastic effects external to the limited scheme employed. The sheer size of such programs, as well as the correlated magnitude of their impact, prompts us to look outside the framework of limited rationality to assess the larger pattern of the interrelation of events.

What Should Be Measured?

Likert employed a somewhat related distinction in discussing two information functions which he felt statistics should perform:

For purposes of easy reference let us call these two kinds of information, respectively, information as to the *nature* of the system and information as to the *state* of the system. By information as to the *state* of the system let us mean the statistical measurements which reveal the current situation of the nation or economy, such as population data, price indices, and measures of the level of business activity. By information as to the *nature* of the system let us mean the basic conceptual model or understanding which serves as a guide to tell what dimensions of the nation, or society or economy should be interpreted in making decisions. This information as to the *nature* of the system includes, of course, both the conceptualizations themselves and the extensive, quantitative measurements which are required for valid conceptualizations.

It is the job of statisticians, in cooperation with other scientists, to provide the two kinds of information needed for effective self-guidance. In the United States . . . and I suspect also in Canada, our attempts to provide both kinds of information have not been equally successful.[4]

Likert concluded that our statistical production is more successful with respect to developing knowledge of the *state* than of the *nature* of the system. We may question this conclusion if we ask, "How can one assess the adequacy of our measures of state when we do not have prior knowledge to guide us in determining what should be measured?"

Prescriptive Approaches

Two alternatives toward answering this question of what should be measured can be distinguished: the prescriptive and the empirical. For the former, there are many historical precedents. It in-

[4] R. Likert, "The Dual Function of Statistics," *The Journal of the American Statistical Association*, 55 (1960), 1–7.

volves specification of the "important" elements and relationships in the social system it represents; and it recommends indicators needed to measure these elements and relationships adequately. Approaches of this type vary in the grandeur of their aspiration, in the theories from which they draw, and in the kinds of data on which they rely.

Some of the recent prescriptive approaches manifest dissatisfaction with the failure of models of national economies to encompass many of the variables on which economic development is clearly dependent. This has led to many efforts to incorporate various demographic, political, and social factors clearly critical to economic life into models of national economies. Other prescriptive approaches, represented for example by Deutsch,[5] seem to spring from attempts by social scientists who are not primarily interested in economics to assimilate to their work the more accessible quantitative, time series data of economics as well as the systematic features of that science.

Both of these types of objectives lead naturally to aspirations for a system of comprehensive social evaluation paralleling the one that exists for the narrow area of economics. The prescriptive approach, as exemplified by Gross's recommendations for "social accounting" in the next chapter, for example, corresponds with some of Mannheim's ideas concerning the extension of substantial rationality in social planning.[6] It involves the systematic attempt toward achieving a coherent grasp of the entire field of social problems with full regard for their interdependence. It leads to the abandonment of artificial compartmentalizations that have grown up to fit the abstract theoretical formulations of the several social science disciplines and the similar compartmentalizations in the institutional organization of human activities. It attempts to identify what Mannheim termed the *"principia media"* of a society (that is, its uniquely crucial regularities and interconnections), and to provide pragmatic, empirical measures of precisely those key aspects of the social process that permit one to chart and forecast social change and to direct or adapt to these changes.

The Empirical, Analytical Approach

The approach I shall take here is empirical and analytical rather than prescriptive. It is in line with another, more cautionary, and

---

[5] K. W. Deutsch, "Toward an Inventory of Basic Trends and Patterns in Comparative and International Politics," *American Political Science Review,* 54 (March 1960), 34–57.

[6] Mannheim, *op. cit.*

not quite consistent vein of Mannheim's later work and thinking, that is, his sociology of knowledge.[7] At times, as in his hortatory discourses on the need for a transformation of thinking, he appeared to assume that "detached intellectuals" might achieve the unified, bias-free, coherent grasp of the essentials of a society and its age, such as is implied in an attempt to devise a national social account. The assumption seems to be at least partially in conflict with his own study of the sociology of knowledge, in which he assumed all knowledge to be determined by the social and historical position of its producers. Presumably the best way to free oneself from the social and historical factors that shape one's perspectives is to begin by analyzing and understanding their influence.

My approach, therefore, recommends the application of the perspectives of the sociology of knowledge to the evaluation of the adequacy of social indicators for assessing and directing the social consequences of large-scale programs, such as the space effort. Extensive consideration of social indicators from this viewpoint can (1) contribute to extension and improvement of the application of statistical indicators to problems of policy, and (2) provide chastening checks against their abuse. (There has always been some dissatisfaction with the term "sociology of knowledge." A more specifically descriptive and appropriate term for the field of study being proposed here would be a "sociology of societal data.")

Extending the Use of Statistics

In the following pages, I shall illustrate how studying social indicators from the perspective of the sociology of knowledge may extend and improve the use of such data by

1. Identifying institutional, political, and other barriers that are responsible for gaps in data about crucial social phenomena. These findings may point toward ways of increasing the correspondence of available measures of aspects of the society with their perceived importance and desired state.

2. Identifying barriers to the comprehension and use of data in planning and administration.

3. Identifying sources of distortion and bias in the recording and reporting of social data.

4. Pointing to neglected pertinences of data to social values.

Cautionary Contributions. In a chastening vein, I shall attempt to show how this approach toward social indicators may guard

[7] K. Mannheim, *Ideology and Utopia: An Introduction to the Sociology of Knowledge* (New York: Harcourt, Brace and Company, 1951).

against ill-advisedly arrogant impositions of some single system of indicators for universal use as a measure of the state of the society. I shall also argue against any possible tendency toward considering only the formal, technical, or scientific adequacy of societal data in deciding which data should be taken into account in forming policy. I shall attempt to show, for example, that certain value perspectives are more likely to be reflected in "good" statistical data than others of equal legitimacy.

Another relevance of the approach to be pursued here derives from the possibility that an examination of the manner in which a society takes account of itself may provide important indicators of the state of that society.

Limited Objectives. This discussion does not aspire to offer, in itself, any definitive assessment of the adequacy of the social indicators currently employed. A comprehensive consideration of major indicators that are or could be applied requires far greater amounts of time, knowledge, wisdom, and audacity than any one scholar, or at least this particular one, could bring to bear. The limited objectives here are to indicate some neglected ways in which the adequacy of the currently available pool of indicators might be assessed, and to illustrate by simple exercises some of the orientations and approaches that might serve such an assessment.

The kinds of assessments I have in mind, further, do not include technical statistical ones as most contemporary statisticians think of the technical aspects of statistics, although they are statistical in an archaic sense of the term. My concern is with questions of substance, such as the pertinence, scope, emphases, value implications, and biases (in the ordinary rather than statistical sense) of indicators, rather than with such questions as the operational adequacy of samples, data collection methods, or statistical analyses. The technical imperfections of indicators are of interest in the present context only as they reflect differences in the regard given to questions of substance. Pertinent to such inquiry are questions about the inevitable choices that are made in determining what facets of reality the indicators should reflect accurately, less accurately, or not at all; about the molehills of error over which the statisticians or their clients feel impelled to ponder; and about the mountains of error they can easily overlook.

A premise of this inquiry is that in the historical development of the field of statistics, questions of substance have come to be neglected relative to those of technique and method. In Mannheim's terms, the field has developed with increasing specialization and functional rationalization, and with decreasing attention to substantially rational considerations.

Statistics as a Measure of Society

Until relatively recently, the term "statistics" still retained its original historical meaning — a meaning more or less identical with the subject of this present study. Both the Statistical Society of London and the American Statistical Association in their early days defined statistics as ". . . the association and bringing together of those facts which are calculated to illustrate the conditions and prospects of society."[8] The term "statistics" is derived from the Latin phrase *ratio status* and its Italian equivalent, *ragiono di stato*. These terms were coined during the Middle Ages to designate the study of practical politics, as distinguished from historical and philosophical approaches to the state. Achenwall, in the eighteenth century, coined the term *Statistik* as the German equivalent of *ratio status*, and from Achenwall's term the English equivalent reportedly was derived.[9]

Quantification was not until fairly recently an essential element of the definition of statistics. Quetelet, for example, wrote: ". . . among the elements which statistics should comprise, some can be expressed in figures and others can in no way be reduced to numerical expression."[10]

The rise of the numerical study of society is said to stem from the gradual growth of the influence of the seventeenth-century school of thought known as "political arithmetic." In the present century, the reversal has become complete. That the numbers treated in statistics must be numbers relevant to "the condition of the state" no longer has definitional relevance for statistics.

The essential definition of statistics has shifted from its original focus on the kinds of data that should be collected and the ends for which they should be analyzed to the current concentration on technical methods quite independent of content and purpose. Most of the vast current assortments of statistical data now have only limited bearing on central questions of "the condition of the state."

[8] W. J. Cohen and L. W. Stringham, "Statistics for Health, Education, and Welfare Legislation," *Proceedings of the Social Statistics Section, American Statistical Association*, September 7–10, 1962, pp. 238–242.

[9] W. F. Willcox, "Statistics: History." *Encyclopedia of the Social Sciences* (New York: The Macmillan Company, 1934), Vol. 14, pp. 356–360.

[10] A. Quetelet, *Recherches Statistiques sur le Royaume des Pays-Bas* (Brussels, Belgium: 1829), quoted by Willcox, 1934.

Further, the number of such questions for which readily available data provide an answer is also severely limited.

Evaluative Schemes

More than a century ago, Herbert Spencer advocated the following criteria for statistics:

> We want all the facts which help us to understand how a nation has grown and organized itself . . . not only the nature and actions of the central government, but also those of local governments, down to their minutest ramifications. . . . Let us be informed of the control exercised by class over class . . . customs which regulated the popular life out-of-doors and in-doors including those concerning the relations of the sexes and the relations of parents to children . . . what was the connection between employers and employed . . . the intellectual conditions of the nation in its various grades . . . the kind and amount of education . . . the progress made in science . . . the degree of aesthetic culture . . . the daily lives of the people — their food, their homes, and their amusements. . . . These facts, given with as much brevity as consistent with clearness and accuracy, should be so grouped and arranged that they may be comprehended in their ensemble, and contemplated as mutually-dependent parts of one great whole. The aim should be so to present them that men may readily trace the consensus subsisting among them, with the view of learning what social phenomena coexist with what others.[11]

During many subsequent decades, the work of even the empirically oriented social scientists involved strong evaluative components — social problems for some, the theory of progress for others. Devising comprehensive schemes for the evaluation of entire societies was fashionable. Dozens of such schemes, in addition to Spencer's, could be cited, varying greatly in the number and types of indexes each involved. A monotonic path of social development was typically assumed in these efforts, with the onward and upward line defined by the primitive past, the present state of whatever Western nation the author inhabited, and the utopian future presumed by his ideology.

Comprehensive Models

In the most recent past both increasing specialization of social scientists and the dominance of a nonnormative stance have made the pursuit of such ambitions relatively rare. World War II, by

[11] H. Spencer, The Study of Sociology (New York: Appleton & Co., 1914), "Introduction," pp. iv–v.

shattering belief in the "idea of progress" and other ideological faiths, may also have helped render obsolescent simple ideas of the measure of the goodness of a society. Attempts to sum up evaluatively the state of a nation have usually been presented as highly personal and unique tours de force, rather than as schemes for routine and universal application.

Predictive and analytic objectives, rather than normative ones, usually characterized the important comprehensive conceptual models of social systems produced in the postwar period, the most noted of which has been that of Parsons and Shils.[12] This scheme (and others) is directed toward understanding what exists and anticipating what may happen rather than specifying what *should* happen and *should* be.

Various developing interests have led to renewed attention to broad systems of social indicators. Important among these is the interest in the comparative study of contemporary nations, particularly with regard to the need and potential of less developed countries to approach the state of the more highly developed ones. The critical role of factors that elude traditional economic measurements, such as political and economic organization, psychological attitudes, and human resources, have led inquiries concerning economic development to be extended into a broad array of social indicators in their search for predictive models and typologies. The development of computer technology, with its potentialities for handling complex, multivariate problems, has also reduced the premium on the scholar's restricting himself to the barest minimum of indexes. Ambitious simulation models of entire social systems are being constructed which, in turn, are creating a hunger for empirical values that can be "cranked in" for their many variables and parameters.

While a large part of the interest in systems of societal indicators has arisen in connection with comparative economics, politics, and general sociology, I am restricting my attention in this chapter to the United States. Further, to narrow my focus, I have arbitrarily excluded consideration of indicators of the relation of the United States to other countries, and, despite the frequent use made of comparisons between American and foreign societies to evaluate the state of this nation, I shall also avoid here this aspect of the complicated issues of comparative statistics.

[12] T. Parsons and E. Shils, eds., *Toward a General Theory of Action* (Cambridge, Mass.: Harvard University Press, 1951).

Vindicators and Indictors

As Lipset pointed out, there have been quite an extraordinary number of books published in recent years that have sought to provide general evaluations of American society.[13] Among the most widely read of recent evaluations of American society, Lipset cites the works of Vance Packard, especially *The Status Seekers;*[14] C. Wright Mills, *The Power Elite;*[15] William H. Whyte, *The Organization Man;*[16] David Riesman, *The Lonely Crowd;*[17] R. L. Bruckberger, *Image of America;*[18] Max Lerner, *America as a Civilization;*[19] and Eric Larrabee, *Self-Conscious Society.*[20]

On the one hand, according to Lipset, there are the writers who have negative views, such as the following:

America suffers from elaborate corruption in business and labor, and in law enforcement practices; from a growing concentration of business power; from the influences of mass media run by business tycoons who satisfy the lowest common denominator of public taste; and from the wasteful expenditure of resources directed to the enhancement of social status.

Others perceive America differently:

America is an affluent, highly democratic society in which the distribution of income, of status symbols and of opportunities for social mobility is becoming more even-handed all the time; in which tolerance for differences in culture, religion, and race is growing; and in which demand for the best in art, literature, and music is increasing.[21]

The supply of statistical indicators is large enough (and many are ambiguous enough) to enable writers of both varieties of books to find a sufficiency of either of the two major types of social indicators to suit their purpose. These types might be termed "social vindicators" and "social indictors," respectively.

To Lipset's listing of those in the latter class, I might add some other at least equally popular statistical indictors, such as crime, delinquency, divorce, mental disease rates, nonvoting, unemploy-

---

13 S. M. Lipset, *The First New Nation: The United States in Historical and Comparative Perspective* (New York: Basic Books, Inc., 1963).

14 New York: David McKay Company, Inc., 1959.

15 New York: Oxford University Press, 1956.

16 New York: Doubleday and Company, Inc., 1957.

17 New Haven, Conn.: Yale University Press, 1950.

18 New York: The Viking Press, Inc., 1959.

19 New York: Simon and Schuster, Inc., 1957.

20 New York: Doubleday and Company, Inc., 1960.

21 Lipset, *op. cit.,* p. 2.

ment, the rise of the public debt, and the constant swelling of the public payroll. Among the list of common statistical vindicators, there are, in addition to the areas mentioned by Lipset, those asserting a revival in religion, the conquest of disease, and the mounting popular quest for knowledge and education.

A few indicators are up for grabs as between social Cassandras and Pollyannas — their implication can depend on the valuation context in which they are used, for instance, changes in the number of automobiles registered or miles of paved highway in use; changes in age at first marriage or age of mother at birth of last child.

General evaluative works on American society, a number of writers have concluded, have by and large tended to dwell on the statistical data with indicting rather than vindicating implications (see Winick, Bell, Bauer and Bauer, Berger, Biderman).[22] Indeed, the socially vindicating musterings of statistics appear to be a relatively recent reaction to what have been felt to be ideologically slanted indictments of American society, or modern society in general.

Obstacles to Consensual Evaluation

The existence of decidedly contradictory interpretations of the state and tendencies of American society as a whole can be contrasted with the relatively great degree of consensus that exists regarding the state of and recent changes in the economic system. It is considerably easier to get both experts and laity to agree on whether "times are good," and whether they have gotten better or worse during, say, a ten-year period, than it is to get them to agree that the society is improving or is going to hell in a handbasket.

A variety of difficulties stand in the way of the formation of consensus regarding the state and trends of the society as a whole. It is part of the temper of our times to regard these difficulties as stemming from technical imperfections in our systems for developing and using societal knowledge — obstacles that will be overcome by improvements in our craft and the spread of a rational approach

[22] Charles Winick, "The Remora Syndrome: Sick Characteristics in Search of an Author," *Business Horizons, 6* (Winter 1963), 63–72; D. Bell, "Twelve Modes of Prediction — A Preliminary Sorting of Approaches in the Social Sciences," *Daedalus, 93* (Summer 1964), 845–880; R. A. and Alice H. Bauer, "America, 'Mass Society' and Mass Media," *The Journal of Social Issues, XVI* (1960), 3–66; B. M. Berger, "The Myth of Suburbia," *The Journal of Social Issues, XVII* (1961), 38–49; A. D. Biderman, "Dangers of Negative Patriotism," *Harvard Business Review, 40* (1962), 93–99.

to the problems of society. Among these technical obstacles to an adequate and agreed-on system of indicators are deficiencies of the following types:

1. Invalidity.
2. Inaccuracy.
3. Conflicting Indicators.
4. Lack of Data.
5. Incompatible Models.
6. Value Consensus.

A sociology of knowledge approach to these imperfections assumes that they arise only in part from the limited potentiality of our sciences to know and do better. In many instances, we know better than we do. In others, we could readily learn to do better if we tried.

There is, of course, a general readiness to admit that technical deficiencies are not the only obstacles to a consensus in evaluating the state of our society. Irreconcilable differences in values, preferences, rankings, tastes, and the like also block ultimate consensus. It is my contention here, however, that the stock attribution of the obstacles to "differences in values" misdirects attention. It misdirects attention first of all by begging key questions. Second, there is considerable indication that at the level of generality at which many societal-level judgments are made an exceedingly broad level of value agreement exists among Americans, and, indeed, for some issues among most men.

Let us consider each of the types of difficulty just listed to see if there is purpose in raising the question: "Why do particular instances of this difficulty exist and persist?" In each instance, our eyes should be turned toward how the development and use of information regarding a particular aspect of society is embedded in social structure and process.

1. Invalidity

This difficulty stems from the limited validity of available indicators as indexes of the social conditions they purport to measure. By this I mean the correspondence of the index with the conception of its phenomenological meaning that figures in inference and judgment. For example, the use of a family income ceiling of $2,600 to define those living in poverty includes many who are not experiencing the suffering associated with the judgmental meaning of the term "poverty" and excludes many who are. Similarly, educational attainment corresponds imperfectly with concepts regarding the distribution of knowledge and skills among the population. Yet, educational attainment is used as an indicator of such knowledge and skills.

In some cases, the difficulty lies in the contradictory factual interpretations placed on the best available indicator. An example is the controversy over whether the declining rate of patenting manifests a decline in the creativeness of American technologists.[23]

Many of the difficulties stem from the attempt to make scientific use of data that are the by-products of administrative activities. Categories, area boundaries, and unit measures of such data may fit sensibly the laws, regulations, or administrative practices of some organization, but may make little sense outside of the system. A government official, for example, in recounting the difficulties experienced by the Department of Defense in its attempt to evaluate the effects of defense spending, said that analyses of its present contracts showed Manhattan Island as the greatest oil-producing area in the United States because most of the oil contracts are signed in New York and it is to New York that the Department sends the payments for these oil bills.[24]

Similarly, in a discussion of domestic transportation statistics at the Eighth Annual Meeting of the Federal Statistics Users Conference in 1964, it was lamented that the major series on interregional movement of goods still used geographic areas based on the division of the nation into army areas in World War I and that the area location of a carrier was determined by the site of its home office. Categorizations of goods, of course, to the extent a uniform principle is applied, follow the tariff schedules rather than any concept meaningful for a model of the economy.

I am interested here in developing understanding of such matters as (1) the meaning of events that generate data within the system in which they occur, and the relationship of these events to the meanings attached to the data thus generated; (2) the conditions under which an indicator is regarded as bearing a satisfactory relationship to a concept; (3) reasons for the persistent use of an indicator by users who recognize its invalidity; and (4) the effect over

---

[23] S. C. Gilfillan, "An Attempt to Measure the Rise of American Inventing and the Decline of Patenting," *Technology and Culture*, 1 (1960), 201–214; I. J. Kunik, "A Patent Attorney Takes Issue," in *ibid.*, pp. 215–226; and "Dr. Gilfillan's Reply," *ibid.*, pp. 227–234.

[24] Quotation from Adam Yarmolinsky, Special Assistant to the Secretary of Defense, in *Board of Trade News* (Washington, D. C.: Metropolitan Washington Board of Trade, December 1964), p. 9.

time that the use of an indicator may have on the original concept that led to its use.

2. Inaccuracy

Accuracy is affected by errors of measurement, sampling, enumeration, and so forth. The demands of accuracy are particularly great when data are to be used to indicate short-term fluctuations in some social condition. Oskar Morgenstern[25] has called attention to the inaccuracies in the economic time series that are in greatest use in making judgments regarding fluctuations in the economy. He shows, for example, that subsequent revisions in each year's reported U.S. gross national product exceed the magnitude of the changes in this indicator from year to year that have been assumed in reaching influential conclusions regarding the economy. He gives numerous other examples of indicators used to make important inferences regarding fluctuations of the national economy from year to year, or even month to month, where the reliability of the indicator is sufficient at best for judgments regarding changes over a five- or ten-year time span. The major point to be learned from Morgenstern's critique is not that there are errors in indicators. Errors are inevitable. The point rather is that accuracy that is adequate for some purposes, such as measuring long-term trends, may not be adequate for other purposes, such as measuring trends over a shorter period.

In examining the degree of accuracy manifested by various indicators, as I have stressed, my interest in the present connection is not with technical problems of accuracy but rather with the social conditions that determine tolerance or intolerance of inaccuracy; with the determinants of the allocation of attention and effort toward curtailing particular kinds of inaccuracy rather than others; and with similar questions.

3. Conflicting Indicators

Social indicators that have a bearing on the same judgment may have conflicting import. Published data on church attendance, as a case in point, have led to the conclusion that there has been a great revival of religious interest in America. But, while one survey shows that increases in church membership have been keeping pace with growth of the population, another concludes that the

---

[25] Oskar Morgenstern, *On the Accuracy of Economic Observations* (Princeton, N.J.: Princeton University Press, 2nd ed. rev., 1963).

number of Americans not affiliated with any church has been growing by about a million persons a year. These contradictory findings are reported by Petersen,[26] who adds many other instances of contradictory data concerning the religious activity of Americans. His findings support Charles Glock's contention that "none of the work done to assess the state of religion in America currently or historically meets even the minimum standards of scientific inquiry."[27]

The existence of conflicting and competing data often provides a ready basis for examining divergent social perspectives toward a phenomenon.

4. Lack of Data

Even greater latitude for contradictory assertions exists in areas for which there are no usable statistical data whatsoever relating to critical judgments about the state of the society. For many years, for example, it was almost taken for granted that a vast increase in mental disorder was associated with the strains and disorganization of contemporary urbanized society, as compared with its bucolic past. When many of the obstacles to adducing statistical evidence to support this contention were surmounted by the arduous and careful study of the mental hospitalization records of one state for a whole century, the conclusion was reached that there had been no appreciable change in the frequency of psychoses.[28] We are still left without pertinent evidence one way or the other regarding trends in the incidence of neurosis, however, despite the millions of inventories of neuroticism that have been administered in the last few decades. There is complete latitude for contradictory assertions as to whether neuroticism is becoming more or less prevalent, or neither.

Here, we are interested in what accounts for the scope of currently available statistical data. We may ask which ideas about the importance of a social phenomenon are influential in generating indicators of that phenomenon; which characteristics of a phenomenon, other than various parties' estimations of their importance, determine whether they will be reflected in indicator series rather than noncomparable one-time studies.

[26] W. Petersen, "Religious Statistics in the United States," *The Journal for the Scientific Study of Religion, 1* (1961), 165–178.

[27] Charles Glock, quoted in Petersen, *op. cit.,* p. 172.

[28] H. Goldhamer and A. Marshall, *Psychosis and Civilization: Two Studies in the Frequency of Mental Disease* (Glencoe, Ill.: The Free Press, 1953).

5. Incompatible Models

The abstract conceptual systems applied by different individuals in social evaluation differ in the significance they attach to various social elements, in the manner in which they bundle phenomena together in the form of concepts, and in the relationships they affirm as existing among these conceptualized phenomena.

Thus, the economist lumps together and handles in terms of simple assumptions the very core of the questions that the psychologically oriented observer may wish to raise about the society.

In evaluating the effects of the mass media on the general culture, to use another example, Bauer and Bauer[29] conclude: "Because of the intricate interrelationship of causal factors, we probably never will be able to say with confidence just what impact the mass media have on popular taste and values." Nonetheless, they do proceed to make various assertions with varying degrees of apparent confidence regarding such impacts of the mass media. They are able to do this within the framework of particular models that separate out from the welter of phenomena a few to which some singular pertinence is attached and among which some coherent pattern of interrelationships can be stated and empirically tested. They aver that were they to choose different models, their evaluative conclusions might well be different also. Others, indeed, incline toward different models in appraising the effects of the media.

To be useful, each indicator must relate to a concept about the society that is a part of an explicit or implicit theory of the society. The theory abstracts from this complexity certain relationships as the important ones — important both in the sense of value significance and the relatedness of things.[30] Depending on which of various contending theories of society one selects, one will seek indicators for different concepts regarded as fundamental.

Three decades ago, Eubank[31] gave a classic demonstration of the lack of agreement that may exist as to which concepts are basic in theories of society. He selected eight volumes purporting, by their titles, to serve as general treatises. All were by eminent sociologists (of the ten authors and coauthors represented, nine were past

29 Raymond A. Bauer and Alice H. Bauer, "America, 'Mass Society' and Mass Media," *The Journal of Social Issues*, XVI (1960), 3–66.

30 J. Fourastie, "Statistical Measurement of Various Material Aspects of Economic Progress," *International Social Science Bulletin*, 6 (1954), 171–175.

31 E. E. Eubank, *The Concepts of Sociology* (New York: D. C. Heath & Company, 1932).

presidents of the American Sociological Society and the tenth was its permanent secretary). For each volume, he listed the concepts given major emphasis in the treatise — the range of basic concepts per volume varying from 31 to 53, with only three of the volumes having less than 40 such concepts in his listing. All told, 146 different basic concepts were found in the eight volumes, of which only 63 (fewer than half) appeared in more than one list. Not one appeared in all eight; only one, the concept "society," in seven; and but two others, "group" and "control," in as many as six. Only 38 of the 146 concepts were common to three or more of the books.

The situation has changed with the rapid development of the social sciences in succeeding decades so that now, doubtless, a greater number of concepts is generally accepted as fundamental; but this has taken place only with a corresponding proliferation of the total number of concepts in widespread, not to speak of idiosyncratic, use.

In the context of the present discussion, I am primarily interested in why it is that certain models, rather than others, influence the production of national statistical data; the correspondence between those which guide the statisticians and those used in decision making; and the consequences.

6. Value Consensus

This difficulty exists because of the limited agreement on preferences, standards, tastes, and abstractly intellectualized values. Such agreement that exists regarding which conditions are good and bad, better and worse, ultimately limits the agreement that can be reached from social indicators on the condition of the society. Proliferation of the automobile and the mass media of communication are cases in point: some see in them the sinful, heedless pursuit of crass values; others, the spectacular largesse of technology and the free enterprise system.

Values help account for the choices made among alternative and conflicting descriptive models. Lipset, in discussing the conflicting conclusions of the several general examinations of American society discussed earlier, believes that the contrasting interpretations arise from the existence of two not fully compatible but fundamental American values — equality and achievement. Egalitarian principles conflict, for example, with the regard that achievement values demand should be accorded to achievers.

In addition to treating equality and achievement as values applied in judging the society, Lipset uses them, in effect, as *principia media* for explaining "what makes America tick."[32] His approach may make one aware of how American society can be devalued when indicators that are designed to be responsive to the achievement system of the society are appraised in terms of egalitarian values, and when indicators of its egalitarian functioning are appraised in terms of achievement values.

Valuation, in the broad sense of motivation, also enters as a psychological factor into all of the obstacles to consensus on fundamental social indicators that I have been discussing. The psychologists, and before them Bacon, have illustrated profusely the dependence of perceptual and cognitive processes on motivation. Believing is seeing, just as much as seeing is believing. The discipline of scientific method curbs but does not eliminate such effects. I shall avoid delving directly into questions of bias, false perception, consciously and unconsciously motivated error, because these are of a priori, rather than explanatory, importance to the topics of present concern.

Indicators and National Goals

In posing the mission and work of the inquiry regarding space efforts and society, Bauer and his associates suggested that lack of consensus on the goals, purposes, and nature of society accounts for the lack of definitive indicators of "good" and "bad" trends.[33] It can readily be observed, however, that various attempts toward formulating statements of goals and purposes for American society have been accomplished with considerably greater ease and met with greater consensus than have efforts to match these goal statements with acceptable statistical indicators of how the nation is doing with regard to these goals. Indeed, in stating social values and goals, people seem to apply standards of what is important that are somewhat different from those they use in compiling indicators of society's state and trends. This is true despite the influence that available indicators — such as gross national product — have on goal formulations. These points may be illustrated by the following discussion.

[32] Lipset, *op. cit.*, p. 2.
[33] Raymond A. Bauer *et al.*, *Space Efforts and Society: A Statement of Mission and Work*, unpublished memorandum (Boston, January 1963).

Indicators for the 1960 Report

Of the several recent attempts at compiling statements of national purposes and values, the most renowned is that of the President's Commission on National Goals in 1960. Let us examine the major statistical sources to see how well they match the areas considered important by this commission.

An examination of the commission's report reveals that the members agreed on 82 quite explicit statements of specific goals in each of 11 domestic areas (I have ignored, for the time being, foreign affairs).[34]

Two sources, the *Statistical Abstract of the United States 1962*, and *Historical Statistics of the United States: Colonial Times to 1957*,[35] were examined to see for how many of the commission's goals any relevant indicators could be found. The loosest criterion of relevance was applied; the only objective was to determine whether the indicators in these volumes were related to phenomena that were at all pertinent to each goal statement. The indicators did not need to be in any sense an index of attainment of the specific goal.

For only 59 per cent of the goal statements are any indicator data in these sources judged pertinent. Table 2.1 lists the numbers of indicators available in the *Statistical Abstract* and *Historical Statistics* for the goals in each of the eleven *major* goal areas treated in the commission's report. Interestingly, the two domestic goal areas probably most directly related to space activity — "arts and sciences" and "technological change" — are among those for which these sources provide the least indicator coverage.

Indicators for the 1933 Report

My impression was that the data contained in the *Statistical Abstract* and *Historical Statistics* would provide far better coverage of a list of national goal statements prepared several decades ago. Therefore, a subsequent check was performed on the national goal statements in the summary of the report of the committee appointed by President Hoover in 1933 to examine recent social trends in the

[34] President's Commission on National Goals, *Goals for Americans* (Englewood Cliffs, N.J.: Prentice-Hall, Inc., 1960). The goal statements identified and a more detailed breakdown of goals and indicators are contained in the appendix to the chapter. The very loose criterion of relevance is also illustrated.

[35] U.S. Department of Commerce, Bureau of the Census (Washington, D. C.: U.S. Government Printing Office, 1962 and 1960, respectively).

TABLE 2.1

AVAILABILITY OF INDICATORS IN *Statistical Abstract of the United States*
OR *Historical Statistics of the United States* RELEVANT TO NATIONAL
GOALS FORMULATED BY PRESIDENT'S COMMISSION

Goal Area	Number of Specific Goals	Number of Goals to Which Some Indicator Is Relevant	Number of Goals to Which No Indicator Is Relevant
The individual	6	3	3
Equality	3	2	1
Democratic process	11	5	6
Education	5	5	0
Arts and sciences	8	2	5
Democratic economy	9	5	5
Economic growth	9	9	0
Technological change	5	1	4
Agriculture	5	4	1
Living conditions	10	2	8
Health and welfare	10	10	0
Total	81	48	33

Sources: President's Commission on National Goals, *Goals for Americans*
(Englewood Cliffs, N.J.: Prentice-Hall, Inc., 1960); President's Research Com-
mittee on Social Trends, *Recent Social Trends in the United States* (New York:
McGraw-Hill Book Company, Inc., 1933).

United States. This check revealed 37 specific goal areas comparable
with the 81 specific goals in the 1960 report of President Eisen-
hower's Commission on National Goals (see Table 2.2). Relevant
data were found more frequently for the national goal statements
made in 1933 than for those of 1960: 73 per cent of the old goal
statements were matched with one or more indicators, as compared
with 25 per cent in the case of new goal statements in the 1960
report (see appendix).

It is not that the institutional questions to which the data pertain
are not still major issues, or that the volumes have not been kept
up to date. The Bureau of the Census constantly and intelligently
updates these volumes to incorporate data relating to modern developments and to discard others that are no longer timely. What
makes the *Statistical Abstract* as a whole seem somewhat archaic
today is a pervasive change in the broad nature of issues that are
salient in the present as compared with the past. One facet of this
change has been the diminished salience of questions relating to
the fundamental adequacy of the economy for producing and dis-

TABLE 2.2

GOALS STATED BY PRESIDENT'S COMMISSION, 1960, THAT ALSO FIGURE
IN *Recent Social Trends*, 1933

	Number of Goal Areas, 1960	Goal Areas also in 1933 Report
The individual	6	2
Equality	3	1
Democratic process	11	4
Education	5	0
Science	8	1
Democratic economy	9	6
Economic growth	9	5
Technological change	5	1
Agriculture	5	1
Living conditions	10	6
Health and welfare	10	10
Total	81	37

Sources: President's Commission on National Goals, *Goals for Americans* (Englewood Cliffs, N.J.: Prentice-Hall, Inc., 1960); President's Research Committee on Social Trends, *Recent Social Trends in the United States* (New York: McGraw-Hill Book Company, Inc., 1933).

tributing basic consumer goods and services. As I shall discuss, questions of order, integration, and quality appear to have come more to the forefront.

In comparing the scope of indicator sources with statements of consensual national goals, I do not mean to imply that this norm is in any way exhaustive. Such statements, even if they reflect the national consensus most thoroughly and validly, obviously should not be the sole basis for the selection of indicators or the emphasis placed on them. A pluralistic society also needs indicators that allow more parochial interests and viewpoints to measure the society from their perspectives.

Other Indicators

The appendix to this chapter presents some results of a preliminary examination of the scope of two additional government-produced indicator sources. These are the *1962 Supplement to Economic Indicators* and *Health, Education and Welfare Trends*.[36]

As can be noted by inspection of the chart in the appendix, the additional indicator sources have much the same scope in relation

[36] U.S. Department of Health, Education and Welfare (Washington, D. C.: U.S. Government Printing Office, 1962).

to the goal areas as does the *Statistical Abstract*. The specific goal statements to which their indicators relate are largely the same ones for which relevent data are contained in the *Statistical Abstract*.

The appendix also presents an examination of one privately compiled effort — Gendell and Zetterberg's attempt to develop *A Sociological Almanac for the United States*.[37] Although this almanac contains only 90 tables, it presents data judged relevant to precisely as many of the 1960 commission's goals as do the 1,263 tables of the *Statistical Abstract*. One source of the greater pertinence of Gendell and Zetterberg's selection of indicators will be examined in another context near the end of this chapter.

Presidential Regard for Indicators

The foregoing analysis of the availability of indicators illustrates one approach through which we might gain an understanding of the implicit views of society that influence persons making general judgments about its state and tendencies. The simple availability of statistics regarding the society does not ensure that they will be used as indicators in any particular attempt to sum up the country's state. I believe, however, that the incorporation of a particular kind of data in a compendium like the *Statistical Abstract* tends to make legitimate certain views of society that stress particular social processes or subsystems. Without doubt, judgments of statisticians and their disciples concerning the significance of statistical indicators influence the opinions of others of what are the essential elements of the society. As President Kennedy remarked in his "State of the Economy" address:

I know that statistics and details of the economy may sometimes seem dry, but the economy and economic statistics are really a story of all of us, as a country. And these statistics tell whether we are going forward or standing still or going backwards; they tell whether an unemployed man can get a job, or whether a man who has a job can get an increase in salary or own a home, or whether he can retire in security or send his children to college. These are the people and the things behind statistics.[38]

This comment about the importance and human meaning of statistics would have been more notable if it had been made within the context of the late President's State of the Union message rather than that on the State of the Economy. Although President Kennedy

[37] New York: The Bedminster Press, Inc., 1961.
[38] "Address to the Nation on the Nation's Economy," *Congressional Quarterly Almanac* (August 13, 1962), p. 920.

and President Johnson made considerably greater use of statistical indicators in their State of the Union addresses than did their predecessors, their uses of these indicators have been predominantly in setting forth the economic facets of the nation.

The messages of Presidents on the State of the Union constitute a possible source for examining the changing regard for statistical statements of the "condition of the state" and the particular facets of the national life that Presidents have felt could most readily be grasped by a statistical statement.

An examination of State of the Union messages since Washington delivered his first on Wall Street in 1790 suggests that until relatively recently statistics (in the present meaning) occupied a peripheral place in Presidential attempts to indicate the critical facts about the state of the country. Frequently it was some unique condition, rather than one that could fit meaningfully into a standard category of a time series, that was the most significant fact in these messages: the threat of war or the actuality of war, the seizure of the Isthmus of Panama, Jefferson's new policy pronouncement on immigration and naturalization, or the setting off of the gold rush by Polk's confirmation of the rumor that "an abundance of gold" had been discovered in California.[39]

Use of Quantitative Statements

To give an accurate reflection of the more recent State of the Union messages, which have made greater use of indicators, I selected 48 messages. Using a table of random numbers, I took one-half of the messages of the post–World War II period; one-third of those between the Civil War and World War II; and one-sixth of those before the Civil War. War years were excluded because of the restriction of our interests to domestic affairs.

As might be expected, it was found that there has been considerably greater use of quantitative indicators in the recent messages. In Table 2.3 I have grouped messages by time periods chosen to reflect trends in the average number of indicators used per message. The increase in indicators per message has actually been more uniform through time than the table reflects. This is due to the fact that prior to the present century the messages included reports on the affairs of each of the executive departments. In subsequent years, the Presidents have relegated these reports to appendixes and

[39] See E. Boykin, *State of the Union* (New York: Funk & Wagnalls Co., Inc., 1963).

special messages that have not been considered in the present analysis.

As Table 2.3 shows, the average number of indicators per State of the Union message has grown from 3 in the first half of the nine-

TABLE 2.3
FREQUENCY OF INDICATORS, STATE OF THE UNION MESSAGES*

Number of Indicators per Message	1794–1843	1844–1893	1894–1946	1947–1964
0	1	0	3	0
1–5	5	7	5	1
6–10	2	8	5	3
11–15	0	1	2	3
16–20	0	0	0	1
21–25+	0	0	0	1
Total number of messages in sample	8	16	15	9
Mean number of indicators per message	3	6	5	11

* War periods excluded from sample.

teenth century to 11 in the period since World War II. The current trend appears to be an accelerating one, with 28 indicator statements appearing in the 1961 message alone.

Shifts in Indicator Emphasis

As has been suggested, indicators have been used in State of the Union messages predominantly with reference to economic matters. Over the entire time span of the sample, almost half of the 306 indicator uses identified were economic. The trends over time have been interesting, however. The proportional use of indicators reflecting noneconomic affairs of the society was greatest in the first hundred years of the history of the republic. Only 42 per cent of all indicators used were economic during this period. The attention to economic matters increased during the present century, with 60 per cent of the indicators used from 1903 to 1948 reflecting these matters. Most recently, the scope of indicators has begun to broaden again, with only 47 per cent of the indicators in messages sampled for the past ten years being economic. These trends are shown in Table 2.4.

The shifts in emphasis observed suggest that the increasing availability of noneconomic indicators was not immediately reflected in their increasing use. Rather, as the more specific categories shown in Table 2.4 reveal, indicators have been selected to illustrate the major preoccupations of the time. In the early period (1794–1894), this involved establishing a national economy around a sound cur-

TABLE 2.4

TYPES OF SOCIAL INDICATORS IN STATE OF THE UNION MESSAGES

Social Indicators	1794–1894 (25 Messages)		1903–1948 (16 Messages)		1954–1964 (7 Messages)		Combined (48 Messages)	
	No.	Per Cent	No.	Per Cent	No.	Per Cent	No.	Per Cent
Economic indicators	55	42	55	60	40	47	150	49
Total activity and income statistics	12	9	7	8	4	5	23	7
Markets and production	4	3	15	16	12	14	31	10
Income (distribution)	3	2	21	23	10	12	34	11
Productive resources	4	3	2	2	3	3	9	3
"Sound" currency	15	11	2	2	2	2	19	6
Employment rates	2	1	8	9	9	11	19	6
Surpluses (Treasury)	5	4	0	0	0	0	5	2
Debts	8	6	0	0	0	0	8	3
Sales of public lands	2	1	0	0	0	0	2	1
Noneconomic indicators	75	56	36	38	45	52	156	50
Population	15	11	8	9	6	7	29	9
Technological advances	0	0	0	0	17	20	17	5
Education	7	5	3	3	4	5	14	4
Military appropriations	5	4.	0	0	6	7	11	4
Utilities and transportation	4	3	4	4	1	1	9	3
Governmental growth	28	22	2	2	1	1	31	10
Natural resources	3	2	6	7	3	3	12	4
Welfare†	6	4	3	3	3	3	12	4
Other	7	5	10	10	4	5	21	7
Total	130	98°	91	98°	85	99°	306	99°

° Percentages do not total 100 in every case due to rounding error.
† Fewer than six cases: includes deaths and accidents, industrial disputes, lynchings, penal codes, health, voting statistics, and disease control measures.

rency, populating the vast expanses of the nation, and the growth, as well as fears of the growth, of governmental institutions. In the middle period (1903–1948), the production of distributive commodities was the dominant interest. Most recently (1954–1964), it

has been technological change, with particular regard to its significance for national security and prestige.

Relevance to Goals

These shifting emphases are perhaps shown better by a reclassifi-
cation of the indicators in accordance with the scheme used earlier;
namely, their pertinence to the particular national goal areas of the
1960 President's Commission report. Table 2.5 shows the indicators

TABLE 2.5

INDICATORS IN STATE OF THE UNION MESSAGES 1794–1964 RELEVANT TO 1960
NATIONAL GOALS FORMULATIONS BY THE PRESIDENT'S COMMISSION

Goal Area	1794–1894 (25 Messages)		1903–1948 (16 Messages)		1954–1964 (7 Messages)	
	No.	Per Cent	No.	Per Cent	No.	Per Cent
The individual	3	2	14	15	4	5
Equality	3	2	1	1	0	0
Democratic process	13	10	0	0	1	1
Education	2	1	1	1	2	2
Arts and sciences	5	4	0	0	17	20
Democratic economy	0	0	3	3	1	1
Economic growth	2	1	14	15	22	26
Technological change	0	0	0	0	0	0
Agriculture	0	0	1	1	1	1
Living conditions	0	0	5	5	4	5
Health and welfare	0	0	2	2	6	7
Relevant	28	22	41	43	58	68
Not relevant	102	78	50	55	27	32
Total	130	100	91	98*	85	100

* Percentage does not total 100 due to rounding error.

in each of the same three time periods that have relevance to the
various areas of the 1960 goals statement. As is to be expected, the
time trend in indicator use is toward greater relevance to these contemporary goals. Almost half of the 127 indicators in the sample
that were judged relevant to these goals were found in the messages
of the last ten years. The shift of indicator attention from the goal
area of "democratic process," in nineteenth-century messages, to
those relating to the individual (in particular, his free choice in the
market) and economic growth, in the first half of the present century, is shown in Table 2.5. In the decade 1954–1964 there is decreased attention to the area of the individual, increased attention

to economic growth, and revived interest in the "arts and sciences" (actually almost exclusively sciences).

Indicators of Progress and Problems

Analysis of the direction (positive or negative) of the indicators contained in State of the Union messages yields an additional dimension for historical comparison. Tables 2.3, 2.4, and 2.5 demonstrate the frequency, type, and contemporary relevance of the social indicators, respectively. Table 2.6 is a corollary of Table 2.5 in that the same types of social indicators are examined, but with a view toward determining which types of social indicators, if any, have been used to point to "progress" or to "problems." This was accomplished by grouping the indicators according to whether they were used to describe a desirable, undesirable, or neutral condition.

Thus, for example, the area of governmental growth emphasized in the first hundred years was found to use indicators in a predominantly negative way. Of the 28 indicators used, 19 were in the vein of "government is a necessary evil."

Except for the 1954–1964 decade, there is little over-all difference in the total positive-negative balance of the messages. This period, however, contains twice as many positive as negative indicators, which may suggest that the messages have become more of a political, self-congratulatory, vindicating vehicle than an evaluational one. For example, of the 17 indicators in this period that are concerned with technological developments, all 17 are presented as evidence of national progress.

Generally, the economic indexes used (as compared with the non-economic ones) tend to be more positive than negative. The greatest differences occurred in the last decade when 28 out of 40 economic indicators were used to document "progress." It should be noted that using economic indicators to show "progress" rather than "problems" continued throughout the 1903–1948 time period, including the years of the Great Depression. In fact, one-third of the positive economic indexes used in this period are found in the 1930 State of the Union message. This message may be viewed as a direct prototype for later vindicating types of messages. With respect to unemployment, for example, the emphasis was on the amount of employment that *did* exist rather than on the employment that did not exist.

Production and Use of Indicators

There is a high degree of interaction between judgments of the importance of a phenomenon and the existence of measurements of

TABLE 2.6

DIRECTION OF SOCIAL INDICATORS: STATE OF THE UNION MESSAGES

Indicator Direction

Index	1794–1894 (25 Messages)			1903–1948 (16 Messages)			1954–1964 (7 Messages)			All Periods (48 Messages)		
	Progress	Problems	Neutral	Progress	Problems	Neutral	Progress	Problems	Neutral	Progress	Problems	Neutral
Economic indexes	26	28	1	34	21	0	28	12	0	88	61	1
Total activity and income statistics	8	4	0	3	4	0	4	0	0	15	8	0
Markets and production	1	3	0	11	4	0	10	2	0	22	9	0
Income (distribution)	0	2	1	11	10	0	8	2	0	19	14	1
Productive resources	2	2	0	1	1	0	2	1	0	5	4	0
"Sound" currency	5	10	0	0	2	0	2	0	0	7	12	0
Employment rates	0	2	0	8	0	0	0	7	0	10	9	0
Surpluses (Treasury)	2	3	0	0	0	0	0	0	0	2	3	0
Debts	6	2	0	0	0	0	0	0	0	6	2	0
Sales of public lands	2	0	0	0	0	0	0	0	0	2	0	0
Noneconomic indexes	33	39	3	8	28	0	29	13	3	70	80	6
Population	6	8	1	2	6	0	0	3	3	8	17	4
Technological advances	0	0	0	0	0	0	17	0	0	17	0	0
Education	5	1	1	0	3	0	2	2	0	7	6	1
Military appropriations	5	0	0	0	0	0	2	4	0	7	4	0
Utilities and transportation	1	3	0	1	3	0	1	0	0	3	6	0
Governmental growth	9	19	0	1	1	0	0	1	0	10	21	0
Natural resources	3	0	0	0	6	0	2	1	0	5	7	0
Welfare	1	4	1	3	0	0	3	2	0	7	4	1
Other*	3	4	0	1	9	0	2	2	0	6	15	1
No.	59	67	4	42	49	0	57	25	3	158	141	7
Percentage	45	52	3	46	54	0	67	29	4	52	46	2

* Fewer than six categories each; include deaths and accidents, industrial disputes, lynchings, penal codes, health rating statistics, and disease control measures.

it. We attempt to observe and comprehend those aspects of reality that are important to us, but, at the same time, the aspects that we are best able to observe and comprehend seem to be those that become important.

With the growth of the complexity of society, immediate experience with its events plays an increasingly smaller role as a source of information and basis of judgment in contrast to symbolically mediated information about these events. The vast amount of information that must be digested places a premium on the selectivity, rapidity, condensation, and generalization of knowledge. Numerical indexes of phenomena are peculiarly fitted to these needs.

The result is not only that social bodies seek to devise numerical indexes to gauge those phenomena that are important to them, but also that those phenomena for which a satisfying numerical index exists assume a special influence on judgments. Sibley remarked:

Statistics published in the chaste and solemn 8 pt. and 6 pt. of the Government Printing Office possess a persuasive quality to which even the most rigorous academic discipline does not produce complete immunity.[40]

If incorporated in the important statistical sources and in Presidential pronouncements, this persuasive effect presumably extends to the significance of the data, as well as to its reliability.

Factors Affecting the Production of Statistics

A consensus of the entire society or of any given social group within it concerning the significance of certain phenomena does not mean that these will be reflected by available indexes. There are other factors determining the availability of indicators. Among them are (1) measurement technology, (2) social observability, and (3) data-agency perspective. Let us look briefly at each of these more closely.

1. *Measurement technology:* the susceptibility of the phenomenon to accurate measurement, given the current state and resources of statistical science. It is easier to develop data on changes in the wealth of the population than in their virtue or happiness; on the number of TV sets per family than on the number of close friends.

2. *Social observability:* the susceptibility of social phenomena to measurement, in turn, is dependent on whether the social processes involved are organized, consciously or not, to permit such mea-

[40] E. Sibley, "Conceptual Integration and Government Statistics," *The American Sociological Review*, 6 (1941), 860–863.

surement. Better data are available on legal than illegal economic transactions. Openness versus secrecy, centralization versus decentralization, standardization versus variation, represent alternative dimensions of organization that affect susceptibility to measurement.

3. *Data-agency perspective:* this factor constitutes differentiated social groups with their own perspectives toward the phenomena in question — perspectives that are only partially determined by a sharing in society-wide consensus, or by the value outlooks of the consumers of their product. In addition to special aspects of the recruitment and social position of statisticians and other indicator producers, other factors affecting their product derive from the values of their craft, for example, aesthetic standards, which regard the elegance of formulations and the prides and vanities of the professional group as well as the rationally technical standards of the profession. The statistician is not a "mere technician." He is a technician with certain backgrounds and standards, working in an agency with its own traditions and interests.

The producers of indicators include the institutions that sponsor or perform the tasks of data collection, measurement, and analysis. The subject of observation may be some aspect of their own operation or some external subject. All groups in the society must rely on others, at least in part, to produce important information and communicate it to them. In addition, the information and index functions are usually the task of specialized institutional components. The statistical profession and related ones constitute particularly important agencies of measurement. Choices with respect to what should be measured, and how, are greatly influenced by the special perspectives and interests of the producing agencies. The nature and magnitude of the effects of these special viewpoints are reduced, but not eliminated, by standards of objectivity, disinterestedness, and verity. The agencies also differ in the extent to which they are constrained by such standards with respect to any given measurement function they perform. The constraints may operate because of the instrumental significance of telling the truth to the producing agency, ethical identification with the norms of science, or the need to maintain the repute of the agency or of its product.

That these three factors are of importance is obvious when one examines critically a specific indicator or the indicators available in some specific field. Each type of factor is also a matter of frequent discussion among the users and producers of indicators.

To the extent that there is novelty or virtue in the discussion of these factors here, it lies in the attempt to consider them as part of a general scheme for evaluating the present state of social indicators and the appropriate roles of indicators in the society.

How Indicators Evolve

Lowry has given some indications of the way in which new federal statistical series evolve:

The procedure for determining priorities is complicated and imperfect. It starts with something like the list before us which has been distilled from an even longer list. The specific items get on the list for a variety of reasons: because of inadequate data which have adversely affected some Federal program or some business operation; because important political issues have thrust particular problems to the fore; because of the particular analytical bent of some advisor or advisors to the President; because of the interest of some articulate, hard-driving bureaucrat or academician; because of the interest of some Congressional committee or some individual Congressman; because of the activities of some outside group; because of the technical review of important statistical programs by qualified individuals or committees.

The way in which priority needs are selected from this list and are pushed forward includes some elements specifically related to the Budget process such as: the relative strengths of the most important officials within a particular statistics-producing agency; the attitude of the Department head toward the statistical agency or agencies under his supervision; various balances of pressures within the Bureau of the Budget; the authority exercised by the Bureau of the Budget in determining the statistical program in any given year; the skill or ineptitude of the head of a statistical agency in explaining his program to Congressional appropriations committees; the attitude of Committee chairmen toward statistical programs; the degree of outside interest in or opposition to particular proposals; and the way in which the head of a statistical agency apportions his money among various projects. And at every stage, from the statistics-producing agency to the Congressional committee, the question of possible public reaction to the collection of data requested is a factor of conscious or unconscious importance.[41]

Scientific Uses of Indicators

Scholarly evaluations of social indicators have largely been restricted to considerations of their manifest functions, that is, representing the extension to the social realm of the modern drive toward

[41] R. L. Lowry, "Federal Statistics for the Sixties," *Proceedings of the Business and Economic Statistics Section, American Statistical Association*, September 7–10, 1962, pp. 86–90.

scientific understanding and control.[42] If we confine ourselves to questions of how accurately indicators reflect the realities they aspire to measure and how good a basis for control of these realities they provide — to what we shall call here "scientific uses" — we shall have gained only a very partial understanding of their nature, scope, and social functions. Indeed, very little is known systematically about the extent and ways in which indicators are actually employed by policy makers and administrators in the practical, decision-making manipulations of the realities that the indicators reflect.

This is manifest in a preliminary report by a task force of the Bureau of the Census[43] the purpose of which is to undertake a study of the uses of census statistics. The task force attempted an extensive review of all studies of uses of census statistics that had been made either in the Bureau of the Census or by others. Insofar as the uses of social statistics for the indicator functions — to which our attention is given here — are concerned, almost none of the sixty-odd studies the committee discovered were concerned with this kind of function. Among the few that did, rarely did they pose questions relevant to actual uses in practical decision making.

The meaning of "use" in the studies covered by the committee was far broader than I intend here. Most of the investigations of uses of census statistics uncovered by the committee were actually surveys or compilations of expressions of interest in, or need for particular items of, information by customers of the Bureau, without indication of the source of the need in the decision-making problems of the clients. Among these were compilations of recommendations and requests regarding the inclusion of items and tabulations in censuses.

Another meaning of use is that exemplified by the various guidebooks to particular series. Here, use means how to locate and interpret particular kinds of information in the published data, or to manipulate them in the process of generating other data.

Still another major class of uses identified by the studies was to meet legal requirements, such as those involving the allocation of state funds to localities on the basis of population. A few, notably Hauser and Leonard's *Government Statistics for Business Use*,[44] provided recommendations on practical uses that could be made, with illustrations.

[42] D. Bell, "Twelve Modes of Prediction — A Preliminary Sorting of Approaches in the Social Sciences," *Daedalus*, 93 (Summer 1964), 845–880.
[43] U.S. Department of Commerce, Bureau of the Census, *Interim Report of the Task Force of Uses of Census Statistics* (October 18, 1963), unpublished litho document.
[44] New York: John Wiley & Sons, Inc., 1956.

In the realm of economic statistics, a somewhat better picture of use can be developed — this largely from the "how to" literature of business and economic forecasting. The bulk of the business and public administration literature, however, appears to be exhortatory — offering advice on how indicators can be used in policy and administration rather than in empirical surveys of the nature and extent of its actual uses. This literature contains an occasional case document of a particularly successful use, and also retrospective examinations of the predictive value of a particular business indicator, such as stock market forecasting indicators.

It is clear that the problems would be complex of conducting a study of what constitutes the rational employment of social and economic statistics in policy formulation of any large institution. Millikan discusses at length how difficult it is to pinpoint the ways in which social data are taken into account in the policy process. "We must recognize," he writes, "that every practical judgment in policy affairs is based on a structure of concepts that is largely implicit and poorly understood."[45]

The Task Force on Uses of Census Statistics found it "one of the thorniest problems" to identify types of uses and to investigate their importance:

Census Bureau statistics may have indirect use in creating other statistics — as a benchmark for projecting a series, as a basis for setting up a sample survey and collecting new statistics, as a component in a more comprehensive measure or index (such as gross national product or the index of industrial production), or as a means of presenting data for analysis (such as putting other figures on a per capita basis). These are uses, but their importance depends on the usefulness of the new statistics.

Similarly, use in solving a problem, developing a theory, or proving a point is only as important as the problem, the theory, or the point. Evaluation of this use is difficult. In one case, certain statistics may be critically important in developing a policy that affects a small group of people; in another case, other statistics may be of minor importance in developing a policy that affects a large group of people.

Publication of statistics in statistical compendia, newspapers, or magazines is use that is difficult to evaluate. This publication is evidence that an editor considered the statistics useful to his readers. If he was right, it may result in some good "hard" use.

Mailing lists, libraries, and field offices are good leads to users, but the Task Force believes that not all important users are at the end of the Bureau's mailing lists or at the desks of the libraries that stack the reports.

[45] M. F. Millikan, "Inquiry and Policy: The Relation of Knowledge to Action," *The Human Meaning of the Social Sciences*, D. Lerner, ed. (New York: Meridian Books, 1959), pp. 158–182.

Many of them are concealed behind secondary sources of Census Bureau reports (such as trade journals) or behind the publication of statistical series of which the Census Bureau data are components. In some large business organizations, the men who make the important decisions get the statistical information they need from their own research groups, which may or may not report the primary source. The Task Force suspects that users who do not show up on the Bureau's mailing lists and users who do not know they are users may be significant groups.[46]

Thus, the difficulty in demonstrating scientific uses is not that such data fail to be used and proved useful in policy and strategy, but rather that it is difficult to trace through any concrete instance the precise ways in which the various inputs of knowledge affect given outcomes. Subsequently, there remains the greater difficulty of summative examination of these processes in a wide variety of decision-making contexts.

It is perhaps for reasons such as Millikan discusses that examinations of social data programs provide such scant concrete demonstration of their management value: for example, indications of how specific decisions have followed from considerations of specific indicators. In perusal of reports of examinations of federal statistics programs, such as hearings of the House of Representatives Subcommittee on the Census and Government Statistics, I find a great deal of general comment on the *scientific* value for administrative and policy uses of the data under discussion. It is my impression that the more concrete testimony in support of, or in opposition to, specific proposals for the development of indicators, rests on the nonscientific uses of such data.

Nonscientific Uses of Indicators

The types of nonscientific uses of indicators that figure most importantly in these settings are derived from the assumed *scientific* value of the statistics. However the nonscientific uses are not identical to and can be partially or wholly independent of their scientific usefulness. They are the roles data play as (1) the bases of claims against resources according to allocative devices established by law or custom, (2) as ammunition for the various parties to the adversary procedures of intraorganizational and interorganizational politics, (3) as the cohesion of organizational alliances, (4) as symbols for the persuasion of publics, and (5) as new grounds for national and institutional creeds.

---

[46] U.S. Department of Commerce, Bureau of the Census, *op. cit.*, pp. 5-6.

Typically, the party that introduces a given indicator into the discussion of a specific policy is not primarily concerned about learning the actual state of affairs. The fact that he may have complete prior conviction regarding what that state is places him in no less of a need for the indicator. His primary need is to get some other party to act on the premise that a certain state of affairs exists.

It is belaboring the obvious to point out that a suburban county commissioner can more easily satisfy his own need to know how much population growth has taken place in his county than he can meet the statutory requirements on the basis of which state and federal funds are parceled out to local jurisdictions.

To gain support, the sponsor of a retraining program must produce the indicators demonstrating the employability of the prospective trainees. The journalist needs to spark his reader's attention and interest. The political candidate seeks indicators to show that crime has mounted during the incumbency of his opponent. The do-gooder tries to show the need for reform; the patriotic orator, his country's greatness; the ideologist and the utopian, their country's decadence.

All of these functions of social indicators, as well as their purely scientific use by policy makers, planners, managers, and scholars, must be considered if we are to appreciate the role of social indicators in society and if we are to seek to improve their manifest functions. These nonscientific functions are, of course, legitimate. Numbers are rightfully both a device whereby an individual brings order to the world in which he must act and a means of communicating his view of the state of affairs to other people. As I have stressed, such nonscientific functions of indicators play, of course, a great role in bringing social statistics into being.

Knowledge Versus Certification

The relative influence of scientific and nonscientific uses of statistics on the data activities of the federal government was illustrated in hearings conducted by the House Subcommittee on Census and Government Statistics in a number of cities in connection with the proposed mid-decade census.[47] The administration and the Director of the Census were opposed to replicating the Census at mid-decade. They argued that a far greater return of knowledge about the population and business of the nation could be gained by the

---

[47] U.S. Congress, House of Representatives, Committee on Post Office and Civil Service, Subcommittee on Census and Government Statistics, *Mid-Decade Census*, Hearings, 1961–1962.

large number of special, sample-survey studies that could be conducted with the same funds as would be required for a complete, census-type enumeration. The most vociferous representatives of user groups, however, were strong proponents of the complete enumeration. These were primarily state spokesmen who were faced with laws that involved apportioning legislative representation and allocating funds on the basis of census figures. True, there were also proponents of the complete enumeration who had scientific purposes: for example, those who had the need to identify specifically the blocks that should be targets of renewal activity in a city. They included also the statisticians who needed more up-to-date block statistics of cities as the basis for their own population samples, and they included representatives of the retailers who needed to know where to locate their stores.

There is good reason to believe, however, that among those who represented their need as one of developing knowledge there actually was a more preponderant need for certifying facts which they already knew. One function of the complete enumeration of the population in a census is that its results are more widely credited as accurate than those of sample surveys. It seems almost certainly the case (and now the position of the Census Bureau), however, that the practical difficulties of carrying out the complete enumeration constitute sources of errors of greater magnitude than the combined error due to sampling and data gathering in the large, highly professional sample survey. (In large, properly drawn samples, the sampling error is negligible, while the lesser load of not doing a complete enumeration makes it possible to do a better job of gathering data from individuals and of reaching hard-to-get persons who are a source of errors in both a census and a sample survey.)

In considering social indicators, the separate functions of developing knowledge of the state of the society and that of certifying what is already known both need to be considered. The latter function involves one party communicating information to another which the receiver accepts as valid and pertinent in the manner intended by the originator.

Indicators are useful as certifiers for scientific reasons, as well as for pseudoscientific and nonscientific ones. Their scientific properties of parsimony, abstraction, generality, communicability, and precision lend themselves equally to the problem of certification and to that of transforming confusion into knowledge. They also possess pseudoscientific advantages, such as the "magic" of numbers and their ability to make an imprecise statement appear to be a precise one. And, as we have illustrated, there are nonscientific advantages, such as the special legal status they may be given.

The discussion here does not begin to exhaust the various functions of indicators as certifiers. A series of case studies of indicators in specific fields would be required to begin to outline how these social aspects of indicators operate and how they vary among many types of indicators.

Earlier in this chapter, in using the terms social indictors and social vindicators, I implied the increasingly significant use of social statistics as objects of expressive behavior. In examining particular social statistics that perform such functions, we may raise questions of the features they have which fit them for the function, and examine what relationships such nonscientific uses may have on the generation and acceptance of scientifically useful statistical indicators.

Indicator Quality and Social Change

The space program is singularly innovational in the nature of many of the activities that comprise it and, presumably, in the nature of the impacts it will have on society. Among the most influential early conceptualizations advanced for understanding the social problems raised by innovations were those of Ogburn. Different types of institutions and cultural elements, according to Ogburn, change at different rates in response to technological innovations affecting them: in particular, the "material culture" changes more rapidly than the associated aspects of "nonmaterial culture," such as beliefs, values, customs, and patterns of social organization.[48] The consequent strain and maladaption among differentially changing elements — the "cultural lag" — provided for Ogburn a diagnosis for many, if not most, social problems.

Strain on Rationality

Although these ideas are regarded now as trite by many social scientists, they nonetheless are quite congruent with a common outlook toward some of the problems discussed here. It is a common opinion that techniques for collecting, ordering, and analyzing social data have developed more rapidly than has the ability of society in

[48] William F. Ogburn, *Social Change* (New York: Dell Publishing Co., 1964).

general, and of the planning and operational units of organization in particular, to take advantage of this knowledge in ordering social affairs.

Nevertheless, there are those persons in positions of responsibility who seek "hard" answers to specific practical problems from the social scientists. They lament the primitive state of the development of social science knowledge, which usually makes it necessary for them to rely on seat-of-the-pants judgment to take account of "the human factor" or "the social factor."[49]

The truth of the matter is that both are right in considerable measure. Statistical knowledge regarding the society has developed more rapidly than appreciations, understandings, and social arrangements that could profit from it. The seeker for practical answers, at the same time, is also right in his finding that the hard answers that can be provided are usually answers to questions he has not asked. It is not simply that the two types of social activities — knowledge producing and knowledge using — change at different rates, but also that they change along somewhat unrelated paths. The paths of both types of efforts toward rational coping with the changing social world also change in imperfect consonance with the demands on rationality presented by the changes of that not very rational world.

The social scientist bears a special burden in the quest for keeping rationality abreast of social change — in recognizing the lags and disparities among the outlooks of social participants and between outlooks and realities. While he has the burden of pointing out to others the false and peculiar perceptions that stem from their distinctive social position relative to other groups and the existential world, this is a burden he tends to assume more willingly than the one of applying the same questioning attitude toward his own activities.

Lags and Indicators

Social statistics also manifest cultural lags. Three kinds of lags affecting the appropriateness of indicators occupy our attention here:

1. Indicators fail to keep abreast of the techniques of statistical measurement.

2. New indicators are not developed to meet new needs for information.

[49] Millikan, *op. cit.*

3. Indicators fail to change in the manner needed to reflect alterations in the nature of the phenomena for which they are an index.

Many of the indicators most frequently used for important judgments concerning the state and trends of the society are certainly misleading. This is true not only where the best indicators provide inexact or ambiguous measures of the magnitude of change, but also where they leave doubt about the direction of change. Just one abstract on a particularly well-developed field, demography — Bogue's summary of knowledge of the U.S. population — provides many such examples. The following are illustrative:

> The known weaknesses of the divorce rate as a measure have caused disputes as to whether the incidence of divorce has increased, decreased, or remained the same since 1950.
> The rapid growth of urban population . . . was temporarily slackened by a combination of business depression and inadequate census definitions.[50]

There are great deficiencies, which make interpretation difficult, in many other types of statistics that are frequently used in making judgments about the state of the society — statistics on health, crime, skill, culture, and others.

An Illustration — Unemployment

As a society changes, the social phenomenon an indicator measures may undergo a metamorphosis. In form and in significance, the phenomenon may alter radically while the same meanings continue to be associated with the indicator.

The measure of unemployment may be taken as illustrative. At a given juncture in our history — the Great Depression, for example — unemployment statistics reflected primarily the magnitude of the failure of the society to make economic use of its manpower resources. This was also one of the major meanings attached to it in interpreting its significance for public policy. It was also generally interpreted as a measure of how widespread economic hardship was among the population. Such significances still tend to be attached to gross measures of unemployment, although the social phenomena reflected by the measures are quite different than they were in a declining or stagnated economy.

To a great extent, unemployment today reflects the increasingly

[50] D. J. Bogue, *The Population of the United States* (Glencoe, Ill.: The Free Press, 1959).

efficient use society makes of manpower. Most of the short-run changes in the indicator, upward or downward, do not reflect developments that can be translated into the question of whether more or fewer citizens are experiencing economic hardship. Rather, it reflects the entrance or withdrawal from the labor force of various categories of persons who are marginal to it, particularly women and students, whose income from work is not the primary source of their own or others' sustenance.

To some extent, gross unemployment may rise with increasing economic opportunity. This can come about when a visibly favorable economic climate encourages large proportions of such marginal groups to seek active employment. Since much larger proportions of such groups will fail to find satisfactory work than is the case with stable members of the labor force, the gross percentage of the labor force that is unemployed will show a rise.

In the opposite direction, the gross figure of total unemployed does not represent a full measure of the number of citizens experiencing hardship. Those urging "antipoverty" and "full-employment" policies emphasize that the much used figure of "per cent unemployed" does not reflect those who need full-time work, but are employed only part-time, and the "hard-core" unemployed who have "left the labor force" after despairing of finding a job.

Unemployment statistics are an instructive example because they involve a type of lag that is thoroughly appreciated by the producers of the series, as well as by many of its users.[51] The long-standing importance of the phenomenon, the vast amount of continuing research directed toward it, its prominence in more rationalized areas of policy consideration, all have developed a high degree of sophistication toward this indicator in both its production and use. The lag is in large measure an illustration of a gap between the producer and the user, particularly politicians and publicists. The Bureau of Labor Statistics series presents fairly detailed breakdowns of the gross unemployment fluctuations, which permit identification of the particular kinds of members of the labor force who constitute the "unemployed": identifications by which one can gauge the significance of considerations such as I have just discussed.

There is also considerable appreciation of the altered significance

---

[51] See U.S. President's Committee to Appraise Employment and Unemployment Statistics, *Meaning of Employment and Unemployment* (Government Printing Office, Washington, D.C.: 1962).

of unemployment statistics in examining their implications for public policy. This is manifest in the attention devoted to such proposals as those for creating more jobs by curtailment of hours of work and retirement plans, eliminating teen-age idleness (to offset psychological demoralization and juvenile delinquency rather than to stave off economic want), deferring entrance of the youth into the labor force by extending the normal period of education, and providing "meaningful" roles for housewives and the aged.

The sophisticated use of qualitatively elaborated unemployment statistics has also served to pinpoint the problems of economic and social hardship that are very much a part of the current economic order — the "pockets of poverty," the lack of fit of various categories of unskilled men and women with the demands for skilled workers created by the contemporary economic apparatus.

Sophisticated uses and production of unemployment series, however, coexist with obsolescent and simplistic ones — in newspaper copy, in political rhetoric, and in serious national policy proposals. It might also be ventured that inertia due to long-rooted concepts and vested interests retard the thoroughgoing rationalization of the indicator. Perhaps only a renamed indicator could free the series from the dead weight of a term so imbedded in the ideologies of the past.

Another Illustration — Education

Educational statistics illustrate a somewhat different type of lag when we consider a common interpretation made of them. In the recent past, the formal and systematic imparting of knowledge and skill was almost exclusively performed by what is termed the educational system. Its units are schools or educational institutions, and curricula. The major type of indicator used to form judgments regarding how much was being done in the nation to impart knowledge and skill was some kind of count of the time people spent as students in an educational institution. The major type of indicator of what kinds of knowledges and skills were being imparted was some kind of count of the time people spent as students of one or another curriculum. These are still the major indicators used for these judgments.

There have always been organizations, apart from the educational system, that have performed functions indistinguishable from some of the varieties of functions basic to the school. The apprentice system of the crafts is thought of as having continuity since the Middle

Ages. On-the-job training is not a new invention. Master-pupil relationships, such as that of the neighborhood music teacher or the artist with his disciples, have a long and continuing history.

Increasingly, however, we find activities going on outside of the educational system that in format and physical aspect, as well as objectives, are even less distinguishable from what goes on within units of that formal system. The armed forces certainly comprise by far the largest "educational institution." But only a very small part of even those activities in the armed forces that involve an instructor talking before a group is counted in the educational statistics.

Similar institutional illustrations could be added indefinitely. If my impression is correct that there is a proliferation of variegated institutional arrangements, for instance, within NASA and within the plants of all of its large industrial contractors, that are assuming increasing importance for imparting knowledge and skill among the population, how do we go about evaluating educational statistics as an indicator of how extensively such functions are being performed in the United States?

Adult education and training are taking place outside the formal school system — most intensely in those institutions associated with especially rapid technological change, among which the aerospace industry is pre-eminent. Hence, this deficiency of educational statistics is of special pertinence in evaluating the social impact of the space program.

Expert Judgments as Indicators

Some attempts have been made at various times to combine the virtues of hardness and quantification with the scope, discriminatory power, and sensitivity of informed human judgment. Currently, a notable example is work at the RAND Corporation toward investigating the systematic uses of panels of experts to develop quantitative estimates of phenomena.[52]

The systematic use of expert opinion was also endorsed recently as a remedy for dissatisfactions with the scope and quality of indicators used in cross-national comparisons — dissatisfactions apparently quite similar to some voiced here toward indicators of conditions in the United States. In an unsigned review of the *World Handbook of Political and Social Indicators*,[53] developed by the

[52] See Bernice Brown and O. Helmer, *Improving the Reliability of Estimates Obtained from a Consensus of Experts* (Santa Monica, Calif.: RAND Corporation, September 1964); and O. Helmer and N. Rescher, "On the Epistemology of the Inexact Sciences," *Management Science*, 5 (1959).

[53] B. M. Russett *et al.*, *World Handbook of Political and Social Indicators* (New Haven and London: Yale University Press, 1964).

Yale Political Data Program, the following comments appeared in the *American Behavioral Scientist:*

Now let us get to the crux of the matter of statistical indicators. As they are to be discovered in semi-complete status by even the best-trained researchers, they are often wide of their mark; they simply do not measure what they purport to measure and moreover vary from one place to another. Secondly they do not indicate the proper things. Although we have here a well-executed set of practically all the world political-social-economic, that is, public policy, indicators that can be found in a semifinished condition, many of them, perhaps over half, are nearly useless. Those that are the more useful wobble as they move from one nation to another. . . .

Still speaking in terms of the conventional framework of such statistical knowledge, the Yale group should give teleological form to its activity. Why do they want to find what indicates what? Only if the goals for which the evidence is sought are known can the right indicators be found. . . .

More likely, the Yale political data group should execute a holding action on the conventional front, which must depend upon unreliable census-takers from everywhere, and should seek to develop a new methodology of indicators. How long would it take and how much would it cost to set up a world policy inventory system that would be based on expert opinions and sample surveys? Both "expert opinion" and "sample surveys" are so much more rapid, cheaper and flexible than censuses that ultimately they must replace them for the greater number of useful profiles of international conditions. . . . The panel technique needs to be perfected for cross-national comparisons. We can imagine a conversion of expert opinions into a quantitative ordering of unemployment phenomena that would be incomparably richer in meaning and in its own way much more "accurate" than the present set of data. The science of appraising conditions is well organized in welfare, mortgage-banking, and other occupational areas. Perhaps the Yale group might ponder the need for training social and behavioral appraisors to provide an adequate supply of standardized judgments on a large number of specified policy conditions.[54]

A Case Example: Crime Rates

The limitations and developmental lags in indicators, I submit, can be sufficiently serious (and frequently are) so that we might in many cases be better off with no indicators at all than with the highly misleading ones that are used.

This would be the case where we conclude that things, on

[54] " 'What Indicates What?' *World Handbook of Political and Social Indicators*," *American Behavioral Scientist*, 8 (December 1964), 29–31.

balance, are going well when they are going ill, or vice versa. I shall illustrate this by considering at some length the problem of crime.[55] Crime statistics have been chosen for a number of reasons, including the following:

1. Crime rates are a much used indicator of basic social problems in the nation.

2. They have been subject to extraordinarily great attention in recent public discussion.

3. They illustrate the special kinds of difficulties that occur where the data are developed by, or from, agencies of social policy and action that are involved with the social phenomenon measured.

4. They constitute an illustration of the possibility of an indicator being poorly adapted to reflect the nature and significance of social changes, with the result that it conveys sometimes one-sided, sometimes reversed, value implications.

5. They have been subject to extensive scholarly examination.

Crime data also have a peculiar relevance to the space effort.

Crime and the Space Effort

At first blush, the problem of crime may seem remote from the problems of evaluating the social consequences of the space program. Actually, the more remote of such influences seem to come first to mind. Space activities and space discoveries, some fear, may have an upsetting effect on established conceptions of the natural order of the world, as the Age of Exploration is said to have upset notions of the natural order that had been established in medieval times. There are speculations and theories that link the attachments of people to the moral order with their sharing of sets of assumptions about space and time.

An intellectually and temporarily less remote association exists between the space program and the incidence of crime. Urban areas affected by the rapid growth of new industry and new population are those that register the sharpest increases in "crime rates," as compared with areas of relatively stable or declining "population rates." Because of this factor, one could show an association between concentrations of space program expenditures and high and increasing crime rates. For example, the Florida east coast and the Southern California and Nevada areas, along with Houston, Texas, all have rates among the highest in the nation.

[55] All crime statistics discussed in this section are drawn from *Uniform Crime Reports, 1963* and previous annual numbers.

Meanings Attached to the Crime Rate

We tend to regard the incidence of crime as probably the most critical manifestation of the failure of social organization. Crime involves a rejection of the moral code of the society. Various popular theories contend that an increased incidence of crime indicates the failure of society to function properly; a decreased incidence, a more effective society.

Some theorists emphasize the psychological element, the success of the society at inculcating its moral norms. Others stress the social organization and the opportunity structure, the ability of a society's members to live satisfying lives within the rules. Still others place greater stress on the effective operation of more formal control, the law, law enforcement, and the penal systems.

Thus, some attribute increases in crime to the failure of agencies of socialization — home, church, school, and community — to develop moral standards and respect for the law. Others attribute it to poverty and the lack of opportunities for social mobility. Still others ascribe it to the weakening of systems of control and sanctions.

In recent years, there has been a dramatic increase of interest in the most widely publicized of all sources of information regarding crime in the United States: the Crime Index prepared by the Federal Bureau of Investigation and published in its annual *Uniform Crime Reports for the United States*.[56] This has excited alarm about trends in our society among holders of each of the points of view toward crime that I have just sketched.

Misleading Nature of the Crime Index

While the FBI's *Uniform Crime Reports* has a technical section that gives definitions and caveats against misinterpretation, the Crime Index receives its greatest public attention in the long, but less cautious, summary section of the report and in the mass media publicity that immediately follows its release each year. A number of properties of the report contribute to this special attention.

First of all, it provides a basis for statements of the sweeping type, such as "Crime has increased ——— per cent in the United States."

Second, the index is restricted to selected "serious crimes." The adjective "serious," however, is not stressed as much currently in describing the Crime Index as it was in earlier years, partly be-

[56] Washington, D. C.: U.S. Department of Justice.

cause it excludes many types of crime that the law and the public regard as more serious than some of the types it includes. There is also dispute about the relative seriousness of some of the reported offenses included, particularly those classed as automobile theft.

Third, it is indeed the most adequate general measure available of changes in the incidence of criminal behavior. As serious as its failings are — and there are a host of other failings we cannot encompass in this discussion — it is less subject to variations in definition and administrative practice than other measures. It is based on "crimes reported to the police or coming directly to their attention" rather than on arrests, trials, or convictions. Being thus derived from the data "closest to the act," the index is least subject to the selective underenumeration that characterizes other sources.[57]

The technical section of the 1963 FBI *Uniform Crime Reports* is more cautious than the long summary section. The caveat in the technical portion of the report that the crime-rate tables aim at the most reliable data for the current year, and that "care should be exercised in any direct comparison with previous issues," is not heeded in the summary. The technical section points out that "changes in crime level may have been due in part to improved reporting procedures," but this comment also is not presented in the summary.

Yet, in terms of public and official attention, the *Uniform Crime Reports* is among the most influential of noneconomic indicators. This is true at both national and local levels. It is among the noneconomic series most frequently cited by the press. It forms the basis for many far-reaching proposals for changing laws. The 1963 *Uniform Crime Reports* itself was published with a preface that includes an attack by the Director of the FBI on "many impassioned pleas . . . on behalf of the offender tending to ignore the victim . . . which are made despite a rapidly rising victim risk rate."[58]

The FBI report fosters an image of an uncontrolled surge of crime. Such an image contributes to citizens deserting their cities, streets, and parks. Presumably, it gives comfort to those lawbreakers who conclude that what they do is innocent relative to the type of crimes "everyone else" commits. To my knowledge, no one has investigated whether the image of rapidly and constantly mounting crime contributes more to support of constructive measures against

[57] T. Sellin and M. E. Wolfgang, *The Measurement of Delinquency* (New York: John Wiley & Sons, Inc., 1964).
[58] *Op. cit.*, p. vii.

crime than to despair and distrust of the mechanisms for coping with it.

This raises the question of whether the availability of an inaccurate indicator is better or worse for the society than having no indicator at all. The availability of a simple indicator may, indeed, lead to the smothering of more accurate but complex information concerning a problem area that might otherwise gain a hearing in public consideration of the problem.

Conclusions Regarding Errors

Criminologists are aware of many ways in which the *Uniform Crime Reports* grossly distorts the incidence and loci of crime in the United States (the same is true of juvenile delinquency statistics collected by the Children's Bureau).[59]

I contend that most of the sources of error operate to inflate the newer figures relative to the older ones, resulting in a false picture of rapidly increasing lawlessness among the population. With respect to most of these sources of error, it is extremely difficult and sometimes impossible to give quantitative expression to the factor.

Nevertheless, in examining several published criticisms of the index, and in subjecting it to my own critical examination, I believe that the following three conclusions emerge:

1. The errors and biasing factors affecting the Crime Index largely operate to show spurious increases, rather than decreases, in the rate.

2. The Crime Index does not provide a sound basis for determining whether criminal behavior is increasing, or decreasing, in the United States.

3. The Crime Index is highly sensitive to social developments that are almost universally regarded as improvements in the society. Thus, it is altogether possible that year-to-year increases in crime rates may be more indicative of social progress than of social decay.

These conclusions are particularly true with regard to precisely those three aspects of society that figure in popular theories of the causes of crime. I shall show that increases in the crime rate may stem from (1) more widespread and intense identification with the norms of the national society, (2) greater integration and effectiveness of the economic and social systems, and (3) more effective

[59] See H. A. Bloch, "Juvenile Delinquency: Myth or Threat," *The Journal of Criminal Law, Criminology and Police Science, 49* (1958), 303–309.

operation of the formal agencies of control, such as the police and courts.

However, before discussing each of these aspects of society, let us first turn our attention to two important points that must be understood about the index.

The Crime Index and Violence

The Crime Index is based on voluntary reports from police agencies of the incidence of serious crimes. This is useful selectivity since the image conjured by the word crime is heavily weighted with conceptions of the more grievous and violent offenses against public morality. However, the contribution to the over-all index of various categories of crimes tends to be in inverse proportion to their importance in the public image of crime.

The first important point that must be understood about the Crime Index is that it is based on reports of only seven of the many types of crime — criminal homicide, forcible rape, robbery, aggravated assault, burglary, larceny (involving property worth $50 or more), and automobile theft.

Various types of embezzlement, forgery, narcotics violation, kidnaping, tax and insurance fraud, extortion, prostitution, arson, and many other categories of crimes are *not* included.

Any statistics of known crimes based on reports by the police fail to reflect the area that is of particularly serious social concern and public attention. This is "organized crime." Very few of the crimes committed by racketeers — the "crime syndicates" — ever appear in criminal statistics. The success of the fight against organized crime cannot be gauged by looking at any statistical crime index. Change in the index does not reveal whether more or fewer of the businessmen of the nation can do business without making "payoffs" to racketeers and corrupt officials; whether more or fewer of our citizens avoid supporting organized crime by not making illegal bets; whether more or fewer unions are "fronts" for racketeer enrichment rather than democratic organizations to protect their members' interests.

A second important point about the index that must be understood is the contribution to the totals of each of the seven types of crimes included.

The inclusion of the most heinous crimes — murder and rape — accentuates the grave impression the index creates. Since these most violent of all crimes are part of the index, the rise in incidence is sometimes cited to give the impression that violence is becoming more rife. However, relative to all the other types of crime that comprise the index, there are very few murders and rapes. In 1961, for example, the number of murders, nonnegligent manslaughters, and rapes comprised just a little over 1 per cent of the indexed crimes. These are so few that the changes up and down in the number of such crimes that occur each year have no numerical effect whatsoever on changes in the total Crime Index.

This would be true even if the rate of occurrence of such crimes changed greatly from year to year, which, in fact, never happens. The rate of murders reported in the index has shown a continual slow decline since the earliest attempts at national crime reporting, and the downward trend has continued in recent years. The FBI estimates that the criminal homicide rate is now 40 per cent lower for the nation as a whole than it was about thirty years ago. Its annual figures showed a decline of 2 per cent in 1963, as compared with the rate for the preceding three-year period.

Relative to population, the number of reported forcible rapes has been just about constant during the past few years — moving up or down by just one occurrence for every million inhabitants each year. If we consider the large increase in the proportion of the population in the younger age ranges that have always accounted for the large majority of the rapes, it is clear that this kind of aberration is becoming increasingly rare among Americans.

Possibly, one reason why these two major crimes show tendencies opposite to those of other crimes in the FBI index is that they are far less subject to "paper" increases: in particular, they are affected less by more complete reporting and stricter applications of the definition of the crime. For many of the interpretations of social change that are usually made from the total Crime Index, the murder rate by itself would be a far better indicator, subject possibly to periodic correction to reflect improved police and coroner practice, on the one hand, and medical practice, on the other.

There are two other types of violent crimes that figure in the Crime Index — aggravated assault and robbery. An assault is called aggravated when it is decided that there was an intent to kill or to inflict severe bodily injury. It is, therefore, not as objective a category as murder. In many cases, the offender's weapon is taken as revealing his intent; in other cases, less objective evidence or peculiarities of legal classifications discriminate aggravated assaults from other acts of violence that are not included in the report, such as simple assault, assault and battery, fighting, and so forth.

Taking all of the crimes of violence — the crimes against persons

— that figure in the total Crime Index, we find that they constitute only a small proportion of the whole: just 12 per cent of all the reported crimes. This means that an 8 per cent change either way in violent crimes registers only a negligible 1 per cent change in the total Crime Index. Since the present system of crime reporting was instituted, the rate for all the crimes of violence has not changed enough to affect the Crime Index by more than 1½ per cent.

So, an important key to interpreting the uses of the Crime Index is to recognize that, even though crimes against persons are included in its computation and in newspaper write-ups about "crime increases" based on the annual FBI reports, year-to-year or city-to-city variations in the total Crime Index reveal little about whether people are becoming less safe from crimes of violence in their own everyday existence.

Only the rates for the specific crimes give us any inkling regarding changes in crimes against persons. Looking at the rates of incidence for these violent crimes in the FBI report shows that they have not involved the dramatic kind of increase of the index as a whole: the dramatic rise is in the rate of crime against property.

Crime Rates and Prosperity

Crime is widely held to be a product of poverty. There may well be truth in this proposition. Insofar as the FBI Crime Index is concerned, however, increases in the rate of crime seem more likely to stem from increased prosperity than from increased poverty.

About half of all indexed crimes are in the categories of larceny and automobile theft. More than half of the rise in the index in recent years — the basis for the alarm expressed about the "mounting crime rate" — comes from increases in the reports people make to the police about things being stolen from them. (This does not include reports of the crimes of burglary and robbery in which an additional violation of morality is involved: that is, either force, the threat of force, or "breaking and entering.") To be reflected in the index, a reported theft has to involve the stealing of an automobile or of something else worth $50 or more. The Crime Index climbs not only when more things get stolen, but also when more of such things that are stolen have a value greater than $50.

Economic developments that multiply the number of valuables worth more than $50 that thieves can steal will thus boost the crime rate, given the same propensities for theft among the population. In recent years, there have been two such economic developments:

affluence and inflation. In the ten-year period from 1953 to 1963, the "average value" of stolen objects reported to the police (including nonindexed petty larcenies as well as indexed crimes) rose from $43 to $82 according to the FBI report. Since the distribution of the value of objects involved in reported thefts is roughly pyramidal — there are about three times as many petty larcenies reported as there are indexed larcenies — one would expect inflation to be reflected exponentially in the rise in the Crime Index. The proportion of index larcenies to all larcenies has stayed just about constant, however, which suggests the possibility that more small thefts are being reported and thefts of valuable objects are becoming relatively less frequent.

The hazards of the uncritical use of indicators to evaluate the consequences of programs of social action can be readily illustrated by considering the possible application of changes in the Crime Index to measure the success of President Johnson's "War on Poverty." The curtailment of crime is one of the pronounced justifications of such a program. Consider the consequences of success of this program on the crime rate in those "pockets of poverty" where currently few of the inhabitants possess anything not nailed down that is worth more than $50.

The effects of affluence on reported larcenies also operates in a number of indirect ways. Part is in the value of the "liftable" or mobile possessions that are in abundance in this modern period of affluence, as compared with Jean Valjean's stolen loaf of bread, the Wild West desperado's stolen horse, or the peasant's stolen plow. A major contributor to increased larcenies currently comes from children's possessions. This is manifest in the one such item for which the FBI's report provides specific information: namely bicycles. Stolen bicycles alone accounted for 20 per cent of all reported larcenies in 1963. In the period of increasing prosperity between 1960 and 1963, reports of stolen bikes increased by 40 per cent.

An unknown but decided influence on the Crime Index comes from another feature of affluence. As more of the population own more things, they come to need and to be able to afford insurance against theft. Quite apart from the magnitude of their need, the insurance industry has become progressively effective in selling them such protection: notably, through the spectacular promotion in the past few years of the comprehensive homeowner's policy. While there has been a steady rise in the number of ordinary burglary and theft premiums written, the bulk of such protection is now incorporated in these "multiple-line" coverages. Multiple-line premiums written each year increased twenty-fourfold between 1955 and 1964.[60] When a theft occurs to an insured homeowner, he is less likely just to curse his bad luck and more likely to conform to the reporting requirements for establishing an insurance claim. The rise in the crime rate attributable to this factor is a useful indicator for measuring the burden of work placed on the police but not for indicating how much lawbreaking is occurring in the United States.

Crime Rates and Automobiles

The proliferation of insured property plays a role in the single social development most responsible for increases in the Crime Index — that is, the ubiquitous automobile. The large percentage of automobiles insured against theft, however, is just a minor feature of this singular commodity that makes it loom so large in the increase in the index of crime.

While the Crime Index is not intended to reflect "white collar" crimes it may actually do so indirectly when individuals erroneously report property loss by burglary, larceny, or theft in an attempt to defraud an insurance company or the tax collector. The worn-out mink and the sold jewelry may be reported as stolen. Some false reports of auto thefts doubtless arise from youths who abandon their parents' car and allege that it has been stolen, rather than "face the music" for themselves when they have smashed it or stripped its gears. What may have been unclaimable damage thereby may also become a claim against the company holding the parents' comprehensive automobile policy.

The central fact about the automobile is the sheer rise in the distribution among the population of a consequential, stealable item of property. In 1963, the number of registered motor vehicles in the United States increased by 4½ per cent. Another special feature of the automobile, however, is that the legal controls pertaining to it now make car theft seemingly less subject to errors of underreporting than any other category of crime against property. (It is subject to various errors of false overreporting and multiple reporting, however.) The system of almost universal and unique registration of automobiles and the legal responsibility of the owner for use made of the vehicle registered to him doubtless lead victims to report auto theft promptly, whether or not the car is in-

[60] Insurance Facts 1965 (New York: Insurance Information Institute, 1965), pp. 17, 23.

sured. The automobile thus figures in the index not only because it is so valuable, so readily movable, but also because it is so reportable. Car thefts account for about one-sixth of all indexed crimes.

Another feature of the automobile as a target for theft is that it is property frequently "left about" among strangers. This is one of the reasons that most of the stealing reported in this country is either the theft of a car or of something out of, or off, a car. Leaving aside thefts of automobiles themselves, about 60 per cent of all reported larcenies in the FBI's 1963 statistics were thefts of something from automobiles. Since the FBI report does not include a breakdown of the classes of items involved in these larcenies, we can only conjecture about the role that the glamorization of the wheel cover has had in boosting the Crime Index. A stolen set of these shiny objects — treasured by juvenile delinquents — is valuable enough to count as a grand larceny in the FBI report.

It is interesting to note that coincident with the popularization of the austerely trimmed compact car there was a drop in the number of reported thefts of automobile accessories: the number fell 4.6 per cent between 1960 and 1961, and 6.9 per cent between 1961 and 1962. The next year the trend reversed: auto accessory theft rose 8.2 per cent in the FBI's report. But the style in autos had changed, too; the compacts were now more glamorously trimmed and intermediate lines of fancier models had displaced the basic compact in sales to a considerable degree.

Some criminologists have suggested dropping automobile theft from the index because of the varying significance of the acts contributing to the reported offenses. One indicator of this is the high recovery rate: 91 per cent of cars reported stolen in 1963 were recovered, 64 per cent of them within forty-eight hours, according to the FBI. This high recovery rate is generally attributed to the large contribution to the incidence of auto theft by teenagers who "borrow" a car for joy riding. Some reported thefts might be more meaningfully reported by the label "unauthorized use," or even "disputed use" as in the case of employees' use of employers' vehicles. The rate is probably boosted also by ex-partners of a marriage, or of similar but less formalized joint property arrangements, where one takes the car owned by the erstwhile partner. (Of persons arrested for auto theft in 1963, only 19 per cent were found guilty as charged; 58 per cent were referred to a juvenile court.)

Unannounced finance company repossessions are said to contribute to the incidence of reported auto thefts in some cities where lax record keeping does not "unfound" the report of theft by the registrant when the police receive notification of repossession. Unfounding of reports of thefts probably also varies where the "thefts" in actuality involve absentminded old ladies who forget where they have parked or the owners of cars hauled from restricted tow-away zones.

Police have sometimes been accused of laxity in failing to unfound false reports of automobile thefts because of the importance of the statistic of the dollar value of recovered automobiles toward justifying the economic value of a police force. For example, the FBI's 1963 "Crime Capsule" — twenty-three lines of type highlighting the "general crime picture" — announces: "Stolen property loss cut to 46 cents on each dollar by police action." From the figures given in the report for the total value of stolen property and the valuation of recovered stolen automobiles, it can be deduced that 43 of these 46 cents is attributable to recovered autos.

The FBI's tally of auto thefts for the nation, however, has risen more rapidly than the human and the automobile population. Unlike other types of crime reflected in the index that are subject to large fluctuations in definition and reporting, and which we shall discuss presently, it does not seem to be the case that spurious factors can account for all of the increase in auto thefts. Presumably, an actual increase in incidence has been taking place. But, again, a factor associated with social progress in the United States would lead us to expect a very sharp increase in the recent past and in the near future. This factor is the change in age structure of the American population.

Demography and Crime Rates

As Americans emerged from the Great Depression, they began having more babies, as well as acquiring more automobiles. During periods of war scarcities, they continued having babies even when they could not get cars. As a consequence of a quarter-century of growing prosperity, a continually enlarging proportion of the population is in the young age groups. These groups, whose members range in age from ten to twenty-five, have always been only partially tamed by the society, and they appear to contribute disproportionately to the incidence of crime.

To reflect meaningful changes in the public morality for which the Crime Index is a frequently used indicator, the index would have to be adjusted to the changing age composition of the population. This cannot be done very precisely because the identity of the offenders is unknown for the large majority of indexed crimes: the index is based on reports of crimes for many of which no suspect is ever identified. If we judge by the age distribution of persons arrested for indexed crimes, almost three-fourths of the incidence would be ascribed to people under twenty-five years of age. Estimating the age incidence from arrest data is imprecise, at best. On the one hand, it presumably tends to exaggerate the role of young people, in that their inexperience and imprudence probably leads to their more frequent apprehension by police than is the case with older offenders. On the other hand, there are many factors tending to understate such an estimate. The protective attitude in law and practice frequently leads an act to be defined as other than a crime when it is known to have been committed by a young person, while it would be defined as a crime if the offender were unknown or known to be an adult. Juveniles also figure less in total arrests than they presumably contribute to the occurrences of all such crimes, because the juvenile rate is lowest in the case of crimes of violence and highest in the case of crimes against property. The large majority of crimes of violence are cleared by arrests, but only a small proportion of the crimes against property. As a consequence, persons over twenty-five probably figure more prominently in arrest data than in the incidence of all reported indexed crimes.

Continued prosperity has been associated with continuing high birth rates. There will be a continuing problem from the high proportions of the population that remain to be fully socialized to the norms of the community. During the last few years, however, change has been more acute, because of the entrance into adolescence and young adulthood of the large baby crops of the 1940's following the unusually low ones of the Depression.

Another aspect of social progress has accentuated the impact of boom-period birth rates on crime statistics. This has been the marked reductions in infant mortality rates. The rate has fallen off particularly rapidly among the urban Negroes. The Public Health Service reports that the mortality rate of Negro males under one year of age fell from 101.2 per 1,000 in 1940 to 59.9 in 1950. In 1963, it was down to 44.8. Since Negroes figure in exceedingly high disproportion in crime data, this means that 50 more Negro infants of every 1,000 now born can reach an age where they have a chance of contributing to statistics on crime and delinquency.

Negro birth rates, which have been consistently higher than those of whites, have also risen in the last two decades, particularly between 1940 and 1950. The Negro population has been growing somewhat disproportionately, and the increase is particularly pronounced in the younger age groups. While Negroes constitute slightly more than 11 per cent of the total population, about 15 per cent of the age group between ten and nineteen is Negro. This partially accounts for the disproportionate presence of Negroes in the FBI statistics on arrests: 27 per cent relates to Negroes.

Crime Statistics and Integration

The changing position in America of Negroes and other groups that have been at the fringes of the society may explain more about changes in crime statistics than changes in their proportionate numbers. Here, too, we may see that developments regarded as progress can produce apparent increases in crime.

During the 1964 national political campaign, the rise in the crime rate was linked, both by innuendo and explicitly, to the extension of civil rights to Negroes. Propaganda of this kind helped call attention to some of the remarkable properties of the Crime Index as a social indicator. The proud and true claim of Mississippi's white supremacists that their state had the lowest crime rate in the nation was particularly instructive, in that certain factors in this low rate are immediately apparent.

The poverty of the population of the state — the fact that so many, both black and white, have little of value that can register in an index of theft — explains only part of this low crime rate.

The publicized lopsided justice of the state also is a contributing factor, but probably a relatively minor one insofar as the total index is concerned. The substantial immunity enjoyed by whites who offend against Negroes doubtless reduces substantially the registration by the index of crimes of violence in Mississippi. In other states, as we have stressed, crimes of violence constitute only a small fraction of all indexed crimes. More important is that where offender and victim are known, the bulk of offenses are not interracial. Offender and victim usually are members of the same race. The most apparent source of the low crime rate for Mississippi is that crimes of Negroes against Negroes have been of little official concern to the all-white police forces of that state. Furthermore, police practices have done little to develop the attitude among the Negro population of the state that it is wise or moral to report to the police the offenses they suffer or witness.

It is not so long ago that much the same sort of situation prevailed in northern cities. But things have been changing recently.

The concept of civil rights means a whole different set of attitudes toward people who once were more outside of the society than in it. What are now regarded as serious crimes were once thought of as just "the way those people act." The standards of "those people" have changed, too. Many of them who used to inhabit the slums and tenant shacks, and many more of their children, have moved out to neat suburban subdivisions and respectable apartment developments.

As people who once felt they were outside of the society feel more and more that they are part of it, and as our law enforcement officials come to judge them by the same standards and give them the same protections as the middle class, we shall go through a period of decreasing crime but of increasing crime statistics. There will not be more crimes but more *recorded* crimes.

Crime Statistics and Police Practices

Improvements in police practices toward "minority group areas" from the traditional combination of terror, containment, shunning, and exploitation are one of a number of manifestations of increasing police professionalism.

This increasing professionalism of the police is one of the biggest factors in the increase in *reported* crimes. First of all, participation by police departments in the FBI voluntary system of national uniform crime reporting itself is a mark of the up-to-date professional police department. Each year since 1957, more and more of the police agencies in the country have been reporting in keeping with the FBI's uniform national standards and definitions. The FBI now gets reports covering about 8,000 jurisdictions, whereas in 1957 only 7,000 reported. In progressive states, practically all of the agencies report their crime figures to the FBI: in a state such as Mississippi, a large proportion do not. (The FBI gets information from police jurisdictions representing only 28 per cent of that state's rural population.)

Furthermore, as every criminologist knows, the more professional a police department and the more complete and thorough its record keeping on crime, the less likely it is that justice will be dispensed on the spot in drumhead fashion rather than through the legal processes of investigation, arrest, arraignment, and trial. There is also less likelihood that crime will be kept from the record for the political reason of "keeping things from looking too bad." There was an 83 per cent increase in major crimes known to the police in

Chicago between 1960 and 1961 when the new police superintendent, O. W. Wilson, reformed procedures. As the citizenry develops more confidence in, and less fear of, the police, more of the crimes that occur in a community will be "crimes known to the police," which make up the Crime Index.

The Crime Index and Everyday Beliefs

We have advanced various considerations suggesting that changes in the Crime Index provide images of social change that are, in many ways, analogous to a movie negative. Various changes in the society are reflected negatively, and vice versa. These, and certain other considerations of bias and artifact in the Crime Index, lead us to question the commonly accepted conclusion that the steady rise in the index in recent years can be accepted as indicating increased lawlessness in the United States. On various theoretical grounds and inferences from qualitative evidence, I find good reason to suspect that, on the contrary, social controls and private dispositions against crime may be functioning continually more effectively in American society.

It would seem that these contentions are less likely to be persuasive than would be the case were they to represent merely a challenge to the statistical index. I would venture that they are more likely to be dismissed by a reader as farfetched, not because of any great confidence he may have in the accuracy and validity of the FBI's Crime Index, but rather because they run counter to a host of impressions derived from more immediate experience and from the mass media — impressions that develop what appears to be an almost universally held belief that crime is on the increase.

Looking at the matter from a slightly different angle, the Crime Index shares with many indicators the property of owing much of its credibility and popularity to its being consistent with beliefs formed by everyday experience. Many an indicator favored for revealing key conditions of the society derives this favor precisely from the fact that it confirms and reinforces existing conceptions rather than augments or alters them. The indicator serves as a shorthand certifier of beliefs, rather than as a shaper of them. In the cases where it lacks this resonance with everyday, qualitative, global, and spatial impressions, the indicator is likely to be rejected. Thus, few would accept the Crime Index as a valid representation of the relative level of criminal behavior in Mississippi, for example, as compared with the other states.

This point, I believe, deserves more stress in the consideration of social indicators than the specific contentions I have advanced about the actual trends in criminal behavior in the United States.

Public Virtues and Statistical Vices

I have tried to show how crime statistics are at one and the same time a measure of several different things, in addition to their manifest role of serving as an indicator of the number of violations of the standards of decent conduct in which almost everyone believes.

First of all, changes in crime statistics reflect, in many different ways, the amount of organized attention the society gives to violations of its standards: by keeping good records about them, by enforcing those standards more efficiently, rigorously, and impartially, and by expecting more and more of its people to live up to them.

Second, the most frequently used crime statistics are largely composed of recorded offenses against property. As such, they are highly affected by changes in the amount and value of property possessed by the people of a community or nation.

And, third, crime statistics reflect proportions of the population who are, so to speak, new members not fully tamed to its ways. In the United States, these new members are primarily young people.

In each of these ways, the growth and progress of our nation has increased the amount of crime we have on paper, even though the large majority of our citizenry has become increasingly law abiding.

Nonscientific Uses of the Crime Index

The Crime Index illustrates in a refined way the kind of social indicator that is highly adapted to nonscientific and pseudoscientific uses. Indicators connoting social conditions that are regarded intensely and with uniformity as "good" or "bad" have this applicability. As I have discussed elsewhere,[61] and as others such as Winick[62] have also, the indicator of the negative condition in society is particularly good for such use.

Another virtue of the national Crime Index, as I have attempted to show, is that, within the range of readily predictable social change, it is an index that can be depended on to keep rising. Under most foreseeable circumstances in the near future, it can fall only by redefinition. Since it is so readily available to prove a sensational

[61] See my article, "Dangers of Negative Patriotism," *Harvard Business Review, 40* (November–December 1962), 93–99.

[62] C. Winick, "The Remora Syndrome: Sick Characteristics in Search of an Author," *Business Horizons, 6* (Winter 1963), 63–72.

point, it is much used and, hence, quite familiar. The journalists and politicians know they can use it and know where to find it.[63] Its frequent use, presumably, accrues for it further popularity.

It is also useful because its implications are ambiguous. In the absence of a consensus on causality, and given the large degree of behavioral ambiguity in the categories of acts that comprise it, changes in the index are open to interpretation as being causally related to whatever development in society a given critic wishes to deplore. It is as open to the interpretations of the political utopians that poverty, social oppression, or free-enterprise materialism breed crime as it is to the ideological interpretations in the preface of the *Uniform Crime Reports* that I have noted earlier. In this respect, it departs from indicators relating to widely accepted concepts that are parts of more closed-system models such as, for instance, the supply and price data of economic indicators.

A fourth utility the index has for nonscientific and pseudoscientific use stems from the many factors contributing to its large, but unknown and unknowable, degree of invalidity and unreliability, internal and temporal. These factors include, for example,

1. The unknown characteristics of the people who contribute the acts that are reflected in the index, since the persons committing most offenses are unknown.

2. The reporting and definitional differences from place to place.

3. The wide range of behaviors that are covered by its constituent indexes.

These and other factors render the data susceptible to such a large variety of spurious correlations that almost any critic can find a phenomenon correlated with the index in a manner suited to his purpose. These same factors baffle attempts at making definitive, scientific assessments of the data that might discipline the nonscientific ones.

Yet another advantage the Crime Index has for nonscientific use is that everyday experience affords opportunities for a pseudo check on the implications read into the index. For very much the same fundamental reasons as I have discussed in examining the index, the pseudo check with "everyday" experience provides pseudo confirmation of the rapid "rise in crime."

A final utility for nonscientific uses of a social indicator — one

[63] N. E. Isaacs, "The Crime of Present Day Crime Reporting," *The Journal of Criminal Law, Criminology and Police Science,* 52 (1961), 405–410.

that cannot with great confidence be attributed to this particular index — is that it should have a self-fulfilling nature.[64]

These are some of the factors contributing to inverse relationships between the scientific and nonscientific usefulness of indicators. They should lead us to expect to find a sort of Gresham's law[65] of indicators in operation. The curb on the operation of such a law is the ethical and practical acceptance of scientific principles throughout so much of the society. For the curb to operate effectively, however, scientific understanding of the uses and abuses of indicators, as well as abstract devotion to the norms of science, is required.

Social Considerations Regarding Indicators

I have used the Crime Index to illustrate various characteristics of indicators and their interpretation that detract from the rational consideration of a phenomenon. The special utilities of bad indicators for the many nonscientific uses that generate demands for statistical production may operate so that bad indicators drive the good ones from the market. Deliberate efforts are needed to curb such developments.

Proposed Curb on Bad Indicators

An institutionalized curb has been suggested by a statistician in his presidential address to the American Statistical Association:

I propose that there be created a new United States Statistical Commission, with responsibility for audit of statistical series, similar to an accounting audit, empowered to put a "certified" label on a statistical product. It should also be charged with investigation of methods, scope, and suitability of statistics, and with making recommendations for future improvements and developmental work. Such a Commission in some respects would be similar to the "Boards of Visitors" which some universities have organized to report to the Board of Trustees; in others like the Inspector General of the Army; and in others like the present Research and Development Board in scientific fields.

. . . in making an audit of an important series, such a Commission should rely on sample checks to verify the accuracy of the basis data and the calculations, and should carefully examine the established procedures to see whether they are being followed scrupulously. It should devote a

[64] See R. K. Merton, *Social Theory and Social Structure* (Glencoe, Ill.: The Free Press, 1957).

[65] Sir Thomas Gresham, 1519–1579, who advanced the popular principle that bad money will drive good money from the market.

good share of its attention to making suggestions for changes in procedures, if those currently in vogue are not in accordance with the best methods known at the time of review, and to considering whether the data are technically adequate for the uses which are being made of them. After such an examination the Commission should be in a position to give these statistics a stamp of approval — ("Certified Public Statistics") — or to withhold that stamp awaiting improvement — and say why. I, for one, would welcome the constructive suggestions and the heightened public interest that would come from such a review. Private statistical series might also be reviewed by the Commission, on request.[66]

Possible Consequences

Were such a proposal to be translated into practice, it would presumably elevate the weight given to the formal, technical adequacy of an indicator in considerations of information by the policy process. The degree of technical perfection of an item of information, however, is only one of the considerations applicable in deciding how much weight it should be given in relation to other informational inputs bearing on a given decision. Two types of hazards of an established statistical orthodoxy might well occupy the attention of such a statistical commission and those who might be guided by its certifications. Early in this chapter I discussed various selective factors that determine the scope, form, and emphasis of statistics. Among these factors is the hazard of the properties of phenomena that lend themselves well or less well to good treatment using the current models and techniques favored by statisticians. A second hazard is the ability of particular interest groups to command the considerable resources necessary for the production of a technically adequate time series that will measure a phenomenon in which they have a special interest.

These factors operate so that the availability of a good statistical indicator for a social phenomenon is only imperfectly correlated with the importance of that phenomenon from the standpoint of any particular value perspective. The exception, perhaps, is the value perspective of a technician whose overriding preference is that things be as neat as possible.

The following discussion illustrates one facet of the selective influence of good statistics on policy.

Group Power, Feedback, and Indicators

An inspection of the major statistical indicators suggests that, with some major exceptions, indicators revealing adverse conse-

[66] A. J. Wickens, "Statistics and the Public Interest," *The Journal of the American Statistical Association*, 48 (1953), 1–14.

quences of government programs on certain segments of society are most likely to exist where they are least essential for feedback. The greater the organization, self-awareness, and political power of interest groups, the more likely we are to find statistical and other systematic indicators relating to the social and economic conditions and trends that these groups believe affect their welfare.

Furthermore, it is more than likely that the indicators will reflect the dominant ideological orientations of the most powerful and articulate groups affected by the phenomena measured. At the same time, of course, we are more likely to get feedback on adverse developments affecting well-organized and powerful groups than on those affecting diffuse, less-organized, or low-power groups.

Indicators showing unsought or undesirable social consequences of a program are bases for attacks against the program or for advocacy of what Thompson calls "counterprograms" — measures to compensate for the adverse effects of a program.[67] The elaboration and proliferation of indicators have recently increased awareness of such secondary effects. Thus:

The heavy drain on the country's scientific resources for work on military and space programs generates powerful feedback from the academic community on which these programs depend. As a counterprogram, the academic community seeks sponsorship for basic research and tolerates, if not encourages, other devices by which more traditional scholarly interests profit from "spill-over" from applied research enterprises.

Despite a tendency toward "poor-mouthing," the scientific community is a powerful, well-organized, and articulate group. It is also well endowed with statistical and other indicators to demonstrate its contentions regarding the impact of applied research on traditional, scholarly activities.

A case from recent history can indicate the opposite situation — where indicators are scanty and the affected group is powerless. For instance:

The Agricultural Adjustment Act of the New Deal displaced a large proportion of southern farm labor. Farm owners, who were paid to take land out of cotton production, had no further need for hired labor. Farm workers, however, (and, illegally, many farm tenants) did not share in the cash benefits of the acreage control programs.

---

[67] V. A. Thompson, "Feedback in the Bureaucratic Organization," unpublished paper prepared for the Committee on Space Efforts and Society, American Academy of Arts and Sciences (undated).

The dimensions of the ensuing displacement of the rural population, and the individual and regional consequences of this mobility, were only dimly seen at the time, masked as they were by the more pervasive dislocations of the Depression. Consequently, the unorganized, impotent state of those most desperately affected made for feeble feedback and even feebler counterprograms.

Some major exceptions to these generalizations involve inertias both in the political system and in the production of, and attention to, statistical indicators. Once a problem area has generated enough support to receive the attention of a program and the establishment of an indicator, both programs and indicators may persist long after the interest group and the social phenomena that brought them into being have attenuated. Thus concern with homeless orphans and industrial child labor has persisted in indicators and programs long after the incidence of these problems has receded close to insignificance.[68] We can probably expect the same of infantile paralysis.

It is, of course, true that many other sources of feedback and influence are subject to the same principles. The purpose of stressing the illustrations given is to correct any assumption that the effects of the extension of science in social affairs are automatically in the direction of great equity and evenhandedness in policy.

Quantitative Versus Nonquantitative

The hardness of data is one determinant of their acceptability to policy makers who seek dependable social indicators. Questions for which relevant hard data are available are debated and deliberated differently from questions on which our information is impressionistic, intuitive, selective, or qualitative.

If we take quantification as the index of hardness, we find wide disparity among various aspects of society for which hard data are readily available. This is reflected in the discussion in the report of the 1960 President's Commission on National Goals regarding the nation's position with respect to various goals. Table 2.7 gives a rough measure of the disparate attention given to quantitative indicators in the discussions of each of the types of goal areas that the commission considered.

As an exercise, we might well consider to which problems our attention would be directed if we were to base our judgment of society only on quantitative indicators. Merely as an illustration, and without any probative intent, I have analyzed the use of quan-

---

[68] See Bogue, *op. cit.*, pp. 287, 424.

titative and nonquantitative indicators in two recent year-end magazine reviews by John Gunther on "where we stand."[69]

First, as was to be expected, quantitative indicators were used much more frequently to describe our domestic than our international position (see Table 2.8). The difficulties of gaining cross-

TABLE 2.7

PER CENT OF PAGES PER CHAPTER ON WHICH QUANTIFIED INDICATORS APPEAR IN REPORT OF THE 1960 PRESIDENT'S COMMISSION ON NATIONAL GOALS

Chapter	Per Cent
Agriculture	57
Economic growth	33
Living standards (urban society)	33
Health and welfare	33
Science	29
Technological change	20
Education	18
Foreign affairs	16
Federal system	10
Individual	8
Culture	6
Democratic economy	0
Entire work	21

TABLE 2.8

QUANTITATIVE AND NONQUANTITATIVE INDICATORS IN JOHN GUNTHER'S ASSESSMENTS OF THE DOMESTIC AND THE INTERNATIONAL SITUATION

	Type of Indicator				All Indicators	
	Quantitative		Nonquantitative			
Assessments	No.	Per Cent	No.	Per Cent	No.	Per Cent
Domestic	31	62	20	18	51	32
International	19	38	90	82	109	68
Total	50	100	110	100	160	100

Sources: John Gunther, "A Quarter Century: Where Has it Left Us?" *Look*, January 2, 1962, pp. 72–78; and "Where We Stand: The World," *Look*, January 15, 1963, pp. 20–24.

national comparability in quantitative data are, of course, notorious.

To determine whether the selective coverage of quantitative indicators tends to give us an overly optimistic or an overly pessimistic view of where we stand, all of Gunther's statements of social change were rated according to whether I regarded them as changes for the

[69] John Gunther, "A Quarter Century: Where Has it Left Us?" *Look*, January 2, 1962, pp. 72–78; and "Where We Stand: The World," *Look*, January 15, 1963, pp. 20–24.

better or for the worse. I have classified his indicators of these changes as "quantitative" and "qualitative." As Table 2.9 shows, Gunther used quantitative indicators somewhat more frequently to document favorable judgments than unfavorable ones, which gave

TABLE 2.9

QUANTITATIVE AND QUALITATIVE INDICATORS AND THE FAVORABLENESS
OF JOHN GUNTHER'S JUDGMENTS OF "WHERE WE STAND"

Social Change Judged as:	Quantitative No.	Per Cent	Qualitative No.	Per Cent	All Indicators No.	Per Cent
For the better	33	62	61	55	94	58
For the worse	20	38	49	45	60	42
Total	53	100	110	100	154	100

Sources: See Table 2.8.

both of his articles an over-all balance toward a favorable view of the nation's situation.

Expanding the Scope of Measurement

Social scientists generally agree that the "objectivity" of data regarding a particular problem does not result from anything intrinsic to the phenomena in question, but rather it stems from the state of development of our ways of making and expressing observations of it. Lundberg stated this view as follows:

The superior development of positive, verifiable, sociological knowledge in the field of demography has erroneously led to the assumption that data of the type mentioned above are in some *intrinsic* sense more "objective" than it is possible for certain other data of social behavior to become . . . however, objectivity is not a quality or an attribute of data *per se.* Objectivity refers rather to the character of the symbols with which we communicate about phenomena. When these symbols have verifiably similar meanings to all men, we call the phenomena to which the symbols refer objective. It is not necessary to deny that such *objective designations* may be easier to invent for some phenomena than for others. To approach this question profitably, however, we would need to know the amount of time and effort devoted to such attempts for different types of phenomena throughout the centuries. It is sufficient for our purpose to point out that the advancement of science has consisted of gradually rendering "objective" increasingly large areas of traditionally "subjective" phenomena. . . . This process will continue also in the future and especially in the social sciences.[70]

[70] G. A. Lundberg, *Social Research: A Study of Methods of Gathering Data* (New York and London: Longmans Green & Co. Ltd., 1942).

Developments in the social sciences in the two decades since Lundberg wrote this have, indeed, seen an enormous broadening of the scope of phenomena subjected to objective observation.

Kecskemeti has discussed several ways in which applications of such developments become material for policy making.[71] Elaborating slightly on his distinctions, I can specify three ways in which this takes place.

First, and most important from the standpoint of our present concern with accurately charting important trends in the nation's social well-being, *the continual, standardized collection and analysis of data may become a regular, routine function of the administration.* Examples are the work of the federal Bureau of the Census and the Bureau of Labor Statistics, or the routine audience-measurement activities of the mass media.

Second, *there is the project approach — special, usually one-shot, ad hoc studies — to shed light on particular problems.*

Third, *the language and concepts of the professional specialist move from the realm of esoterica into the general culture.* The wide familiarity with an application of the Freudian "defense mechanism" concepts provide one illustration of a technical concept being taken over by the general culture, although in simplified and altered form. Formal educational institutions provide one means of this transmittal. Another mode of application of indicator data is the use of the professional consultant.

Series and Special Projects

For the purposes of the development of sound impressions regarding the significance of changes in the society, we may consider a quasi hierarchy of sources of information. First, and least efficient, comes impressionistic observation that is guided by common-sense concepts, juxtaposed with similar observations by others in the past. Second comes impressionistic observation that is guided and ordered by theoretically rooted concepts and defined so as to involve less ambiguity than common-sense terms. Third is the application of theoretical concepts that use systematic collection procedures as, for example, in the impressionistic survey. Fourth is the fairly rigorous, but one-shot, quantitative survey, which is interpretively compared with such data regarding the past as may be available. Fifth is the specific attempt at replicating the procedures of

[71] P. Kecskemeti, *Utilization of Social Research in Shaping Policy Decisions* (Santa Monica, Calif.: RAND Corporation, Report P. 2289, 1961).

some earlier study to determine change. Sixth is the data from statistical time series, such as those from administratively collected data, which require quantitative and qualitative correction and reinterpretation to accommodate changes in definition, completeness of enumeration, and other factors deriving from the lack of standardization of collection procedures. Last there are those regular series that involve collection procedures specifically designed to maximize the reliability and validity of the data for the specific statistical purpose in mind.

This hierarchy is termed quasi because it does not automatically rank data in terms of their usefulness or accuracy. The hierarchy is based on the fact that each successively higher level is characterized by fewer types of errors. However, in an individual instance a specific indicator may involve a degree of error more serious than the errors of all types associated with an indicator at a lower level. For this reason, good impressionistic observations, for example, may provide a more accurate and pertinent portrayal of some significant social change than does a poor statistical study that attempts to get at the same matter.

In considering the adequacy of indicators, it is important to discriminate between two types of error that may be involved in observations: defined and undefined error. To illustrate: it is a characteristic of statistical work that we are willing to disregard much of what we know about the object of our measurements so as to concentrate on what we can measure accurately and economically. We must tolerate a greater amount of total error in order to be able to define and establish a quantitative probability value for the error of our procedures.

Since approaches to perfection, nonetheless, require the reduction of error of all types, this type of scale can be applied in evaluating the indicators that are used to form judgments about the significance of social trends. An interesting exercise is to determine what aspects of social change can be judged on the basis of higher-level indicators, and for which ones only "lower-level" bases are available.

I have already illustrated a manner of approaching the problem by the use of quantitative and nonquantitative indicators in John Gunther's summary articles on the state of the nation. For simplicity, I have limited this to a distinction between data from *ad hoc* studies and those from regularly collected series. I have examined the sources of data used in Gendell and Zetterberg's *Sociological Almanac* from this standpoint.

I noted earlier that the effort of Gendell and Zetterberg to compile a *Sociological Almanac* resulted in more exhaustive coverage of national goal statements than did far more voluminous treatises such as the *Statistical Abstract*. This result is possible only because these authors use a great deal of data developed by *ad hoc*, one-shot projects. They did not, as does the *Statistical Abstract*, restrict themselves to standardized, regularly collected series. In 48 per cent of the matches found between indicators in their *Sociological Almanac* and the national goal statements, the data were not those of a regularly collected series.

The broad scope of the almanac is, at the same time, a major source of its deficiencies. For many key tables, the compilers have had to draw on obsolete data, on information from highly inconvenient points in time, and on data difficult to arrange in series because of the differences in definitions or approaches of the various investigators who collected them.

An extreme example is their table on the occupational background of political decision makers in the United States, which they derive from Matthews.[72] The table gives data on (1) the occupational background of presidents, vice presidents, and cabinet members for the period 1877–1935; members of Congress for 1949–1951; state governors for 1930–1940; and state legislators for 1925–1935; and (2) a comparative base of the whole labor force for 1940.

Many of their tables present data for only a single point in time such as, for example, membership in voluntary associations for 1954–1955. For their table on the income of artists for 1950–1954, they use data from a highly selective sample study of three hundred painters who exhibited in New York City.

Reliance on project data was found in all of the goal areas touched on in tables of the almanac, as is shown in Table 2.10. It was particularly heavy in the goal areas "health and welfare" and "economic growth." In the area of "arts and sciences," the compilers used data from regular series to a surprising extent.

The achievements of the project approach have, in the past, been forerunners of systematic data series that provide accurate long-range information in areas that are now well charted. The project approach can also serve as a guide when determining the feasibility of innovating new series so as to extend the scope of needed social indicators.

An examination of current fruits of the project approach suggests likewise that the short-term, sporadic, shifting, and piecemeal sup-

[72] D. R. Matthews, *The Social Background of Political Decision Makers* (New York: Random House, Inc., 1954), p. 50.

port of many areas of study generates considerable waste. In addition, the way in which much of social science activity is institutionally organized and supported frequently precludes the consistent, long-term observation required to develop needed series of indicators.

Cultural Features and Indicator Reflections

The major statistical indicator series reflect certain dominant sociocultural features of America and the institutional conceptions associated with them. Following are some of these and their reflections in indicator series:

Features of American Culture	Reflectors in Indicators
Egalitarian	Economic models and statistics are well adapted to accounting for the production and distribution of nonpublic distributive goods and services but poorly adapted to public nondistributive goods; equal weighting of individuals (or families of firms) in statistics.
Federalism	The autonomy of state and local jurisdictions is reflected in definitions and systems of reporting in such areas as crime and education.
Freedom	In contrast to societies which exert greater centralized surveillance and control over the lives of individual citizens and enterprises, in the United States after-the-fact indicators are required to measure matters that in centralized societies are outcomes of planning decisions.
Objectivity and thing-orientation	A distrust of the reliability and validity of subjective data is evident; emphasis is on material production and consumption in indicator series.

Existing Space Indicators

Some ways in which such considerations can guide our study of indicators, describing the social impact of space programs, are illustrated in the following discussion.

In considering indicators that will provide measures of the secondary effects of the space program, it may be profitable to give some attention to more immediate indicators of its social impact. In a number of respects, the conventional types of indicators provide poor reflection of the significance of space activities for the society.

General statistical treatises now provide three kinds of data concerning space activities: (1) space probes and manned flights by country, (2) satellites in orbit by country, and (3) federal budgetary authorizations and expenditures.

TABLE 2.10

USES OF INDICATORS FROM REGULAR SERIES AND FROM SPECIAL PROJECTS
BY *A Sociological Almanac* IN TABLES RELEVANT TO
SPECIFIC "NATIONAL GOALS"

Goal Area	Number of Relevant Tables from Series	Number of Relevant Tables from Special Projects	Total Relevant Tables
Individual	7	7	14
Quality	14	10	24
Democratic process	10	11	21
Education	5	6	11
Arts and sciences	11	3	14
Democratic economy	5	6	11
Economic growth	7	9	16
Technological change	0	1	1
Agriculture	0	0	0
Living conditions	7	3	10
Health and welfare	5	9	14
Total	71	65	136

We can expect a certain amount of conservatism in any institutional system, including one that is devoted to the production and reporting of social data. We can, therefore, also expect a considerable lag in registering the activities and consequences of a highly innovational complex, such as space activities.

This is particularly true when the new phenomenon is not a replacement for some older one. Space-program planners envision some substitutive developments: future statisticians may chart, for example, a decline in the number of point-to-point messages transmitted by cable associated with an increase in the use of satellite relay. Space voyages, on the other hand, are completely innovational. Therefore, comparing their frequency with that of more conventional means of travel would be pointless, to say the least.

Type and Focus of Value

The space program represents a radical departure from the past, not only in its application of innovational science and technology, but also in its emphasis on areas of previous social de-emphasis. The immediate goals of the space program involve the following:

1. The production of public, nondistributive goods, rather than private, distributive ones.

2. The production of a relatively small number of unique, large, complex, integrated systems, rather than repetitive production processes employed in the case of consumer goods and services.

3. Activities organized at national and international rather than at state and local levels.

Despite recurrent attention to spill-over benefits from the space program to the distributive economy, the primary products of this program, and probably most secondary effects as well, involve the creation of public goods to a far greater extent than of private goods. According to Bator:

A good or service is defined as public if X's consumption of it leads to no subtraction from what is left over for consumption by Y and Z. Radio programs, the services rendered by the beacon atop the Statue of Liberty, the protection provided by the Strategic Air Command are some examples.[73]

Most of the values spoken of in discussions of the goals and benefits of space activities are examples of public goods, such as national prestige, improved communications by means of satellites, and that most economically pure of such goods, the advancement of fundamental knowledge.

This is reflected in my analysis of speeches given in a recent fourteen-month period by the director of the National Aeronautics and Space Administration, James E. Webb. His speeches, covering a period of sixty-seven weeks, were examined for statements enunciating goals of the national space program. About one-fourth (20) of the goals guiding this program coincided with specific national goal statements in *Goals for Americans* (see the appendix to this chapter). Of these 20 goals, 16 were judged to involve public values, while only 4 involved individual, private values.

Our economic system provides us with some (although frequently highly inexact) methods of accounting for allocations of resources to the production of public goods, but no accurate measure of the value in consumption of such goods. Indeed, the only measure we have of the value derived from public goods is the willingness of the public to endorse the allocation of scarce resources to their production. The processes that result in allocative decisions for or against

73 F. M. Bator, *The Question of Government Spending: Public Needs and Private Wants* (New York: Collier Books, 1960), p. 97.

the production of various public goods are, in political doctrine, the legitimate measure of this willingness. This begs the question of what shapes the perceptions of the public, or of the institutional decision makers to whom they delegate allocative functions, concerning the merit of any public goods.

Consequently, indicator series are decidedly weighted against public goods. The measures of public activities present us with fairly satisfactory indications of what we give up to gain such values but no conception of the satisfactions we gain from them. Whether public-goods creation is undertaken by government or by any of a great variety of nongovernmental organizations, neither the market economy nor marginal-utility economics provides us with good measures of their value.

The Problem of Countable Units

The tables devoted to or mentioning space activities in the *Statistical Abstract* indicate another way in which conventional data series fail to reflect the effects of space programs. Statistics involves counts of a great many identical units. Many social and economic activities lend themselves to this type of measurement — the number of babies born, neckties manufactured, miles traveled, welfare cases handled, and many others. The units in these examples also have an independent human significance, apart from their significance in broader systemic configurations, as in the case of babies in the population distribution, neckties in a wardrobe, miles in the transportation system, or welfare cases in urban organization.

In the case of much of the space program, however, the problem of identifying countable significant units is extremely difficult. Indeed, counts are irrelevant to indicating the scope, success, nature, and value of many of the systems involved, or to answer almost any other significant question about them. NASA programs most frequently involve the production of fairly unique, large, costly, complex, and highly integrated systems, rather than the quantity manufactured of large numbers of like or similar units.

For some of the important problems involved in space systems, indicators more meaningful than those currently employed could be presented — for example, improvements in the accuracy and reliability of space-probe guidance systems. A spherical trigonometry accuracy measure would assuredly be most unusual in a rundown of where we stand as a nation, yet such a figure might gauge the success of a major national effort much more accurately than the counts of satellites and their weights that currently appear.

Level of Organization

A third characteristic that sets space programs apart from other large-scale efforts is the considerable extent to which they are organized at national and international rather than at state and local levels. It is at these lower levels of impact that many of our national statistical measurements are taken.

Here we may draw an analogy to public, nondistributive goods and private, distributive ones. To an extent, we maintain appreciation of, and demand for, public goods by attaching to them, through the operation of the federal system, some elements of distributive goods. Sectionalism and localism substitute to a degree for private interest. People and legislators are more responsive to questions concerning "What is my state getting?" or "How is my city faring?" than they are to "How does the whole nation benefit?" Some general psychological factors, referred to as "scope of affiliation,"[74] operate in the same direction, as does the organization of the political system. In a national program for parks or health facilities, localities can receive their tangible pieces of the benefit. However, this is not the case with most *products* of space development.

Our measures of the costs of NASA programs — that is, how many dollars for what purposes get spent where — are susceptible to the regional, state, county, and city reporting characteristics of most series in our major indicator sources. Persons with a local point of view frequently regard these costs of the program as its major benefits. From statistical series available to him, a congressman is able to estimate how many jobs the space program has created in his district. He cannot, however, judge the benefits accruing to it from such things as improved weather prediction, vicarious participation in astronauts' adventures, greater understanding of the universe we inhabit, and so forth.

For some of these questions statistical data could be made available. They would, however, be so-called "subjective data" in that they would consist of the citizenry's responses to questions about their individual behavior and feelings. With only one exception, such data have found no place in the major statistical series.[75] The

[74] G. W. Allport, "A Psychological Approach to the Study of Love and Hate," in P. Sorokin, ed., *Explorations in Altruistic Love and Behavior* (Boston: Beacon Press, 1950), pp. 145–164.

[75] Economic optimism and intentions in the consumer surveys conducted until recently by the University of Michigan for the Federal Reserve Board. See George Katona *et al.*, *1961 Survey of Consumer Finances* (Ann Arbor, Mich.: Survey Research Center, University of Michigan, 1962).

resistance to the use of subjective data as indicators is, in itself, a large question that must be considered in a broader examination of the conjunctions and disjunctions of our national concern and our national measures.

Indicator Quality and Acceptability

As we have seen, there are broad areas of agreement concerning national interests and phenomena that promote and inhibit these interests. No one is averse to seeing a greater total volume of production, regardless of what type of goods it comprises; hardly anyone opposes the idea of advancing knowledge; nearly everyone, including perhaps many a criminal, would be dismayed by an increase in the frequency of violent crime. There is also, although somewhat less, consensus regarding causal relationships, or at least interdependence, among social phenomena — money in circulation and inflation, unemployment and crime, and higher education and technological development.

Policy makers often fail to use available indicators relevant to these consensual problems because they doubt their validity. Similar doubts prevent them from sponsoring data collection in areas that are not currently the objects of regular inquiry. We should recognize, however, that attacks on the validity of indicators regarding a phenomenon are a recurrently convenient political device to prevent the policy apparatus from taking account of that phenomenon.

It is important, therefore, to consider, both separately and together, the questions of what it is that we must measure and of how well we can measure it. No measurement or index is ever totally free of error. The proper question is, "Will there be greater error if we use some explicit, systematic indicator than if we rely on intuitive, impressionistic, or qualitatively summative judgment?"

Certain needs for indicators become so strong and nearly universally apparent that we consent to accept them despite their technical drawbacks. The most hallowed example is the acceptance of the election returns as the indicator of *vox populi*. (The problem in predicting election returns by public opinion polling is not that of gauging the distribution of preferences for the candidates among geographical distributions of the adult citizenry at a point in time. The survey method can make this measurement with far greater accuracy than the electoral mechanism. What is more difficult for the opinion poller is to determine how this measurement will be made by such an erratic, clumsily complex, and inefficient measuring device as the varied election systems of fifty states, the thousands of districts, and the "get-out-the-vote" efforts of many political organizations.)

The use of the Bureau of Labor Statistics' "cost-of-living" index as a wage escalator in collective bargaining agreements is an example of a more technical indicator that achieves a consensus for administrative purposes, despite its known (and fought-over) technical deficiencies. The measure of the gross national product, despite its historically proved inadequacy for such use,[76] has sanctified respectability as a measure of short-range fluctuations of our economic health and growth.

In examining the deficiencies in the scope of the social indicators that are brought to bear on problems of policy, we can weigh the possible technical inadequacies of indicators that might be developed and used against their potential utility.

National System of Social Indicators

In the narrowly economic area, it was possible to develop and gain acceptance of a system of national evaluation (accounting), doubtless because of the relative ease of achieving a broad degree of consensus regarding what was important to measure and the significance to be attached to variation in one or another direction on that measurement. Producing more goods has been acceptable as an ultimate good. The apparent ease and accuracy of the quantitative expression of economic values in terms of the common monetary unit, however, have been equally important. The same features of a consensus regarding significance and the apparent simplicity of the quantitative unit have also facilitated the development and acceptance of demographic indicators. People are important and they can also be counted.

The national economic account has been suggested as a model for a broader system of social accounting. In the chapter that follows, Bertram Gross develops this suggestion extensively.

However, there is some reason to question using the national economic account as a model for a system of social indicators. The acceptability and uses of the economic account may rest on its insulation from social areas that are important enough but that involve quantitative untidiness and value disagreement.

[76] See Morgenstern, *op. cit.*

Much of the burden of the present discussion is that we must balance our recognition of the value of descriptive and evaluative systems, and our striving to perfect their scope and accuracy, with recognition of their imperfections, in particular, appreciation for the importance of what they leave out.

It is doubtful that a singular, systematic model can ever be constructed that can fit all needs, purposes, and perspectives; all the pressures that are thrust up to national policy levels; all the divergent conceptions there are of national purposes and performances; or all the systems models that are now used in attempts to view the society in terms of a particular aspect of its essentials.

While it is possible that a comprehensive system of social indicators may someday be introduced by fiat, it seems more likely that various systems will evolve slowly. They will represent products of the interaction of theoretical and technical developments of statisticians and social scientists, on the one hand, and of various social, political, and administrative forces that determine the demand for, and acceptance of, data as indicators, on the other.

The Role of the Social Scientist

Social scientists can contribute to the rational development of sets of standard social indicators in several ways. Among them are the traditional activities of identifying the significance of social phenomena and their interrelationships; devising and refining the conceptual and technical apparatus for the measurement of these phenomena; educating the citizenry for social indicators regarding the meanings, uses, and abuses of social indexes; and lobbying for data series in areas in which they are lacking.

However, I propose another relatively undeveloped role that the social sciences can play. It involves the study of social indicators themselves as institutional products and social objects.

This study would aim at developing understanding of how particular indicators come to be generated, who uses them and *how*, the aspects of society they reflect strongly and those they do not reflect at all, the attention and inattention they receive from various publics, and the interests they sustain or threaten.

Statistical indicators are a growing, but probably still minor and peripheral, mechanism by which societies take account of themselves. Scholarly attention to statistical indicators could profitably be integrated with far broader attention to the many other mechanisms that influence ideas of what is going well or ill in the society.

APPENDIX

The body of this appendix consists of a table showing in detail (1) the specific goals and goal areas into which the statements of the President's Commission on National Goals are classified; (2) the corresponding goal areas in the report of President Hoover's Committee on Recent Social Trends in the United States and in speeches on the space program; and (3) the indicators in each of five sources that were judged as having some relevance to each specific goal. The chart shows those goals for which one or more indicators were found in the given source that were judged relevant to that goal.

The coding of indicators for their pertinence to goals was performed independently by two judges in the case of the *Statistical Abstract*. Only a negligible number of disagreements in judgments were reported. These were subsequently resolved in a discussion between the two coders in which the basis for their judgment of pertinence was explained, and they would report their consensus as to whether a given indicator could be judged relevant to a particular goal.

In the summary tables in the body of the chapter, which report the number of specific goals for which a source contained pertinent indicators, only the goals of the second order of the outline in the chart have been counted. A third order of specificity, however, is shown in the chart for goal areas such as "Equality" and "Education." In these cases, the President's Commission's discussion involved a special degree of explication of specific facets of the goal. To have enumerated these third-order goals would have given undue weight to the area, relative to its role in the commission's report. They are retained in the chart in this appendix, however, for the additional information they convey about the indicator sources.

The tallies by specific goals, of course, do not reflect the *quantity* of information nor the *degree* of pertinence of the indicators available in a given source. Thus, for example, the commission states the goal of improving products of manufacturing through basic research, rather than devoting resources to producing superficial changes of style. This goal was matched by three, indirectly pertinent, tables in *Historical Statistics* (private industry's expenditures and federal expenditures and obligations for research and development). The same source provided twenty-one tables pertinent to the goal of improved communication.

TABLE A.1

NATIONAL GOAL STATEMENTS, CORRESPONDING TO GOALS IN 1933
STATEMENT AND IN SPEECHES ON THE SPACE PROGRAM, AND
CORRESPONDING INDICATORS AVAILABLE IN FOUR SOURCES

National Goals as Stated by President's Commission	Value Statements		Indicator Sources			
	1933 Statements[a]	Space Goals[b]	Hist. Statistics & Stat. Abstract[d]	Economic Indicators[e]	HEW Trends[f]	Sociol. Almanac[g]
Individual						
Status of individual			X		X	X
Individual dignity						
Development of individual capabilities	X	X	X		X	X
Free economic choice						X
Nonconformity, tolerance of willingness to express	X					X
Responsible exercise of personal power		X	X			
Equality						
Eliminating religious discrimination						X
Legal						X
Voting and office holding						
Access to education						X
Access to employment						
Occupational access and promotion						
Home ownership						
Community participation						
Equality of sexes	X	X	X			X
Legal						X
Voting and office holding	X					
Access to education			X		X	X
Access to employment		X	X			
Occupational access and promotion		X	X			X
Community participation						
Eliminating racial discrimination	X		X			X
Legal						X
Voting and office holding						
Access to education			X			X
Access to employment			X			X
Occupational access and promotion						
Home ownership			X			
Community participation						

TABLE A.1 — *Continued*

National Goals as Stated by President's Commission	1933 Statements[a]	Space Goals[b]	Hist. Statistics & Stat. Abstract[d]	Economic Indicators[e]	HEW Trends[f]	Sociol. Almanac[g]
	Value Statements		*Indicator Sources*			
Democratic process						
Informed, involved citizenry		X	X		X	X
Participation in choice of representatives			X			X
Quality of executive office holders						X
Congressional process						X
Information media: quality	X		X			X
Information media: coverage	X		X			X
Legitimacy of pressure group operation			X			X
Broad interest representation in pressure groups						X
Civil service quality						X
Dispersion of power: state and local jurisdiction					X	
Equitable geographic representation	X					
Education						
Teaching techniques improved/salaries			X		X	X
Retain, strengthen local control of education			X			X
Consolidation						
Strengthen school boards						
Increase junior colleges						
Double graduate capacity						
Extend high school completion to two-thirds of youth; college entrance to one-third			X		X	X
Extend adult education		X	X			X
Financing double expenditures by 1970 from all sources			X		X	X
Arts and sciences		X				
General improvement of		X	X		X	
Health	X					X
Economic growth						
Military power		X				

TABLE A.1 — *Continued*

National Goals as Stated by President's Commission	1933 Statement[a]	Space Goals[b]	Hist. Statistics[c] & Stat. Abstract[d]	Economic Indicators[e]	HEW Trends[f]	Sociol. Almanac[g]
Basic research for understanding world should govern such programs as space		X				
Basic achievement preference in funds over "spectaculars"		X				X
Ensure access to scientific training for the able		X			X	X
Use manpower efficiently, on basis of capacity not formal training						X
Strengthen administration of scientific and technical programs		X				X
Humanities, social sciences, and natural sciences require support, also arts		X	X			X
Foreign language skills need improvement						
Democratic economy				X		
Government regulatory agencies independent of private interests	X					X
Collective bargaining set wages and working conditions	X		X			X
Labor-management-public conferences for mutual understanding of economy	X					
Corporations and unions limit influence over private lives of members	X					
Unions develop better grievance and legitimate opposition procedures	X					
Professional organizations and trade associations should operate on a democratic basis						
Faster and fuller pension rights to improve employee mobility			X			X
Remove barriers to employment for women	X		X			X
Older worker employment expanded			X		X	X

TABLE A.1 — *Continued*

National Goals as Stated by President's Commission	Value Statements		Indicator Sources			
	1933 Statements[a]	Space Goals[b]	Hist. Statistics[c] & Stat. Abstract[d]	Economic Indicators[e]	HEW Trends[f]	Sociol. Almanac[g]
Economic growth				X		
Maximum rate consistent with maintaining free enterprise and avoiding inflation	X	X	X			X
Full employment; 13.5 million new workers in 10 years	X		X	X		X
Tax overhaul to encourage new ventures with high risk and growth potential	X		X			
Improve standard of living	X	X	X	X	X	X
Improve products through basic research		X	X			
Assure U.S. competitive strength		X	X	X		X
Education aims at more flexible work force		X	X			X
Forced savings and reduced consumption if GNP does not grow at 5 per cent			X	X		X
Growth rates needed to meet goals for defense, education, healthy private economy, rising living standards, foreign aid	X	X	X	X		
Technological change						
Promoted with planned impact	X	X				
Retraining by firms or by locally managed programs						
Financed by state or federal funds						
Severance pay						
Military management to avoid waste of manpower, especially scientists and engineers				X		X
Encourage technological change in Department of Defense						
Decrease lead time for new weapons						
Encourage civilian decision in inter-service disputes						
Relocate some industry in depressed areas		X				

TABLE A.1—*Continued*

National Goals as Stated by President's Commission	1933 Statement[a]	Space Goals[b]	Hist. Statistics[c] & Stat. Abstract[d]	Economic Indicators[e]	HEW Trends[f]	Sociol. Almanac[g]
Agriculture						
Market demand with fair return achieved gradually			X	X		
New opportunities for farmers through retraining and relocation of industries; new jobs locally for 1.5 million farm operators						
Retire farm land			X			
Reduce farm surpluses by improving nutrition			X			
Price supports to cushion transition without fundamental adjustments			X			
Living conditions				X		
Relieve crowding of low-income and minority groups in city slums	X					X
Stop haphazard suburban growth	X					
Equate service costs to city and suburbs						
Urban centers with mixed population and rounded sets of institutions						X
Parks and recreation	X		X			
Urban renewal at $4 billion yearly			X			
Purchase city land and clear dilapidation						
Use for residential and commercial building						
Increase construction of low-income homes and apartments						
Housing, nondiscriminatory, subsidized; services to slum dwellers, especially education	X					X
Effective regional planning		X				X
Roads and rapid transit planned and financed as a unit						
Make local use of federal housing assistance	X			X		X

TABLE A.1 — *Concluded*

National Goals as Stated by President's Commission	Value Statements		Indicator Sources			
	1933 Statements[a]	Space Goals[b]	Hist. Statistics[c] & Stat. Abstract[d]	Economic Indicators[e]	HEW Trends[f]	Sociol. Almanac[g]
Financial innovations to provide moderate cost housing	X					X
Health and welfare					X	X
More doctors, nurses, etc.	X		X		X	X
More hospitals, clinics, nursing homes: better use	X		X		X	X
Increased federal support of construction of medical facilities and training	X		X		X	
Reduce cost of medical care; equalize coverage of social insurance institutions	X		X		X	
Welfare objective: causes of and prevention of juvenile delinquency, family breakdown (mental research)	X		X		X	X
Jobs for growth yet maintaining labor standards					X	
More social workers: strong churches	X		X			
Require states to provide with unemployment tax a minimum standard of benefits levels: duration, fiscal solvency	X		X	X	X	
Sick-time income improved	X		X		X	

[a] *Recent Social Trends in the United States*, report of the President's Research Committee on Social Trends (New York: McGraw-Hill Book Company, 1933).

[b] Addresses by James E. Webb, March 16, 1961–June 27, 1962.

[c] U.S. Department of Commerce, *Historical Statistics of the United States, Colonial Times to 1957* (Washington, D. C.: U.S. Government Printing Office, 1960).

[d] U.S. Department of Commerce, *Statistical Abstract of the United States*, 1962 (Washington, D. C.: U.S. Government Printing Office, 1962).

[e] *1962 Supplement to Economic Indicators: Historical and Descriptive Background*, prepared for the Joint Economic Committee by the Committee Staff and the Office of Statistical Standards, Bureau of the Budget, 87th Cong., 2nd Sess. (Washington, D. C.: U.S. Government Printing Office, 1962).

[f] U.S. Department of Health, Education and Welfare, *Health, Education, and Welfare Trends* (Washington, D. C.: U.S. Government Printing Office, 1962).

[g] M. Gendell and H. L. Zetterberg, *A Sociological Almanac for the United States* (Totowa, N.J.: The Bedminister Press, Inc., 1961).

ACKNOWLEDGMENTS

Grace S. Malakoff performed the content analyses of indicator sources and national goals reported in this chapter, with the exception of the analysis of State of the Union messages. The latter was done by Bettye Eidson. Carole Wolff performed the reliability check of indicator coding reported in the appendix.

The writer has profited from discussions with Raymond A. Bauer, Louis A. Dexter, and Edward E. Furash.

3

The State of the Nation: Social
Systems Accounting

Bertram M. Gross

INTRODUCTION: A SOCIAL SYSTEMS MODEL

How can we best appraise the state of a nation? How can we outline the major elements in any broad program or plan for the future
of a country? How can we ascertain the various effects — primary
and secondary, favorable and unfavorable, anticipated and unanticipated — of a new program and of other national goals?

These are important questions for the large organization whose
future is closely linked with that of the nation (or nations) in which
it operates.

They are much more vital for the higher officials of national governments. In the United States the President is required by the
Constitution to present to Congress an annual report on the "State
of the Union." In other countries, with or without a constitutional
requirement, chiefs of state and ministers of finance customarily
discharge a similar responsibility and render a public accounting of
their stewardship. This responsibility is most keenly felt in any
nation committed to national planning of its future growth.

Such questions are even more important at the supranational level
of the United Nations, its Economic and Social Council, its regional
organizations, and its specialized agencies. The state of the world
inevitably resolves itself into a composite picture of the states of
nations.

Economic information by itself cannot fully answer these questions. In addition to economic aspects, every situation has political,
social, cultural and biophysical aspects. Moreover, qualitative information may be fully as important as quantitative information. Over-
emphasis upon statistics, because they seem more precise, or upon
economic data, because they may be more readily available, often
yields a narrow or unbalanced view of the state of a nation.

A broader and more meaningful view can best be obtained, in my judgment, through a system of national social accounting[1] that brings together in an integrated fashion the relevant concepts developed by economists, political scientists, sociologists, anthropologists, psychologists, and social psychologists. The great advances in the social sciences during recent decades make it possible to establish such a system. The needs of administrators, government leaders, and international agencies make it imperative.

The major purpose of this document is to open up intensive discussion of the subject by setting forth a general model for an international system of national social accounts.

Accordingly, in Part I of this chapter, I introduce a model of a social system at the national level. This model incorporates the major concepts traditionally used in national economic accounting but broadens them from a set of economic indicators alone to a set of social indicators. According to this model, the state of any nation at any period of time — past, present, or future — can be analyzed in terms of two interrelated, multidimensional elements: system structure and system performance. The elements of system structure deal with the internal relations among the system's parts, the elements of system performance with the acquiring of inputs and their transformation into outputs. Both involve relations with the external environment. This model, or any part thereof, may be flexibly applied to describe the unique characteristics of any country whatsoever, no matter what the level of industrial development or the type of political regime.

The major dimensions of each of these two elements are set forth, respectively, in Part II and Part III of the chapter. These structure and performance dimensions provide a conceptual framework for ordering any information, both qualitative and quantitative, on national purposes and the extent to which they are or are not being achieved. The material in Part III is based on my Leatherbee Lectures on administration, which were given in November 1962, at the Harvard Graduate School of Business Administration. Parts II and III together represent an extension of the system concepts presented in the more narrow context of single organizations in Parts Four and Five of my book *The Managing of Organizations*.[2] These

---

[1] A terminological warning bell must here be sounded. Some writers — particularly in Britain — use "national *social* accounting" to refer to national income analysis of a strictly *economic* variety. The term is herein used to describe a form of national accounting that goes far beyond economics.

[2] New York: Free Press of Glencoe, Inc., 1964, 2 vols.

same concepts — once again at the level of single organizations — have also been presented in more concise and rigorous form in "What Are Your Organization's Objectives? A General Systems Approach to Planning."[3]

In Part IV, I discuss the difficulties involved in developing and using social indicators on the basis of this (or any other) model. Major emphasis is placed upon selectivity in developing "unique models" and "special purpose models" as distinguished from "ideal types." Suggestions are then offered as to how private, national, and international agencies may promote the development of social indicators during the coming decade.

At first glance, the approach herein presented may seem breath-takingly — if not outrageously or even dangerously — ambitious. This is because of the inherent potentiality of any accounting system to be used as an instrument of *prediction* and *control*. A second glance, however, will indicate that what I have thus far done is extremely — if not excessively — modest. My strategy has been to concentrate upon *description* and thereby prepare a foundation for *explanation*. This has meant studiously resisting the temptation to leap precipitately into premature use of the proposed accounting system for the purpose of *prediction* or *control*. It has also meant deferring for the time being the important questions involved in the use of electronic computers for the processing of the large amounts of quantitative and qualitative information required by the system.

This modest effort at developing a descriptive social accounting system has been possible only because of the pioneering work of many social scientists during the past fifteen years in developing ways of comprehensively ordering complex information on national societies. Many exciting and fruitful partial system models have been developed to stand alongside the traditional models of economic systems. Daniel Lerner has applied a model of social change to fifty-four societies, "traditional," "transitional," and "modern."[4] Gabriel Almond has presented an input-output model for the political systems of "developing" countries.[5] David Easton has offered a more sophisticated input-output model applicable to all polities.[6] Fred Riggs has worked out, with considerable illustrative detail, a

[3] *Human Relations, 18* (1965), 195–216.

[4] Daniel Lerner, *The Passing of Traditional Society* (Glencoe, Ill.: The Free Press, 1958).

[5] Gabriel A. Almond and James S. Coleman, *The Politics of Developing Areas* (Princeton, N.J.: Princeton University Press, 1960).

[6] David Easton, *A Framework for Political Analysis* (New York: Prentice-Hall, Inc., 1965); and *A Systems Analysis of Political Life* (New York: John Wiley & Sons, Inc., 1965).

model dealing with historical changes from less to more differentiated societies.[7] Karl Deutsch has set forth a cybernetic model of communication channels in society.[8] Meanwhile, on a much larger scale, econometricians throughout the world have been forging ahead in the development of increasingly sophisticated economic models.[9]

This rich work with partial system models makes it easier to think of more powerful models that bring economic, political, sociological, and cultural variables together into a general systems framework. Indeed, earlier work by Parsons and Shils had already suggested the desirability of bringing households, economy, polity, and culture together into a general social system model.[10] An influential "structural-functional" model has been presented by Marion Levy.[11] Robin Williams, in his classic study of American society, has already demonstrated the utility of dealing with all aspects of social structure, including physical resources, technology, and economic institutions as well as other matters customarily dealt with by sociologists.[12] The need for proceeding more vigorously along these lines has been suggested by Everett Hagen[13] and Saul Katz.[14] Neil Chamberlain has tended toward a general systems approach in his analysis of national planning as the managing of national assets.[15] Alfred Kuhn has suggested a unified way of thinking about society in terms of transactions and organizations, with support from the

[7] Fred W. Riggs, *Administration in Developing Countries* (Boston: Houghton Mifflin Company, 1964). Riggs uses the term "diffraction" instead of "differentiation" and defines a continuum stretching from "fused" (nondiffracted) through "prismatic" to "diffracted" societies.

[8] Karl W. Deutsch, *The Nerves of Government* (New York: Free Press of Glencoe, Inc., 1963).

[9] Bert G. Hickman, ed., *Quantitative Planning of Economic Policy* (Washington, D. C.: The Brookings Institution, 1965).

[10] Talcott Parsons, *The Social System* (Glencoe, Ill.: The Free Press, 1951); and Talcott Parsons and Edward A. Shils, eds., *Toward A General Theory of Action* (Cambridge, Mass.: Harvard University Press, 1954).

[11] Marion J. Levy, Jr., *The Structure of Society* (Princeton, N.J.: Princeton University Press, 1952).

[12] Robin Williams, Jr., *American Society* (New York: Alfred A. Knopf, Inc., 2nd ed., revised, 1960); and "Model of Society: The American Case," paper prepared for the Arthur F. Bentley seminar on the Great Society, Maxwell Graduate School of Citizenship and Public Affairs, Syracuse University, October 1965.

[13] Everett Hagen, *On the Theory of Social Change* (Homewood, Ill.: Dorsey Press, Inc., 1962).

[14] Saul M. Katz, "A Systems Approach to Development Administration," Special Series in Comparative Administration, Paper No. 6, Comparative Administration Group, American Society for Public Administration, 1965.

[15] Neil Chamberlain, *Public and Private Planning* (New York: McGraw-Hill Book Co., Inc., 1965).

concepts of *transformations, decisions,* and *communication.*[16] A vigorous boost to the study of social systems has been provided by the fundamental — and still broader — work of James G. Miller across all levels of *living* systems.[17]

In its initial stages, at least, much of this work in both partial and general systems analysis has involved considerable borrowing, with too little adaptation, from the "hard goods" models of systems engineers and cybernetics. Yet there is now increasing awareness that social systems are much more complex than machine systems, other nonlife systems, or nonhuman systems. There is increasing willingness to face up to this complexity, even though the price may be the additional effort involved in using "soft data" and impressionistic judgments as well as "hard" statistics.

While social systems models are seen as guides to the gathering and processing of relevant information, Robin Williams — with the advantage of concentrating upon the United States — is the only one who has made a serious effort to bring together comprehensively both quantitative and qualitative information. In the U.S. government a major forward step toward the systematic ordering of noneconomic data has been taken by the Department of Health, Education and Welfare. Its monthly "Health, Education and Welfare Indicators," together with its annual "Trends," provides a valuable supplement to the Council of Economic Advisers' monthly "Economic Indicators." On the other hand, the obvious importance of "getting the facts" on a transitional basis has led to many pathbreaking compilations. Banks and Textor have provided 57 kinds of "hard" and "soft" data on 117 countries.[18] Russett and associates have presented 75 political and social indicators — selected for their presumed reliability and comparability — for a basic list of 133 countries.[19] The United Nations has looked at the problem of measuring "living standards" around the world[20] and has attempted a series of information reports reviewing the "world social situation."[21] While most of this work suffers from the lack of a conceptual frame-

[16] Alfred Kuhn, *The Study of Society* (Homewood, Ill.: Irwin and Dorsey Press, Inc., 1963).

[17] James G. Miller, "Living Systems: Basic Concepts," *Behavioral Science,* 10 (July 1965), 193–237.

[18] Arthur S. Banks and Robert Textor, *A Cross-Polity Survey* (Cambridge, Mass.: The M.I.T. Press, 1963).

[19] Bruce M. Russett, Hayward R. Alker, Jr., Karl W. Deutsch, and Harold D. Lasswell, *World Handbook of Political and Social Indicators* (New Haven and London: Yale University Press, 1964).

[20] United Nations, *Report on International Definition and Measurement of Standards and Levels of Living* (New York: United Nations, 1954).

[21] United Nations, Department of Social Affairs, *1963 Report on the World Situation* (New York: U.N. Publications, 1963).

work into which information may be fitted, it provides additional stimulus to those interested in building such frameworks. It also serves to ease the conscience of anyone who, like myself, prefers to concentrate attention for the time being not upon the compilation and processing of specific data but rather upon the general types of data to be compiled and processed.

Within the brief confines of this study, unfortunately, there will not be space to summarize the thinking of the partial and general system theorists and those who have initiated compilations of social indicators. Nor shall I be able to compare their approaches with the model herein presented. For the time being I can merely hope that the materials herein presented may be regarded as a small partial repayment on intellectual debts incurred.

Finally, let me acknowledge the considerable encouragement and constructive criticism I have received in this project from Gerhard Colm, who served as Chief Economist at the President's Council of Economic Advisors when I was the Council's executive secretary; from my associates in the study of national planning in various countries, Zygmunt Bauman, University of Warsaw, Michel Crozier, Center for European Sociology in Paris, Eric Trist and David Armstrong, Tavistock Institute of Human Relations, John Friedmann, formerly of M.I.T., now chief of the Ford Foundation project on urban and regional planning in Chile, and Milton Esman, University of Pittsburgh; from my colleagues at the Maxwell School, S. M. Miller, Warren M. Eason, Jesse Burkhead, Jerry Miner, Ronald G. Ridker, Robert J. Shafer, and Victor A. Thompson; and from Stephen K. Bailey, Dean of the Maxwell School, and Irving Swerdlow, Associate Dean for Research and International Programs, who jointly encouraged the 1965–1966 Maxwell faculty seminar on the Great Society. One of the major questions discussed at this seminar (planned by a faculty committee composed of Jerry Miner, S. M. Miller, Robert J. Shafer, and myself) has been "How can we best measure desired and actual change in *any* society?" Above all, I am indebted to Raymond A. Bauer, whose questions concerning the possibility of social indicators accelerated a line of thought that I had been pondering for many years; to Arthur F. Bentley and John Dewey, whose joint work on the study of man and society has long served as a valuable inspiration and guide; and to Imogene Bentley, widow of the great philosopher, who provided the financial support for the Great Society seminar as an inquiry into the usefulness of social systems models as well as into the future of the American society.[22]

[22] The papers presented at this seminar will be published in the volume,

PART I. STATES OF A NATION

The task of this part is to set forth in broad sweeping terms the major outlines of what is involved in describing a social system at the level of the nation-state.

Before plunging into this task, however, it is first desirable to introduce the "system state" concept, to identify the growing role of national economic accounting in analyzing system states, and to discuss the factors making for the "organized complexity" of any national society.

It will then be clear that any general model capable of reflecting the complexities of a national society must also have some applicability to the subsystems contained within it. Thus the model introduced at the end of this part is "general" in a double sense. In addition to transcending partial models of a national society, it may be applied — with certain adaptations — to less inclusive social systems.

System States: Past, Present, Future

Consider the case of any two individuals — be they presidents, prime ministers, bureau heads, corporation executives, or plain citizens — who reflect on the condition of their country. One of them is convinced that things are going along very well indeed and that no major changes are necessary; the other is quite dissatisfied, believing it imperative for the government to initiate major new programs of far-reaching social impact.

Despite their divergent views, these two individuals — at a certain level of abstraction — have many things in common. Each has looked at information bearing on certain aspects of life in his country. To justify his views and act on them, each needs better information on those aspects that he regards as relevant. Each must beware of unpredicted or unsought consequences of situations or actions that, on the surface, seem favorable or unobjectionable. Each must guard against being smothered by such an overload of information that he will see trees alone and not the forest. In short, each needs a set of concepts bearing on the condition of his country and on the supply of information fitting into those concepts.

Or, to state the point more technically, each uses some model for the structuring of complex information on *states of the system*, both

---

The Great Society (New York: Basic Books, Inc.), to appear by the end of 1966 or early 1967.

past and present as well as desirable and undesirable. These system state concepts provide the conceptual link between statements concerning future goals (or purposes) and either descriptive or evaluative statements concerning actual action (or performance) toward or away from achieving such goals. Some degree of clarity concerning these concepts is a prerequisite for the collection of any relevant information, whether statistical or barely qualitative.

This point may well be illustrated by three concepts from national income accounting: per capita gross national product (GNP), net investment in relation to GNP, and the balance of international payments on current (or commercial) account. Each is widely used in economic analysis and national economic planning. In each case the collection of relevant data (even rough and ready estimates) presupposes a considerable degree of conceptual sophistication. Thus, clear distinctions must be made between GNP and national income, net and gross investment, current and capital account aspects of the balance of international payments.

Once these concepts have been carefully defined, they then become useful tools for reporting on present performance, for stating future purposes, and for formulating criteria for the evaluation of performance. This multiple use of system state concepts is shown in Table 3.1.

TABLE 3.1
MULTIPLE USE OF SYSTEM STATE CONCEPTS

System State Concept	National Performance	National Goal	Criteria	
			Critic A	Critic B
Annual increase in per capita GNP	2%	4%	5%	4%
Net investment in relation to GNP	12%	12%	10%	15%
Balance of payments, current account ($ millions)	−200	−250	0	−300

On each of the horizontal lines in Table 3.1, the identical concept has been used in different ways. In the first case of "per capita increase," the goal has exceeded performance. In the second, the "net investment" performance has equaled the stated goal. In the third, the "balance of payments" performance has exceeded the goal in terms of reducing the deficit. In the case of "per capita increase," Critic A has used a higher goal, thereby implying that in his judgment the goal itself should have been higher in the first place. In the "net investment" and "balance of payments" cases, the critics have adjusted the relevant concept upward or downward in formulating their criteria. Thus, in all cases, the same concepts are applicable to the formulation of goals, to the analysis of performance, and to the specification of criteria for the evaluation of performance that may differ from the original goals themselves.

What is evident with respect to these selected indicators is also true with respect to any larger set of indicators. Thus, a full system of national social accounting will supply the concepts needed to (1) structure information on the past or present; (2) formulate goals (desired future system states toward which commitments are made); and (3) establish criteria of evaluation. Such system state descriptions will thereby provide the substantive content of problem defining and decision making, the informational content of communication processes, and the specific measures of social change and influence.

National Economic Accounting

National economic accounting is one of the great social inventions of the modern world. Its origins go back to the *Political Arithmatick* of William Petty (1623–1687), an English physician, and to the *tableau économique* of François Quesnay (1694–1774), the French physiocrat. Quesnay saw the preparation of economic tables as an aid in the strengthening of agriculture. He and his followers were greatly influenced by the rise of business accounting in the great trading companies and by the historic work of Colbert (1619–1683) in developing accounting methods for governments.

The idea of preparing tables to give a statistical view of the total output and income of a nation was further developed by the so-called "classical" economists. It received its greatest impetus from the Cambridge school under Alfred Marshall (1842–1924) and, somewhat later, under John Maynard Keynes (1883–1946), two of the great line of British economists.

The great surge in national economic analysis took place — at an accelerating rate — during the three periods of the Great Depression, World War II, and the period of postwar reconstruction and expansion. During each of these periods, national economic accounts were seen as an instrument of national economic planning. In the United States and England, however, the sophistication of national economic accounting went far beyond its immediate practical usefulness. Indeed, economists who favored more national planning busied themselves in developing new accounting concepts that could be used when the opportune time came. In the Soviet Union under Stalin, conversely, where a limited form of national economic accounting was in daily use, the creative development of new accounting tools was often discouraged.

Content of Economic Accounting

The essence of national economic accounting is that it provides a way of looking at the total sum of a country's economic activity in at least two ways:

1. The total output of goods and services (GNP) by types of expenditures and products.
2. The distribution of national income by sectors of origin and types of income.

Each of these separate "accounts" adds up to a total for the entire nation. Through a few additions and subtractions each may be adjusted to equal any of the other totals. Thus, GNP can be converted to national income by subtracting capital consumption allowances (which gives net national product), indirect business taxes, business transfer payments, and current surplus of government enterprises, and by adding government subsidies.

More important, each account provides a significant cross section of the "economic system." Their use facilitates many kinds of analysis, prediction, and control that would otherwise be impossible. They also tie in with other basic sets of economic statistics and analyses.

Thus, the GNP, through the net export item, is related to a nation's international balance of payments. The national income by sectors of origin ties in with data on employment in divisions of production. With some slight adjustments a government's budget can be fitted into the GNP by types of expenditures, while its revenue calculations can be based on estimates of the national income by types of income (see Table 3.2).

Many forward steps are constantly being made in national economic accounting — both in developing ever more refined concepts and in collecting information to fit the new concepts. One basic area of improvement is in the collection of price data and the development of indices that make possible the expression of quantity information in terms of "stable" (that is, theoretically stabilized) monetary units. Perhaps the greatest area of progress is in the field of input-output analysis, as developed by Wassily Leontief,[23] Henry Lee Professor of Economics at Harvard University, and a host of his followers in many countries. The input-output matrix

TABLE 3.2
MAJOR NATIONAL ECONOMIC ACCOUNTS

GNP by Types of		Distribution of National Income by	
Expenditures	Products	Sectors of Origin	Types of Income
Personal consumption	Durable goods (exc. construction)	Agriculture, forests, fisheries	Compensation of employees
Gross private domestic investment	Construction goods	Mining Manufacture	Business and professional
Government	Nondurable goods	Construction	Income of farm proprietors
Net exports of goods and services	Services	Transportation and communication	Rental income of persons
		Electricity, gas, water	Net interest
		Trade	
		Finance	
		Government	
		Other services	

provides a useful way of detecting inconsistencies or bottlenecks in any national program for the expansion of investment or production.

Its Double Role

National economic accounting plays two increasingly important roles in public affairs, one analytical and the other social.

The first role — technical analysis — provides the following:

1. A method of ordering vast quantities of information on monetary aspects of economic phenomena.

2. A doorway through which one can enter and explore a vast

[23] The classic work in this field, *The Structure of the American Economy 1919–1939* (New York: Oxford University Press, 2nd ed., 1953).

domain of social phenomena, including those that are but imperfectly reflected in economic terms.

3. Some indication of possible interrelations among various policies and programs.

4. A language for the expression of many important objectives and aspects of performance.

5. An impetus to fact-orientation by policy makers and the collection of desirable data.

The second role — although intimately associated with the first — is a social one. In this sense, national economic accounting provides

1. A dramatic way of expressing objectives, one that capitalizes on modern-day "number magic."[24]

2. Stimulus to the formulation of objectives by providing professional legitimation of various desires and aspirations.

3. A unifying language for a professional elite of trained economists.

4. Opportunities for economists to win limited access to central points of power, thereby often bringing into the public service people with a greater variety of social backgrounds and with a dedication to the possibility of more rational efforts at decision making.

These factors help explain the widespread use of national economic data by political leaders (including some who do not understand them) as well as the frequent propensity of some economists and statisticians to use such data without indicating the tremendous margins of error that often exist.

Large Margins of Error

As pointed out by Oskar Morgenstern in *The Accuracy of Economic Observations*,[25] there are three principal sources of error in national income statistics: (1) inadequate basic data, (2) the fitting of the data to the concepts, and (3) the use of interpolation and imputation to fill gaps. The weighted margin of error for such estimates has been estimated as ranging from 10 per cent to 20 per cent. Yet, most of the collection agencies do not make — or else refuse to release — estimates of margins of error. The behavior of

[24] The nature of modern "number magic" is discussed in "The Clarity-Vagueness Balance," in Gross, *The Managing of Organizations, op. cit.,* pp. 494–501.

[25] Princeton, N.J.: Princeton University Press, 1963, rev. ed., pp. 242-282.

economists and statisticians in exaggerating the quality of national income data would in itself be a revealing subject of social — even statistical — research.

In his attack on the accuracy of economic statistics, Morgenstern analyzes the many reasons for error in economic statistics. One of the most pervasive sources stems from the fact that

economic statistics are not, as a rule, the result of designed experiment. . . . In general, economic statistics are merely by-products or results of business and government activities and have to be taken as such, even though they may not have been selected and designed for the analyst's purpose. Therefore, they often measure, describe, or simply record something that is not exactly the phenomenon in which the economist would be interested. They are often dependent on legal rather than economic definitions of process.[26]

Morgenstern also points out that in the physical sciences "it is customary to report data together with their carefully determined errors of observation. . . . In the social sciences such habits have not been developed. . . ."[27] His conclusion is that most economic statistics should not be stated in the manner in which they are commonly reported. It is, therefore, essential "to insist that economic statistics be only published together with an estimate of their error."[28]

In presenting his viewpoint, of course, Morgenstern is thinking of the analytical, not the social, role of the data. For purposes of achieving important social goals, economists often feel it essential to use highly inaccurate data. This use is particularly justified as a way of educating people on national income concepts and developing the demand for better data. Thus, in contrast to the "Morgenstern doctrine" of "truth in packaging," we find the "Malenbaum doctrine," as proclaimed in a discussion of India's national income statistics, that "lack of precision is not a sufficient explanation for the failure to use them."[29]

The "New Philistinism" in Accurate Economic Data

Yet, as against the dangers flowing from errors in economic statistics, I must also point out, as no less dangerous, the bias resulting from accurate economic statistics. Greater accuracy may easily

26 *Ibid.*, pp. 13–14.
27 *Ibid.*, p. 8.
28 *Ibid.*, pp. 304–305.
29 Wilfred Malenbaum, *Prospects for Indian Development* (New York: Free Press of Glencoe, Inc., 1962), p. 199.

bring with it greater irrelevance. For example, the most accurate part of a company's balance sheet is its statement of cash on hand. To focus on this alone would be a ridiculous way of analyzing a company's financial position. The balance sheet, as a whole, does not reflect the assets that the company enjoys in the form of its clients' good will and the support of its cooperating organizations. These "intangible" factors, however, cannot be dealt with as quantitatively as the estimated value of inventories and receivables. Hence, they tend to be ignored by executives who are hypnotized by the quantitative data in the balance sheet. (To repeat what has been said before, the fact that a variable can be quantified — by present techniques — may be illusory or deceptive.)

Similarly, the highly quantitative economic data in today's economic survey documents tend to detract attention from ideas that cannot be so readily expressed in quantitative terms. When a statistical indicator has been established — whether it is for gross national product or a cost of living index — it tends to take on a lifelike character of its own. Attention is inevitably directed to the small changes that take place from time to time in the selected indicator while other important and relevant aspects of the situation are neglected. Economic statistics, as a whole, emphasize the monetary value of goods and services. By so doing, they tend to discriminate against nonmonetary values and against public services for which costs invariably serve as surrogates of output value. Because figures on health and life expectancy are not directly incorporated in national economic accounts, progress in these areas may be seriously ignored, either in formulating goals or in evaluating performance. Let us suppose that during a given period of time the incidence of disease in a certain country will decline sharply and life expectancy will rise. During the same period the growth in gross national product will be less than that provided for in the plan. In this case the regular economic statistics will reveal a "shortfall." In other words, the larger aggregation of quantitative data will draw attention away from other indicators. Similarly, the size of this shortfall will not change one iota, moreover, if during the same period the public sector, with no increase in expenditures, succeeds in providing a larger quantity of essential services in education, health, and related fields.

In short, national economic accounting has promoted a "new Philistinism" — an approach to life based on the principle of using monetary units as the common denominator of all that is important in human life. The "new Philistinism" shows up in different forms:

1. The cost-benefit analysts who recognize no benefits (or dis-benefits) that cannot be expressed in dollars and cents.

2. The econometricians still operating on the ludicrous premise that there is, or should be, a "single-valued, objective welfare function" by which one could judge alternative courses of action.

3. The pathetic effort in the United States to debate policies for the "Great Society" and the "quality of life" on the basis of concepts developed decades ago to fight depression and provide minimum material sustenance for the population.

Statisticians have too little interest in removing bias of this kind. True, in the early days, statisticians were vitally interested in the kinds of data to be collected. More recently, however, their major concern has been on "technical matters of 'how' quite independent of content and purpose."[30]

This bias can be overcome only by persistent efforts to develop broader models that include many more variables than those thus far used by economists.

Trends toward Broadening

Among the many efforts to introduce technical refinements into national economic accounting, there are certain avenues of proposed improvement that go beyond economics. While they point to certain extensions of economic accounting, they at the same time raise questions that can be dealt with adequately only by some form of social accounting.

First of all, national accounting deals mainly with current performance — measured in terms of output, income, or current investment. Unlike corporate accounting, it does not present a balance sheet showing a nation's accumulated assets and liabilities. Various efforts, however, have been made to develop systems of national capital accounting. One of the pioneering efforts in this field is the work led by Raymond Goldsmith on a national balance sheet for the United States.[31] Technically, one of the great difficulties in this field is how to calculate annual depreciation on natural resources

---

[30] Albert D. Biderman, in Chapter 2 of this book.

[31] Raymond W. Goldsmith, Robert E. Lipsey, and Morris Mendelson, *Studies in the National Balance Sheet of the United States* (Princeton, N.J.: Princeton University Press, for the National Bureau of Economic Research, 1963), 2 vols. Another step in the direction of a national balance sheet is "flow of funds accounting," which tries to summarize all financial transactions and thereby provides a link between income and asset accounts. This work, still in its early stages, was pioneered by Morris Copeland in *A Study of Money Flows in the United States* (New York: National Bureau of Economic Research, 1952).

and government property. In fact, one may seriously question whether such calculations are worth the effort. A much greater problem — not previously tackled — is that of including manpower resources. Economists are generally agreed that manpower and human skills are the most important of all resources. Yet, these cannot be readily incorporated in monetary accounts.

Second, national economic accounting gives but an extremely small glimpse of the structure of an economy. Although Leontief's pioneering book on input-output analysis was titled *The Structure of the American Economy*, his matrix shows only the current interchange of output among sectors. Other conceptual techniques are needed to reveal economic structure in terms of the assets and size of organizations, and the power relations among them. Therefore, any serious effort in this direction must necessarily go in the direction of dealing with the social structure as a whole.

Third, within the area of current economic performance, some of the most fundamental concepts of national economic accounting are being stretched far beyond their traditional limits. The biggest stretch has come in the area of investment, long calculated entirely in terms of hard goods. John Kendrick in *Productivity Trends in the United States*[32] has proposed an extension of this concept to cover two forms of "hidden investment": (1) investment in persons, including education and health expenditures that are traditionally classified as consumption outlays; and (2) intangible investment by business and government in research and development, training, and improved methods. Theodore Schultz in "Investment in Human Capital"[33] has insisted on attention to five categories of "human investment": (1) health facilities and services; (2) on-the-job training; (3) formally organized education; (4) study programs; and (5) migration to adjust to changing job opportunities. In another article, "Capital Formation by Education,"[34] Schultz estimates for the United States that from 1900 to 1956 the annual investment in organized education alone rose from one-tenth to one-third of all investments in physical assets. This proposed extension may lead one day not far off to major changes in the structure of national economic accounts. It may even strengthen the case for "asset accounting" in human terms. At the same time, it may reach inevitably into areas of analysis far wider than economics that cannot be dealt with readily in monetary terms alone. Con-

[32] Princeton, N.J.: Princeton University Press, 1961, pp. 104–110.
[33] *American Economic Review*, LI (March 1961), 1–17.
[34] *Journal of Political Economy*, 68 (1960), 571–583.

ceivably, still another "stretch" may be imminent in the concepts relating to output. One of the weakest points in present-day output accounting is the lack of sufficient attention to quality.

Thus, as economists have long pointed out, there is an "upward bias" in the price indices for almost every category of expenditure. For commodities, it exists because quality changes and the introduction of new products cannot be integrated adequately into the price data. For services, it exists because, by and large, the value of services is assumed not to increase, although Richard Ruggles, in "The U.S. National Accounts and Their Development,"[35] presents strong evidence that it does. Peter Wiles, after developing a similar line of thinking in considerable detail in *The Political Economy of Communism*, finds in it "a disagreeably large revolution in statistical theory. Its consequences, if correct, will reverberate very widely, since it demonstrates that nearly all existing output and cost of living indices are wrong. The latter rise much too rapidly, and the former much too slowly." Wiles maintains that all data on national output should be adjusted to take into consideration changes in utility resulting from quality changes or innovation. Recognizing that any such adjustments may mean the use of guesswork instead of accurate information, he takes his stand by favoring imprecise answers to the right questions, as opposed to precise answers to the wrong questions.[36]

It is likely that the collectors and analysts of national economic data will move slowly and cautiously in this direction. But in so doing they will be deserting the area of data on directly observable transactions in monetary terms. From this, it is not a far cry to dealing more directly and openly with the nonmonetary indicators of human satisfaction.

The measurement of the quality and quantity of nonmarketed output becomes particularly difficult in the growing area of non-marketed government services. In national economic accounting, the volume of this service output is calculated by the monetary cost of input. This may easily result in a serious underevaluation of output in the public sector. Various ways of adjusting such output figures upward could be devised. For example, when expenditures for education remain stable while the number of students, curriculum hours, and graduates rises, the expenditure figures could be adjusted upward to give a better monetary representation of the total educational output. Yet, it might make more sense, instead of

[35] *American Economic Review*, XL (March 1959), 94.
[36] Cambridge, Mass.: Harvard University Press, 1962, pp. 246–247.

relying entirely on adjustments in monetary measures, to use some form of nonmonetary account that would deal directly with various social measures of educational output.

In general, the effort to squeeze all relevant information on action under national planning into an improved system of economic accounts would be tortuous. It would seem much more fruitful to build a broader system of national social accounts that, while not limited to calculations in monetary aggregates, would nonetheless include — and capitalize on — the basic concepts of national economic accounting. This would make it possible to deal more systematically with information that goes beyond the data in the economic accounts, and help to explain the whys and wherefores of economic performance.

The Complexity of a National Society

The major difficulty in understanding social behavior is the great complexity of human beings, groups, and formal organizations, of the subsystems within them, and of the intricate clusters, constellations, and macrosystems into which they combine. Here one finds that a tremendous number of variables interacting simultaneously in many subtle ways produces what Weaver has referred to as "organized complexity." This is far more difficult to understand than the "disorganized complexity" of most nonliving systems, which is susceptible to statistical analysis based on probability theory.[37] This organized complexity — difficult enough at the level of smaller social systems — becomes still more formidable in the case of such territorial entities as cities, urban areas, and nation-states. These are complex aggregates of smaller systems, with varying degrees of cohesion or integration. Thus any effort to understand a national society requires that one deal with the interrelationships among different kinds of subsystems.

From Partial to General Models

To cope with this complexity social scientists have followed the logical path of dividing the labor and concentrating upon small and more manageable aspects. This has meant increasing specialization of labor within such established disciplines as psychology, economics, political science, sociology, anthropology, history, and geography. It has given birth to valuable new specializations in

[37] Warren Weaver, *1958 Annual Report of the Rockefeller Foundation* (New York: Rockefeller Foundation, 1959), pp. 7–15.

management, organization theory, decision making, linguistics, cybernetics, and computerization.

The progress made in these many fields, however, has itself added to the complexity. We now have a growing wealth of theory and research (particularly in economics) based on partial, segmental models, each concentrating on a small number of variables, and providing little or no information on how to build the bridges needed to connect it with other models or with the "real world" of political leaders and administrators. With increasing output in research and theory, this can mean declining marginal benefits in each specialty and rising costs for all who try to utilize the output of many specialties.

On the other hand, the growing field of systems theory is a specialization that offers exciting possibilities of synthesis. By providing a common language and techniques of conceptual economizing, general systems concepts can help bridge the gap among partial models and — through the construction of "unique models" — narrow the gap between model and reality. These possibilities, let it be emphasized, exist only because there is a great deal of material worth synthesizing. They can be fruitfully developed only as specialization increases, thereby contributing to — and in turn being illuminated by — the synthesizing process.

In its initial phases systems theory has itself started with gigantic oversimplifications. This has meant considerable borrowing, with too little adaptation, from the "hard goods" models of cybernetic engineers. It has meant considerable obeisance to the mystique of tight little models that can be presented completely in mathematical notation, if not through mathematical operations. But there is now less effort to define social system models in terms of a single type abstracted from its environment, describable with only a few variables, static or homeostatic, or — at least theoretically — completely predictable. There is more willingness to regard social systems as varied, open, dynamic, and, in a certain sense, "unsystematic."

The Variety of Subsystems

An introductory view of the variety of social systems can be obtained by examining the rows and columns of Table 3.3.

The first row deals with the simplest forms of social systems, from the human personality to different forms of small groups, formal organizations, and territorial entities. In this context they may be called "microsystems."

As one reads from left to right, one moves from the less to the

TABLE 3.3
VARIETIES OF SOCIAL SYSTEMS

Levels	People*	Groups*		Formal Organizations*				Territorial Entities†
		Informal Groups	Families	Associations	Enterprises	Government Agencies	Governments	
Microsystems	Individuals	Small groups	Nuclear families	Single associations	Single enterprise units	Single agencies	Local governments	Villages / Local communities / Neighborhoods
System clusters		Mobs / Crowds	Extended families	Local, state, and regional federations	Multiunit enterprises or groups	Agency groups	Intergovernmental bodies / State and regional	Towns and cities / Metropoli / Megalopoli / Intranational states and regions
System constellations			Tribes	National federations	National multiunit enterprises or groups	Nationwide agencies	National states (unitary) or federal	Nations
Macrosystems				International federations	International multiunit enterprises or groups	International agencies	International regions or systems / "Worldwide" governmental federations	International regions / World

* These columns include only *simple* systems. *Complex* systems are networks composed of formal organizations (usually different types), groups, and individuals.

† As here defined, "territorial entity" includes a variety of other social systems within its spatial boundaries. Almost every territorial entity is a complex system.

173

more inclusive microsystems. Groups include individuals. Formal organizations include individuals and small groups. Each of these, of course, being located in space-time, has certain geographical dimensions: a base (such as a dwelling place, office, or factory) and a range of operations. A "territorial entity" at the microsystem level includes within a relatively small spatial area the bases of individuals, groups, and formal organizations. Its spatially defined boundaries, however, do not necessarily delimit the operational range of these other systems, whose people, goods, and messages may move back and forth over much larger areas.

Descending from top to bottom, we find increasingly larger spatial areas. Small groups become crowds or mobs. Nuclear families are transformed into extended families. Single organizations are combined into clusters with bases that may be widely dispersed. From the village, local community, or neighborhood, we move to towns, cities, and larger subnational regions. At this level the geographical entity may include many bases (often only minor field offices) of organizational clusters, constellations, and macrosystems with bases dispersed across the nation or the world. This tends to modify seriously — or perhaps destroy — any organic unity or deep sense of community that may have existed in smaller geographical entities.

At the national level we find geographical entities with varying degrees of unity and sense of community: at one extreme, hyper-nationalism, and at the other, states still engaged in nation building. The macrosystems are represented by international organizations and the world itself.

Even the smallest microsystems are internally differentiated, with various kinds of component subsystems brought together through various roles, hierarchic relations, polyarchic relations, and codes of behavior. As systems become larger and more differentiated, these roles, relations, and codes tend to become more complicated, divergent, and internally conflicting.

The table itself, however, concentrates upon *simple* systems. As indicated in the footnote, *complex* systems are networks of inter-related organizations, groups, and individuals. The American banking system and air transport system are complex constellations— each one an intricate network of relations among government agencies at various levels, private organizations, trade associations, international bodies, employee and professional groups, informal groups, and individual clients. A village may be a complex microsystem, a city a complex cluster, and so on.

System Openness

Every social system is an open system. In other words, certain activities cut across its boundaries and connect it with its social, biological, and physical environment. The environment, in turn, is made up of other systems, social, biological, and physical.

There are four kinds of boundary-crossing activities:

1. *Entries and Exits.* Entries into families and informal groups — and their subsystems — are determined by birth, marriage, aging, acceptance, or cooption. Entries into formal organizations — and their subsystems — are achieved by recruitment, joining, seniority, promotion, or merger. Entries into geographical entities are accomplished by birth or migration. Exits are provided by death, resignation, termination, demotion, dissolution, and emigration. The significance of entries and exits is underscored by "rites of passage." These are particularly important in formal organizations, which (their parts being infinitely replaceable) have a potentiality for immortality.

2. *Multiple Membership.* Most individuals play roles in different groups and organizations. These multiple roles cannot be completely segregated within the human personality. In fact, they invariably lead to role conflicts and divided loyalties. They therefore bring to one system some appreciation of the objectives and values of other systems. This is particularly true of subsystems included within larger systems.

3. *Resource Exchange.* This involves the acquisition of inputs (goods, services, or information) and the delivery of outputs (goods, services, or information that have been processed in some form) through a clientele network. Many subsystems in a large organization will receive inputs from internal suppliers and transmit outputs to internal clients. Many large organizations have input-output relationships extending across their country and the world.

4. *Influence.* Every system exerts a certain amount of influence (or power) beyond its boundaries and is influenced by other systems. These reciprocal influence relations (rarely balanced) take place not only with suppliers and clients but also with controllers and controllees, associates and adversaries, and miscellaneous publics — as illustrated in Chart 3.1. A system's range of operations beyond its own bases may be measured in terms of its influence and its input-output relations.

Obviously, the varying extent of these complex boundary-crossing activities results in different degrees of openness — with more

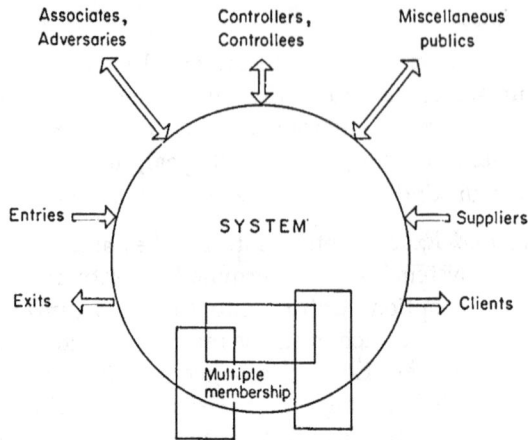

Chart 3.1. System in environment.

highly isolated systems at one extreme, and at the other those boundaries at the point of crumbling.

System Dynamism

With the passage of time, a social system moves from one system state to another. These system states are never identical. There are always certain changes taking place in at least some dimensions of some subelements. Some of these changes may, over small periods of time, be of little significance or — as is often the case with the continuing changes in system structures — may be hidden from view. Others may accumulate in small, marginal increments that one day suddenly yield a major change: what Hegel referred to as "the transformation of quantity into quality."[38] Some may seem — at least in certain respects — repetitive or cyclical, while others may reveal entirely new system state profiles. Many changes are the result of unconscious, automatic processes of development[39] and decay. Others — probably far less than intellectuals would like to think — are the product of conscious, goal-oriented performance. Still others are the unforeseen consequences of system interaction. Above all, the various elements and dimensions of system and subsystem change at differential — and differentially changing — rates of change.

Conflict among and within systems is probably the greatest

[38] Most large-scale system transformations — including revolution and dissolution — probably come about in this manner.

[39] The word "development" is here used in the sense in which psychologists distinguish biological development from learning.

source of continuing change. Internal conflicts are inescapable even in the "normal" personality. They are created by the multiplicity of competing or even contradictory human interests, social roles, and group attachments. Similar conflicts develop among and within the subsystems of all systems. The common interests and goals that keep a system together are always imbedded in a network of divergent and competing interests and goals. Conflict usually becomes more dramatic in the intersystem relations of rivalry, competition, and combat. Extreme forms of conflict, of course, may readily undermine or destroy a system. On the other hand, some degree of conflict — both internal and external — is an essential stimulus to system adaptability and creativity.

Although any social system may be regarded as a system of power, no social system has the power to resolve all conflicts through victory. All systems must lose on some occasions to win on others. They must frequently compromise: bargaining and negotiation are a way of life in social systems. At times, by redefining their interests and broadening the agenda, they may be able to achieve an integration of interests whereby no one loses and everyone gains.[40] They must often avoid issues or tolerate sustained deadlock. Thus "conflict dialectics" is far more complex than envisioned by Marx. On the one hand, there is no simple two-element "thesis" and "antithesis." On the other hand, any synthesis may be a complex outcome composed of varying elements of victory (or defeat), compromise, integration, avoidance, and deadlock. It will usually have both "good" and "bad" aspects. Yet every outcome will itself generate new forms of conflict and serve to push forward (for better or worse) the multidimension of dialectics of change in both system structure and system performance.

Theories of equilibrium and disequilibrium are ill-suited to deal with the dynamics of change in social systems. As Karl Deutsch has pointed out, "the concepts of equilibrium and disequilibrium are now most useful as descriptions of temporary states of small components of such systems, while the systems themselves are recognized as engaged in dynamic processes of change which go well beyond the classic equilibrium image."[41]

The cybernetic model of the "controlled feedback" or "self-governing" system has already become the new classical image in systems theory. In a cybernetic system a "governor" (or "selector")

[40] The concept of conflict integration, first developed by Mark Follett, is interpreted in a broader context in Gross, *The Managing of Organizations, op. cit.,* Chapter 11, "The Conflict-Cooperation Nexus," pp. 265–270.
[41] *The Nerves of Government, op. cit.,* p. 186.

acts to achieve a certain goal through an "effector." Through a "detector" it obtains information on the results of its own action. It then automatically modifies its subsequent behavior in order to achieve the goal. The chances of success in goal attainment usually vary inversely with the amounts of *information load* in the feedback channels and of *lag* in response to such information. They vary positively to the system's *lead* (that is, the effectiveness of its predictive processes). Up to a point corrective action (or gain) will help attain the goal; beyond this it increases the probability of oversteering.[42]

The sophisticated development of cybernetic models in systems engineering has been a major factor in the rapidly moving automation revolution. This revolution, it must be noted, applies not only to the processing of hard goods, but also — through computers — to the processing of information. This has involved the computerized simulation of man's cognitive processes. It is leading to ever-increasing efforts to develop cybernetic or computer models of man and of social systems. Efforts along this line are encouraged by the obvious fact that "cybernetics offers not only a gain in technical competence but also a possibility of restoring to problems of purpose their full share of attention."[43]

Further progress in this direction will require a greater recognition of social system complexity. Easton has already pointed out the need to think in terms of "multiple feedback loops." In view of the interrelations among complex systems, we must also think of "coupled feedback" among cooperating-competing systems. We must be able to think of "feedforward loops" that provide a flow of information on reciprocal expectations of future behavior. As Deutsch has suggested (among many other pregnant suggestions), we must devise models not only of goal-seeking feedback but of goal changing, a complex form of learning. Above all, we must be prepared to cope with the dynamics of changing a multiplicity of mutually constraining and often conflicting goals. This means that we must be willing to bring into our system information that may be qualitative and impressionistic, rather than limiting ourselves to "hard data" of limited significance.

Unsystematic Systems

The term "system" often gives one the impression of referring necessarily to a tight set of relationships that are fully deterministic,

[42] *Ibid.*, pp. 186–187.
[43] *Ibid.*, p. 91.

predictable, or controllable. Actually, models in natural science are mainly probabilistic rather than deterministic. The models of the cybernetic engineers not only deal with probabilities, they also include "black boxes" to indicate areas of ignorance and presumption. Any realistic social system model must be still looser.

A social system is rarely a taut system. A change at any one point does not necessarily mean a significant change at some other point. There is usually considerable slack in the system.

A social system is only partially knowable. There are not merely "black boxes" but "black regions" with amorphous boundaries. There are always unforeseeable (not merely unforeseen) consequences for good and evil (and usually both together). Although myths of perfect knowledge, wisdom, or infallibility may be cultivated by some governors, central omniscience by them or anyone else is impossible.

A social system is never fully controllable. The myths of central omnipotence always hide imperfections; internal disunity lurks behind the façade. Perfect coordination can be achieved by neither hierarchy, bargaining, nor any combination of the two. There are always uncontrollable aspects of the biological and physical environments in which social systems are imbedded. Tight control of some elements may usually be achieved only at the cost of diminished control over others.

In sum, social systems are so loose that one may well ask skeptically, "Is this a system?" Perhaps the best answer is, "An unsystematic one."

Let us now try to define a social system more carefully.

The Structure-Performance Model

The term *system* has a number of meanings. There are systems of numbers and of equations, systems of value and of thought, systems of law, solar systems, organic systems, management systems, command and control systems, electronic systems, even the New York Central system.[44]

Although the common meaning is "some set of interrelated elements," it is obvious that there are many kinds of systems. One kind, not the center of attention here, is a system of rules or procedures influencing behavior, some "systematic" method (whether rational or psychotic) of doing things.

As elucidated by James Miller, there are three other major meanings:

[44] Miller, "Living Systems: Basic Concepts," *op. cit.*, pp. 200–209.

1. *Concrete system,* a "nonrandom accumulation of matter — energy in a region in physical space-time, which is nonrandomly organized into coacting, interrelating subsystems or components."

2. *Abstracted system,* the units of which are "relationships abstracted or selected by an observer in the light of his interests, theoretical viewpoint or philosophical bias."

3. *Conceptual system* (sometimes called "analytic system"), the units of which are "terms, such as words (commonly nouns, pronouns and their modifiers), numbers or other symbols," with relationships "expressed by words (commonly verbs and their modifiers) or by logical or mathematical symbols. . . ."[45]

I concur with Miller's judgment that "behavioral scientists, if they deal with abstracted systems, easily forget the intra-system relationships in concrete systems which influence processes within and between these systems."[46] In my judgment a model of a national society is a *conceptual system* through which people try to represent *concrete systems.* Such systems may be partially represented by concepts dealing with abstracted systems or with systems of rules or procedures.

The Duality Principle

The state of any social system may be expressed in terms of two types of concepts: those relating to structure and those relating to performance.

Some analysts prefer to concentrate their attention on structure. System performance is taken for granted or set aside for later attention. This will yield a rather static representation of reality unless attention is given to the changes in system structure. More serious, national leaders often plan for major changes in structure without considering what kinds of performance are needed to bring about these changes or how such changes affect subsequent performance.

Other analysts prefer to concentrate on performance, or activity. System structure is taken for granted — or else various structural elements are introduced whenever it is obvious that performance cannot otherwise be rationally discussed.[47] At the level of national

45 *Ibid.,* pp. 200–209.
46 *Ibid.,* p. 208.
47 David Easton, *A Systems Analysis of Political Life, op. cit.* Concentrating upon input-output analysis, Easton affirms that he "shall not be directly concerned with exploring a conceptual framework for the analysis of political structures and their interrelationships" (p. 13). Subsequently, however, it proves impossible to escape dealing with the question, "input into what?" and "output from what?" (Chapters 11, 12, 13, 27, and 28)

policy, leaders often plan for major improvements in performance (particularly economic growth) without considering the structural changes that are prerequisites of improved performance.

Any well-rounded view of a social system must deal with *both* structure and performance — although at any particular time there may be reason to emphasize one rather than the other. This duality of approach is well recognized, of course, in enterprise accounting. Here the balance sheet presents a monetary summation of the company's financial structure (various kinds of assets and of claims against them) at some point in time. The income statement (or profit-and-loss account) summarizes the company's financial performance over a given period of time. This duality is also recognized, at least in part, by the "structural-functional" school of analysis. The difficulty here is that many structural-functionalists emphasize the former to such an extent that their concepts become unduly static. "Function" is often regarded as referring more to a "state of affairs" or "potential" than to action, operating or functioning.[48] This danger might be avoided by using the term "structure-functioning." The term "structure-performance" expresses the same idea, but with less embarrassment from the many confusing meanings that have been attached to the word "function."[49] At the purely physical level the distinction is similar to that between *matter*, anything that has mass and occupies space, and *kinetic energy*, which is action. At any level both structure and performance are aspects of process. The former may be regarded as "slow processes of long duration," and the latter "quick processes of slow duration."[50]

This interrelated duality may be illustrated graphically by any typical chart showing input-output transactions between a system and its environment. Chart 3.2 also identifies a number of subsystems and illustrates their interaction in transforming inputs into outputs. Although this chart resembles a cybernetic model, it is more than that: inputs and outputs may include people, goods, and services as well as information. It is also less than that: the "feedback loop," with all the necessary details on different kinds of feedback and on indirect or broken linkages, has not been completed.

[48] Levy, *op. cit.*, pp. 55–62.

[49] A stimulating critique of the term "function" in "structural-functional" analysis may be found in Ernest Nagel, *The Structure of Science* (New York: Harcourt, Brace & World, Inc., 1961), pp. 520–535.

[50] Ludwig van Bertalanffy, *Problems of Life: An Evaluation of Modern Biological Thought* (New York: John Wiley & Sons, Inc., 1952), p. 134.

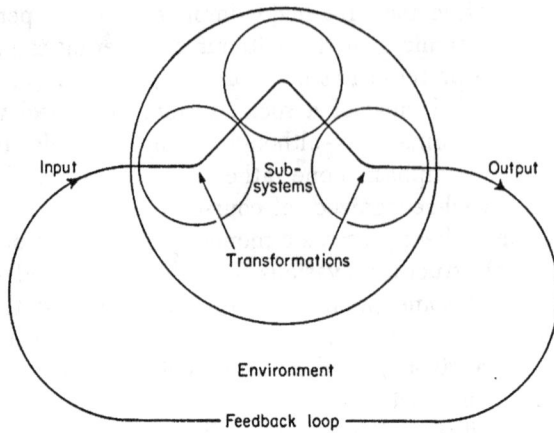

Chart 3.2.   General system model.

The Structural Elements

There are so many aspects of the structure of a national social system that no one need feel particularly unhappy if he cannot make a complete list of all of them. Indeed, a *complete* list would be impossible, since someone could always get new additions through subdivision or combination. Even if possible, such a list would be too burdensome and complicated for most uses.

It is both possible and desirable, however, to develop a list that goes far toward meeting two requirements: (1) providing a set of general categories in which all conceivable aspects can somehow or other be fitted, and (2) providing a useful and reasonable ordering of the categories. Indeed, such a set of structural elements will be *much more than an ordinary list*. Rather, it will be a major part of a conceptual model that represents concrete systems.

Let us now go back to the commonly accepted concepts of concrete systems. These concepts are related to some set of interrelated elements in an environment. If we spell these concepts out a little more clearly, we get the following:

1. Differentiated subsystems.
2. Internal relations.
3. External relations.

To deal properly with the first of these elements, we must now make four additional distinctions. First, as we look at the great variety of subsystems in a national territorial aggregate, as described in Table 3.3, there is some merit in distinguishing between people as individuals and people as members of informal groups and organizations. In demography, vital statistics, and other important calculations we must deal with various categories of people apart from their participation in larger subsystems.

Second, we must recognize that all subsystems are intimately associated with physical, nonhuman resources. This makes all social systems *man-resource systems.*

Third, all social systems have some kind of guidance system (or subsystem) to maintain the internal relations necessary to prevent system disintegration and to influence system performance.

Fourth, all subsystems are guided by various values. In addition, there are usually some minimal values common to the social system as a whole. Hence these two merit separate attention, particularly since there are so many kinds of values and value conflicts in any national society.

We thus find that our simple set of three elements is now expanded into seven interrelated elements. These may be set forth in the following proposition concerning social system structure:

The structure of any social system consists of (1) people and (2) nonhuman resources (3) grouped together into subsystems that (4) interrelate among themselves and (5) with the external environment, and are subject to (6) certain values and (7) a central guidance system that may help provide the capacity for future performance.

Each of these seven elements, of course, is itself multidimensional. Many investigators may spend decades investigating just one or two dimensions of one subelement. Any comprehensive analysis of these elements (no matter how ordered) might be regarded as a "balance sheet" that presents a system's human and institutional assets as well as its physical and financial assets.

Each element of system structure has certain spatial and temporal dimensions. The most obvious of these are the geographic extension of a society's land mass and the geographic distribution of people and critical types of nonhuman resources. There are spatial aspects, in terms of both "home base" and sphere of operations of every subsystem. All elements of system structure are located at specific points in time and tend to change over time.

The Performance Elements

The obvious starting point for analyzing system performance is the input-output concept. This, also, may be spelled out in terms of three initial elements:

1. Acquiring inputs.

2. Producing outputs for external use.

3. Investing in the system, that is, producing outputs to maintain change or increase the system's future performance.

Here again four additional distinctions are helpful.

First, there is a major difference between information developed to describe the kind, quantity, and quality of output of a system (e.g., the health services available at a hospital or the educational activities at a university) and the actual welfare, utility, or benefits generated by such services.

Second, there is considerable value in giving special attention to information on the extent of economizing on input use: that is, to various input-output relations (variously referred to as "efficiency," "productivity," or "profitability").

Third, an extremely important aspect of performance is the extent to which the system and its components conform to various behavioral codes (legal, moral, organizational, professional, etc.).

Finally, these aspects of performance, both separately and in combination, may be viewed in terms of information on their degree of rationality. There are advantages in dealing separately with information on this also.

Once again, for purposes of both convenience and completeness, three elements have now been expanded to seven. These may now be put together in the following proposition concerning the performance of a social system:

The performance of any social system consists of activities (1) to satisfy the interests of various "interesteds" by (2) producing various kinds, qualities, and quantities of output, (3) investing in the system's capacity for future output, (4) using inputs efficiently, (5) acquiring inputs, and doing all the above in a manner that conforms with (6) various codes of behavior and (7) varying conceptions of technical and administrative (or guidance) rationality.

Each of these elements, again, is itself composed of multidimensional subelements and sub-subelements. Any comprehensive analysis of such elements (irrespective of the ordering pattern) might be regarded as a system "performance statement." Indeed, it would necessarily include much of the information customarily provided in economic accounts (for either an organization or an economy) and revenue-expenditure budgets.

As with system structure, each element of performance also has its own spatial and temporal dimensions. Rapid changes in temporal dimensions are sometimes so important that attention is distracted from the spatial dimensions, even though they may be changing also.

Structure-Performance Relations

The relations between structure and performance are even more intricate than those between an enterprise's balance sheet and income statement. Almost any aspect of system performance will have some effect on various aspects of system structure: investment performance, of course, has the most direct effects. Any important plans for changes in future performance inevitably require significant changes in system structure. Changes in system structure, in turn, always have implications, often extremely hard to predict, for future performance.

An infinite number of permutations may be created by combining various elements and subelements of structure and performance. In this way the system states of nations, as well as their major subsystems may be described for any period of time, past, present, or future. In broad terms, these system descriptions may indicate the general characteristics of many systems. In more specific terms they may define the special, or even the unique characteristics of the specific systems with which one is concerned.

A complete system state analysis, however, is never needed, and would in most cases probably be impossible. For any particular purpose, whether action or research, only a selected number of cross-sectional statements are needed. The value of a general system approach to all possible variables is that it provides a background for selecting those variables most appropriate to specific situations and for changing one's focus as the occasion warrants. It can prevent *ceteris paribus* from becoming *ceteris incognitis*.

As here presented, the major elements of both structure and performance have been presented at too high a level of generality to be meaningful.

It is now imperative to define each element more carefully and indicate some of the major subelements and dimensions of each.

This is the task of the next two parts of this chapter.

PART II. SYSTEM STRUCTURE

The structure of a social system invariably enters into debates and proclamations concerning national plans and policies. Sometimes the avowed purpose of national leaders or planners is to change an old social system, achieve "institutional reform," or set up a "socialist society." Occasionally the avowed purpose of national policy — particularly where national planning is formally disavowed — is to maintain "free enterprise," save "capitalism," or build a "mixed economy."

But discussions of social structure — particularly in the context of national policy and planning — are apt to be dealt with in oversimplistic terms. On the one hand, there is the old dichotomy between capitalism and socialism, or — as it is often put — between free enterprise and collectivism, or between freedom and security. In the communist countries the avowed aim is to move from capitalism to socialism and then from socialism to communism. But in the modern world these distinctions are fading in significance. They are based mainly on nineteenth-century concepts of nationalization and, in the era of the administrative revolution, deal only with the peripheral aspects of social structure.

Of more central relevance are the three dichotomies between (1) democracy and totalitarianism, (2) independence and subservience (either as colony or satellite), and (3) the "haves" and the "have nots," or the "developed" and the "developing."[51]

All of these have meaning as aspects of social structure. Yet there is a tendency to deal with each of them in glittering generalities abstracted from concrete data, to regard them separately, without an appreciation of their interrelations as part of a broader system. This can best be combated by looking at these matters — and the capitalism-socialism dichotomy as well — within a system framework.

One way of doing this is to deal separately with the "economic structure" and the "political structure." Structural aspects that are left over can then be thrown under the heading of the "culture" or "society." This approach, however, is inevitably one-sided, as each analyst may leave major aspects of his subject to others and ignore the interrelations between the separate parts. This, in turn, may also encourage the multiplication of specialized approaches and bodies of information accessible only to specialists working in isolation from one another.

In contrast, it is often more useful to look at national structure as a whole. This approach brings together under the rubric of "social structure" all the basic ideas dealt with in separate disciplines.

---

[51] In many contexts the term "developing" refers to industrial development, in some contexts to changes in political institutions. In a more fundamental sense, "development" may refer to any aspect of change in social structure or performance — often with the implication that it is desirable or induced.

It may thus provide a way of reformulating existing concepts and information in a much simpler fashion. The seven structural elements mentioned in the preceding part provide a way of doing this. These, too, of course, must be dealt with separately as well as in combinations. Their subject matter may indeed be separately referred to as a nation's population structure, resource structure, group (or institutional) structure, the structure of internal and foreign relations, value structure, and guidance (or control) structure. The concepts of "economic structure" or "political structure" cannot be fitted into any one of these categories. Each is a "cross-sectional"[52] conceptual system drawing upon various components from many of the seven structural elements.

Before discussing each of these elements separately, it may be useful to refer to Table 3.4, which presents a selected list of subelements. This table also illustrates, in a parallel column, how the same subelements may be adopted to describe the structure of some major formal organization — let us say, a defense ministry or a steel manufacturing enterprise — in the same society.

Let us now take a brief look at each of the seven elements and then suggest how they may be used to analyze the major processes of historical change from preindustrial to postindustrial societies.

People

The basic element of system structure in any nation is the people[53] of the country. They are the basis of the entire social system. Land, minerals, and man-made facilities are "resources" only because the people find them useful. Groups exist only because of the interrelations between individual human beings. Social power is exerted by, with, on, and for people individually, and by people acting together in groups. External relations are relations among people. Social and cultural values are never disembodied; they exist only because people hold them. Thus, all the other five elements of system structure are merely ways of elaborating on certain stable characteristics of, and interrelations among, people.

As a basis for understanding these characteristics and interrelations, it is necessary to deal analytically with the population struc-

---

[52] The importance of "cross-sectional" analysis was first pointed out by Arthur F. Bentley in his classic, *The Process of Government* (Bloomington, Ill.: Principia Press, 1908).

[53] One may refer to people, of course, as "human resources." But there is much more to be said about people than is usually comprehended under the term "resources."

TABLE 3.4

SYSTEM STRUCTURE: ILLUSTRATIONS FOR ORGANIZATION AND NATION

Structural Elements	Organization	Nation
1. People		
Number	Total number by grade or rank, salary, full-time or part-time, tenure, age, sex	Total number by age, sex, race, religion, occupation, employment status
Characteristics	Education, health, experience, abilities	Education, health, abilities
2. Nonhuman resources		
Physical assets	Land, buildings, equipment, machinery, materials	Natural resources (soil, water, flora, fauna, minerals, man-made resources)
Monetary assets	Cash, bank deposits, receivables, securities	Domestic money supply, foreign currency reserves
Claims against assets	Equity, debt	Equities, domestic debt, foreign debt
3. Subsystems		
Types	Units with various roles; by location	Territorial entities, formal organizations, groups (and clusters and constellations of same)
Structural forms	Divisions and subdivisions, committees, informal groups	Legal basis, the government-nongovernment continuum
Differentiation	Degree of subdivision and specialization	Degree of subdivision and specialization
4. Internal relations		
Cooperation-conflict	Scope and intensity of internal conflicts	Scope and intensity of internal conflicts
Hierarchy	Extent of conflict resolution	Extent of conflict resolution
Hierarchy	Network of superior-subordinate relations	Network of superior-subordinate relations
Polyarchy	Internal bargaining procedures, committees	Markets, intergovernmental bargaining, representative assemblies
Communication	Formal and informal communication networks	Mass media, informal networks

TABLE 3.4 (*Continued*)

Structural Elements	Organization	Nation
5. External relations		
External systems	Territorial communities, formal organizations, groups, individuals	Foreign nations, international organizations, blocs, and coalitions
External roles	Controller-controllee, client-supplier, associate-adversary	Controller-controllee, client-supplier, associate-adversary
Environmental	Dispersed or clustered, placid, disturbed or turbulent	Dispersed or clustered, placid, disturbed or turbulent
6. Values		
Internal-external orientation	Esprit de corps, organization aggrandizement, public service	National identity, nationalism, internationalism
Activism-passivity	Instrumental activism, stability, routinization	Instrumental activism, stability, fatalism
7. Guidance cluster		
Internal structure	Role differentiation, occupants, tension, and integration	Role differentiation, occupations, tension and integration
Links with system and environment	Support base, entry channels	Support base, entry channels

ture by itself — that is, with the types, quantity, and quality of people.

Types or Categories

By "types" reference is made to such classification categories as age, sex, race, religion, geographical location, and occupation. With subgroups within these categories as rows and with quantity groups as columns, a full set of matrices can be developed to indicate the "population structure" of any society. By "population structure" I mean, therefore, the quantitative distribution of the population across the various relevant categories.

Age and sex distributions of the population are elements that are usually taken as "givens" rather than objects of planned change. In a society that has an unusually high proportion of young people or old people, such a "given" may be of tremendous importance for planners. The same is true in any other society in which there is a disproportionate number of one sex — as in the U.S.S.R. after the loss of millions of males during World War II. Race and religion are important characteristics in societies where interracial or religious tensions are high. Another important element is the geographical structure of any country in which the seats in representative bodies are distributed on a popular basis. Increased population in certain less populated regions may become a vital national goal, whether for purposes of military strategy, resource development, or internal political support.

Any serious program for economic growth or development invariably involves major changes in occupational distribution. In industrially underdeveloped countries the shift is from agriculture to construction, industry, and services. In well-developed industrial societies the major change is from goods to services. Whichever the case, there seems to be an inevitable occupational redistribution from agricultural and rural areas to metropolitan and (in the larger countries) "megalopolitan" areas.

Quantity or Population Size

As a whole, apart from various subgroups, population size is a major consideration in any country where there is a danger of overpopulation in relation to available resources, or underpopulation in relation to external enemies. It is also related to the size of present and potential markets and the ability of the country to benefit from mass production and competitive enterprises.

A "population policy" may be developed by measures directed at the birth rate, the death rate, and immigration or emigration. Efforts to increase population, as in Israel and Australia, have been relatively rare. They are usually undertaken through the promotion of immigration and health measures to extend the life span. Occasionally, resort is made to subsidies for larger families. In industrially underdeveloped countries the major emphasis has been in the direction of public health measures and improved living standards that have reduced the death rate. Together with high birth rates, this has often exerted tremendous pressure on natural resources and slowed down the rate of per capita increase in national output. Under such circumstances "planned parenthood," in the sense of birth control, is being increasingly viewed as a major part of national policy, with birth rates and reproduction rates becoming important social indicators.

Quality

The most obvious aspect of population quality is health. A healthy population is one of the greatest of all natural resources. Yet the only indicators of health that have thus far been developed are statistics on the incidence of disease. These must be handled with extreme caution. The increased incidence of certain diseases may be the result of better diagnosis, improved systems of data collection, a reduction in infant mortality, or a larger relative role for the degenerative diseases (in itself a *positive* index of health resulting from a decrease in other diseases).

It would also be helpful to have broad information on the interests, abilities, and knowledges of various groups in a population. Yet detailed information on these matters is usually available only for certain "captive groups" of a population, such as members of the armed forces and children in public schools. For these groups, information is often available not only on health and physical attributes but also on personality characteristics and the ability to pass intelligence and aptitude tests.

The most significant and most readily available information on population quality is that dealing with formal education. The total population — or a segment of it such as the labor force over a certain age — can be represented in terms of the numbers of people with varying amounts of schooling. In a more refined way, information can be compiled on the distribution of advanced degrees and the numbers of people in professions calling for special training or skills.

Reference is often made to a society's "accrued knowledge" or stock of "technical know-how." These terms refer to valuable human assets. Both are often used in a way which seems to assume that knowledge and know-how may somehow or other be disassociated from "people who know." This assumption is rooted in the rather conspicuous fact that libraries, filing systems, and other document repositories are aids to, and extensions of, human memory. One may, therefore, reach the false conclusion that accumulated knowledge and know-how are in some way embodied in *them*. Yet both knowledge and know-how are characteristics of human nervous systems. These assets are *human* capacities. The libraries, files, and archives are resources only when there are people available who know how to use them. In other words, the level of technology in any society is a dimension of human ability. Yet this dimension does not lend itself to direct measurement. It can be characterized only by rather indirect surrogates in the form of information on educational levels, occupational breakdowns, organizational demography, and the extent of document repositories.

Nonhuman Resources

The nonhuman elements in man's environment have always been an integral element in social structure. These are sometimes referred to as *physical* resources to distinguish them from people. Yet even poets, preachers, and philosophers — no matter how disembodied their thoughts may occasionally seem — are also physical entities. It seems more appropriate to describe man's biophysical environment (apart from the people in it) as *nonhuman* resources.

As already indicated, however, nonhuman resources have no existence *as resources* apart from people. Physical objects can become resources only when two conditions are met: (1) when there are people with certain interests to be satisfied, and (2) when there are people with the knowledge and technological know-how required to use such physical objects for the satisfaction of such interests.

Natural Wealth

"The most important resources," notes Richard L. Meier in *Science and Economic Development*,[54] "are those which are most common and are noted only upon their loss or absence." Among these are air, light, water, soil, minerals, flora, and fauna. The availability

[54] New York: John Wiley and Sons, Inc., 1956 (paperback edition, Cambridge, Mass.: The M.I.T. Press, 1966).

of air and light depend to a large extent on climate considerations. Air and light tend to be taken for granted except in cases of air pollution or when people turn to solar energy or air currents as a source of power. Special configurations of soil and water give rise to rivers and natural harbors. The amount and quality of soil, together with the availability of water, provide the basis for agriculture, forestry, and animal husbandry. Minerals provide materials for construction machinery, tools, and consumer products, and the fuels that (apart from muscle power, water power, and wood burning) are the greatest sources of energy in modern civilization.

There are tremendous variations in the amount and quality of information on natural resources. In countries that are well explored and industrially developed much data are available. In the rest of the world little is known. It is in those countries where technology is progressing the most rapidly and where the possibilities are the greatest for new technological methods that valuable resources will some day be made out of materials now regarded as worthless. It should be pointed out that estimates of natural resources may in complex ways be a function of their development. Thus estimates of oil reserves are dependent on the extent of exploration, which, in turn, will be dependent on the resources available for exploration.

Man-Made Assets

Man-made resources are easier to identify and quantify. These may be classified as follows:

1. The physical infrastructure composed of roads, bridges, dams, harbors, buildings, and houses.

2. Farms (with or without livestock), timberlands, and fisheries.

3. Energy-producing facilities that can supplement the muscle power of people and animals.

4. Machinery and tools that use such energy in agriculture, mining, manufacturing, construction, transportation, communication, and other activities.

5. Stocks of consumers' and producers' goods held for future use.

Despite the high visibility of these assets, comprehensive information is rarely available. Individual organizations may keep detailed records on their own facilities and stocks. But aside from an occasional housing census, governments rarely keep accounts of their own holdings, let alone assemble the data of nongovernment organizations.

Claims Against Resources

For the various inhabitants of a country, a larger supply of domestic currency usually implies the power to acquire a greater amount of those resources for sale, rent, or hire. For the country as a whole, however, too large a supply of domestic currency may result in runaway inflation.

The situation is somewhat different, however, with respect to foreign currency. A larger supply of foreign currency reserve is not ordinarily a direct source of inflationary pressure. First and foremost, it is an insurance of the nation's ability to obtain needed imports from other countries.

In addition to money, ownership (or property) rights represent the other significant form of claim against resources. The resource structure of a country is always paralleled by an ownership structure that determines the distribution of wealth among individuals, families, organizations, or classes.

Exact information on the distribution of ownership is practically never available on a comprehensive basis. The only highly organized data on this important aspect of resource structure are those relating to (1) land ownership, which is rather conspicuous and on which information is sometimes fully recorded in land registries, and (2) the book value of corporate assets, as revealed in the reports of private corporations to tax collection agencies and in the reports of public corporations to higher control bodies. Indirect information on the distribution of wealth can be obtained from data on income distribution. Quantitative information, which often has a powerful influence on public policy, can be obtained from general observations concerning the housing and the living standards of the conspicuously wealthy.

Subsystems

In discussing the population structure earlier, we divided human beings into various classification categories. These categories are less significant, however, than those which describe the way people act together in subsystems or smaller groups of various types. It is the intricate network of these subsystems that, more than anything else, establishes the framework of social structure. We must, therefore, be prepared to identify the various kinds of social groupings: families, communities, employment organizations, associations, and political parties.

Families

Although families are to be found in all societies, there are great variations both in their internal structure and their relation to other social organizations. In agricultural and pastoral societies the basic family unit is the "extended" family. In the most primitive societies the family may be the only significant organization, with larger groupings composed of clusters of extended families. With the growth of social development, other organizations come into being, particularly governments, armies, churches, and trading groups. But families become — and for a considerable time tend to remain — the dominant control units in such organizations. Thus, we have governmental dynasties, hereditary priesthoods, and patrimonial business enterprises. With the development of industrial civilization, these organizations tend to detach themselves from family influence. Concurrently, the extended family begins to break down and the basic family unit tends to dwindle into the "nuclear" family. Under such conditions the last strongholds of traditional family structure are found in those families which operate small farms, small businesses, or control a few large corporations.

Communities

These are groupings of families residing in a given — usually small — geographical area. Community bonds become, and remain, strong when based not only on physical proximity but also on a common mode of making a living, or a common ethnic or religious background. With increasing urbanization and industrialization these bonds tend to break down. In many underdeveloped countries, however, ambitious efforts are made to reconstruct community life through "community development" or "village development" programs.

Employment Organizations

This type of social grouping — that is, the organization that employs people for salaries and wages — is the most significant institution for getting things done in the modern world. It is found in every sector of economic production, from agriculture and mining through manufacturing of goods and supplying of services. The great bureaucratic structures of the modern world, whether civilian or military, are found only in employment organizations or in the employment aspect of associations. It was organizations such as these that — by improving on the functions previously performed by cooperative work groups, by single families, or by individuals acting alone — made the Industrial Revolution possible. The long and sustained growth of employment organizations in total assets, employees, and output resulted in still more organization, more large-scale organization, more bureaucracy, and more administrators, and has, indeed, ushered in an era of "organizational revolution" that is sweeping across the world. Among other things, this revolution has meant a rapid decline in the proportion of the population in agriculture, a rapid growth in the population of urban areas, and increasing specialization and differentiation in and among formal organizations.[55]

Associations

The essence of the association is that its members belong to it on the basis of affiliation rather than of employment. The larger and more important associations also have employed staffs, although these usually represent but a small portion of the total membership. The oldest associations are churches, religious groups, and those based upon ethnic or racial bonds. The most powerful of these groupings — particularly in the industrially developed countries — are usually the trade associations and trade unions.

In many countries there are hundreds of other important associations composed of professional groups, veterans, women, youth, and people interested in various programs for social or political action. The intricate network of such associations provides an important part of the social structure in the industrially developed countries. In many cases, as a matter of fact, the operations of government can never be fully understood without understanding the role played by associations in influencing the actions of executive, legislative, and judicial agencies.

Political Parties

A political party is a special kind of social grouping whose major activity is the effort to place its members in key positions in government. The traditional method of defining the party structure in any society is to do so in terms of the number of parties: one, two, or multiple. Yet a one-party system may be little more than a loose coalition of major factions that might almost be regarded as political parties in their own right. In a multiple-party system one of the

[55] A broad perspective on these vast changes is provided by "The Rise of the Administered Society" (Chapter 2) and "The Challenge of the Administered Society" (Chapter 30), in Gross, *The Managing of Organizations, op. cit.*

parties (although it may have much less than a majority of the popular vote) may be able to achieve sustained dominance by organizing a stable series of coalitions. When this does not happen in a multiple-party system, then the individual parties often behave as little more than narrow associations.

A more useful typology of party structures has been provided by Milton Esman:

1. Conservative oligarchies, such as in Iran, Ethiopia, Northern Nigeria, Afghanistan, and Peru.

2. Competitive interest-oriented parties, such as in the Philippines, Brazil, Greece, Chile, Malaya, and Jamaica.

3. Authoritarian military reformers, such as in Pakistan, Burma, South Korea, Thailand, and the Sudan.

4. Dominant mass parties, such as in Mexico, India, Egypt, Algeria, Puerto Rico, Tanzania, Tunisia, and Guinea.

5. Communist totalitarians, such as in China, the Soviet Union, and the Communist countries of Eastern Europe.[56]

Government-Nongovernment Continuum

Another important structural aspect is provided for by the continuum running from government organizations at one extreme to nongovernment organizations at the other. Within any single country the one extreme is represented by the national government itself, its regional or local subdivisions, or (in the case of federations) by member states, and the many separate agencies of national and local government.

At the other extreme stands the nongovernmental organization. This includes not only individual and corporate enterprises but also such public service bodies as private schools, hospitals, and welfare agencies.

In the middle of this continuum are a host of quasi-governmental organizations. These include (*a*) regional and international organizations formed by governments, but far from being federated governments; (*b*) mixed agencies formed by governmental and nongovernmental organizations; (*c*) government-established agencies on whom governmental authority is bestowed; and (*d*) those political parties that install, or try to install, their members in positions of power within governmental organizations.

---

[56] Milton Esman, "The Politics of Development Administration," occasional paper prepared for the Comparative Administration Group seminar, Boston, 1962.

It should be kept in mind that the distribution of organizations along this continuum in any society does not automatically give a picture of the market system or of the extent of government control. Many government organizations sell their services in the same way as private corporations. Under such circumstances they are part of the market system. Many nongovernment organizations are subject to detailed control and regulation — and, at times, the burden of such control may become much greater than that on certain government corporations which operate with relative freedom from governmental control.

Internal Relations

While it is the various interrelations that make a system out of a large number of subsystems, these interrelations are extremely hard to depict in comprehensive and specific terms. Often the best that can be done is to produce a series of general statements of a qualitative nature. With the further development of the social sciences, however, it should be possible within a decade or two to describe the more important of these in quantitative terms.

Integration-Conflict

By itself subsystem differentiation seems divisive. The system as a whole exists only to the extent that the parts are integrated through some network of internal relations.

The first element in internal relations is cooperation or integration among and within the subsystems. This integration must be based upon certain commonly accepted values or some degree of perceived interdependence, if not mutually acceptable objectives. A large part of this integration may derive from routinized and habitual activity and expectations.

Beyond the minimum requirements for an operative system, there are tremendous variations. In societies with little polyarchy, few linkages, scant multiple membership, and little mobility, there is a very low level of integration and little communication among various groups. There may be no common language, little common understanding, and serious separatist movements. This is particularly true of multiracial, multilingual societies in which the majority of the people make a living through subsistence agriculture and play little part in the monetized economy. The more integrated societies are welded together not only by common language but by the interdependence of a highly specialized market economy, by mass media of communication covering the entire country, and by an educational system that promotes mobility.

At the same time cooperation is always associated with conflict relations within and among subsystems. If carried too far, conflict and tension may impair, even destroy, internal structure. Within limits they may help to invigorate it. Under certain circumstances, social conflict among competing groups may itself be an integrating factor, since it gives each side a stake in what it hopes to get from others.

An important factor in subsystem integration is the linkage provided by multiple membership. Most people belong to a number of different, and sometimes competing, groups. Thus, in addition to his family and employment organization, a person may also belong to a religious group, a professional group, a recreational group, or a cultural group, and a trade association or trade union. This phenomenon of multiple membership leads to competing loyalties in the lives of individuals and to internal conflicts within many organizations. Yet by making the members of one group more sensitive to the interests of other groups, it also serves as a balancing force in the social structure.

Still greater integration is provided by organizational links. Among business enterprises this is often done through subsidiaries, holding companies, interlocking directorates, cartels, and trade associations. Among other groups, including governments, this may be done through federations, blocs, and alliances. Sometimes these linkages are clearly visible to any observer. In other cases, only insiders may know of their existence.

When viewed internally, any large and powerful group may be seen as a coalition among its various subgroups and members. Similarly, any such group will usually seek to extend its power by various forms of coalition with other groups. This leads to the loose arrangements referred to as "log rolling." It also leads to complex clusters and constellations — such as the "American banking system" or the "air transport system." At the level of national policy considerations, these are often referred to as "alliances" or "blocs." When these are "general," covering all possible issues, they result in major cleavage within a society. Often, however, they are "partial," covering only one or two issues, or "shifting," with major groups entering one alliance on certain issues and an entirely different alliance on other issues. In either case, they are major centers of power and comprise the major participants in social conflict.

The internal relations of a society can be fully understood only in terms of the distribution of power among its subsystems. This, in turn, gives us the best idea as to where any society stands on the continuum stretching from democracy to dictatorship. The position on this continuum indicates who has power to determine what within the system. Basic differences exist between power, as the ability to influence events, and formal authority and legal rights. Both of these latter may be important sources of power. But neither is a sufficient source. Each may be an empty formality.

Hierarchy and Polyarchy

In any society there are certain groups that stand in a superior-subordinate relationship to other groups or to unorganized publics. This hierarchic relationship is evidenced in the relation between government agencies and those subject to governmental controls, in the structure of formal organizations, and in status ranking throughout a society. In some societies hierarchic relations are much more highly developed than in others. This is particularly true whenever there is a caste (or class) stratification of the population or an effort made toward total domination by a single political party.

Without some degree of hierarchy most societies would probably disintegrate. The upper positions in a hierarchy provide valuable points for conflict settlement and important symbols of organizational unity. The lines of hierarchic authority provide formal channels of internal communications and ladders for career advancement. At the same time, the growing role differentiation in modern organizations leads inevitably toward the subdivision of hierarchic authority and the growth of "multiple hierarchy."[57]

Hierarchic status relations are often described in quaint, nineteenth-century language that distinguishes between upper, middle, and lower classes. This distinction is based on a rather simplistic idea of group structure. It brings together under the rubric of a single class a great variety of disparate groups. Thus, the much abused term "middle class" has been used to refer to such divergent groups, both organized and unorganized, as small shopkeepers, government bureaucrats, various levels of army officers, members of established professions such as law, medicine, engineering, and teaching, members of "emerging professions" — such as social work-

[57] See Gross, "The Law of Multiple Hierarchy," in "People-in-Organizations: Formal Aspects," *The Managing of Organizations, op. cit.*, pp. 377-379.

ers, statisticians, and economists — scientists, "humanist" intellectuals, and artists.

Yet, hierarchy is always accompanied by polyarchy, that is, by an intricate set of relations outside of the superior-subordinate mold. In fact, no hierarchic system could operate without lateral relationships of this type. These polyarchic relations are based on both "joint responsibility," in which different groups operate together as equals (often in committees or councils), and "dispersed responsibility," in which the various groups negotiate and bargain with each other. Market relations are an outstanding example of the dispersed responsibility form of polyarchy. These relations are so important that they will be discussed separately.

Markets

The term "market" refers to some pattern of transactions between buyers and sellers. Because of economists' preoccupations with "perfect competition" and a few variants thereof, there has been little empirical analysis of actual market structure. Yet, we can readily distinguish the more important variables: the number of buyers and sellers, their price strategies, controls over markets, and the extent of nonmarketed products. Other variables in market situations relate to the homogeneity, heterogeneity, or uniqueness of the products involved; the supply situation; the extent of actual cooperation or organization among few or many sellers or buyers; the availability of information on cost, output, and related matters; and the ease of entering the market as either a buyer or seller.

Buyer-Seller Lineup. The first aspect of any market structure is provided by the number of buyers and sellers. Economists use the terms "monopoly," "oligopoly," and "polyopoly" to refer respectively to situations of one, few, and many *buyers.* Since any number of sellers may confront any number of buyers, there are nine major situations that may be discovered in examining various markets. These are shown in Table 3.5.

Price Strategies. Market transactions may also be analyzed in the approach taken to the bargaining on prices or the fixing of prices. An extremely perceptive effort to distinguish among alternative price strategies has been provided by Peter Wiles[58] in his typology of (*a*) primitive higglers, (*b*) price takers, (*c*) full-cost chargers, (*d*) continuous producers, and (*e*) marginal-cost chargers.

[58] Peter Wiles, *Price, Cost and Output* (Oxford, England: Basil, Blackwell, 2nd ed., 1961), pp. 4–5.

TABLE 3.5
MAJOR SITUATIONS OF VARIOUS MARKETS

Buyers	Sellers		
	One	Few	Many
One	o, o	o, f	o, m
Few	f, o	f, f	f, m
Many	m, o	m, f	m, m

o = one; f = few; m = many.

Controls Over Markets.   All types of markets — no matter what number of buyers or sellers — are subject to various controls. Internal controls are those effectuated by buyers or sellers themselves. These are the most significant when the buyer or seller group is small or highly organized. External controls are those exercised by government. The most direct government controls are those effectuated through the setting of maximum or minimum prices, or by government participation as a buyer or seller. Less direct controls take the form of fiscal or monetary policy, or policies that affect the structure, bargaining power, and methods of buyers and sellers.

Nonmarketed Products.   In a subsistence economy, a large proportion of agricultural products are consumed on the farm. Also, clothing may be made and construction work performed by family or volunteer labor, rather than by hired labor. In all highly industrialized societies, entirely apart from the extent of nationalization, a growing proportion of vital services consist of nonmarketed products. Like educational and public health services, they are distributed not on the basis of sale to individual purchasers but rather through systems of rationing, random access, or nonprice bargaining. Under such circumstances there is no direct price that provides a monetary measure of the quantity or quality of output. A similar situation exists with respect to the output of most units within all employment organizations, including the component units of business enterprises. In these circumstances, administered systems of "shadow prices," and "internal pricing" may be devised as a means of obtaining monetary measures of output.

Communication-Mobility Networks

The communication network is an all-pervasive part of internal relations. As already noted, a role in this network is always played by the lines of hierarchic authority. But many other multidirectional channels and media — some of them informal — are also needed. Although face-to-face, word-of-mouth communication is vital in all societies, a growing role is played by the telephone, radio, television, cinema, and newspaper networks and by rapid transportation facilities.

Communication links are extremely weak in preindustrial societies with many languages and national cultures and high degrees of illiteracy. Even in urban areas there is a great gap between the literate modern sectors and the illiterate traditional sectors. The gap is still greater, as Almond has pointed out, between the urban centers and the rural and village periphery. "Here the problem of interpretation is a massive one. The interpreter, whether he be a bureaucrat, interest group leader or party leader, cannot readily find equivalents in language, values and cognitive material to make an accurate translation. . . . No real penetration by communication is possible, and the audience of the polity consists of a loosely articulated congeries of subaudiences."[59] The introduction of radio (or even television) may extend the communication system, but on a one-directional basis only and at the risk of considerable misunderstanding at the receiving end. The most reliable communication links may often be a network of traditional and antidevelopment subsystems, as with the Catholic clergy in many Latin-American countries.[60]

Another dimension of internal relations relates to barriers that tend to "freeze" people or channels that help them move more freely, either horizontally or vertically. Horizontal mobility occurs when people move from one geographical area or employment organization to another; vertical mobility when they move to higher or lower positions of power, prestige, or income. In almost all societies there are discriminatory barriers against upward mobility. These may be based upon caste, race, religious or sexual differences. To the extent that these discriminatory barriers are weak, large-scale bureaucracies provide significant opportunities for upward mobility through career advancement. The ability to take advantage of such opportunities depends to a large extent on the size and openness of the educational system.

---

[59] Gabriel A. Almond, "A Functional Approach to Comparative Politics," in Almond and Coleman, eds., *The Politics of Developing Areas, op. cit.,* pp. 50–51.

[60] George L. Blunksten, "The Politics of Latin America," in Almond and Coleman, eds., *op. cit.,* p. 519.

External Relations

No nation is a closed system. It operates within a world environment. Its relationships with the rest of the world are expressed in terms of both trade and influence — as well as the movement of people and ideas.

These external relations may be expressed in terms of three sets of overlapping roles played by external actors:

1. *Controllers and Controllees.* The controllers are imperial powers or big powers that organize spheres of influence. The controllees are colonies, satellites, and camp followers. On this dimension plans may be oriented toward freedom from external controllers, control of others, or both.

2. *Associates and Adversaries.* The associates are partners or allies, both of whom are usually needed to build up external power. On the other hand, the adversaries are those against whom such power may be used. They range from rivals and competitors to openly belligerent opponents or enemies.

3. *Clients and Suppliers.* The clients are those who receive goods, services, and ideas, while the suppliers are those who provide them. When countries are seriously dependent on external sources of supply, they usually orient their planning activities toward the development of a larger external clientele. The suppliers also include those who furnish financial assistance, technical aid or advice, and general support.

All of the nations playing any of these external roles may be active in trying to influence a given system. Any serious efforts at influence call not only for external persuasion and pressure but also for various forms of internal penetration. Similarly, resistance to external influence involves countermeasures of persuasion, pressure, and penetration. Both kinds of efforts require the formation of blocs, alliances, and coalitions. The shifting patterns of these complex clusters and constellations help determine the structure of power and the loci of conflict in the world system.

Values

Every society exhibits a complex and shifting structure of values. This value structure may be regarded as a patterned set of general attitudes toward what is desirable or undesirable. It indicates the different ways in which people in different societies try to satisfy universal human interests.

Parsons' "Pattern Variables"

Although the delineation of value patterns has been one of the great achievements of anthropology and sociology, no widely accepted taxonomy has yet been devised. One approach is that of Talcott Parsons who suggests that any structure of cultural values can be defined by a society's position on the continuum between five dichotomies.[61] These five "pattern variables" are presented as applicable not only to cultural systems but also to social systems (that is, specific organizations) and personalities:

1. *Affectivity-Affective Neutrality.* The extent to which people are expected to act in such a way as to achieve immediate gratification or else discipline themselves to renounce immediate gratification.

2. *Self-Orientation–Collectivity Orientation.* The extent to which people are expected to serve private or collective goals.

3. *Universalism-Particularism.* The extent to which people are expected to act in accordance with general standards rather than in the light of particular cases.

4. *Ascription-Achievement.* The extent to which people are expected to judge others on the basis of their attributes or their actual performance.

5. *Specificity-Diffuseness.* The extent to which people are expected to act toward others on the basis of narrowly defined spheres or without such confinement.

National planners often aim at changing these pattern variables. Sometimes these objectives are implicit, without being openly stated. Generally speaking, the major orientation in modern society is toward the strengthening of affective neutrality (particularly when current satisfactions must be sacrificed on behalf of long-range investment or national defense), collectivity orientation, universalism, achievement, and specificity.

Kluckhohn's Variables

On the basis of a more elaborate empirical study of five cultures and much wider general experience in the analysis of cultural values and rules, Clyde Kluckhohn proposes the use of thirteen dichotomies (appearing in three clusters).[62]

[61] First set forth in *The Social System* (Glencoe, Ill.: The Free Press, 1951); and further developed by Talcott Parsons and Edward Shils, with the assistance of James Olds, in *Toward a General Theory of Action*, Part 2, "Values, Motives and Systems of Action," pp. 47–243.

[62] "Toward a Comparison of Value-Emphases in Different Cultures," in

Man and Nature

1. *Determinate-Indeterminate.* The extent to which people believe in orderliness in the universe, as opposed to chance or caprice.
2. *Unitary-Pluralistic.* The extent to which the world is divided into such separate realisms as "mind" versus "body" and "sacred" versus "profane," rather than being seen as a whole.
3. *Evil-Good.* The extent to which nature and human nature are seen as basically good or evil.

Man and Man

4. *Individual-Group.* Much the same as Parsons' self-orientation and collectivity-orientation pattern variable already mentioned.
5. *Self-Other.* The degree of relative emphasis on one's self or on loyalty or devotion to other individuals.
6. *Autonomy-Dependence.* This is similar to David Riesman's "Inner-Directed"–"Other-Directed" polarity.[63]
7. *Active-Acceptant.* This is the contrast between accepting one's fate or trying to help determine it.
8. *Discipline-Fulfillment.* This is the "Apollonian-Dionysian" contrast between safety, control, and adjustment on the one hand and adventure, expansion, and self-realization on the other.
9. *Physical-Mental.* The extent of emphasis on sensual versus intellectual activities.
10. *Tense-Relaxed.* The extent to which tension of any kind is pervasive or is counterbalanced by a sense of humor and calm easy-goingness.
11. *Now-Then.* The extent to which emphasis is placed on the here-and-now, as opposed to either past or future.

Both Nature and Man

12. *Quality-Quantity.* The extent of measurement or other standardization beyond purely qualitative considerations.
13. *Unique-General.* The extent to which the world is seen in terms of the concrete, the literal, and the unique, rather than in terms of abstraction and universalism.

Kluckhohn goes on to state that the dominant value-emphases are often taken for granted and not readily verbalized. Moreover, they are "felt" primarily as seekings or avoidances, as in the "do's" and "don't's" of every culture.

From the rich assortment of cultural values, there are some that

---

Leonard White, ed., *The State of the Social Sciences* (Chicago, Ill.: University of Chicago Press, 1956), pp. 116–132.

[63] David Riesman, Nathan Glazer, and Reuel Denney, *The Lonely Crowd* (New Haven, Conn.: Yale University Press, 1951).

appear more than others as manifest or latent objectives of national planning and policy.

In so far as the Man-Nature cluster is concerned, national planners usually aim at developing beliefs in the orderliness of the universe and in the basic goodness of nature and human nature. Of the Man-Man variables the ones that are most relevant to planned objectives are those that emphasize group and other (rather than self) orientations, activity (rather than acceptance), discipline, tension (under the pressure of planned objectives), and the future (rather than past or present). Of the Nature-Man variables the emphasis is usually on quantity and generality, both of which are basic to the growth of science and technology.

Modes of Communication

At the same time, there are probably many other cultural values that are not even hinted at by the systems of dichotomies of Parsons and Kluckhohn. For example, one area of considerable importance — and too complex to be handled by a simple dichotomy — is that of modes of communication. National planning efforts in different cultures may be deeply affected by the balance between verbal and nonverbal communication, the pace of communication, the balance between honesty and deviousness, and the degree of indirectness or directness. Peter Hammond points out that indirectness in communication is highly institutionalized in non-Western societies. In contrast, he finds (although without indicating that he has examined the American scene carefully enough) that it "is negatively sanctioned in American culture and must be relied upon covertly."[64]

In his study of friction between Americans and Mexicans in Mexico, John Fayerweather reports a difference in degree; that is, in Mexico indirectness is used more than in the United States as a means of avoiding tensions and conflicts.[65] The formalities of etiquette, protocol, and organization rituals — which differ extensively from country to country — are themselves often devices for channeling communication toward relief from tension and conflict.

While national policy makers must perforce adapt themselves in many ways to existing values concerning communication, the policy process itself often leads them toward changing such values. The

---

[64] "The Functions of Indirection in Communication," in *Comparative Studies in Administration* (Pittsburgh, Pa.: University of Pittsburgh Press, 1959), pp. 183–194.

[65] *The Executive Overseas* (Syracuse, N.Y.: Syracuse University Press, 1959), pp. 163–166.

most common changes are probably in the direction of more highly developed verbal and written communication, faster communication, honesty, and directness. These may be coupled with new organizational roles and rituals that provide relief from inevitable tensions.

Guidance System

Some degree of system integration is usually provided by common values, by the unifying influence of external adversaries, and by mutual adjustment — both routinized and spontaneous — among the subsystems themselves. But sufficient capacity for survival, let alone for effective performance, is not possible without a special subsystem with responsibility, authority, and power for system guidance. In the rather vague terms of jurisprudence, this subsystem is often called "the state." More specifically, however, it is something less than that, if by "state" one refers to the entire set of government agencies or even the agencies of central government alone. It is, rather, the central control system of central government.

The membership of this system may include people and groups outside of formal government (as with political parties, business interests, trade unions, churches, etc.) or from foreign governments (as in the guidance systems of colonies and satellites). It may include legislators and judges (although the tendency in the central guidance system is usually obscured by the myths of governance, the censorship and deception invariably used in the guidance system, and the mystic aura that invariably surrounds any major center of national power.

Central Guidance Clusters

Some parts of a guidance system play important symbolic roles. Thus the "chief of state" serves as a valuable symbol of national unity. This role may be performed by a constitutional monarch who "reigns" but does not "rule" or by a president or prime minister involved in "ruling" as well as "reigning." Similarly, a national planning authority (or board, commission, or council) may symbolize dedication to the guidance of rapid economic change. But the agency itself may be merely a minor part of the central mechanism for guiding such change. Indeed, there is a general tendency for these symbolic rules to obscure the fact that the central guidance system is invariably a complex cluster (or constellation) of interrelated subsystems.

All members of a central guidance cluster play various roles in decision making and communication with respect to formulating and reformulating objectives, activating people and groups, and evaluating both objectives and action taken toward achieving them. More specifically, these roles may be broken down formally into five general categories: (1) general leadership roles, (2) financial management roles, (3) critical problem roles, (4) special staff roles, and (5) general staff roles. The major roles in each of these categories are shown in Chart 3.3. A more detailed discussion of each of these roles, with special reference to economic planning, is provided in my "The Managers of National Economic Change."[66] In any particular society some of these roles may be developed more fully than others. The detailed roles are always distributed among various people, groups, and organizations in different ways. The formal roles are always associated with a variety of informal, ritualistic, or ceremonial roles. Many of the key actors wear many hats.

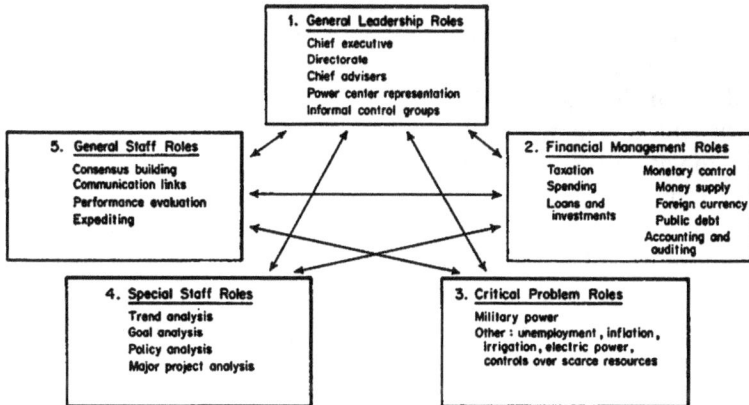

1. General Leadership Roles
Chief executive
Directorate
Chief advisers
Power center representation
Informal control groups

5. General Staff Roles
Consensus building
Communication links
Performance evaluation
Expediting

2. Financial Management Roles
Taxation
Spending
Loans and investments
Monetary control
Money supply
Foreign currency
Public debt
Accounting and auditing

4. Special Staff Roles
Trend analysis
Goal analysis
Policy analysis
Major project analysis

3. Critical Problem Roles
Military power
Other : unemployment , inflation , irrigation , electric power , controls over scarce resources

Chart 3.3.   Central guidance cluster roles.

The internal relations within a central guidance cluster — as with any system — are characterized by both integration and conflict. The multiplicity of these various central guidance agencies creates the inevitable problem of coordination within the guidance system: "Who shall coordinate the coordinators?" Simple hierarchic control by chief executives will never suffice by itself. A high degree of mutual understanding and spontaneous cooperation is also required,

[66] In Roscoe C. Martin, ed., *Public Administration and Democracy*, Essays in honor of Paul H. Appleby (Syracuse, N.Y.: Syracuse University Press, 1965), pp. 101–127.

qualities that develop very slowly indeed in a situation where each central guidance agency must protect itself against role encroachment by others. Indeed, actors and new agencies in a central guidance cluster must usually concentrate major attention upon establishing themselves; mere survival in a highly competitive and politically sensitive area is not an easy matter. Thus we see constant reorganizations, liquidations, mergers, and amalgamations, a constant rise and fall in the importance of specific individuals, and a succession of new and old actors.

Relations with Other Subsystems

A central guidance cluster can be effective only if embedded in a network of relations with other subsystems in the society. Its most direct relations are usually with large "intermediary" subsystems (such as major ministries or departments of government, regional or local governments, organized economic "sectors") and representative assemblies that may have formal authority over the guidance system itself. In order to obtain feedback information on the results of their actions, however, many actors and agencies will circumvent these intermediaries and develop direct communication links with the broader masses of the people and specific organizations and communities. The multiplicity of these links tends to recreate within the central guidance cluster (albeit with considerable distortion) the group conflicts and value conflicts within society as a whole.

An important aspect of central guidance is the balance between centralization and decentralization. In times of stress and challenge — as with war, planning for accelerated growth, building a new nation, or effectuating a social revolution — a major increase in centralization is needed. Yet with a large society, and particularly one in which there is an increasing differentiation among subsystems, effective central guidance is impossible without widespread decentralization of responsibility, authority, and power. This requires the central promotion of conditions under which subsystems can develop their own capacity and initiative and the more capable subsystem leaders may hopefully aspire toward entry into the central guidance cluster.

Individual Democracy

An important measure of the centralization-decentralization balance in any society is the extent to which individual systems enjoy "democratic rights." This has been expressed traditionally in terms relating to the citizen's participation in public politics. Although this is an important consideration, it is only part of the entire picture; it deals mainly with the individual's occasional and limited participation in great decisions affecting himself and his family. If we look at the nature of individual participation more broadly, we find at least five dimensions of democracy or of a democracy-dictatorship continuum. Thus, the power distribution within any given system can be expressed in terms of its POISE profile: that is, the extent to which it rates high or low on each of the following:

1. Political democracy, which provides for the participation in the decisions of state agencies by adult members or citizens of the state.

2. Organizational democracy, which provides the members of organizations with the opportunity for participation and self-development and recognizes their individual rights and responsibilities.

3. Individual democracy, which provides individuals with the rights of juridical self-defense.

4. Social democracy, which provides guarantees that political and economic rights shall not be impaired because of a person's color, race, religion, national origin, or sex.

5. Economic democracy, which provides full opportunities for useful employment and for at least minimum standards of food, shelter, clothing, medical care, education, and recreation.

The fact that a society enjoys a high degree of political democracy does not necessarily imply that its rating is high on other scales in the POISE profile. Under certain conditions social or economic democracy develops more rapidly. Organizational democracy often seems to develop most slowly. In any case, any serious effort to appraise the democratic nature of a society requires the collection of information on all five types of individual participation in the system.

From Preindustrialism to Postindustrialism

Some of the most impressive and significant work in the social sciences — from Marx, Spengler, and Toynbee to Lerner, Rostow, and Riggs — has dealt with the changing structure of societies. Much of this work, however, has been unidimensional, concentrating upon one major aspect of social structure. One of the advantages of a multidimensional structural analysis, along the lines set forth in the preceding parts of this chapter, is that it facilitates any effort to synthesize the results of unidimensional theory and research.

Still more important, however, it provides a useful instrument for escaping the "present as culmination" illusion that seems to have dominated most thinking on changes in social structure. Just as Hegel interpreted all of world history as culminating in the German state of his day, modern theorists have tended to interpret economic and social change as culminating in their version of the present-day "modern" society. Thus for Lerner, Rostow, and Riggs, respectively, societies that are "traditional," "underdeveloped," or "fused" (undifferentiated) move through "transitional," "take off," and "prismatic" stages until they finally achieve "modernity," "mass consumption," or "refraction" (high differentiation). This modern-day "Hegelism" allows investigators from "developed" societies to escape tensions and frustrations at home by concentrating on "underdeveloped" ones. It promotes a satisfying sense of superiority among their compatriots, relieving them of the uncertainties involved in trying to understand the nature of social change in their own country. But if we conscientiously look at the various elements in the social structure of "developed" societies, we can hardly escape the overwhelming facts that point to multidimensional processes of extremely rapid social change. These changes are so great that, indeed, we must regard the United States and all the countries of Western Europe as "transitional" societies.

But toward what are these societies in transition? The old terms "capitalist" and "socialist" no longer have much relevance. More specific terms — but only partially appropriate — might be the cybernetic, the service, the affluent, the secular, the technopolitan, the megalopolitan, the intellectual, the leisure, the planning, the information-overload, the long-lived, or (if we consider the growing potentialities in military technology) the suicidal society. Perhaps the most general term is the "great society" — as earlier discussed by Graham Wallas and John Dewey. The use of the term by Lyndon Johnson presages the growing political necessity in industrial societies to offer policies that go far beyond the "welfare state" and deal with the "quality of life." A less colorful term — which at least has the advantage of dramatizing a major contrast with the recent past — is "postindustrialism."

Any analysis of the present transition to postindustrial societies, however, as with any comparison with preindustrialism and industrialism, is meaningful only if it serves to illuminate the changes in various elements of social structure and performance. An illustration of how such a multidimensional analysis might be initiated is provided by Table 3.6. This multidimensional view, however, does not justify a vision of unidirectional change. Both industrialism and postindustrialism contain many alternatives and contradictions. Each has many phases, none watertight, some of which may be "leapfrogged." Also, "progresses"[67] may be marred, matched, or overwhelmed by retrogressions.

To go much further in depicting the nature of postindustrialism, however, we must turn to system performance.

PART III. SYSTEM PERFORMANCE

Information relating to system performance plays a more vital social role than that bearing on system structure. Performance goals are usually far more specific than structural goals. Performance itself — generally through a series of steps — is usually the only way to bring about any changes in social structure. The most accessible and the most frequently collected statistics relate to past and present performance. In fact, many aspects of structure, such as accumulated assets in any important sector, can most conveniently be estimated by aggregating data on current investment performance over a period of time.

As with system structure, there are many oversimplistic ways of thinking and talking about system performance. Politicians and philosophers may speak abstractly of a system's performance in enlarging human happiness or serving the general welfare. Both will often maintain that welfare is best served by actions that enlarge human freedom and opportunity (without realizing that both concepts are subject to a wide latitude of definitions). Economists often write about "growth" and "development" — with the former referring to industrially developed and the latter to industrially underdeveloped countries — which may be contrasted with "stagnation" or "decline." What grows or develops is usually described as national output or income, although emphasis is often placed on the use of such output or income in consumption or investment. When pressed, many economists invariably state that the *raisons d'être* of output, income, and investment are consumption and the human welfare, which presumably derives from consumption. Some, how-

[67] "Not progress, but progresses, is what we find in man-society." Arthur F. Bentley, *Relativity in Man and Society* (New York: G. P. Putnam's Sons, 1926), p. 191.

TABLE 3.6

NATIONAL STRUCTURE: PREINDUSTRIAL, INDUSTRIAL, POSTINDUSTRIAL

	Preindustrial	Industrial	Postindustrial
People	Low life expectancy at birth	Higher life expectancy	Life expectancy above 70–75
	Low education	Much more education	Highly educated population
Nonhuman resources	Little development of natural resources	Large-scale development (and waste) of natural resources	Large-scale conservation of natural resources
Subsystems	Relatively little differentiation (fused)	Considerable differentiation (refracted)	Still more differentiation
	Agriculture more than 60 per cent of labor force	Agriculture below 30 per cent of labor force	Agriculture below 10 per cent of labor force
		Manufacturing 15–25 per cent of labor force	Manufacturing below 10–15 per cent of labor force
			Services (public and private) above 60 per cent of labor force
	Small government sector	Large government and mixed sector	
External relations	From colonialism to independence	From empire to bloc or commonwealth	Extensive transnational, intersecting and interpenetrating relations
Internal relations	Centrifugal tendencies	More integration with growth of nationalism	Less integration with growth of transnationalism
	Weak communication and transportation networks	Highly developed communication and transportation networks	Still more highly developed communication and transportation networks
Values	Localism	Nationalism	Transnationalism
		Cosmopolitanism	Megalopolitanism
		Activism	Humanism
Guidance	Restricted elites	Multiple elites	Dispersed elites
		National planning systems	Transnational planning systems

TRANSITIONAL   TRANSITIONAL

Notes to Table 3.6

To help round out the items in the table, the following points may be added:

People: a more **specialized** and professionalized society with "continuing education" tending to absorb at least 10 per cent of the work year.

Nonhuman resources: major "cybernation" systems, based on coupling of electronic computers with power-driven machinery.

Subsystems: further extensions of the organizational revolution and the growth of complex clusters and constellations. More blurring of distinctions between government and nongovernment organizations, with more "mixed" enterprises. Great expansion in absolute size and relative importance of metropolitan areas and megalopoles.

External relations: greater degrees of penetration of and intervention in other societies — and vice versa; with transnational legitimation of such activities and provision for cooperative transnational actions.

Internal relations: high mobility and integration, together with intense conflicts and shifting conflict patterns.

Values: growing secularization, with potentialities for more widespread and deeper humanism. Values reflecting growing material abundance — as contrasted with (*a*) "zero-sum" nonredistributive values of preindustrial societies (based on their limited productive potentials), and (*b*) the "scarcity economics" and "zero-sum" redistributive ideologies in industrial societies (increasingly out of keeping with growing productive potentials).

Guidance: high differentiation means elite dispersion and major emphasis on polyarchic bargaining relations in social system guidance.

ever, place major emphasis on the system's performance in providing employment, maintaining stable prices, producing favorable change in the balance of international payments, or achieving a balanced government budget. Many social reformers are particularly interested in the distribution of income and in the provision of social justice. Others are more concerned with investing in a system's capacity to survive.

A more comprehensive view is provided by the seven performance elements listed in the last section of Part I of this chapter. In Table 3.7 these are set forth with a selected list of subelements for each of the categories. As in Table 3.4, a parallel column is also provided here to illustrate how these subelements may be concretized to describe the performance of a formal organization within the broader social system.

When viewed abstractly, these various performance elements may seem to fit together neatly and consistently. In actual life, however, they invariably present a pattern of divergence. There is always considerable conflict among the various elements — as when rationality interferes with the observance of established codes, or efficiency interferes with the satisfaction of human interests. There are even more glaring conflicts within the specific elements, as when technical rationality clashes with administrative rationality, morality with legality, output per worker with costs per unit of output, and satisfactions for one sector of society with satisfactions for another sector.

In addition to these more substantive conflicts there are invariably many cross-purpose disputes in any society. As illustrated in Table 3.8, these take place when a critic charges failure with respect to certain elements of performance and a defender responds by discussing other elements. "Talking to the point" may perhaps be facilitated by more widespread acceptance of a system's approach to the multidimensionality of performance.

Satisfying Interests

In a very fundamental sense social systems exist to serve human interests or needs, or at least to provide conditions under which these interests may be reasonably satisfied. The performance of any family, group, or formal organization — no matter how it may be ranked — is inevitably associated with the satisfaction of certain human interests. The same is true of a national society, as with *any* territorial entity.

TABLE 3.7

SYSTEM PERFORMANCE: ILLUSTRATIONS FOR ORGANIZATION AND NATION

Performance Elements	Organization	Nation
1. Satisfying interests		
The "interesteds"	Members, clientele network, controllers, more groups	People, groups, organizations, committees, foreign clients, suppliers, and associates
Their interests	Employment, working conditions, high income, interesting work, participation in management, status, respect	Full employment, fair employment, high income, leisure, health, social participation, human dignity, the "general welfare"
Extent of interest satisfaction	Opinions expressed, choices, payments, results	Opinions expressed, choices, payments, results
2. Producing output		
Output mix	Types of end products (functions, missions)	Types of end products of each sector; output not reflected in economic accounts
Quantity	Monetary: value added, total	Monetary: GNP, total transactions
Quality	Satisfactions given, product characteristics, production processes, input quality	Satisfactions given, product characteristics, production processes, input equality
3. Investing in systems		
Hard goods	Land, buildings, equipment, machinery, materials	Resource development and conservation; buildings, etc.
People	Training	Education, health
Subsystems	Improved organization	Institution building and adaptation
External relations	Building support base	Dividing adversaries, building alliances and international organizations

TABLE 3.7 (*Continued*)

Performance Elements	Organization	Nation
4. Using inputs efficiently		
Achieving potential	High utilization of capacity, low waste	High utilization of capacity, full employment level of output
Profitability	Total or unit profits, related to net worth, total assets or sales (only for organizations selling products)	Not relevant
Costs per unit	Total unit costs, cost of inputs not paid by organization	Total unit costs, direct and indirect
Partial input ratios	Ratios between output and labor, capital or materials	Ratios between output and labor or capital
5. Acquiring resources		
Money	Revenues, loans, investments	Foreign trade, foreign investment, taxation
People	Recruitment	Immigration, population growth
Goods	Procurement	Foreign trade, conquest, expropriation
6. Observing codes		
External codes	Conformity with or deviating from regulations, laws, morality	Conforming with or deviating from international law and morality
Internal codes	The organization's rules	National constitution and law
7. Behaving rationally		
Technical rationality	Using relevant science and technology	Advancing and using science and technology
Administrative	Using best possible methods of managing organization	Using best possible methods of guiding nation

TABLE 3.8

NATIONAL PERFORMANCE: CROSS-PURPOSE DISPUTES

	Critic:	Defender:
Satisfying interests		
Certain interests		We survive and grow
Other interests	You do not improve income distribution	
Producing output		
Quantity		We provide a rising GNP
Kind	You do not provide enough peacetime, public services	
Investing in system		
Hard goods		We build up the country's capital plant
Institutions	You do not modernize the country's institutions	
Using inputs efficiently		
Achieving potential	You do not make optimum use of resources	
Partial input-output ratio		We get more GNP per man-year
Acquiring resources		
Foreign currency		We get a high margin of export revenues over import payments
People	You do not open the door to valued immigrants	
Observing codes		
Internal codes		We uphold the Constitution
External codes	You do not observe international agreements	
Behaving rationally		
Technical		We advance modern technology
Administrative	You do not give enough attention to long-range planning	

Yet even at the level of simpler and less inclusive systems, interest satisfaction is the most difficult kind of performance to conceptualize and the most baffling to measure. The most accessible information may be false and the most accurate information misleading. At the level of the nation these difficulties are often compounded.

Mysteries of Interest Satisfaction

Let us begin by acknowledging that this harmless term "interest satisfaction" includes within its scope all that philosophers have referred to by "happiness." It includes the rather disembodied satisfactions dealt with by economists and mathematicians under the name of welfare, benefits, utility, utiles, or (in the hard language of game theorists) "payoffs."[68]

Before plunging into this difficult and controversial area, we must recognize at least five major difficulties.

First of all, there can be no interests without "interesteds," that is, people, groups, organizations, and territorial entities with interests. Any nation is a remarkably complex set of "interesteds." Many of these are — for most observers — only partially visible, if not hidden. The great contribution of "interest group theory," in political science has been to direct attention to groupings that might otherwise remain unseen.

Second, the actual interests of individuals and larger social systems are themselves extremely complex. In every case, they are multiple, divergent, internally and externally conflicting, and changing over time. Indeed, "they cannot be directly seen or counted . . . they can only be inferred. When we attempt to analyze them, we are brought willy-nilly into some of the deepest mysteries of human behavior."[69] The probing of these mysteries has been one of the great contributions of psychiatry and psychoanalysis, human relations research and industrial psychology. The great limitation of interest group theory has been the reluctance of Bentley and most of his followers to plunge directly into the interests of interest groups.[70]

---

[68] The use of "payoffs" in referring to all sorts of nonmonetary benefits is an interesting example of how innovating theoreticians try to win social acceptance for their ideas by using the "hard" language of the market place.

[69] Gross, "Satisfaction of Interests," *The Managing of Organizations, op. cit.,* p. 506.

[70] This reluctance is evident throughout Arthur F. Bentley's great classic, *The Process of Government* (Bloomington, Ill.: Principia Press, 1908, reissued 1949). In his later years, however, as indicated in my correspondence and discussions with him in the 1950's, he realized the necessity of going further. Yet there is little of anything that might be called "motivational analysis" in

Third, satisfactions and dissatisfactions are often inextricably connected. Satisfaction vanishes when it reaches the point of satiety, as suggested by the tendencies referred to by the economists' "law of diminishing returns." The existence of some degree of dissatisfaction — with its attendant tensions and frustrations — is basic to social system efforts to achieve future satisfaction. At times, the "tensions themselves may be a very satisfying part of human existence, particularly when associated with partial attainments and satisfying forms of activity."[71]

Fourth, since satisfactions and dissatisfactions are almost impossible to observe directly, we must use a wide variety of "surrogates," that is, indirect indicators that serve us as quantitative substitutes or representatives of the phenomena we want to identify or measure. Indeed, any element of system structure and any element of system performance, other than satisfying interests, may be used as a "remote surrogate" of interest satisfaction or dissatisfaction. This is shown in Table 3.9. The difficulty of inferring actual satisfactions from any single "remote surrogate" suggests the desirability in most cases of using a varied set of such indicators.

Within the field of interest satisfaction itself, we may use a variety of "close surrogates" in the form of various kinds of behavior from which inferences on satisfaction and dissatisfaction may be made.

1. The choices made among various alternatives;
2. The monetary payments made for services or goods that may be purchased (in most circumstances, a specialized form of choice);
3. Opinions expressed, whether solicited or unsolicited; and
4. The presumed results of any activity.[72]

Fifth, there is a natural tendency for greater attention to be given to the more "objective" interests at the expense of "subjective" interests. The former may be more readily quantified. The latter are harder to describe, let alone measure. Discussion of them tends to degenerate into the empty phrases and glittering generalities of propagandistic perorations. This becomes another illustration of the

---

David Truman's "modern" reformulation of Bentley's approach to interest groups in *The Governmental Process* (New York: Alfred A. Knopf, Inc., 1951).

[71] Gross, "Satisfaction of Interests," *The Managing of Organizations, op. cit.*, p. 512.

[72] Specific illustrations of each of these surrogates — together with an identification of the peculiar advantages and disadvantages of each — are given in "The Surrogates of Satisfaction and Dissatisfaction," *The Managing of Organizations, op. cit.*, pp. 530–537.

TABLE 3.9
SURROGATES OF SATISFACTION

	Structure		Performance
People	Population change	Satisfying interests	
Nonhuman resources	Stock of housing; securities	Producing output	Per capita level of, or increase in, national income or output
Subsystems	Stronger associations	Investing in system	Hard goods investment
Internal relations	Upward mobility	Using inputs efficiently	Extent of waste
External relations	Freedom from foreign control	Acquiring resources	Balance of payments
Values	Respect for human life	Observing codes	Law and order
Guidance system	Broad-based	Behaving rationally	Science-technology advances

"new Philistinism" referred to in Part I of this chapter. We thus find a modern-day, double-barreled Gresham's Law under which monetary information tends to drive out of circulation quantitative information of greater significance, and quantitative information of any kind tends to retard the circulation of qualitative information.

To help restore a balance between the two, let us now look briefly at each.

The More "Objective" Interests

By referring to certain interests as "more objective," there is no intention of suggesting that they are less significant than others. The term "objective" merely indicates that it is easier to identify them and appraise the extent of their satisfaction or dissatisfaction.

Indeed, in a certain sense these interests are more fundamental than any other. They include the most elementary biological needs of the human organism and the most elementary survival needs of larger social systems. Whenever they are largely unmet, they are *the most important interests at that time*. To the extent that they are gratified, they usually begin to lose their significance. In all cases, of course, gratification for some people and groups is usually associated with much lower degrees of satisfaction for the social system population as a whole.

Hence the importance of seeking information that provides — in the forceful formulation of Russett and associates — "not just the *mean* of a certain value for a country, but also the *median*, the *mode*, and the range of the distribution, as well as the frequency and the physical and social location of various levels."[73]

Activity, Employment, Leisure. Some form of activity is an essential need of all human beings. "The human organism is not designed for complete idleness. Either body or mind, and usually both, must reach some minimum level of activity. Under special conditions induced by drugs, hypnosis or perhaps extremely low temperatures, it may be possible to maintain human life for long periods with little or no activity. But under usual conditions, inactivity means decay, disintegration and death. People simply must do something."[74]

Employment is one of the most important forms of human activity. It is a basic source of both income and output, particularly in the modern, monetized society. Moreover, people who are gainfully employed — no matter how much they may complain about working conditions or income — belong to something larger than themselves. They are needed and feel they are needed. In contrast, those who seek employment without finding it for long periods of time — and even more, those who give up seeking and are thus regarded as no longer in the "labor force" — are displaced persons. They do not belong and they are not needed. Their inactivity may well mean decay, disintegration, and living death. Thus one of the most important of all human interests is dealt with by the Employment Act of 1946 in its historic declaration on the responsibility of the U.S. government for "creating and maintaining . . . conditions under which there will be afforded useful employment opportunities, including self-employment, for those able, willing and seeking to work . . ."[75]

In addition, there are many forms of activity that are extremely "gainful" but are not calculated as "gainful employment." Some of these activities — such as the housework of housewives, political activity, and volunteer services — are every bit as satisfying (or dissatisfying) as paid work.

Respite from work is in itself one of the great human satisfactions.

[73] Russett *et al., op. cit.,* p. 5.
[74] Gross, "The Human Beings," *The Managing of Organizations, op. cit.,* p. 323.
[75] Similar commitments are found in the constitutions of many countries, in "white papers," and in various declarations of the United Nations.

It also provides an opportunity for activities that satisfy many needs which cannot be met during actual employment. Indeed, it presents an opportunity for renewal of employment-spent energies. In this sense, it is a prerequisite of productive employment and useful output.

The expansion of human leisure may be measured in terms of the declining number of work hours per day and in the declining number of days worked per week. It may also be expressed in terms of longer vacations and more holidays — particularly those with pay.

Leisure is not an unlimited source of satisfaction, however. On the one hand, involuntary leisure is just another term for unemployment. On the other hand, there are those for whom voluntary leisure provides "dead time" that cannot be filled by satisfying forms of activity. One of the great problems in this age of automation and computerization, with their great potential for the replacement of manpower, is the expansion of the more satisfying and meaningful leisure-time activities. The solution to this problem will probably lead to a breakdown of the old distinctions between education and play, and between work and education.[76]

Survival and Health. Here we enter a realm with a wealth of nonmonetary statistics compiled over long periods of time.

As a U.N. Committee of Experts has pointed out, one of the most important measures of interest satisfaction is the average expectation of life at different ages. "The length of the individual's life is not only a result of such factors as medical services, food, clothing, housing and fuel, but also takes into account such other factors as education, security, moral and spiritual values and the desire for living. Of all the needs and values relating to levels of living the most universal, both historically and culturally, is the desire for life itself, the fulfillment of which may be expressed by expectation of life at different ages."[77] Unfortunately, the committee did not directly recognize the importance of getting behind averages and noting how life expectancy differs for different groups in the popu-

[76] A remarkably stimulating attempt to calculate the amount of leisure, together with a "national time budget," is provided by Marion Clawson in "How Much Leisure, Now and in the Future?" *Leisure in America: Blessing or Curse?* Monograph 4 (Philadelphia, Pa.: The American Academy of Political and Social Science, 1964). Both Clawson's study and those of his coauthors in the same volume are largely relevant to other industrial and postindustrializing societies, not only to the United States.

[77] Committee of Experts, *Report on International Definition and Measurement of Standards and Levels of Living* (New York: United Nations, 1954), p. 53.

lation. Thus in the United States the average life expectancy at birth of the female *non-white* population was 10 per cent lower in 1962 than that of the female white population.[78]

The U.N. committee did point out, however, that "the lengthening of life by modern medical techniques does not necessarily imply the improvement of living in other respects.[79] Thus considerable attention is often given to the infant mortality rate, which, according to Russett and his associates, "gives the best overall measure of national health that we have."[80] More specific measures of health are those dealing with the incidence of various types of disease, injuries, and accidents. Information of this type is meaningful only when related to the number of people in various groups. Accidents and fatalities must also be broken down by type (motor vehicle, airplane, etc.). When not carefully related to the total amount of activity in which they took place (for instance, passenger miles), this information can be very misleading. Success in improving recordkeeping invariably tends to give an upward bias to all such data.

Beyond such commonly kept data, there is also a need for improved information on injuries and deaths in riots and other forms of domestic violence.[81] The need is still greater for the regular compilation of information on deaths and injuries resulting from wars. These are the best measures — negative though they may be — of domestic tranquility and international peace, two of the greatest interests of all mankind.

Income and Consumption. Income may be defined as the net increment during any given period of time in a person's command over resources. This includes all income, whether in the form of money, fringe benefits, interest, or profits of capital appreciation.[82]

---

[78] U.S. Department of Health, Education and Welfare, *Health, Education and Welfare Trends* (1964 ed., Washington, D. C.: Government Printing Office, 1964), p. 13. This differential, it should be pointed out, represents a marked reduction over what it was in previous decades. Similar data for various groups in other countries — particularly contrasts between the rich minorities and the large masses in preindustrial societies — would probably show far greater differentials.

[79] *Report on International Definition and Measurement of Standards and Levels of Living, op. cit.,* p. 54.

[80] Russett *et al., op. cit.,* p. 199.

[81] See discussion and data in *ibid.,* pp. 97–100.

[82] This definition of income is based on the concept set forth in Richard Titmus, *Income Distribution and Social Change* (London: George Allen and Unwin, 1962), Chapter 2, "The Problem of Definition: Income and Income Units," pp. 21–35.

Estimates of national income provide a way of calculating for any particular period the total increment in command over resources. In aggregate terms they differ very little from estimates of national output.[83] Some of the problems at this level will be discussed in the subsequent section on "producing output." In component terms they indicate the way in which monetary income from the production process is distributed among different recipient groups in such forms as wages and salaries, corporation profits, income from unincorporated enterprises, interest, and rents. Such data are important largely because they indicate changes in the potential of the society as a whole and of various income recipients to use money to satisfy various interests. At the same time, in a monetized society money income is such a powerful symbol of status and power, as well as of the things that can be bought with money, that it comes to serve as a direct indicator of interest satisfaction. Increases bring gratification, and decreases deprivation. In both cases, the absolute figures may be less meaningful than those bearing on "relative deprivation" or "relative gratification." Unfortunately, income distribution data are notoriously unreliable. Great attention has thus far been centered mainly on the most intolerable inequities represented by the conspicuous incomes of the ultrawealthy and on the conspicuous destitution of those with insufficient income to survive at a minimum standard of living. Many new concepts, as well as a large amount of data collection, are needed to provide meaningful information on changes in income distribution between the extremes of the ultrawealthy and the ultradestitute.

To see how national income affects personal consumption, we must first reduce it to total personal income. This may be done by deducting such items as corporate profit (and social insurance payments) and adding such others as dividends and government transfer payments. At this level, data on distribution has a major bearing on living levels. Minimum living standards or "poverty lines" are usually defined in terms of the personal income of different groupings of individuals or families. The minima have traditionally been established on the basis of calculating the costs for a so-called "subsistence" level of food, housing, apparel, transportation, health, and recreation. The subsistence level, of course, is one determined by the resources of the society, the pressures exerted by the poor, and

[83] To move from gross national product to national income, the national economic accountants subtract depreciation (which gives net national product), and then subtract indirect business taxes and the surplus of government enterprises, and add subsidies.

the political judgment of those involved in the calculations (not only technicians but the political leaders who may use the calculations in decisions on welfare payments). The persistent reference to minimum living standards in terms of a "basket" of goods and services — particularly in the United States — serves as an amusing reminder that ideas concerning these minima derive from the image of the charitable upper-class lady of the nineteenth century who went into the slums to deliver a "basket" of food to the poor at Christmas. The minima proposed by the U.N. Experts get away from this confining heritage by including essential material items that cannot very well be placed in a basket: education, working conditions, employment situation, and aggregate consumption and savings.[84]

More direct information on consumption is provided by statistics on expenditures rather than income. These are particularly revealing when broken down by specific categories of expenditure. In the absence of such breakdowns, consumption may be inferred from breakdowns on the output of specific types of services and goods and, as in the case of housing, on the total supply of assets. Still more specific information may be provided in terms of calories or proteins consumed.

A sound approach to the measurement of "material well-being," however, can never be made in terms of income (or expenditures from it) alone. Whether we are concerned with establishing minima or calculating the extent of opulence, it is essential to recognize that the material well-being of individuals and families is three-dimensional. Full command over material resources is an aggregate of (1) income, (2) assets, and (3) public services that are not bought. To some extent these are interchangeable. More assets in the form of savings, insurance, and property may make up for a deficiency of income. More public services in the form of free education and health services may make up for deficiences in income and assets. We must begin to think of poverty in terms of income poverty, asset poverty, and public service poverty, with minimum standards for each developed in terms of a country's productive capacity and adjusted to rising price levels. Opulence and gross inequities in distribution of full command over resources must also be calculated in three-dimensional terms.

---

[84] *Report on International Definition and Measurement of Standards and Levels of Living, op. cit.*, pp. 28–47. A nonmaterial item, human freedom, is also included, but without any serious effort to identify its various aspects.

The More "Subjective" Interests

In dealing with the more subjective interests, we touch upon the most difficult facets of system performance. Here, more than in any other field, considerable theoretical work is needed by psychologists, sociologists, anthropologists, political scientists, and philosophers before greater conceptual clarity may be attained.

An impetus toward such theoretical work has undoubtedly been provided by the emergence in the United States of the "Great Society" vision. Thus, in a series of historic statements President Johnson has introduced the more subjective interests into the realm of national politics and national policymaking:

The Great Society is a place where "the least among us will find contentment, and the best among us can find greatness. All of us will respect the dignity of the one and admire the achievement of the other."[85]

We can open the doors of learning, of fruitful labor and rewarding leisure, not just to the privileged few, but we can open them to everyone.

These goals cannot be measured by the size of our bank balances. They can only be measured in the quality of the lives that our people lead. Millions of Americans have achieved prosperity, and they have found prosperity alone is just not enough. They need a chance to seek knowledge and to touch beauty, to rejoice in achievement and in the closeness of family and communities.[86]

The Great Society asks not only how much, but how good; not only how to create wealth but how to use it; not only how fast we are going, but where we are headed.

It proposes as the first test for a nation: the quality of its people.[87]

To the jaundiced observer these statements by an American President might be regarded as merely campaign slogans — slogans with the special purpose of allowing a formerly rather conservative southerner to broaden his support among American liberals. They might also be regarded as indications that, in their attention to education and the arts, the United States is beginning to catch up to where Western European governments were generations ago.

In a still more fundamental sense, however, they represent the effort of American elites — not just a President — to develop the politics of an affluent society. With minimum material security already provided for the great majority of their citizens, the leaders of the most industrialized societies can no longer develop any wide

[85] *My Hope for America* (New York: Random House, Inc., 1964), p. 2.
[86] Remarks of the President, Madison Square Garden, October 31, 1964.
[87] State of the Union Message, January 4, 1965.

enthusiasm for programs designed merely to provide greater economic security. In the United States, the major horizon of future economic performance is the curtailment of poverty: mainly among urban Negroes, the aged everywhere, and people living in depressed rural areas. But if the U.S. government leaders had placed major emphasis upon this "antipoverty" program, they would have been appealing to the interests of a minority only, and — in terms of organizational and political power — a weak minority. Hence, it became essential to develop a political appeal to broader interests of the entire population. Less dramatic steps in this direction have already been taken in other countries. Indeed, one may confidently predict that by the 1970's there will be various "Great Society" programs — under many different labels — throughout both Western and Eastern Europe.[88] Just as the earlier national goals of "economic stability" were broadened to the present goals of "economic growth" (or development), these present goals are bound to be broadened to various forms of "the good life."

On the theory that political necessity serves as a major stimulus to the theory and research needed to explain, justify, and improve the policy commitments of national leaders, one may predict that during the next two decades there will be a considerable maturation of "great society" and "good life" concepts. In the meantime, let me set forth one way of looking at interest satisfactions in this area.[89]

Belonging, Participation, Affection. As a social animal, man is interested not only in meaningful activity, survival, and material consumption but also in being a part of something larger than himself. Belonging and togetherness have value in themselves, apart from their clear contribution to security. People obtain gratification from merely being members of a family, a work group, a nationality group, a political party. They obtain more direct satisfactions from belonging to some one or some group that will meet their needs "to be nursed, supported, sustained, surrounded, protected, loved, ad-

[88] A unilateral intimation of this was provided in a statement before the U.N. Assembly by U.S. Ambassador Arthur J. Goldberg: "In my own country we are embarked under the leadership of President Lyndon B. Johnson in a search for a 'Great Society'. . . . Nor is the vision it proclaims exclusively American. It is a vision common to all mankind. . . . So what we seek for our own people in a Great Society at home, we seek for all mankind." (September 23, 1965)

[89] The subsequent discussion is an extension of the concepts developed in "The Human Beings," *The Managing of Organizations, op. cit.,* pp. 321–330. These concepts represent a synthesis of the motivation theories of A. H. Maslow, Karen Horney, Henry A. Murray, Kurt Goldstein, Erich Fromm, and Hans Selye.

vised, guided, indulged, forgiven, consoled."[90] Valuable indicators with respect to the satisfaction of these needs can be found in statistical data on family formation and breakdown, "fatherless families," and the types and memberships of associations, and through research surveys on morale and informal groups in employment organizations.

Being a part, however, may vary from being a meaningless cog to an active participant. The idea of "social participation" if developed in a more sophisticated manner could be used to obtain information on the kind of belonging that goes beyond mere conformity.

Status, Respect, Power. But satisfaction of togetherness needs is rarely enough. People want to be *apart from,* as well as *a part of.* Thus a variety of "differentiation interests" — status, respect, and power — enter the picture. It is their satisfaction that provides the *dignity of man,* and their denial the indignity of life for millions of men, women, and children.

Status ranking is an inevitable part of any society's social structure. It may be affected by birth, wealth, income, occupation, membership in an ethnic or religious group, organizational affiliation, innate capacity, achievement, and power. Many of these determinants may be measured or estimated. Status, in turn, has an important bearing both upon self-respect and upon respect in the types of others.

The sharpest form of differentiation is found in the wielding of power. Human interests in power may take many forms. For all those who yearn to shape great events, there are probably far more who feel an equally deep need to dominate just a few other people. In the case of a parent, it may be a need to dominate a helpless child, or an equally helpless mate. Or it may take the more positive form of nurturance needs, the needs "to give sympathy and gratify the needs of a helpless other: an infant or another that is weak, disabled, tired, inexperienced, infirm, defeated, humiliated, lonely, defeated, sick, mentally confused. To assist another in danger. To feed, help, support, console, protect, comfort, nurse, heal."[91]

In a somewhat broader context, the power of people to make decisions affecting their own lives may be measured in terms of the five elements in the POISE profile of individual democracy, as presented in Part II of this chapter. In still broader terms, the dis-

[90] Henry A. Murray *et al., Explorations in Personality* (New York: Oxford University Press, 1938), p. 182.
[91] Murray *et al., op. cit.,* p. 182.

tribution of power in society must be seen in terms of the interrelations between its various subsystems and, particularly, the extent of participation by other subsystems in the guidance system and their influence upon the central guidance cluster.

Self-fulfillment, Beauty, Creativity. Increasingly psychologists have found it necessary to use such concepts as self-fulfillment, self-actualization, and self-development. These concepts relate to the gratification of interests that, while closely related to those discussed above, are nonetheless different from them. They deal with the tremendous satisfactions obtained from learning, creativity, aesthetic experience, scientific and intellectual exploration, and creativity in any form, be it ever so humble.

While activity for its own sake may be demeaning, while the struggle for survival may wreck others, while the pursuit of belonging and differentiation may produce unending frustration, while the piling up of material benefits may lead to satiety, there are less of these undesirable indirect results in the pursuit of self-development, beauty, and creativity. Even in its more modest forms, it is usually noninjurious to others. At its best, it becomes self-development in behalf of interests larger than the self.

Indirect information in this area is provided by data on the arts, the humanities, education, science, and research, and — inversely — on the despoliation of natural and urban beauty by man's uglier artifacts and more harmful waste products.

Security, Freedom, Challenge

"Security" is often used in the narrow sense of referring to (1) the steady provision of a bare minimum of economic subsistence, or (2) protection against domestic violence or external attack. In a broader and more fundamental sense, however, security relates to the future probability of satisfying various interests. In subjective terms a high degree of security is the expectation that a range of interests will probably be satisfied. Insecurity is the expectation that they will probably be frustrated. In objective terms security and insecurity may be measured in rough-and-ready probability estimates of what might happen (apart from what people think may happen) and by facts on what has happened. In either case, employment and income security is very different from security with respect to status, power, and opportunities for creativity. Progress in raising the former may under many circumstances (particularly under so-called "welfare" programs) serve to reduce the latter.

Like security, "freedom" is also an extremely important concept that is often used too narrowly or too vaguely. When used in the anarchistic sense of freedom from all constraint, the term may mean freedom for the strong to tyrannize the weak and freedom for the poor to starve. The term has more significance only when used to refer to the freedom *of* specific *interested groups from* certain things and *for* specific *things.* Thus the great historic freedoms are *from* slavery, tyranny, fear, monopolistic restrictions, discrimination, and poverty and *for* speech, thought, religion, educational opportunity, assembly, and organization.

When used in this more meaningful sense, the freedoms provided by any society may be seen to depend, to a very large degree, upon a reasonable degree of security with respect to both objective and subjective satisfactions. At the same time, too high a degree of security with respect to the entire range of interest satisfactions would unquestionably curtail the extent of freedom. Both security and freedom are more meaningful when associated with continuing challenge. Such challenge is provided not only by the new internal and external problems of every society but by the leadership and vision of subsystem and system leaders.

The "Public Interests"

In many discussions of past or future social performance, references are continuously made to the "national interest," the "general *welfare,*" or to the *"common good."* But there can never be any broad agreement on the precise nature of the national interest, the general welfare, or the common good. These terms are meaningful only in so far as they refer to some integration of various interests of various interested groups and to different ways in which these many interests are satisfied. A more useful term would be the "public interests." The plural form emphasizes the great multiplicity of the interests that the people of any society have in common. It also suggests that the extent to which public interests are served can be appraised only by looking at the satisfactions provided for a great variety of interesteds throughout a society.

One of the outstanding characteristics of the twentieth century has been the increasing orientation of associations, organizations, and national leaders toward the satisfactions of more interests of larger publics. This tendency has resulted from such factors as increased education, greater material abundance, and greater organization of hitherto unorganized interesteds. It has also pointed toward ever-increasing disputation among competing interesteds, interests, and conceptions as to how divergent public interests may best be integrated. Cynical commentators have often reported that they cannot find any "public interest." "The difficulty here, whether we have reference to a community, a nation or the world itself, is not the absence of any common interests. It is rather the profusion of common interests, a profusion so rich that it can never be expressed, without serious distortion, in a single formula."[92]

Although the term "general welfare" may be regarded as referring to some synthesis of public interests, the concept of "welfare state" is much more narrow. Thus far it has been used to refer to national governments that aim to provide a minimum basis of material welfare by eliminating destitution, starvation, and mass unemployment. This kind of government, while a large advance over those that did not care too much about these things, addresses itself only to man's more obvious and elementary needs. A true "welfare state" — one oriented toward promoting the general welfare in the sense in which the term is used, say, in the U.S. Constitution — would be oriented toward providing conditions under which the full range of human interests might be developed and gratified.[93]

Man's deeper interests have often appeared as strongly expressed demands. A powerful way to assert a demand is to proclaim it as a right. During the "Enlightenment" period of the eighteenth century the "rights of man" were proclaimed as a part of "natural law." Subsequently, the natural law foundation of these rights was shaken, at the very same time that the asserted demands became increasingly concretized in legal rights, with appropriate organs of enforcement and appeal. In the decades that lie ahead the foundations of man's rights in natural law may conceivably be rebuilt by the findings of social scientists as they devise principles that explain human nature and social systems. The rights of man, we may eventually learn, are grounded on the needs of men and the common interests of mankind.[94]

Producing Output

The output of a system is composed of those products that make it available for use by its members or by the external world. These may consist of services (tangible or nontangible) or goods.[95] In

---

[92] Gross, "Satisfaction of Interests," *The Managing of Organizations, op. cit.*, p. 525.

[93] *Ibid.*, p. 526.

[94] *Ibid.*, p. 529.

[95] I prefer the order "services and goods" (in contrast with the usual "goods and services") because of (1) the increasing importance of services, and (2) the fact that the production of goods is essentially a process of transforming raw materials through the performance of certain services.

either case they are the most direct instruments for the satisfaction of human interests. It is inconceivable that human interests could be satisfied by social systems without the production of various services and goods; it is these — together with the many satisfactions associated with their production — that meet basic human needs. Accordingly, indirect information on interest satisfaction may be provided by the great amount of information usually available on the kinds, quantity, quality, and monetary value of output.

This close relationship between output and interest satisfaction readily leads to two kinds of confusion. On the one hand, information on the former may too quickly be regarded as a conclusive measure of the latter, as when increases in police or military services are regarded as indications of a reduction in crime or in the danger of war. Even with such outputs as medical services, it is more reasonable to look also at the data on disease and mortality. On the other hand, the producers of intangible services — particularly those that are not bought and sold — often face great difficulties in identifying their output. These difficulties may be evaded by focusing attention on certain interests they aim to satisfy. Thus officials of certain government agencies may say that their purpose is "safety," "larger exports," or "national security" without any clear specifications of just what it is that *they* contribute — as distinct from the contributions of many others — toward attaining such objectives. In both cases, dealing separately with interest satisfaction and output can avoid confusion and facilitate a better understanding of the relations between these two elements of system performance.

The Output Mix

One of the great values of national economic accounting is that it provides certain monetary measures of the composition of output, that is, the "output mix."

One way of looking at the output mix is to compare output among the various "sectors" of production. These sectoral distinctions are primarily based on differences between the products produced. One of the distinguishing characteristics of modern societies is a decline in the relative significance of agricultural production and an increase in manufacturing. This transition usually requires expanded performance in construction, transportation, communication, and other support sectors.

Another way of looking at the output mix is to make a broad distinction between services on the one hand and goods on the other.

Once manufacturing performance has reached high levels, the tendency in a well-developed industrialized economy is for an increasing proportion of the national product to be composed of services. A distinctive characteristic of French national planning in recent years, for example, has been an outspoken acceptance of the necessity for this shift in economic performance.

As already pointed out in Part I, national economic accounting — based primarily on marketed goods and services — provides inadequate attention to other kinds of output.

First, in preindustrial societies, there is a large "subsistence" or "nonmonetized" sector. Although this sector is found mainly in agricultural areas, it includes not only agricultural output for home use, and clothing produced on the farm but also structure and other capital improvements produced by family labor. This excluded area of performance can be dealt with crudely by rudimentary "guesstimates" that place a monetary value on such outputs. These have little meaning, however, unless supplemented by qualitative descriptions of the various kinds of outputs.

Second, national economic accounting gives an inadequate picture of the growth of nonmarketed government services in industrializing and highly industrialized societies. These are incorporated into national economic accounts only by using input value as a surrogate for output. In Part I, the distortions thus created are illustrated with respect to the output of educational services. To these may be added the problem of military services, whether potential or actually used in combat operations. These may be identified most accurately as "destructive services." They may best be classified by the objects and methods of destruction and best be measured by the extent of potential destruction in various areas of operation under specific conditions. An increasing proportion of natural output allotted to such services may — in the case of the many smaller nations — result in military services whose destructive potential declines in relation to that of the "big powers." In the largest and richest societies — as in the United States — rapidly "advancing" technology makes it possible to produce continuing increments of "overkill" with a declining proportion of national output allocated to military services.[96]

The growth of nonmarketed services is not, however, limited to

---

[96] Under various circumstances, of course, an increasing output of destructive potentials (no matter what the proportion of national resources used) may contribute to national and international *insecurity* rather than helping to satisfy common interests in security and peace.

government. One of the distinguishing characteristics of industrial and postindustrializing societies is the "highly capitalized family." Thus huge amounts of "hard goods capital" are increasingly invested not only in housing and furniture but also in transportation equipment (automobiles and boats today, airplanes tomorrow), communication equipment (radio, television, and libraries), and cleaning, cooking, refrigeration, and storage facilities. These huge investments, together with the unpaid household labor involved in their operation and maintenance, produce an enormous — and growing — volume of output. While some of this output replaces services sold on the market (as in the case of the family automobiles), almost none of this is reflected in the output side of national economic accounts. A similar observation may be made with respect to the "nonpay" informational services provided by private radio and television companies.

Moreover, even within the limits of using inputs as a measure of output, the routinized rigidity of accounting classifications often results in enormous errors. Once again education provides a rather shocking example. Thus in national economic accounting educational services are traditionally based on the expenditures of the "educational establishment" alone: elementary and secondary schools, and accredited institutions of higher learning, both publicly and privately supported. This usually leaves out of the picture the rapidly growing fields of "on-the-job" training in private and public enterprises, management education and adult education generally, correspondence courses, military education, and training in a wide variety of specialized skills. In the United States it has often been estimated that a full calculation of educational expenditures of various types would result in at least a doubling of the figures.[97]

Quantity

Having already touched on one aspect of output quantity, let us now focus on the distinction between "available" and "contributed" output and the problem of measuring the quantity of intangible services.

The most obvious measure of output quantity is the number or monetary value of certain products that an organization makes

[97] Thus Fritz Machlup has calculated total educational expenditures in the United States for 1958 as exceeding $60 billion, *more than twice* the official figures for the "educational establishment." His calculations also include, however, the estimated earnings forgone by high school and college students: *The Production and Distribution of Knowledge in the United States* (Princeton, N.J.: Princeton University Press, 1962), pp. 51–144.

available for use by its clients. Thus the quantity of airplane production may be expressed in terms of the number and sales price of airplanes, and airline services in terms of passenger miles of transportation and the revenues received from passengers.

But the monetary values of output made available to clients by these and other organizations cannot be added up to give the total economic output of a society. To do so would be to calculate many times those sectoral outputs that are used as inputs by other sectors. The total output of an economy as a whole can be reached only by aggregating the "value contributed" by each sector. In monetary language, this is "value added," that is, the value of its sold output *less* the value of all its purchased goods and services. This value-added measure gives a more precise indication of exactly what has been done *by* a sector or organization. In the case of nonmarketed services, where calculations of monetary value are not feasible, it may nonetheless be important to distinguish between available and contributed output.

In countries suffering from a shortage of foreign currency it is often important to extend value-added calculations to "value added to imports." This measure can be broken down into two parts: (1) "foreign currency earned by exports" (or "value added by exports") and (2) "foreign currency saved by replacement of imports" (or "value added by replacement of imports"). In both cases, it is essential to calculate the value of imports on the basis not only of the direct foreign costs paid by any company — including debt service on foreign loans — but also on the basis of all hidden or indirect foreign currency costs. These include the goods and services paid for not only in local currency by a company, but in foreign currency by a company's suppliers. Once this calculation has been made, one can measure the costs in local currency of earning foreign currency with exports or of saving foreign currency by replacing imports.

A far more important and complex problem in all countries (and in the internal management of all organizations) is the measurement of the quantity of intangible services. How can we calculate the output of a foreign ministry, of a research department, of scientific research as a whole, or of a judicial or legislative body?

Here the first problem is not counting but identification. This is extremely difficult in all cases of intangible services with blurred boundaries. It is particularly difficult when — as is usually the case with vital government activities of a regulatory or informational nature — conflicting conceptions of what the service *should* be result in divergent views as to what it actually *is*. Moreover, many advantages to both producers and users are often found in ambiguities and compromises that make it extremely difficult to determine just what services are being performed. Mission definitions and labels (such as the famous "Operation Overlord" in World War II) and the newly developing techniques of performance budgeting are often needed in order to segregate one form of output from another.

But in many cases discrete activities cannot be clearly identified. Under such circumstances, one has no choice but to use one or more "quantity surrogates." The total set of such surrogates is composed of the following:

1. The number of clients (such as students in school and patients in hospitals).

2. The duration of service (such as student-hours or bed-days).

3. The number of intermediate or subsequent products (letters answered, reports prepared, bed pans emptied, and examinations passed).

4. Input factors (number of teachers or doctors, total costs of services provided).

The use of any one of these surrogates by itself, or even a full combination of them, may be misleading, since in all cases they give something less than an incomplete picture. Nevertheless, judicious and skeptical use of them can scarcely be avoided.[98]

Quality

In part, figures on output quantity reflect quality as well. This occurs whenever market prices provide an accurate measure of the additional satisfactions produced by better quality outputs. Whenever market prices fail to provide such a measure, it is possible to calculate arbitrary increments or decrements in quantity as a means of reflecting physical changes in quality.

But physical changes in quality can be appraised only by dealing directly with the extent to which goods and services conform to desired specifications. The highest level of quality specification is the

---

[98] The problem of identifying intangible services and using quantity surrogates, together with more illustrative material, is discussed analytically in "Output: Operations and Functions," *The Managing of Organizations, op. cit.,* pp. 590–617. Special attention is given to the implications of this analysis for mission definition, general statement of function, performance budgeting, and performance rating.

extent to which the interests of various output users are satisfied. This takes us back to the subject of interest satisfaction and the various satisfaction surrogates discussed in the previous section on "The Mysteries of Interest Satisfaction." More technical — although usually less direct — measures may be found in the physical characteristics of various goods and services, the processes whereby they are produced, and the quality of various input factors used in their production.[99]

Changing Monetary Units

Although monetary value is the only practical way of aggregating the quantity of different kinds of output, serious problems are created by price changes. Since these produce changes in the monetary units themselves, corrective measures are needed to get a picture of changes in "real" output.

One way to avoid this problem is to construct a physical output index. For individual items this may avoid monetary evaluation. But when a physical index is prepared for a group of related products — such as "food grains" — it is essential to provide a weighting for each of the component elements. Any such weighting must be made in terms of monetary value. This brings us back — at least in part — to the original problem of coping with changing monetary units.

Any serious effort to deal with changing monetary units requires some form of price adjustment. This requires the use of "deflators" for rising prices and "inflators" for falling prices. Price deflators and inflators may be calculated either by the laborious process of revealing specific quantities of output by the price changes for each item or by the less accurate, but faster, process of using a general price index for large groups of products. In either case, there are many alternative methods of using deflators and inflators, depending on whether one uses base period weights — the "Laspeyres" system, which gives an upward bias to the data — or uses given year weights — the "Paasche" system, which often yields a downward bias.[100]

[99] This subject is presented more fully in the section on "The theory of output specification," in "Output: Quality and Quantity," *The Managing of Organizations, op. cit.* The same chapter includes a pertinent discussion of "quality-quantity conflicts."

[100] For specifications on this and other methods of building indices, see William A. Neiswanger, *Elementary Statistical Methods* (New York: The Macmillan Company, 1956), Chapter 13, "Index Numbers."

A still more difficult problem of adjustment must be faced in making comparisons of output among different countries. The simplest way is to convert value figures of different countries into the currency of one country by using official exchange rates. A more accurate method — but one much more difficult to apply — is to calculate the purchasing power equivalent of different currencies with respect to specific categories of goods. In both forms of adjustment, the margins of error are usually very great.

Production (or Transformation) Processes

Because of the necessary concentration upon output itself it will not be possible to provide sufficient attention to the production processes whereby inputs are transformed into output.

Three concepts, however, must be briefly mentioned. The first is the distinction between end products and intermediate products. This distinction is always a relative one. The end products of a steel company are intermediate products from the viewpoint of national economic accounting.

The second is "work flow," or "product flow." In a complex society with interdependent parts, goods, services, information, and people move through myriad channels as they are transformed from "less processed" to "more processed" intermediate products and finally to "end products." Input-output analysis of the Leontief variety provides one method of tracing these flows.

The third is the nature of the processing that takes place at various stages in the flow. All such production or transformation processes (whether the output consists of services or goods) may be regarded as consisting of some permutation of various services in two broad categories: (1) holding (storage) or moving (transportation and communication mainly), and (2) dividing (separating, reducing, or analyzing) or uniting (linking, assembling, or synthesizing). These services may be applied to inanimate objects (raw materials, machinery, and other goods), living objects (people, and other biological organisms), and information. With modern technology there have been vast changes in the nature of these processes, the most obvious of which have been the replacement of physical labor by machinery driven by electrical energy and of human information processing by electronic computers. These changes in output performance have profound implications for every other aspect of system performance and all aspects of system structure.

Investing in the System

If all resources were devoted to the output of services and goods, a system would soon lose its capacity to survive, let alone grow. Accordingly, an essential part of system performance is the investment of some portion of resources in its own future. The pattern of investment in and by various subsystems, particularly single organizations, has particular bearing on future performance capacity.

Increments in "Hard Goods"

In traditional national economic accounting, investment is calculated in terms of annual increments to the stock of "hard goods," that is, to construction, producers' durable equipment, and inventories other than those of households. When these calculations are made for private and government investment, it is then possible to get an aggregate figure for gross investment by both government and business. The gross figures, obviously, include replacement of obsolescent capital and new additions. By deducting from the gross figure an estimated amount for depreciation, it is then possible to get an estimate of net investment. Far more accurate and much more useful are the gross and net investment data for strategic sectors and for major projects that propose to change the structure of an economy. Most national planning concentrates upon major investment programs.

Investing in People

In the discussion of "Trends Toward Broadening" in Part I reference is made to the contention of modern economists — particularly Kendrick and Schultz — that the investment concept must be broadened to include investment in people. Special attention was paid to such "human investment" as expenditures on (1) education and training, (2) health facilities and services, (3) scientific research and development, and (4) the movement of people to locations with improved job opportunities.

A major implication of this concept is that the strict "either-or" approach to resource use must be abandoned. When considering educational or health services, one can no longer say that resources must be used *either* for consumption *or* for investment. These are services which are immediately consumed: indeed, they enter as much as food into the current pattern of consumption. At the same time, they also have an investment aspect. For the purpose of simple aggregation, they may continue to be classified as consumption.

However, for analysis — and for the many quantitative tabulations needed in analysis — they must be regarded as investment.

Investing in Institutions

In breaking down the prison walls of the "hard goods" concept of investment, it is not enough merely to acknowledge investment in people. It is also essential to recognize that investment can be directed toward changing any aspect of social structure, including organizations and other subsystems, the interrelations among them, external relations, values, and the guidance system. A concept of "institutional investing" is particularly important in relation to any program of economic growth or development. Any significant expansion of economic performance requires greater system capacity. This can rarely be achieved merely through investing in hard goods and individuals. Indeed, this form of investing — when examined carefully — invariably involves changes in the institutional framework within which people and hard goods operate. Such investing activity invariably involves diverting a certain amount of resources from current output. Since here, again, the "either-or" approach to investing must be avoided, this involves certain activities that may have both consumption and investment aspects at one and the same time. The investment aspects, furthermore, may be oriented toward the maintenance, conservation, adaptation, or development of institutional capacities as well as toward replacements or additions.

Any consistent approach to institutional investing, it may be added, requires some orderly way of viewing information on existing assets and the changes brought about in them by investing activities. It is difficult to see any way of doing this except through social accounting for system structure, along the lines suggested in Part II.

Using Inputs Efficiently

When available inputs are perceived as scarce, attention is invariably directed toward making efficient use of inputs relative to outputs. Since there are many ways of calculating input and output, and of relating the two, there are many varieties of input-output relations. The broader ones are those based on the sum of all inputs. The partial relations are those that deal with only one aspect of input — usually either labor or physical capital.

Actual to Potential Output

One of the most significant ways of measuring national efficiency is to start by estimating the optimum output capacity. This can be regarded as the best and the largest product mix that can be obtained with optimum use of the skill and energy of the total labor force and with optimum use of external support sources. One can then subtract from this figure the actual output during a given period. The difference can be regarded as the waste resulting from failure to use available resources. Thus, the Council of Economic Advisers has estimated the potential output of the American economy based on an unemployment reduction of 4 per cent of the labor force and coupled with an average annual increase of about 3½ per cent a year in real gross national product. By comparing actual with potential output, the Council has shown that the waste or "gap" was, in effect, as high as $50 billion in 1961 and $30 billion in 1963.[101]

"Total" Productivity

A somewhat less problematical calculation is provided by Kendrick in his analysis of "total productivity." In an effort to get away from productivity or efficiency measures based on capital or labor inputs alone, he has calculated "total factor input" as a weighted average of both labor and capital inputs. By relating this to "real gross product" he has produced a measure of "real productivity." Kendrick thus comes to the conclusion that in the United States (with an increase in total annual output of 3½ per cent per year over many decades) "About half of the growth in output was accounted for by additions to real capital and labor inputs, and half was contributed by increases in the efficiency with which the inputs were utilized, that is, in productivity."[102]

Social Efficiency

In a broad sense, social efficiency is measured both by the ratio of actual to potential output and by total productivity. In a more narrow sense, social efficiency calculations are also made for specific sectors or projects when use is made of input and output factors that are not customarily recorded in the regular accounts of orga-

[101] *Economic Report of the President* (Washington, D. C.: U.S. Government Printing Office, January 1964), pp. 36–39.
[102] John W. Kendrick, *Productivity Trends in the United States* (Princeton, N.J.: Princeton University Press, 1961), p. 60.

nizations. Thus on the input side, attention may be paid to external unpaid inputs, such as free services provided by government agencies and other external economies. On the output side, attention may be paid both to indirect benefits and indirect injuries or disutilities. In a country faced with a shortage of foreign currency, value added in foreign currency is one way of measuring an indirect benefit, or — if the local currency costs of obtaining additional foreign currency are too high — of measuring indirect injury. Beyond this, almost any other kind of indirect benefit or injury may be used in a social efficiency calculation.

At the level of a sector or organization, as distinguished from a national economy as a whole, one of the best ways of measuring input use is to aggregate all cost factors. This makes it possible to calculate total costs per unit of output, a calculation that is feasible whether or not the product is marketed. Wherever the product is marketed, it is then possible to compare total input with total output by the common denominator of monetary value. This is the essence of a profitability calculation, which may be extremely valuable in judging the efficiency of either a public or private enterprise. Considerable care is needed, however, in detecting the extent to which changes in profitability may be the result of changing definitions of either input or output, of the power exercised by various buyers or sellers, or of changes in the market situation that have little or no connection with the operations of an enterprise.

Labor and Capital Ratios

Since partial ratios are rather easy to calculate, they have been widely used. At the national level, labor output ratios often appear in the form of gross national product per worker or man-year. One of the outstanding characteristics of modern industrialization is the rapid increase in output per man year. Yet, such calculations can be extremely misleading when one loses sight of the fact that increased output per man-year is often associated with — and, in fact, partly the result of — increased capital input.

The capital side of the picture is often presented in capital output ratios. These have been widely used in estimating amounts of physical investment needed to produce the desired volume of total national output. Yet, such ratios suffer from the same defect as labor output ratios: they assume stable factor proportions. Or, what is even less tenable, they are based on the premise that it is capital input alone that determines the volume of output.

Acquiring Resources

Neither producing output nor investing in the system — at any level of efficiency — is possible without resources that can be used as inputs. These must be obtained from the external environment or from within the system. Under conditions of scarcity and competition this requires considerable effort.

For the individual, resource acquisition has generally been seen as a problem of what he can get from nature and from others. At lower levels of civilization this may be done through foraging, theft, and conquest, at higher levels through trading and borrowing. For the organization an important part of resource acquisition is what can be obtained from the energy, devotion, and initiative of individual members. But beyond this, more formalized techniques of resource acquisition are necessary — particularly to get resources from other organizations. At the level of the nation-state these techniques become particularly important — since they relate to both the acquisition of resources from other parts of the world and the acquisition patterns of major subsystems within the society. The major techniques may be listed as in Table 3.10.[103]

TABLE 3.10

TECHNIQUES OF RESOURCE ACQUISITION

	Money	People and Nonhuman Resources
Government organizations	Taxation Money creation	Commandeering Drafting people Expropriating property Rationing goods
All organizations (including government)	Borrowing Selling Leasing property Getting contributions Appropriations Gifts and legacies Subsidies Dues	Borrowing Buying Renting property Getting contributions Gifts and legacies Volunteer services

A full discussion of this subject would have to deal with information bearing on the mobilizing of resources within a society. This would have to include the role of government taxation, borrowing, and money supply in influencing the flow of resources

103 Gross, "Mobilization of Resources," *The Managing of Organizations, op. cit.,* p. 700.

among subsystems. For spatial considerations, however, attention will here be concentrated upon the acquisition of resources from other parts of the world. This aspect of system performance is particularly important in industrializing and postindustrializing societies, for which autarchy would impose severe and costly limits upon all performance aspects.

Imports

Every economy needs certain essential imports from other countries. The growth of modern industry has been associated with a world-wide search for raw materials, particularly oil and strategic materials. This search has often been associated with political and economic imperialism and the subjugation of colonial peoples. Liberated colonies, in turn, such as America after the Revolutionary War, have usually needed large amounts of imported equipment and machinery. In the modern world, such imports are even more seriously needed by the various colonies that have been liberated since World War II. In some cases, both in well-developed and underdeveloped countries, essential foods must also be imported. All of these needs require considerable activity in searching out alternative sources of supply and in trying to obtain essential imports on the most favorable terms.

Balance of Payments

The more fortunate countries can obtain essential imports by using the foreign currency earned through exports. This is often the result of highly organized "export drives." These operations may be based on quality competition, vigorous price competition (often becoming "dumping"), liberal financing, subsidies, or even political control.

Many countries, particularly those at a relatively low stage of industrial development, are unable to earn enough through exports to pay for the imports needed for future growth. This lack of earning capacity is revealed by a deficit in the balance of international payments on current account. Steps must then be taken to finance such a deficit by "capital imports," that is, by a surplus in the balance of payments on capital account. This surplus may take the form of (a) grants or gifts, (b) public or private loans, and (c) public or private equity investments. In many countries, performance in the mobilization of external resources can best be measured by success or failure in obtaining these various kinds of assistance.

The financial terms arranged are always a part of resource mobilization. These include not only such arrangements as interest rates, amortization periods, and the repatriation of invested capital but also the various "strings" or conditions that may be insisted on by the grantors, lenders, and investors.

People, Organizations, Information

Resource mobilization, however, is not limited to the goods and services that appear in the balance of payments. It also includes such valuable resources as people, organizations, and information. Many countries make strenuous efforts to promote immigration of people with special skills and abilities. Conversely, when there is an outflow of such people the government planners will usually take steps to try to curtail the "brain drain." As important as it is for a nation to have brainy people, it is often of greater strategic value to obtain "going organizations" from abroad. This may be done either on a permanent basis or through negotiated arrangements whereby foreign firms contract to establish going enterprises and train local people to manage them. Finally, the flow of scientific and technical information from abroad — even when not accompanied by people or organizations — is extremely important. No society can afford to insulate itself from the new ideas and methods that are being developed in other countries, even though these concepts and procedures may often need considerable adaptation before they can be put to use under indigenous conditions.

Observing Codes

Every society operates in terms of certain codes of behavior. Some of these codes are imbedded in custom, tradition, and widespread concepts of morality. Others are formulated in laws and regulations. Still others are embodied in the organizational codes and professional ethics of specific social groupings.

Despite the tremendous variety of behavioral codes within any society and among the various societies of the world, there is a hard "inner core" that may probably be found in all societies. This core consists of those codes with which observance is essential if the social structure is to hold together and the system to perform with a minimum degree of effectiveness. It is this inner core of behavioral codes that provides the common element in human morality and ethics, irrespective of vast cultural differences. Conformance, however, is always a relative matter. Code conflict and the inevitable weaknesses of human nature make complete compliance impossible. The most that can be expected is that the inevitable deviations be contained within reasonable limits.

Law and Order

No society can function without the maintenance of some minimum degree of "law and order." Such maintenance is one of the most elementary aspects of social performance. The most obvious measures of conformance with the code of order are provided by the extent of disorders of various types, such as theft and riots, and by the effectiveness of law-enforcing organizations. In a broader sense, conformance with a code of order also requires continuous adjustments in the details of the laws, regulations, and principles established in this connection. Rigid order codes and inflexible law enforcers may often lead to an intolerable amount of deviation.

Aspects of Honesty

The inner-core code of honesty has three aspects. All are vital elements in the development of stable interrelations within an interdependent society.

The first is, "Tell the truth or something close to the truth." Truth telling provides the basis of a reliable communication network. When lies or deceptions become widespread, all communication is suspect, and communication becomes intolerably inefficient because of the excessive burden of checking the truth of each message.

The second is, "Keep your word, promise, or contract." Word-keeping or adherence to agreement provides the basis for confidence in the contracts and promises needed to hold organizations together and to allow for fruitful interorganizational contacts.

A third aspect of honesty is, "Thou shalt not steal anything substantial." Widespread deviation from this code would not only undermine the rights of individuals to use their personal property but would also disrupt the major organizations that produce private and public goods and services.

As with the code of order, information on compliance is usually of a negative nature. Moreover, data on corrective action never provide a reliable indicator of the extent of surreptitious violation. Nevertheless, in broad qualitative terms, it is often possible to acquire a sense of the extent of various forms of dishonesty. This is particularly true in countries entering the first stages of industrialization, where many people bring to their dealings with government and business organizations practices based on the deceit, guile, and trickery so often necessary for survival in primitive societies. This is also true in highly industrialized societies where new forms of dishonesty — well calculated to escape detection — are always being devised.

Loyalty

In a minimum sense, the inner core of loyalty provides that the members of a nation place the national interests above any allegiance to some foreign country or organization. In a wider sense, it provides that they subordinate their personal interests to those of the nation under circumstances when some degree of self-sacrifice may be required. The major tests of conformance with the code of loyalty arise in time of external conflict or of civil war.

Codes of Justice

In all societies there are fundamental codes of justice, some embodied in law, many embodied only in widespread popular expectations. A sense of injustice will often contribute to deviations from the inner codes of order, honesty, and loyalty.

"Distributive" justice applies to the distribution of the good things in life, particularly income, wealth, status, and prestige. Distributive justice, however, is rarely conceived in terms of egalitarianism. In traditional societies a just distribution is viewed as one based on hereditary claims and social status. More modern societies base it on demonstrable personal merit or achievement.

"Retributive" justice deals with the distribution of sanctions. Here, the inner-core code usually embodies widespread expectations that the punishment should, more or less, fit the crime, that some degree of mercy be shown, that serious or repeated offenders be "brought to justice," and favored persons be nonexempt.

Behaving Rationally

Although people, organizations, and societies invariably try to behave rationally, it is by no means easy to formulate rationality goals or evaluate the extent of actual rationality. One reason for the difficulty is that rationality is often thought of entirely in the two dimensions of feasibility and consistency. From this point of view, any course of action, even though it may frustrate the most important interests in society, is rational just so long as (1) the means chosen will succeed in attaining certain ends, and (2) there is no inconsistency between it and some other feasible course of action. However, the highest test of rationality is whether a given course of action is desirable, that is, whether it satisfies human interests. Conversely, when people take feasible and consistent steps to frustrate fundamental human interests, this is, by the test of desirability, an illustration of extreme irrationality. Yet, what is desirable is not always feasible, and feasible courses of action are not always consistent with one another.

Thus, a comprehensive test of rational behavior must deal with three dimensions: desirability, feasibility, and consistency.[104] A satisfactory performance pattern, whether in the past or the future, is one that represents an acceptable combination of all three dimensions. Since desirability may, itself, be measured in terms of all of the categories of system performance, the application of this test provides a way of bringing together all the dimensions of system performance.

Rational behavior, however, always includes an intricate combination of routinization and creativity. Routine is essential to allow people and organizations to deal with certain problems through habits, customs, regulations, and established procedures. This, in turn, frees creative energies for dealing with the more baffling array of new problems for which routinization is an irrational approach. These new problems can be dealt with only by the acquisition of new knowledge, new abilities, and new interests. This is the essence of the learning process. A rational society is one in which people and organizations are capable of sustained learning and, in fact, are explicitly oriented toward recreating themselves through sustained learning.

Narrow Rationality

One of the greatest forces for social change in the world has been the remarkable development of modern science and technology. Rational social behavior unquestionably requires the sustained promotion of both pure and applied sciences (social as well as natural) and of the many technologies needed to bring the results of scientific inquiry into contact with the daily lives of human beings. There has also been tremendous progress in administrative rationality, that is, in the world's great fund of know-how and currently useful generalizations concerning the guidance of organiza-

---

[104] A fuller exposition of three-dimensional rationality is set forth in Gross, "Rationality: Satisfactory Action Patterns," *The Managing of Organizations, op. cit.*, pp. 746–757. "Optimality may be used as a way of referring to the most acceptable combination of these dimensions," as explained by Saul Katz in "A Systems Approach to Development Administration," *op. cit.*

tions. It has been the development of administrative rationality that, although lagging behind technical rationality, has made it possible to develop the large-scale complex organizations required for the exploitation of modern science and technology.

Yet, technical and administrative rationalities are rather narrow in scope, tending to deal with a relatively limited number of variables. They may be used for the purposes of destruction as well as construction, war as well as peace, frustration as well as gratification. Both rationalities have often been developed to their highest pinnacle by people and organizations that are primarily concerned with narrow interests, rather than with public interests in the broadest sense of the term.

Broad Rationality

Any truly rational orientation toward the satisfaction of public interests — either at national or international levels — calls for a much broader kind of rationality than is customarily developed by scientists, technologists, or the administrators of organizations. This rationality may be described as the *rationality of the guidance of social systems*. Of necessity, it is a rough-and-ready kind of rationality that deals with a tremendous number of variables — indeed, all the basic interests and groupings in a society — and vast imponderables. Although valuing tight concepts and neat statistical specifics, it is not led astray by sacrificing relevance on behalf of accuracy. This is the broad rationality found in the behavior of statesmen, politicians, and national planners. It is often best concretized in those overriding compromises that, from the viewpoint of a technocrat or an idealist, seem to be logically absurd. In its highest form the rationality of guidance often emanates not so much from preconceived policies and calculations as from the heat of social combat and conflict resolution. At this level of generality, the formulation of meaningful goals and the meaningful evaluation of social performance require a combination of brutal, pragmatic realism and humanistic ideology that places major emphasis on satisfying people's interests.

Industrializing and Postindustrializing

Performance Patterns

At the end of Part II, I indicated how a multidimensional analysis of system structure might be used to provide perspectives on the long-range dynamics of social change. Any full study of this type would have to deal also with the patterns of system performance and with the interrelations between performance and structure. Without presuming to present such a full study at this time, let me merely provide two illustrations of how the performance concepts presented above may be used.

First of all, let us consider certain aspects of the industrializing process in the low-income countries of Africa, Asia, the Middle East, and Latin America. One of the overwhelming facts about social change in these countries is that the majority of their national leaders — and certainly their most vigorous leaders — are committed to very rapid change. They are not interested in recapitulating the slow growth processes that characterized western industrialization during the eighteenth and nineteenth centuries. They aim to be *century skippers*.

The nature of the century skipping objectives may be illuminated by comparing the performance *achieved* by the Western countries over a longer period and the performance *sought* by today's industrializing countries during a shorter period. Some basic starting points for such a comparison are provided by Table 3.11. Even a quick examination of the table will indicate that the century skippers aim at much *more* than the speedier economic development concretized by their objectives for total and per capita increases in the GNP. In contrast with the "black Satanic mills" that characterized early industrialization in Western Europe, today's poor countries aim at some kind of "welfare state" and "social justice." They exhibit a more enlightened view toward investment in the economic "infrastructure" and in people. Neither they nor their political supporters can tolerate the wild and wasteful economic fluctuations that characterized nineteenth-century growth. They cannot reap the benefits obtainable from colonies and dependencies. They cannot justify (although let it be admitted that at times they cannot prevent) the conspicuous and widespread forms of corruption, bribery, and nepotism that characterized Western growth in the nineteenth century. Somehow or other, they must develop the capacity to use — and adapt to their own conditions — the world's great reservoirs of science and technology. The difficulties involved in attaining any such performance pattern and the nature of the strategic decisions needed to overcome them become clearer when one considers the many changes in social structure required to provide the capacity for changed performance.

It is often asserted that people in the highly industrialized countries fail to understand the problems of industrializing nations be-

TABLE 3.11

WESTERN DEVELOPMENT PERFORMANCE AND POOR COUNTRIES' PERFORMANCE OBJECTIVES[*]

	Historical Development of Today's Rich Countries	Objectives of Today's Poor Countries[*]
Satisfying interests	Unhealthy living and working conditions	"Welfare state" standards
	Growth of huge fortunes	Prevention of extreme disparities
Producing output, annual increases, real GNP		
Aggregate	Less than 3 per cent, 1860–1950[†]	At least 5 per cent
Per capita	Less than 1.5 per cent, 1890–1950[‡]	At least 3 per cent
Investing in the system	Capital accumulation at expense of consumption	Both capital and calories
Using inputs efficiently	Vast social waste resulting from wild ups and downs in business cycle	Sustained use of resources
Acquiring inputs	Exploitation of colonies or dependent areas	No colonies or dependent areas
Observing codes	Conspicuous corruption in all walks of life for many decades	Modern standards of integrity in government, business, education, etc.
Behaving rationally	Slow development of science and technology	Catching up on use of rapidly accelerating science and technology of the rich countries

[*] The listing of these objectives, obviously, does not suggest that they have as yet been attained.
[†] European countries from 1860 to 1950 (e.g., U.K., 1.8; France, 1.1; Germany, 2.4; Netherlands, 2.2); R. W. Goldsmith, "Financial Structure and Economic Growth in Advanced Countries," in *Capital Formation and Economic Growth* (Princeton, N.J.: Princeton University Press, 1955), p. 115. The U.S. rate for the same 90-year period, however, was 3.8.
[‡] In most European countries the per capita rate was closer to 1 per cent (e.g., U.K., 1.2; France, 0.9; Germany, 1.4; Netherlands, 0.7). The U.S. rate for the same 90-year period was 2.2. See *ibid.*

cause they can no longer see events against the background of their own painful processes of industrialization. While this is a valid assertion, it does not go far enough in identifying the cultural gap between the highly industrial and the preindustrial societies. The former are also in a state of transition, as pointed out in the final section of Part II. In judging the performance of the latter, they tend to use standards derived not so much from their own historic experiences in the industrializing process as from their present experience in passing from industrialism to postindustrialism.

Some of the highlights on structural changes during the transition from industrialism to postindustrialism have already been suggested (Table 3.6, p. 214). Those structural changes that are already taking place have provided the basis for such performance changes as the following:

Satisfying interests: Eliminating of material poverty at various absolute levels (although not of differential deprivation) and providing substantial security against pestilence, floods, earthquake, and nondegenerative diseases. Providing greater opportunities for leisure, creative work, and personal development, with increased blurring of the lines between work, education, and leisure. Decline in "moonlighting" and rise in "starlighting."[105] Greater opportunities for more people to satisfy the more "subjective" interests.

Producing output: From vast standardization to product differentiation, with ever-increasing attention to quality (including aesthetic aspects as well as durability and service). Vast increases in information output, information "overload," and in nonmarketed services that cannot be reflected in economic aggregates.

Investing in systems: Greater utilization of machine and material inputs, with declines in work year, work week, and involuntary unemployment. Great investment in laborsaving and data-processing hard goods, but with more conscious and explicit attention to investment in people, subsystems, internal and external relations, values, and guidance systems.

Using inputs efficiently: Increasing attention to efficiency in terms of utilizing potentials and developing the quality of output, with

[105] "Moonlighting" occurs when people with full-time jobs take on additional after-hour jobs to augment their salary — a widespread phenomenon in industrializing societies that cannot provide enough wages or salaries to satisfy ambitious workers and professionals. "Starlighting" may be used to describe the postindustrializing phenomenon of professionals and intellectuals extending their regular "work" beyond any definable limits, to satisfy their needs for self-expression and creative activity. The probability is that anyone who has read as far as this is — or will soon become — a "starlighter."

declining attention to efficiency relations calculated in the more limited and old-fashioned terms of capital or labor inputs related to strictly monetary measures of output quantity.[106]

Acquiring inputs: Greater foreign trade and internal capital flows, higher domestic taxes.

Observing codes: Substantial deviation, with changing and clashing codes. More widespread compliance with codes of honesty, truth, equity, and due process.

Behaving rationally: Advancing and using sciences and technologies, with increasing computerization and automation. Developing and using advanced methods of social system guidance — with possibilities of "unitary thought" through general systems analysis. Keynesianism becomes old-fashioned "le Stop Go" (already lampooned in France and Britain), as economic planning is transformed into social system planning.

In comparing today's rich nations with today's poor nations, many economists have wisely noted the growing economic gap that is being created because in terms of annual GNP many of the "developed nations" are "developing" faster than the so-called "developing nations." To see these widening gaps, however, only in terms of output performance, as measured in monetary terms, is to ignore not only the sources and consequences of the phenomenon but also many other gaps. It is more meaningful to focus on the many changing dimensions of system performance — some widening, some narrowing — between national systems in transition toward various phases of industrialism and others in transition from industrialism toward various phases of postindustrialism. Only by so doing can we hope to understand, and hopefully cope with, the discrepancies, conflicts, and misunderstandings created by different kinds and rates of change in our complex world society.

PART IV. TOWARD SOCIAL INDICATORS

In a profound statement that still reverberates in the minds of scientists and philosophers, Immanuel Kant once pointed out that a

---

[106] Galbraith has pointed out this tendency in his contention that "If the things produced are not of great urgency, it follows that the efficiency of the process by which they are produced ceases to be an overriding consideration." John K. Galbraith, *The Affluent Society* (Boston: Houghton Mifflin Company, 1958), p. 287. By using a narrow, single-dimensional concept of efficiency, however, Galbraith has failed to deal with the changing nature of efficiency concepts under conditions of rising material affluence.

percept without a concept is blind but a concept without a percept is empty.

In the preceding chapters I have brought together in a relatively simplistic form the overarching concepts that social scientists have developed as a framework for perceiving the changing states of any nation. While these may be a remedy against blindness, they cannot by themselves protect against emptiness. The boxes must be filled with some kind of information. Indeed, the concepts can be properly sharpened, reshaped, and interrelated only by using them persistently in the handling of concrete data. A few sketchy illustrations of one way of doing this have been set forth in the brief discussions of historical change and "postindustrialism" in the concluding sections of Parts II and III.

Now, instead of carrying forward with the direct collection and analysis of concrete data, I shall discuss some of the social and methodological problems involved in any large-scale efforts to do this.

I shall then conclude with some very specific proposals for practical steps toward the development of "social indicators."

The Social Problems in Social Indicators

In the previous chapters I have assumed that the vast collection of economic statistics during the past few decades has been "good" — except for the bias created by detracting attention from non-economic and qualitative data. I shall now accept as a general premise — subject to occasional qualifications — the proposition that during the next few decades the orderly collection of social indicators on the states of nations will also be "good." In fact, it can contribute to a major improvement in the quality of economic information while at the same time helping eliminate the bias of the "new Philistinism." These value judgments bear some resemblance to those of philosophers and psychologists who have interpreted human progress as a process whereby people become increasingly aware of their environment, or others, and of themselves. They are very close to the common-sense admonitions, "Let's find out where we are," and "Let's try to figure out where we're going."

Yet let us keep in mind that the process of collecting new and broader kinds of information on social systems is itself an aspect of system performance. More specifically, it is a specific kind of output performance initiated by certain elite groups in social science and government during the period of transition from advanced industrialism to postindustrialism. As with any other aspect of social system performance, it involves interest satisfactions and conflict dynamics.

The Interests Involved

The proponents of social indicators include both producers and users. In the early stages the most active people on the producer side are the advocates and designers, those whose interests in self-expression, creative thought, public service, and perhaps even personal advancement lead them to propose new kinds of data collection. The most active people on the user side are those who, like Banks, Textor, Russett and his associates, push existing social data to the limit while urging the necessity of additional data collection. Major government departments, like the U.S. Department of Health, Education and Welfare, operate as both producers (in the sense that they collect and interpret basic data) and consumers (in that they use such data in operating old programs and studying the need for new ones). All these activities inevitably stir up growing interest among other users: government policy makers, leaders in labor, business, and agriculture, professionals, educators, and others.

Most proponents of new indicators, however, are mainly interested in some special category of data: say, educators in educational indicators, psychiatrists in mental health data, sociologists in information on stratification and mobility, political scientists in voting behavior and political attitudes. Activists in all fields are interested in new information that will help vindicate their position or indict the opposition. They want — to use Alfred Biderman's pungent phrase — indicators that serve as vindicators and indictors.[107]

Only a small minority of proponents — whether on the producing or using side — are interested in enough new indicators to provide comprehensive social system accounting. These include a handful of academicians, researchers, and theorists who see in social system accounting a way of counterbalancing — even of fruitfully using — the onsweeping trend toward narrow specialization. Some of these are vitally interested in problems of growth, development, and social change — whether in low-income countries, high-income countries, or both. On the user side there is another minority, one that is much more powerful in the short run. This includes leaders of huge organizations, public and private, whose activities are

[107] See Chapter 2.

inextricably linked with the fortunes of a nation as a whole, or even of nations. It includes the chief executives of many nations, and the advisers and technicians who may work with and for them in planning and implementing major programs of economic and social change. Here the requirements of effective plan formulation and execution invariably point toward the necessity of well-ordered, continuing, and comprehensive information on the state of the nation.

All proposals along these lines inevitably face serious resistance. The initial form of resistance is simple inertia. People and organizations involved in collecting, processing, and analyzing data are as much weighed down by habit and custom as any other subsystem, sometimes, because of professional fastidiousness, a little more so. Any effort to induce new forms of activity may be perceived as contrary to their immediate interests. A more widespread and long-lasting form of resistance is the active fear on the part of many groups that innovations along this line would impair their relative power position. Knowledge is one of the greatest forms of power, and new forms of knowledge always suggest a threat to the existing power structure. If this threat is vague and hard to pin down, that may make it all the more formidable.

Finally, all efforts toward large-scale data collection are inevitably embroiled in the unending social struggle for scarce resources. This struggle among competing interests is more visible in the processes by which governments decide when to add a new item to government statistics. As Lowry has pointed out, specific items get on the list of possibilities for such reasons as the following: "because of inadequate data which have adversely affected some Federal program or some business operation; because important political issues have thrust particular problems to the fore; because of the particular analytical bent of some advisors to the President; because of the interest of some articulate, hard-driving bureaucrat or academician; because of the interest of some Congressional committee or some individual Congressman; because of the activities of some outside group; because of the technical review of important statistical programs by qualified individuals or committees." The decisions on which items are to be selected from the list are influenced by such factors as these: "the relative strengths of the most important officials within a particular statistics-producing agency; the attitude of the Department head toward the statistical agency or agencies under his supervision; various balances of pressures within the Bureau of the Budget; the authority exercised by the Bureau of the Budget in determining the statistical program in any given year; the skill or ineptitude of the head of a statistical agency in explaining his program to Congressional appropriations committees; the attitude of Committee chairmen toward statistical programs; the degree of outside interest in or opposition to particular proposals; and the way in which the head of a statistical agency apportions his money among various projects. And at every stage . . . the question of possible public reaction to the collection of data requested is a factor of conscious or unconscious importance."[108] In other countries, where the specific forms of government are different, the specific processes of bargaining and maneuver are nonetheless similar, exacerbated in many cases by shortages of trained manpower and by the lack of professionalized data collection institutions. Within research institutions and universities, where many pioneering efforts are made to develop new types of data, the interest conflicts are less visible but nonetheless significant.

The Conflict Dynamics of Social System Accounting

Even at this early stage a few predictions may be hazarded concerning the dynamics of social conflict with respect to social system accounting on the states of nations.

The first controversies will center on the question of *whether* this social system accounting should be done. During this stage some of the proponents will exaggerate the need for comprehensive information on the states of nations. Some will oversell the value of the proposed product, following the example of the "hard sell" and "soft sell" methods brilliantly used by the developers of operations research and electronic computers. By so doing, they will draw attention to their proposals and at least escape the dreadful fate of being totally ignored. Others will work in the shadows and, with very little attention at the outset, develop prototypes of the new product. Among both groups there will probably be those who will be interested primarily in "hard" quantitative data, in mathematical computerized operations, and in prediction and control rather than simple description and explanation.

During this stage there will be many forms of opposition, based on inevitable misunderstandings. Many people will be offended

---

[108] R. L. Lowry, "Federal Statistics for the Sixties," *Proceedings of the Business and Economic Statistics Section, American Statistical Association,* September 7–10, 1962, pp. 86–90.

by an approach that gives such major attention to economic variables. Some economists, particularly among the younger generation of narrow econometric technicians, will regard the inclusion of non-economic variables as an attack upon economics. People of more humanistic bent will be offended by the very idea of "social system accounting." Many of them will assume that "system" implies such unpleasant things as rigidity, routinization, and the neglect of human values. Some will rigidly assume that systems analysis implies total central control, or in routinized fashion they will refuse to accept the proposition that social system analysis deals with "unsystematic systems." In very human fashion they will prefer the Cassandra-like role of bewailing the loss of human values as against enlisting in a positive effort to restore human values to a central position in man's thought and action. Slowly and imperceptibly, however, the controversies will center more and more on *how* it should be done. As more information is made available — and the trend in this direction seems inevitable — the disputes will turn on needed improvements in their quality, in interpretation, and in their ordering. These disputes are essential. Official data will always become too "official," reflecting the bias of collection agencies or the institutional rigidities of the major interpreters. The categories themselves will never be automatically adjusted to new types of data and styles of interpretation. Only by continuing debate, review, and recurring reconstruction will it be possible to prevent a "hardening of the categories," the major disease that can afflict any data processing operation.

The Selectivity-Comprehensiveness Paradox

In addition to the difficulties involved in overcoming resistance, there are equally formidable conceptual difficulties confronting any efforts to establish a comprehensive system of social indicators or social system accounting. The selectivity-comprehensiveness paradox is perhaps the most bewildering of these, particularly because it is not often openly discussed. This paradox consists of the tension existing between the following:

1. The necessity that planners and evaluators concentrate their attention upon a selected number of strategic variables instead of dispersing attention comprehensively.
2. The need for a comprehensive view as a background for strategic selection.

Comprehensiveness as a Basis of Strategic Selection

As specialists develop comprehensive ways of looking at systems, they often tend to overemphasize the role of comprehensive objectives in planning. Thus economists often give the false impression that national aggregates of income, product, investment and consumption are the major goals in national policy-making. In the process of "selling their wares," budgeteers and accountants often give the impression that comprehensive projections of budgets, income statements or balance sheets can define an organization's major goals.[109]

The same tendency is inherent in the effort to go beyond economic and financial data and provide still more comprehensive information on the state of a nation and its subsystems. Indeed, even if one is concerned with mere evaluation of where we are, as contrasted with plans for going somewhere else in the future, the tendency is to emphasize the importance of ever more comprehensive information. At times this emphasis may go so far as to suggest a yearning for "complete" or "total" information. Such an objective, if ever achieved, would produce an information overload vast enough, if ever used, to break down the system's channels for information processing. Happily, such an objective is at any rate impossible and the many overloads that occur are disposed of by information wastage. But even without going to such an extreme, a passion for detailed comprehensiveness — by all elements of structure and performance and also by dimensions of major subelements — can readily result in a loss rather than a gain of perspective, in document and data-orientation for their own sake, and in a serious waste of resources.

On the other hand, strategic selection without a comprehensive view is extremely dangerous. Both top policy makers and technicians, whether in central government positions or in peripheral subsystems, may too readily fasten upon a badly selected set of variables. The men of action will tend to focus attention on the kinds of information they have become accustomed to dealing with in the past or which is brought to their attention by vigorous pressures and sharp conflicts. The ablest among them will be intuitively sensitive to new kinds of information but unable to communicate such information explicitly. The technicians will tend to concentrate upon the variables on which they are experts and regard all others as "exogenous." Knowing the value of assuming that "all other

[109] Bertram M. Gross, "What Are Your Organization's Objectives," *Human Relations*, 18 (1965), p. 212.

things are equal," they will tend to ignore the changing and non-equal nature of "all other things."

The great value of social systems accounting and of comprehensiveness information on varying aspects of structure and performance is that they provide *a conceptual and informational basis for economically scanning the array of all possible kinds of relevant data and selecting those that are most relevant under specific circumstances.* This scanning-selection process, in its most rational forms, relates to the following:

1. Criteria for evaluating past and present situations and trends.
2. Strategic objectives for current action.
3. The various remote areas in which there may be third-order consequences or "by-products" of current action.

Thus the combination of broad, systematic scanning and careful strategic selection can enable people to use the *"ceteris paribus"* technique more adeptly. With *ceteris paribus* no longer being *ceteris incognitis,* they may be pushed from the center of attention by a knowledgeable act of specific exclusion rather than a myopic act of tunnel vision.

Frameworks for Special, Unique, and Partial Models

At a very high level of abstraction from detailed information another form of comprehensiveness may be found: the comprehensiveness of the general systems model outlined in Part I. Thus the major elements of structure and performance — in the more general terms set forth in Parts II and III — may be regarded as a comprehensive stereotype of any social system.

At first glance, this comprehensive model may seem to be an "ideal type" that, in the tradition of Max Weber, actually presumes to describe all social systems. In my judgment, however, *any* "ideal type" is always too remote from the actual, the desirable, or the attainable to be of use in indicating what has been or is in any society, or in serving as a guide to the future. If one puts "meat" on the bare bones of the comprehensive model set forth in the previous chapters, one gets a representation not of *any* social system but rather of a group of social systems or of a specific social system.

Thus, when more work is done in analyzing "postindustrial societies" along the lines suggested in the concluding sections of Parts II and III, the result will be a special model that emphasizes the distinctive differences between them and their industrial and pre-industrial forebears. Thus general systems accounting provides a framework for the construction of such *special models.*

Let us carry this line of reasoning one step further. Let us now assume that still more informational "meat" is put on the bones, with appropriate distinctions between the United States, the post-industrializing countries of Western Europe, and the postindustrial future of the Soviet Union. This verges on the development of models dealing not with sets of societies but with unique societies. If the *Commissariat du Plan* in France or the President's Council of Economic Advisers in the United States should develop a model of French and American societies, respectively, these would be unique models. The role of social system accounting in each case would be to provide the framework for constructing a *unique model.*

But progress in understanding society cannot come from general models alone. In fact, as pointed out in the introduction, partial system models have already contributed to the development of more general models. These contributions cannot be regarded as having come suddenly to an end. Indeed, general system models and social system accounting based upon them will undoubtedly promote increasing progress with respect to partial systems. First of all, a partial model may be regarded as a set of elements selected from the full set of general system elements. Indeed, whenever this may be proved to be untrue, the generality of the social system model will have been proved defective and improvements will be needed to restore its generality. Second, the general system model will provide a basis for linking any partial model with those elements of society that have been omitted. Thus social system accounting also provides a framework for the development of new and more powerful *partial models.*

The Abstraction-Specificity Ladder

Another set of conceptual difficulties is found in the problems faced at the various points in the long ladder from vague but grand abstractions down through intermediate abstractions to very specific kinds of information. Some of the grand and intermediate abstractions associated with system performance are set forth in Table 3.12. Chart 3.4 provides a more complete abstraction-specificity ladder for "abundance," one of the simplest of all the grand abstractions.

TABLE 3.12

NATIONAL PERFORMANCE ABSTRACTIONS: GRAND AND INTERMEDIATE

	Grand Abstractions	Intermediate Abstractions
Satisfying interests	Peace, security, freedom, liberty, autonomy, self-determination, equality Tolerance, dignity, honor, prestige, pride Progress, culture, beauty, the arts, self-development	Full employment Fair employment Equitable income distribution Higher living standards
Producing output	Abundance	Growth in national output Output of specific services or goods Price stability
Investing in system	Expansion, unity, national consciousness Saving free enterprise, building socialism or a new or great society	Investment in hard goods Investment in people or institutions Conservation and development
Using inputs efficiently		Productivity ratios Balanced budget
Acquiring resources	Economic independence or self-sufficiency	External assistance Economic independence or self-sufficiency Favorable balance of payments
Observing codes	Justice, equity Democracy Order, duty Obedience to God or gods	Law enforcement Due process Fair procedures
Behaving rationally	Reason Wisdom	Scientific or technological progress Good government or administration

Grand Abstraction
Abundance (plenty)

Intermediate Abstractions

| | Wealth | Distribution of output or wealth | Appropriation (or expropriation) |

Output (or production)

Quantitative Indicator Concepts

Output types	Output quantity	Output quality
Services or goods	End or intermediate products	Gross or net
Physical or monetary units	Time periods Indices	Aggregate,average, or marginal
Current or stable prices	Type base	

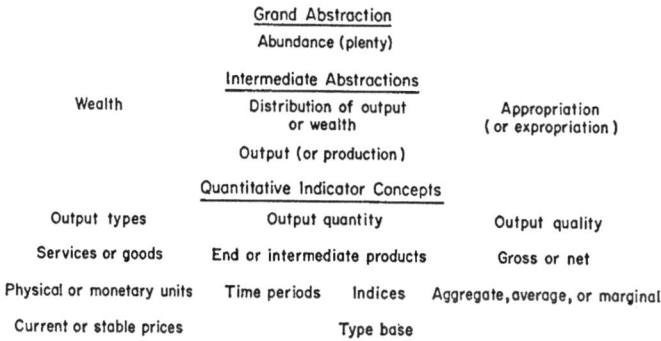

Chart 3.4.   An abstraction specificity ladder.

On the Heights: Meaning and Emptiness

For centuries the "grand abstractions" have been the ideas that have stirred men's souls. "They have become the symbol and inspiration of mass movements, wars and revolutions and the creation of new states. In declarations of independence and national purpose, in constitutions, charters, and solemn covenants, they have become enshrined as national and international goals."[110] Similarly, the "intermediate abstractions" "are those which are the lifeblood of national debates on economic policy. They enter into the language of controversy, planning negotiations and maneuver in bureaucracies, legislatures and courts."[111]

At times both the grand and the intermediate abstractions become "empty shells, devoid of meaning and content" or else a "shoddy façade to disguise tyranny, slavery, prejudice, exploitation, stagnation or intellectual or moral bankruptcy."[112] The continuing strength of the grand abstractions lies in their recurring use to refer to specific interests in specific aspects of system performance. They are "most powerful when rooted in the intermediate abstractions and, through them and along with them, in the deeply felt interests of people and well-organized groups."[113] These intermediate abstractions may themselves be meaningless or fraudulent. They become more meaningful only when supported by more specific indicators at lower levels on the ladder.

[110] Gross, "Satisfaction of Interests," *The Managing of Organizations, op. cit.,* p. 528.
[111] *Ibid.*
[112] *Ibid.*
[113] *Ibid.*

Down to Earth: Precision and Irrevelance

When we come down to earth and spell out just what we mean by a grand abstraction like "abundance," we can now attain much greater precision. This has the great value of providing data that give a better understanding of relations and interrelationships, make it easier to verify or disprove conclusions, and facilitate communications among different people and groups. Such data may also be of considerable symbolic value, sounding more "objective" and "scientific." At the same time, greater precision may eliminate the possibilities for consensus and coalition that stem from vagueness and ambiguity.

At the same time, as we come near the bottom of the ladder, we encounter the phenomenon of the decreasing relevance of any indicator. Thus the monetary value of a certain type of output may give an extremely one-sided or distorted view of events. One-sideness or distortion may occur when an increase in output quantity is used without considering marginal increments; or when one type of index number is used without seeing what happens when other types are used. All these, and many other, possibilities illustrate the danger of focusing on a *single* precise indicator. This danger may be avoided only by using a *set* of indicators.

Multiplicity: Richness and Manipulability

To avoid the danger of irrelevance at the bottom of the ladder, we must recognize the necessity of multiple dimensions, even for such a presumably concrete and homogeneous phenomenon as output. How we select the components of any particular set depends, of course, on the nature of the available data, the cost of obtaining it or improving it, and the particular purpose at hand.

This "horizontal multiplicity," in turn, must be combined with "vertical multiplicity," if the specific indicators are to be linked with the intermediate and grand abstractions. Any rich understanding of a past or present system state or any rich portrayal of future purpose requires one to run up and down the abstraction-specificity ladder. This is the only way to escape the "slippage" resulting from decreased precision as one goes up, and of increasing multiplicity and decreasing relevance as one moves downward.

But a multiplicity of concepts and measures, it must be recognized, always creates new difficulties. The most obvious one is the problem of working them into some manageable pattern rather than allowing them to create confusion by unordered proliferation. The less obvious difficulty is that multiplicity creates excellent opportunities for the manipulation of data to vindicate or indict. Indeed, unless one is prepared to handle a multiplicity of concepts and measures at various levels of the abstraction-specificity ladder, one may be readily misled by those who are more proficient in the arts of data interpretation and presentation.

Surrogates: Necessity and Danger

As already indicated in Part III, some phenomena cannot be directly quantified. We cannot make direct measurements of human satisfactions or of the quantity of certain intangible services. But we can get quantitative measures by using what I call "surrogates." These are indirect indicators that serve as quantitative substitutes for, or representatives of, the phenomena we want to measure. Thus, the price someone pays for something — whether it is an automobile, a wedding license, or a year at college — is a surrogate of human satisfaction. While this may be the best we can do, accepting price as a measure of satisfaction involves the buried assumption that there is a linear relationship between the amount of money spent and the magnitude of the need that is satisfied. As of yet, there is no better *practiced* assumption. Similarly, the number of additional university students in a given year is a surrogate of increased educational output. Both these surrogate figures may be of some use. They may often be used. They may readily be misused, also. They will be misused whenever they are taken too seriously. Thus, any serious effort to reap the advantages of increased meaning, precision, and richness creates the need for considerable imagination in the finding of many new surrogates, and for considerable self-restraint in not being misled by them.

Some Practical Steps

What can be done to develop social systems accounting on the states of nations? Three lines of approach merit attention.

Public Accounting on the States of Nations

In many countries the head of the government is expected to provide regular reports to the national legislature and the public at large on the state of their nation. Thus, under the U.S. Constitution, the President "shall from time to time give the Congress Information of the State of the Union. . . ." (Article II, Section 3) Thus far Presidents have never complied with this mandate in a comprehensive manner. The annual "State of the Union" messages traditionally deal mainly with the country's foreign relations and certain highpoints of domestic policy. They are strongly supported by two information-packed documents: the Budget Message and the Economic Report. "But these massive public documents are out of touch with the great changes in American society. . . . The Budget Message provides little more than a financial, dollars-and-cents accounting of government transactions. The Economic Report is little more than a review of where we've been and a prognosis of where we're going in strictly economic terms. Neither one can deal directly with the 'quality of life' in America, no matter how strong may be the President's desire to get beyond financial and economic considerations alone. Together, they have served to create a narrow and distorted view of reality."[114] This situation can be remedied by broadening the Economic Report to include the major aspects of social structure and performance in which economic variables are embedded. Or else the two back-up reports to the State of the Union Message could be supplemented with an Annual Social Report. In this case the State of the Union Message — in modernized form — could provide the major vehicle for a public accounting on the major trends in the American society, together with the President's goals for future social change.[115] In other countries, where annual messages of this type are not so fully differentiated already, it might be more appropriate to develop comprehensive "white papers," "planning reports," or other surveys to perform a similar function.

If and when such general surveys are made public, it is all the more important to base them upon detailed examinations of specific fields. In the area of economic information, the development of input-output matrices, national balance sheets, and analyses of wealth and income distribution is particularly important. It is even more important to catch up on the huge backlog with respect to noneconomic aspects of system structure and performance. The following are a few of the more important and most feasible areas:

1. The entire range of a nation's educational capacities and activities, where currently available information is usually limited to the "educational establishment."

2. The broad and varied area of the arts and humanities, where little information has been systematically compiled.

---

114 Bertram M. Gross, "The Social State of the Union," *Transaction*, 3 (November 1965).

115 Bertram M. Gross, "Let's Have a Real State of the Union Message," *Challenge*, 3 (May–June 1966).

3. Crime and delinquency, where currently available information is often extremely misleading.

4. The "vital statistics" of organizations and associations, long woefully neglected.[116]

Much of this information can be obtained more economically by recurrent sample surveys than by expensive censuses. Moreover, fundamental distortions can best be avoided by removing the collection tasks from agencies that use the data in operating other programs. Under such circumstances it is a natural tendency for data to be collected, interpreted, and disseminated in a manner guaranteed to help a program agency in its bargaining relations with clients and adversaries and in its efforts to increase its budgetary appropriations. A more objective and generally useful approach may be obtained through professional fact-gathering departments like census bureaus and general statistical offices. Even under such conditions, however, it will prove desirable to arrange for "public inquiries" from time to time into the state of one or another statistical series. These, in turn, will be constructive and penetrating only if a steady stream of criticism and new ideas comes in from university researchers and other independent sources.

State of World Surveys

The United Nations and its various specialized agencies have developed a growing series of increasingly sophisticated factual surveys on economic conditions around the world. To these have been added a number of recurrent reports on noneconomic matters.

One of the most important of these is the *Report on the World Social Situation*, which — in accordance with a recent decision of the Economic and Social Council — is now to be issued biennially. The first of these biennial reports attempts to sum up the major trends in social conditions and social programs since 1950.[117] Unfortunately, this report is unduly confined to the standard-of-living concepts developed a decade earlier. Thus, neither art nor recre-

---

[116] The lack of the most elementary data on the number, size, longevity, and mortality of various kinds of organizations is discussed in the section "Survival or Liquidation," in Gross, *The Managing of Organizations, op. cit.*, p. 662. An important proposal to fill this gap — albeit with respect to public organizations only — has been provided by the sixty variables listed in Blanche Davis Blank's "A Proposal for a Statistical Approach to Comparative Administration: The Measurement of National Bureaucracies," *CAG Occasional Paper* (Bloomington, Ind.: Comparative Administration Group, July 1965).

[117] United Nations, Department of Social Affairs, *1963 Report on the World Social Situation* (New York: U.N. Publications, 1963).

ation, neither stratification nor mobility, neither political nor business institutions are included as part of the "social situation" in any country in the entire world. "Social" is used to refer to certain minimum welfare concepts (as in the phrase "social worker") rather than to major aspects of society.

Accordingly, the United Nations should be expected to broaden the kinds of information to be covered as part of the "world social situation." If this is too much to expect for the world as a whole, it would nonetheless be a tremendous service to most countries if a few "model social reports" could be made for a pilot set of countries.

Another valuable U.N. report is the annual *Yearbook on Human Rights*. This has been issued by the Department of Social Affairs every year since 1946. The last yearbook[118] describes constitutional, legislative, and judicial developments in ninety-eight states, together with information on trusts and nonself-governing territories and international agreements. Special attention is paid to such developments bearing upon the 1948 Universal Declaration of Human Rights. But *no* information whatsoever is provided on the actual extent to which such rights are or are not enjoyed in various countries. It would surely seem that this situation calls for renewed attention in the higher councils of the United Nations and on the part of governments and groups interested in this extremely important aspect of national performance. Naturally, there are serious obstacles involved in the collection of *new* data in this field by international agencies. Nonetheless, it would seem appropriate for the United Nations to assemble and include in its regular surveys the large amount of information that is already available. This would help clarify the need for improved information and, insofar as some countries are concerned, act as an incentive toward such improvements. In some countries, certain kinds of international collection operations may even be welcomed.

A Long-Range Perspective

No matter what may be done in the immediate future, a long-range perspective is necessary. Thus, the pioneering work in national economic accounting in the United States was undertaken through a series of annual conferences under the sponsorship of the National Bureau of Economic Research. A similar series of conferences — both on a national and international basis — could likewise be sponsored on the broader subject of social accounting. Private

[118] United Nations, Department of Social Affairs, *Yearbook of Human Rights for 1961* (New York: U.N. Publications, 1963).

and public foundations and national academies of arts and sciences could play a significant role in the promotion of this intellectual pioneering. Over a period of ten years regular conferences of this type would make considerable progress in grappling with the conceptual difficulties and getting a few preliminary compilations under way.

In any case, *progress in the collection of social indicators will be slow and uneven.* It would be utopian to expect that any government would ever set itself to the task of moving from economic to social indicators in one comprehensive operation. The first social system reports of presidents and prime ministers will be fragmentary and exploratory.

Above all, *the maturation of social accounting concepts will take many decades.* Let us remember that it took centuries for Quesnay's economic tables to mature into national income accounting. In most countries of the world, national income accounting is still at a rudimentary stage. In countries where it is highly developed, national income experts recognize that they face many conceptual problems that still require years of dedicated attention. By contrast, the formulation of national social accounts is a much more complex undertaking. It requires the participation of social scientists from many disciplines and the breaking down of many language barriers among them. The ideas set forth in this chapter provide little more than an initial staking out of the territory upon which vast debates must take place.

4

Anticipatory Studies and Stand-by Research Capabilities

Albert D. Biderman

The Problem

Gross and I, in the preceding two chapters, have written about the desirability and use of regular and continuous trend statistics as social indicators. Such regular reporting series have three limiting distinctions. First, they are, for the sake of reasonableness of cost and effort as well as to avoid an information glut, limited to those phenomena that were important for evaluating a fairly wide range of programs and institutions. Second, they are limited to phenomena that can be anticipated, and anticipated with sufficient certainty to warrant establishing a statistical series. And, third, being a *series*, they do not include unique, noncomparable events.

But the information requirements for evaluating social programs, policies, and institutions are not limited to such regular series. Adequate information systems must also be prepared to gather *ad hoc* data relevant possibly only to the entity being evaluated, and for events that either can be anticipated only dimly or that prove to be entirely unanticipated. Thus in my earlier chapter, on "Social Indicators and National Goals," I suggested that "a spherical trigonometry accuracy measure" might be an appropriate indicator of progress in space science.

Current Indicator Limitations

The facetious aspect of my suggestion is that such an indicator lacks sufficient general relevance to be incorporated in a regular system of social indicators. It is illustrative, however, of the sort of indicator that NASA personnel would maintain routinely and informally — probably without recognizing it as such an indicator — in the course of keeping abreast of knowledge in that area. Similarly, a unique event, such as initial public reaction to the satellite transmission of TV, would not fit into a series.

Specific Difficulties. It is not only the narrowness of applicability of certain information or its uniqueness that militates against incorporating it in a general scheme of social accounting, but the difficulty of anticipating the events that might be observed in order to garner that information. This chapter will concentrate on the events that are unique, or at least do not form a continuous series, and are in varying degrees difficult to anticipate.

Space programs, our own and foreign ones, have been creating a succession of new and dramatic experiences for both the public at large and for groups of people who have specific roles with respect to space activities. Among such groups are legislators, military officers, employees of space programs, scientists, and space "fans." To some extent, the occurrence of these dramatic space events can be anticipated. Our anticipations are limited in several ways, however. We may not know the specific time that a foreseen event will occur or, indeed, we may be uncertain as to whether or not it ever will; we may not know that a foreseen event will have some particular dramatic characteristic; and we may not foresee at all the occurrence of certain events that will in fact occur.

Such unpredictability as this has affected the research that has been accomplished on reactions to space events, and has also left us with no reliable information whatsoever about most events that may have affected conceptions of behavior in this area. But research on reactions to events relating to space is not alone in this regard.

The contributions of research into the impact of immediate events on the behavior of significant publics have generally been limited by the *ex post facto* or *ad hoc* nature of most such research. Only rarely have social scientists anticipated the occurrences or possible occurrence of unscheduled events that might prove to be of research significance. And even more rarely have they begun their work sufficiently well in advance of the event to be able to make precise measurements of change and direct observations of the processes of change while they were occurring.

Inherent Weaknesses. The nature of such research has resulted in characteristic weakness of both method and substance. Methodologically, certain things happen necessarily under these circumstances:

1. An overreliance on *post hoc* reasoning without *ante hoc* observations.

2. An overreliance on the use of retrospective questions.

3. Possibly a source of even greater invalidity, an overreliance on

"retrospective introspection"[1] — that is, "How did you feel?" or "What did you expect before it happened?" — in research procedures.

4. Reliance on data from those sources that leave indelible records, such as newspapers and institutional records, and a concurrent neglect of other sources.

Substantively, the *ex post facto* timing of research may contribute to the dominance of static categories of analysis, such as comparing the differences between persons of dissimilar backgrounds. More dynamic modes of analysis, such as comparing people who played different roles in the event, are presumably used where immediate observations of the processes are possible.

The Requirements

Four requirements must be met to better the situation:

1. We must endeavor systematically to anticipate the occurrence of events that may constitute important objects of research.
2. Research plans must be developed, using to the fullest extent our ability to anticipate the demands that will confront research on the occurrence of the event.
3. Where a study of change caused by the anticipated event is indicated, base-line measures should be made before the event. Such measures should be aimed at both relevant publics and variables.
4. A ready capability must exist for carrying out research observations *where* and *when* events significant for study occur.

The Need for Anticipating Events[2]

The precise measurement of social effects demands *before-after* study designs, but the *before* measure is too seldom made. In addition, a large proportion of social science studies do not involve tests of a specific hypothesis derived from a highly explicit theory of dynamic process. Consequently, even if we have measures *before* and *after* the event, it may be very difficult to infer just what mech-

---

[1] See R. K. Merton, M. Fiske, and Patricia L. Kendall, *The Focused Interview: A Manual of Problems and Procedures* (Glencoe, Ill.: The Free Press, 1956).

[2] The problem of how to anticipate space-related events was a matter of concern in many of the activities of the Space Committee. The entire collection of essays on the early history of the railroad was directed at the use of historical analogy to generate hypotheses about future developments in space exploration.

anisms brought about the change — if a change is observed. Therefore, close observations of the processes of change *during* their occurrence is essential to gain an understanding of the dynamics underlying social effects. The classic model of the research discussed here is the panel study, involving reinterviewing of the same individuals several times in the course of an event; its traditional use has been in political election studies.[3]

The *before-after* (or *before-during-after*) study, with the panel design for carrying out the research, is being used effectively in the social sciences to study the impact of definitely scheduled events, such as elections. Particularly neat procedures for such studies can be and are employed in those circumstances where the requirements for conducting such research are built into the timing and staging of the event that is to be studied. Examples of projects that can be conducted so as to fit the timing of the event to research requirements are "demonstration projects" in the welfare field, market testing of new products, and promotional campaigns.

Anticipatory Studies. The problem considered by the present chapter is that of gaining the advantages of *before-during-after* observations when various degrees of uncertainty exist regarding when, where, or whether an important event will occur or what specific import the event may have. To distinguish the subject of this discussion from the usual *before-after* study, the term "anticipatory studies" can be used for those proposed here.

Such elements of uncertainty characterize many events of the immediate past and indefinite future that may prove to be important as determinants of the social impact of space activities. In the sequence of events associated with innovations, however, there are many signals that, if heeded, can alert researchers sufficiently in advance to permit *before* measures to be made. The following is a conclusion reached a quarter of a century ago from an examination of the impact of technological and scientific development on society:

Though the influence of invention may be so great as to be immeasurable, as in the case of gunpowder or the printing press, there is usually opportunity to anticipate its impact upon society since it never *comes instantaneously without signals.* For invention is a process and there are faint beginnings, development, diffusion, and social influences, occurring

[3] See M. Rosenberg, W. Thielens, with P. F. Lazarsfeld, "The Panel Study," in Marie Jahoda, M. Deutsch, and S. W. Cook, *Research Methods in Social Relations, with Especial Reference to Prejudice* (New York: Dryden Press, 1951), Part 2, *Selected Techniques*, pp. 587–609.

in sequences, all of which require time. From the early origins of an invention to its social effects the time interval averages about 30 years.[4]

By the systematic attempt to anticipate events that can be predicted to be important objects for research, by extensive preplanning for studies of these events, and by organizing ever-ready stand-by capabilities for carrying out research on the occurrence of these events as quickly as necessary, the full potentiality of social science can be brought to bear on understanding the changes wrought by these events.[5]

Opinion Studies. Since efforts to study reaction to dramatic or catastrophic occurrences are focused mainly on *opinion*, and since, therefore, a large number of the examples cited in this chapter are drawn from *opinion* and attitude studies, it is important at the outset to stress that the object of discussion here is in no way confined to the field of public opinion. The objectives that follow are broader than the field of public opinion, as normally interpreted, in several ways. They encompass, for example,

1. The development of data-collecting or data-monitoring activities of a new sort that would permit us to get well beyond opinion.

2. The focus of attention on the relationship between the social structure and the social impact through observations of the process.

3. The collection of data that would permit an analysis in *depth* of shifts in conceptualization and ideology and in definition of situations (in W. I. Thomas'[6] classic term) as these relate to the structuring of behavior.

4. The use of selective studies of key elite groups, such as scientists, administrators, and group leaders, as more productive of knowledge relating to the impact of space developments for purposes of either theory or policy planning.

Need for Advance Planning

Even when the occurrence of events that have proved to be of high research interest have been clearly anticipated, only rarely have the social science researchers systematically undertaken to gather base-line data in advance of the event. And rarely have they

[4] National Resources Committee Subcommittee on Technology, *Technological Trends and National Policy Including the Social Implications of New Inventions* (Washington, D. C.: U.S. Government Printing Office, 1937), p. ix.

[5] A. I. Gladstone, "The Possibility of Predicting Reactions to International Events," *The Journal of Social Issues,* IV (November 1955).

[6] W. I. Thomas and Florian Znaniecki, *The Polish Peasant in Europe and America*, 2 vols. (Boston, Mass.: Richard G. Badger, The Gorham Press, 1918).

been in a position quickly to carry out well-planned research on the event while it was occurring or while the experiences of publics with it were fresh. As a consequence, much costlier studies, and studies producing data in which less confidence can be placed, have frequently been undertaken to fill gaps in knowledge.

Conspicuous Failure. A conspicuous example of our failure to gather base-line data in advance of an event whose occurrence is virtually certain is in our study of the effects of TV. A large amount of research on the impact of TV viewing on Americans is reviewed by Bogart.[7] Only with respect to gross variables, such as the use of other media, do the studies available to him report direct observations *before* and *after* the TV innovation. The bulk of the *before-after* comparisons he discusses are based on responses to *retrospective* questions, or on comparisons between families that had acquired a TV set as of the date of the study and those that had not yet acquired one.

Yet, in the single year, 1951, the percentage of American homes having TV sets rose from 7 per cent to 23 per cent. The advent of TV to an area was known in advance, and for long before students had been discussing the effects the new medium would have on people's lives.[8] *Intensive research to determine the effect it had was rarely based on observations of the same people or of the same community before and after the medium had had an impact.*

The large-scale British studies of the innovation of television did employ a *before* and *after* study initiated prior to the beginning of TV service in the Norwich area. This study pointed to major errors of interpretation that would have been made had the differences between users and nonusers been interpreted as effects of TV exposure.[9]

The initiation of radio to a particular area did provide one early model of the kind of research advocated here. In anticipation of electrification with consequent large-scale adoption of radio in isolated southern Illinois, a careful study was done in the 1930's both *before* and *after* the event.

Exceptional Attempt. The lack of timely planning and the failure to capitalize on fortuitous opportunities with impromptu re-

[7] L. Bogart, *The Age of Television: A Study of Viewing Habits and the Impact of Television on American Life* (New York: Frederick Ungar Publishing Co., Inc., 1956).

[8] National Resources Committee, *op cit.*, pp. 228–229.

[9] H. T. Himmelweit, "A Theoretical Framework for the Consideration of the Effects of Television: A British Report," *The Journal of Social Issues, 18* (1962), 16–28.

search have also led to a paucity of attempts to replicate studies relating to a number of critical propositions. An exceptional case is the study of how members of the public first learn of dramatic news events, and the reasons for this pattern of exposure. This type of information, for reliability, must be developed by immediate interviews. Larson and Hill's impromptu studies on the deaths of President Franklin D. Roosevelt and Senator Robert A. Taft found that these two events differed interestingly in respect to the roles of the mass media and interpersonal communication as disseminators of the news.[10] But further research is needed, and could be done, to clarify the role of such factors as the time of day that an event occurs or is announced, and the human interest value of the event as a determinant of word-of-mouth dissemination of the news.[11]

Similarly, while content analyses have produced some knowledge of the persons who define the "larger significance and implications" of events in mass-media coverage, the reactions of publics to various "issue definers" have rarely been studied.[12] A particularly interesting case study of this problem was Bucher's analysis of the origins of blaming reactions in a series of commercial airliner crashes in Elizabeth, New Jersey.[13]

Feasibility Implications. The space effort itself can be used to illustrate failure to plan for research on a predictable event. The immediate technical feasibility of launching an earth satellite was recognized in 1950. The possibility that the Soviet Union might make such a launch at any time, and prior to a U.S. launch, was also accepted.

Two implications for the present discussion of the feasibility of these anticipations are relevant. First, our knowledge of how Sputnik I affected significant publics is largely based on reconstructed facts. Michael, in concluding his review of the available data about the impact of Sputnik on American public opinion, stated: "the very fact that they [the data] are inadequate . . . should hammer

---

[10] O. N. Larson and R. Hill, "Mass Media and Interpersonal Communication in the Diffusion of a News Event," *The American Sociological Review, 19* (1954), 426–433.

[11] R. A. Bauer and Alice H. Bauer, "America, 'Mass Society' and Mass Media," *The Journal of Social Issues, 16* (1960), 3–66; L. Bogart, "The Spread of News on a Social Event: A Case History," *The Public Opinion Quarterly, 14* (1950–1951), 769–772.

[12] One exception is A. D. Biderman and J. L. Monroe, "Reactions to the Korean POW Episode," paper read at the American Psychological Association, Washington, D. C., September 1958.

[13] R. Bucher, "Blame and Hostility in Disaster," *The American Journal of Sociology, 62* (1957), 467–475.

home once again the need to take advantage of situations which allow carefully planned *before-after* studies. The dubious pleasures of double-guessing the meanings of these data are left to the reader. . . ."[14]

A second implication is the possibility that intensive pre-Sputnik research on how publics would react to satellite launchings might have significantly altered the way the American government talked about space at the time, even though we might not have behaved differently.

Where research is undertaken *before* or *during* the event by or for an agency in a position to influence the event, or where the research itself becomes a matter of public attention, potential indeterminacies are introduced. This has been discussed by Lundberg[15] and others, and is no more than an instance of what has long concerned physicists — namely, that the very art of studying a phenomenon may change the thing being studied. The most often discussed illustrations in the social sciences are pre-election polls and predictions of the outcome of elections.

Mass-Observation. The most extensive precedent for the kind of activity I shall advocate here was the Mass-Observation organization in Great Britain during its early period of operation. It will be seen that this operation did constitute a sort of stand-by research facility. Mass-Observation made use of hundreds of unpaid, volunteer observers — supplemented by full-time observers for some of its important studies — who were recruited through advertisements and newspaper publicity. In 1939, some 1,500 of these amateur observers were providing reports to Mass-Observation, on request, regarding what they had done, overheard, and seen on a particular day. From these reports, analyses were made of public reaction and behavior in response to such events and things as critical political developments leading up to World War II, the coronation, the Lambeth Walk dance craze, behavior in "pubs," and strikes.[16]

Despite the exciting data it developed during its early period, Mass-Observation was overwhelmed by its deficiencies, and the organization moved in more conventional directions. While the *in situ* observations of behavior and the systematic listening to unprompted conversations "gets as near as the outsider can to the

[14] D. N. Michael, "The Beginning of the Space Age and American Public Opinion," *The Public Opinion Quarterly*, 24 (1960), 573–582.

[15] G. A. Lundberg, *Social Research: A Study in Methods of Gathering Data* (New York: Longmans Green & Co. Ltd., 1946).

[16] C. Madge and T. Harrison, *Britain by Mass-Observation* (Harmondsworth, England: Penguin Books, 1939); H. Jennings *et al.*, *May the Twelfth: Mass-Observation Day Surveys* (London: Faber & Faber, 1937).

'frank' level of opinion, and essentially to spontaneous interest and intensity of feeling . . . the chanciness of overhearing and the natural tendency of the observer to select, memorize, and record the more bizarre conversations make it rash to use such material as the basis for generalizations. . . ."[17] These problems were aggravated by the amateur character of the observers, their lack of training, the selective factors in their recruitment, and the lack of planning and system in the research that was done.

Lang and Lang have commented that these shortcomings are not inherent in mass observation as an approach:

Greater resources than Mass-Observation had at the time would permit the use of trained observers, more carefully briefed, working with a clear idea of the information they need, and applying themselves systematically to obtain it. Some kind of mass observation setup, based in university towns, could easily be recruited and used to undertake studies on given occasions. Indeed, the Tavistock Institute of Human Relations in England has used a modified version of this design. The American Political Science Association used it in 1952 to observe the nominating process in American political parties. . . . Margaret Mead and her associates obtained the initial reactions of the launching of the first man-made satellite, before responses were structured as a result of social support or recognition via the mass media and before they had become crystallized into public opinion around the issues of public education and the national defense effort. Such data make possible the observations of the collective process from its points of origin.[18]

Earlier the Langs themselves had been notable in applying some of the principles of Mass-Observation,[19] and had circumvented some of its methodological difficulties by their professional competence and by advance preparation. Also, two studies of mass behavior toward a "miracle" in Puerto Rico,[20] a study of a school desegregation that developed a student strike,[21] and a number of studies of disasters[22] constitute other good examples.

[17] J. Madge, The Tools of Social Science (London: Longmans Green & Co. Ltd., 1951).

[18] K. Lang and Gladys E. Lang, Collective Dynamics (New York: Thomas Y. Crowell Company, 1961).

[19] See their article, "The Unique Perspective of Television and Its Effects: A Pilot Study," The American Sociological Review, 18 (1953), 3–12.

[20] See M. M. Tumin and A. S. Feldman, "The Miracle of Sabona Grande," The Public Opinion Quarterly, 19 (1955), 125–139.

[21] H. Mendelsohn, "The 'Student Strike' as a Socio-Psychological Reaction to Desegregation" (Washington, D. C.: Bureau of Social Science Research, Inc., no date).

[22] C. E. Fritz, An Inventory of Field Studies on Human Behavior in Disaster Situations (Washington, D. C.: National Academy of Sciences–National Research Council, August 15, 1959).

Need for Stand-by Capabilities

The argument of the present chapter adopts from Mass-Observation the importance of having observers ready at all times to make observations but stresses the requirement of their being *professionally* ready, not merely physically ready. Professional readiness presumes the preparation of plans and personnel for carrying out studies that will meet as many of the canons of rigor as possible. These requirements, in turn, depend on the anticipation of events. Professional readiness also requires a willingness to engage in some degree of risk taking — psychological, if not economic — in preparing contingent plans for work that may not be done.

Our argument is that, while there is and always will be a failure to anticipate critical developments, we are not taking full advantage of the anticipations that we do have regarding problems.[23] If such anticipations are to be taken advantage of, they must be organically linked to the responsibility and the capability for taking research action.

Retrospective Questions. The basic purposes of the proposed stand-by capability will be to avoid "missed boats" in future programs of research on reactions to space events and to substitute the presumed more valuable techniques of immediate observation for the current overuse of retrospective methods, which ask people to reconstruct what they did, felt, or thought *before* or *during* some important event.

The limited premeasure of social scientists will always make it necessary to rely somewhat on retrospective data. From a methodological point of view, therefore, it is important to test the adequacy of our methods for developing information by retrospective methods.[24] The panel designs proposed here will afford important opportunities of this kind.

For research activities oriented to the future, there is heavy reliance on asking anticipatory and hypothetical questions. Evaluating the predictive power of inferences drawn from responses to anticipatory questions would be an important task. Here again, the proposed panel design would be particularly pertinent. A project sponsored by the U.S. Air Force Office of Scientific Research, and

[23] A. Kaplan, A. L. Skogstad, and M. A. Girschick, "The Prediction of Social and Technological Events," *The Public Opinion Quarterly, 14* (1959), 93–110. In their study, the authors found that considerable accuracy could be achieved by well-informed persons in predicting technological and social events within time periods and at the approximate levels of specificity that would be involved in the kinds of work discussed here.

[24] Merton, Fiske, and Kendall, *op. cit.*

directed by Jiri Nehnavajsa, has made intensive use of anticipatory and hypothetical questions.[25] These questions bear on potential international developments, and are asked of selected groups of respondents from many nations. This project is also concerned with the impact of actual events on expectations. Various questions relating to possible developments in space affairs have been used in this series of studies, although at a higher level of generality than in the work proposed in this chapter. The distribution of responses to these questions among various world publics can be instructive for the planning of the current work.

Of considerable interest is the comparison of responses to anticipatory questions with the same person's responses to retrospective questions in which they are asked what their expectations *had* been in relation to a certain event. Such an analysis was made of *before* and *after* interviews with persons who were forced to relocate by an urban redevelopment project.[26] The analysis focused on the consistency of the occurrence with the subjects' expectations and the "optimism" or "pessimism" of the original expectation. Retrospective questions yielded answers that correlated more highly with their current attitudes than with the attitudes they had originally expressed and which they were presumably trying to reconstruct.

Janis, Lumsdaine, and Gladstone's study of preparatory communication toward Soviet atomic bomb development provided essentially similar observations.[27] Their results indicate more of a tendency to cling to whatever illusions can be retained than of radical disillusionment when actual events prove to a person that he "has been sold a bill of goods." Such studies indicate that publicists need have less concern about creating "overoptimism" for fear that events will produce disillusioning than is sometimes counseled: see, for example, the report by Michael.[28] This anxiety figures also in the official

[25] See various reports of results of "Project Outcomes," Air Force Office of Scientific Research, Contract AF49(688)-1116 (Washington, D. C., 1960–1962).

[26] R. Bower, A. D. Biderman, and A. Richardson, "Consistency and Inconsistency in Retrospection," a paper read at the 1961 Annual Meeting of The American Association for Public Opinion Research (Washington, D. C.: Bureau of Social Science Research, Inc.).

[27] I. L. Janis, A. Lumsdaine, and A. I. Gladstone, "Effects of Preparatory Communications on Reactions to a Subsequent News Event," *The Public Opinion Quarterly*, 15 (1951), 487–518.

[28] D. N. Michael, *Proposed Studies on the Implication of Peaceful Space Activities for Human Affairs*, report of the Committee on Science and Astronautics, U.S. House of Representatives, 87th Congress, first session (Washington, D. C.: U.S. Government Printing Office, March 24, 1961).

argument against ill-prepared summit meetings because they lead to exaggerated public expectations and radical "let downs" if major agreements are not reached.

Persons with initially favorable expectations tend frequently to attach more favorable interpretations to events that turn out unfavorably than do those who had initially unfavorable expectations. The limits and qualifications of this generalization, and its specific relevance to the expectations and reactions to space events, might be one useful focus of study. Toch, for instance, has drawn many illustrations to show that extensive ideological re-evaluation occurs in events that a person experiences *as a crisis.*[29] The process of re-evaluation itself, however, includes efforts to salvage as much as possible of prior beliefs and also the total rejection of beliefs that have proved to be in error and that may in fact have led to damaging action. Thus studies by the Allies of the attitudes of Germans after the collapse of Nazism found that those who made frequent use of the catch phrase of the time — *"belogen und betrogen"* (essentially "We were lied to and deceived") — tended to be persons who clung to much of the ideology of Nazism.

Impromptu Studies.   There is no need to dwell on the desirability of well-planned *before-during-after* studies. The major burdens of this chapter are to present some indications of the feasibility of such studies, even when the events in question are in some sense or in some degree unanticipated.

It is first of all apparent that, as in the case of Sputnik I, we could frequently have foreseen the occurrence and research significance of events that have been the subject of intensive, impromptu study. As an example, there are the illuminating studies about the functions of the press that have been made where and when strikes have deprived the public of their newspapers for a period.[30] These studies have only been undertaken after the strike has been underway for some time. The studies have been carried out on an impromptu basis. Yet, the newspaper strike is a recurrent phenomenon in the U.S.A. A social scientist wishing to test hypotheses against an event of this class would have to wait at most a few years to have available to him a large city somewhere in the United States with a newspaper blackout. And he could narrow down the possibilities as

[29] H. H. Toch, "Crisis Situations and Ideological Re-Evaluation," *The Public Opinion Quarterly, 19* (1955), 53–67.

[30] B. Berelson, "What Missing the Newspaper Means," in P. F. Lazarsfeld and F. N. Stanton, eds., *Communications Research* (New York: Harper & Brothers, 1949), pp. 111–129.

to the time and place through knowledge of existing labor relations and contracts in different geographical areas. Yet, a replication of Berelson's study made thirteen years later was not begun until the eighth day of the second New York City newspaper strike of recent years.[31]

Disaster Studies.   One class of events has been attacked on the basis of the knowledge that events of the type sought for study would occur frequently, although the specific nature, place, and time could not be predicted. I refer to the studies of domestic disasters carried out for the Army Chemical Center by contract with the National Opinion Research Center (NORC).[32] The innovations of stand-by research capabilities in this instance are attributable to certain characteristics of the interests of the research client; the nature of the event; and, most of all, the frequency with which disasters occur — although at imperfectly predictable times and places. Despite these distinctive features of the case of disaster studies, it nonetheless offers instructive precedents for the present case.

A noteworthy aspect of the disaster study case was the interest in the events *per se,* as opposed to the newspaper strike case mentioned earlier where the interest in the event lay in the opportunity it presented for learning about the role that newspapers played when they were present. For the client of the NORC studies, disasters presented a direct analogy to the potential war-caused devastation in which the Army Chemical Center was interested.

The types of studies we have discussed were similar to each other in that the events to be studied were approached with fairly definite interests. This is not to say that unanticipated aspects of these situations did not excite research interest — for example, the "convergence behavior" that became a key topic of analysis in the disaster field.[33]

Need for Specification of Research Interests

Another type of problem arises in making preparations to study the impact of events on the public when it can be predicted that a certain event is likely to be at the focus of public attention, but when little can be predicted about what specific aspects of the

---

[31] Lazarsfeld and Stanton, eds., *op. cit.;* P. Kimball, "People without Newspapers," *The Public Opinion Quarterly,* 23 (1959), 389–398.

[32] *Human Reactions in Disaster Situations* (Chicago, Ill.: NORC, University of Chicago, June 1954).

[33] C. E. Fritz and H. H. Mathewson, *Convergence Behavior in Disasters: A Problem in Social Control* (Washington, D. C.: National Academy of Sciences–National Research Council, 1957).

event may have great impact or when inaccurate predictions are made. As a possible example, we can consider researchers planning to study a summit meeting at which international space cooperation is to be discussed. An unanticipated spectacular proposal by one side or a dramatic success or catastrophe in some related field could come to dominate the "news" of the event. In such an instance the decision as to what event to study, and when and where to study it, can be planned in detail.

However, the plans as to which aspect of the event to study must be kept flexible. Events are in the habit of being fickle. The present writer took part in some stand-by planning to study the impact of an anticipated surge in the retirement of career military personnel on the twentieth anniversary of World War II. The anniversary year when a large section of the "Class of 1941" became eligible for retirement arrived, but the Berlin crisis and restrictions on retirements from the armed forces came with it. The recognition that the date would be a significant one for research remained valid, however, but the research for which it proved to offer an unusual opportunity was a study of how compulsory retention affected those who planned to "get out," rather than of the predicted large-scale retirement. An important point, however, is that the same kinds of baseline data would have been relevant both to the anticipated occurrence and to the important questions that were posed by its not occurring.[34]

Chart 4.1 may clarify the relevance for stand-by research planning of the two aspects of predictability we have discussed in the foregoing illustrations:

1. The predictability of the time of occurrence of an event calling for research.

2. The predictability of what will be the aspects of the event that are significant for research.

The chart provides a rough guideline for one step in the over-all planning of a program of *before-during-after* studies of significant space events. In this step, the attempt would be made to consider all available anticipations, prognostications, and hunches about possible events in space during, say, the next ten years, in terms of the two dimensions of the chart.

[34] A. D. Biderman, *Needs for Knowledge Regarding the Military Retirement Problem,* summary report of a conference held in Washington, D. C., April 30–May 1, 1960 (Washington, D. C.: Bureau of Social Science Research, Inc., December 1, 1960); and "The Prospective Impact of Large-Scale Military Retirement," *Social Problems,* 7 (1959), 84–90.

Predictability of time of occurrence	Predictability of What Will Be Aspects of Event Significant For Research		
	Significant Aspects Foreseeable	Some Significant Aspects Foreseeable, Some Not	Significant Aspects Not Foreseeable
Definite prediction for specific date	A		D
Contingent prediction for specific date : definite prediction for gross time interval			
Specifically unpredictable, but high probability	C¹		C²
Specifically unpredictable, significant possibility			
Improbabilities and completely unanticipated events		B	

Chart 4.1.   Predictability of events and stand-by research planning.

Type of provision for research: A, conventionally planned and executed "before-after" research; B, impromptu research: formulation in advance of general hypotheses and procedures, mechanisms for prompt funding; C¹, anticipatory studies and stand-by capability for "during" field work; C², anticipatory research planning and field work capabilities; D, versatile research planning capability and stand-by field work capabilities.

Conventional Studies.   Certain events would fall in the upper left-hand area of the chart, in that research planning would relate to a well-defined research interest in events whose occurrence could be definitely anticipated for a given date, and where the interesting aspects of the events could be foreseen. An example would have been the first Telstar TV tests. With respect to problems that fall in this area (A), conventionally planned *before-after* studies are indicated, with priorities determined by the importance of the research questions and the opportunities expected to be inherent in the event. Research in this area of the chart is not the central concern of the present chapter. In over-all research planning and allocations, it is desirable to consider studies that do permit more conventional planning in relation to the needs and opportunities for research on events that fall in other areas of the chart. A large number of evaluation studies of staged and scheduled events provide models here.

However, such studies are routine and do not pose the demands for a stand-by facility and for planning that characterizes studies in the shaded areas.

Events that are considered to be in one part of the chart when research is planned may actually transpire to be in some other area. For example, a research planned for the ill-fated Eisenhower-Khrushchev Paris summit meeting might well have neglected to make provision for pertinent study of the "blow-up" of that meeting. Thus at the time of planning a research study, when both the event and its significant aspects would seem to be quite predictable, some new unsuspected aspect might exhibit itself. Hence, even a conventional *before-after* study should be designed for flexible adaptation.

Anticipatory research — the *before* part of the *before-after* design — or even specific planning for predictions of events that fall at the bottom of the chart (area *B*), and particularly in the lower right corner, are ruled out by the low probability that the research will ever be consummated. When surprising events occur, research must be on an impromptu basis, as, for example, in the celebrated "Invasion from Mars" study by Cantril and others.[35]

Contingency Planning. While it is unwise to make specific plans for exceedingly low probability events, and impossible to plan for completely unforeseen ones, the experience of social science has shown the value of contingency planning. It is both possible and advantageous to plan on the basis of the recognition that impromptu studies are a recurrent need. General requirements for such studies can be anticipated even without advance knowledge of the particular demands.

A primitive but critical need for any study of scope is financing. *Concern for stand-by research possibilities will prove well worth while if it does no more than provide a mechanism whereby funds can be committed instantly to carry out a study of unanticipated events.*

That social scientists are frequently unable to forecast the occurrence of specific events that prove to be fruitful objects of study does not mean that more elaborate planning of impromptu research is not feasible. Both the general requirements of research and the general hypotheses we seek to test against specific events or types of events, if they should occur, provide bases for fairly detailed and advantageous advance planning for even the most impromptu efforts. As a matter of fact, this form of contingency planning, if properly done, demands more elaborate preparation than does planning for research on specifically predictable events.

The NORC plan for the study of disasters, which I mentioned earlier in this chapter, although addressed to a more limited class of events and more specifiable forms of research on them, well illustrates ways in which general methodological requirements are translatable into specific plans for research on an event when its specific time, place, and nature are not known. Such planning in the case of the NORC studies made possible both rapid implementation of

[35] H. Cantril, Hazel Gaudet, and Herta Herzog, *The Invasion from Mars* (Princeton, N.J.: Princeton University Press, 1940).

research and a far higher degree of rigor than would have been achieved in completely unplanned impromptu studies. Thus a division of labor and specification of duties among four members of the research team was prearranged so that various administrative and data-collecting steps of survey research that would ordinarily take place serially could take place concurrently (see Table 4.1, taken from the NORC report).

Much of the ability of the NORC researchers to preplan their studies rested, in turn, on their ability to take what were specific interests of the client and translate them into a limited number of general hypotheses concerning behavior in crises. The subjects of these hypotheses were the following:

1. The reduction and control of panic reactions.
2. Organization and effective leadership.
3. The elimination of confusion.
4. The securing of conformity to emergency regulations.
5. The minimization of discomfort.
6. The maintenance of public morale.
7. Rapid reconstruction.[36]

The formulation of these statements specified criteria for suitable situations for study, and for the aspects within these situations that it would be relevant to study.

This degree of explication and prediction of the kinds of events to be studied made it possible to construct in advance broadly applicable sampling designs, interview schedules, and questionnaires. The NORC group was dealing with problems falling in the central, left-hand areas C^1 and C^2 of Chart 4.1.

The more precisely the social scientist can identify the purpose for studying a particular kind of event, the more capable he will be of carrying out studies immediately when and where the event occurs. Thus the well-defined interests of civil defense in warning systems led to three partially replicating studies of accidental soundings of air-raid sirens, summarized by Mack and Baker.[37]

Before going on to problems in this planning region, certain additional observations should be made about impromptu studies that are shown in area B of Chart 4.1.

Budget Bureau Approval. There is an administrative matter

[36] National Opinion Research Center, *op. cit.*, pp. 196–197.
[37] R. W. Mack and G. W. Baker, *The Occasion Instant: The Structure of Social Responses to Unanticipated Air Raid Warnings* (Washington, D. C.: National Academy of Sciences–National Research Council, 1961).

TABLE 4.1
NORC PLAN FOR DISASTER STUDY FIELD PROCEDURES
Time Schedule and Procedures in Field

Day	Field Director	First Assistant	Second Assistant	Two Chief Interviewers
1	Makes local arrangements, rents office space, begins informal background interviews with community leaders	Begins design of sample	Begins recruitment of supplementary interviewers	Begin informal exploratory interviewing
2	Continues background interviewing	**Continues design of sample**	Continues recruitment	Continue exploratory interviewing
3	Trains pretesters, pretesting begins	**Trains listers; listing begins**	Continues recruitment	Assist in training pretesters, pretesting
4	Continues background interviewing	**Block selection completed; listing sheets prepared**	**Continues recruitment, has recruited sufficient interviewers for listing and pretesting purposes which begin the 4th day**	Continue exploratory interviewing
5	Pretesting continues	Listing continues	**Continues recruitment**	Continue pretesting
6	Pretesting continues	Listing completed; selects sample of dwelling units, begins transcription to enumeration sheets	**Continues recruitment**	Continue pretesting

TABLE 4.1 (Continued)

Day	Field Director	First Assistant	Second Assistant	Two Chief Interviewers
7	Pretesting completed; revises questionnaire, arranges printing of questionnaire and other forms	Completes transcription, prepares individual interviewer assignments	Continues recruitment	Complete pretesting
8	Begins final training	Assists in final training	Assists in final training	Assist in final training
9	Completes final training	Assists in final training	Assists in final training	Assist in final training
10–16: primary interviewing period	Supervision of 27 interviewers, each with quota of 15 interviews	Assists in supervision, continues background interviews	Assists in supervision, continues background interviews	Interview main sample along with staff of 25 interviewers
17–21: clean-up interviewing	Supervision, interviews "hard-to-get" cases, completes background interview	Interviews "hard-to-get" cases, completes background interviewing	Interviews "hard-to-get" cases, completes background interviewing	Interview "hard-to-get" cases

Source: National Opinion Research Center, *Human Reactions in Disaster Situations* (Chicago, Ill.: NORC, University of Chicago, 1954), Appendix A-9, p. 202.

relating to impromptu research undertaken by or for the federal government that must be mentioned first because of its absolutely crucial importance. Possibly, one fact that lead the NORC group to construct their sample design, schedules, and questionnaires in advance was the legal requirement of approval of these by the Bureau of the Budget. Where research on a fast-breaking event has to be done with speed by a federal agency or contractor, the accomplishment of this step after the event may prove impossible in the required time. Consequently, approval by the Bureau of the Budget of a plan for interviewing work is needed even in the case of events that prove to fall in the unanticipatable area *B* of Chart 4.1. This is particularly difficult in the right-hand side of this area, since the specific aspects of the event that will be of interest cannot be foreseen. Because of this, it becomes proportionately more difficult to prepare a questionnaire in advance. *Several* forms may be necessary to provide for a range of contingencies. (Similar administrative difficulties may sometimes arise in research under nongovernmental sponsorship.)

Need for Specification of General Interests

The possible answer to this problem and to the entire question of the feasibility of that seemingly contradictory operation — well-planned, impromptu research — lies in the social scientist being able to spell out what he wants to learn and what kinds of data will provide answers to these questions, even when he is not quite sure what specific types of opportunities will present themselves for developing the data.

The chart on predictability has been constructed, however, to emphasize the limitations in making such definitions. Much of the importance attached to impromptu studies for social science has stemmed from the very fact that researchers do not come to formulate many critical questions until events have rubbed their noses in them. Even if certain questions have previously been of scientific concern, they may be reminded of them only by the press of events.

As an illustration from my own recent experience, the formulation of questions about "sensory deprivation" re-emerged from the Korean War "brainwashing" events, as it had in earlier forms during agitation for penal reform (controversy regarding solitary confinement) in the early nineteenth century and during the period of arctic exploration early in this century. It is my feeling that we are not sufficiently well along in understanding what will be the key questions that we shall eventually be concerned with.

We need to recognize that in the past impromptu research studies have made frequent and important contributions to our knowledge. It has also been true that hindrances to getting such studies "off the ground" have thwarted many other opportunities to make significant contributions. A quick response is vital.

Planning Capability. As we consider events of greater probability than those shown in area *B* of the chart, but regarding which the nature of our research interests lack definition, we begin to enter the zone that curves upward through the chart. Here, stand-by provisions for specific research studies become feasible. Let us assume that the exhibit represents a ten-year planning period. We can then consider as an example research on reactions to an announcement by another country, say Sweden or China, of the discovery of a completely new scientific principle — one that, among other things, will quickly render obsolescent much of the capital investment in rocketry of the United States and the U.S.S.R. (We must assume, further, that such an event could actually have been accepted as a significant possibility for the ten-year interval in the original stand-by research planning step.)

Given the number of ramifications of such an event and the low probability that would have been attached to its occurring, advance planning for research on just this particular event could not have been undertaken previously. General classes of phenomena could have been considered in advance, however, that would be present in this event — for instance, the attaining of significant roles in space by minor powers, developments rendering obsolete vast space investments, public reaction to a sudden drop in America's relative power, and so on.

Research planning that considered potential implications of such developments, and that was oriented toward more detailed planning of research on specific events when they occurred, would presumably be an improvement over completely impromptu responses to the occurrence. A further gain would follow if the group doing this planning had given consideration to the resources available — on a global basis — for carrying out studies of various types.

At the upper right hand of the chart (area *D*) definitely scheduled events are indicated, the impact of which cannot be sufficiently well foreseen to determine definitely whether or not they will be of research interest or what the nature of this interest will be. The case of the summit conference mentioned earlier illustrates an event that social scientists can anticipate will get great public attention, but that suddenly presents an unpredicted, and unpredictable, potential as a research subject. In such cases, where the event is inherently important and presents an unforeseen research opportunity, a versatile research planning capability and staff for field work might be put on an "alert status."

Field-Work Capability. The areas discussed thus far are peripheral to, but convergent on, the subject of this chapter. The major attention, and the major priorities for a program for stand-by research capabilities, should center in the area in which (1) we have fairly definite anticipations that an event may occur within a time period for which we are planning but are uncertain as to precisely when within that period it will occur, and (2) where there are highly significant, well-defined research interests in the event. For work on such problems, the creation of an actual stand-by capability for field work and the detailed planning of alternate approaches are feasible. In the areas (C^1 and C^2) of greatest predictability and determinancy on the chart, anticipatory *before* studies can be undertaken.

We can readily imagine that a "total system" designed to meet all the demands that we might conceive of would be vastly expensive. Our purpose, at this point, is to explore the possibility of more economical arrangements.

Much of what we have learned about the dynamics of reactions to dramatic events has come from the fortuitous opportunities that have been seized by researchers who have been studying particular groups over long periods of time. As an example, where researchers have been making systematic observations of an entire community over a long period of time, they have been in a position to observe reactions in the community when dramatic local political issues happened to arise.[38]

It might be feasible to establish elaborate base-line information and intensive monitorship of several communities specially designed as laboratory communities for the sole purpose of studying their reactions to space events as they occur. They could be communities in which studies have already been made, and these facilities could also be used for the study of reactions to events associated with programs other than the space program.

The NASA grant to the American Academy may possibly be

---

[38] See, for example, A. J. Vidich and J. Bensman, *Small Town in Mass Society: Class, Power and Religion in a Rural Community* (Garden City, N.Y.: Anchor Books, Doubleday & Company, Inc., 1960); and W. L. Warner, *The Living and the Dead: A Study of the Symbolic Life of Americans* (New Haven, Conn.: Yale University Press, 1959).

precedent-making to the extent that it is directed toward consideration of a thorough method of information feedback regarding the social consequences of its program. *It is questionable whether the research demands for pursuing objectives of such scope can be supported by research resources directed solely to the space program, however. It seems rather the case that integration, with work directed toward other objectives having requirements for similar surveys and analyses, would be required.*

Economical Arrangements. Unfortunately, there is a deficiency in the mechanisms that exist for pooling a variety of research interests — and the financial means associated with them — into cost-saving studies pursuing joint objectives, such as, for example, the research the Census Bureau does for work employing economic and demographic data. The public opinion and market research organizations, with national corps of interviewers and preselected samples, offer a partial solution through the incorporation of items for various clients into their regularly conducted polls.

Many of the kinds of data discussed in this chapter can be developed by using the resources of large polling organizations. Through their preselected samples and panels, existing interviewing staffs, and so forth, they offer many potentialities for meeting the requirements for rapidity that have been outlined here. Further, their continued repetition of a number of basic questions relating to attitudes toward current affairs has provided a regularly used, fortuitous index of the impact of unanticipated events.[39]

These advantages of the large polls have been acquired by adherence to one limited method. The methodologies and regular resources of polling organizations will often be inappropriate to NASA objectives. Populations, samples, and observational procedures quite often different from those of conventional surveys will be required.

While other organizations may have equivalent interest in the development of essentially identical stand-by field capabilities — for example, the continuing interest that exists in the study of reactions to disasters and traumatic information — it may be more feasible at the present time to carry out a pilot attempt directed at one problem area than to pursue the difficult administrative task of attempting to coordinate several such interests.

The outlines of a possible pilot project are included in the next section of this chapter.

Priority Considerations. A final decision on a specific program

[39] See, for example, G. A. Almond, "Public Opinion and the Development of Space Technology," *The Public Opinion Quarterly*, 24 (1960), 553–572.

should be made, however, on the basis of a considered review of the priorities for various kinds of knowledge regarding reactions to space events and should also include consideration of the likelihood of particular developments taking place.

I have refrained from elaborating my conjectures on what might be NASA's interests in reactions to, and behavior concerning, space events, and on which domestic and foreign publics might be relevant. Without specification of the nature of the questions that would be posed as events occur, I can give only an abstract and sketchy treatment to the research suggested in this chapter. I feel it is preferable to indicate the needs and opportunities at this general level rather than to burden the treatment with what might be ill-considered speculations regarding the importance of various questions to the Space Agency. But systematic consideration of priorities among possible targets for stand-by research capabilities is an initial step in the work suggested here.

In general, it cannot be stressed too strongly that institutional factors are the major reasons for the neglect of fruitful anticipatory studies rather than the inability to foresee the future targets that are deserving of our research attention.

The Proposal

My ideal for a pilot study is that it should be highly specific, low in risk, and promise a quick and definite result. This should minimize institutional difficulties. Anticipatory studies and stand-by research planning on the other hand, by virtue of being addressed to future problems, cannot be as fully defined in advance. This is because these involve greater degrees of risk and entail a deferred consummation of the interest motivating them. They are essential, however, if our natural and social experiences are to be exploited as natural and social experiments.

An Illustrative Pilot Project

A useful pilot study would undertake work relating to three or four specific, prospective developments in space. It would undertake to investigate both the responses specific to these events — the definitions that come to be attached to them by the public studied — and their impact on a number of general attitudes that may be of interest to NASA. Such attitudes may be the salience attached to space by various publics in their consideration of contemporary affairs, attitudes of optimism and pessimism with respect to future space events, and East-West competition in space.

By incorporating into its planning procedure various general questions concerning space reactions and by establishing a mechanism capable of quickly executing field research, the project would also be prepared to undertake investigations of events that are not anticipated to occur during the study period.

It would be desirable to gain experience in the pilot project with studies involving the following different types of samples:

1. A participant public, such as the staff of NASA headquarters, a space installation, or a large space contractor.

2. A national cross-sectional sample.

3. A multinational comparative sample.

In all cases a six-cell panel approach would be used.[40] In the case of the national sample, a complete panel design would be too elaborate for the pilot phase: it would be preferable for the moment to purchase the inclusion of rider questions for a large-scale sample and to check on these by a more intensive study of a small number of panels. It would probably be advisable to select somewhat different anticipated events as the foci for each of these studies.

Prediction Phase. An initial step of the pilot study would involve a detailed consideration of developments in space that have a reasonably high chance of occurring during the study period (one year to eighteen months). In coordination with representatives of NASA and other informed persons, the researchers would explore the significance of potential reactions to space developments and thus provide final criteria for selecting the problems to be included in the planned study.

In advance of such a step, only illustrative suggestions can be given as to the kinds of events that might figure in the actual studies. As will be noted, different degrees of specification will be possible among the various classes of events that may be selected. Consider:

1. Tiros' contribution to avoiding the impact of a weather disaster.[41]

[40] See S. L. Payne, "The Ideal Model for Controlled Experiments," *The Public Opinion Quarterly, 15* (1951), 557–562.

[41] The original draft of this chapter was submitted to the Committee by the author on July 30, 1962. Only editorial revisions have subsequently been made. It is noteworthy that subsequent to the preparation of the chapter several occurrences have taken place of the specific types of events used as illustrations in the original draft. The following are examples: controversy over inadequate weather warnings in Florida hurricanes (1963), cf. p. 34; the sudden death of a President (1963), cf. p. 9; a prolonged New York newspaper strike (1962–

2. The striking of a populated place by a missile fragment.

3. Announcement of a revolutionary breakthrough in space technology.

4. A report of injury or death of an astronaut as a result of a manned space attempt.

5. Success against odds in a manned space flight.

6. Indications of a radical shift of public mood toward the space programs.

7. A discovery of an unanticipated natural barrier to projected space accomplishments.

8. A successful planetary reconnaissance.

9. Report of a confirmation of extraterrestrial life.

Suggestions of Kaplan, Skogstad, and Girschick[42] regarding the evaluation and the improvement in accuracy of predictions of social and technological events will be followed here. In particular, their finding is relevant that predictions have greater accuracy if made in a group rather than individually.

Research Staff. The demands of the proposed work call for a combination of (1) sophisticated and specific planning of instruments and research resources and (2) rapid, versatile adaptability of these to accommodate unanticipated developments and to profit from specific knowledge as it becomes available. The research director should be assigned the responsibility of developing a study planning group and field staff prepared to undertake the required data-collection work. They must be prepared in two senses:

1. They must be made fully conversant with a number of contingent study plans.

2. They must be willing and able to free themselves on brief notice — within hours — to undertake the research work that will be required.

In the preparation of study designs, and the development of the research instruments and procedures, consideration must be given both to the specifically predicted events and to the tapping of infor-

---

1963), cf. p. 17; Chinese Communist testing of a nuclear device (1964), cf. p. 15; the Beatles (1963–1964), cf. p. 11. When the draft was mimeographed by the Committee just a few weeks later, the editor felt it necessary to add a footnote to the first page to explain that the manuscript had been prepared before the Cuban missile crisis.

These instances are mentioned not to suggest that the writer of the chapter possesses any particular prescience but to illustrate the feasibility of the kind of anticipatory research planning recommended.

[42] *Op. cit.*

mation relating to broad interests of NASA and other agencies in public reactions to space events.

The commissioned research organization should be able to make modifications in preplanned instruments and procedures and to communicate these to field associates within twenty-four hours after a study has been initiated (for some events, even more rapid initiation of the research work would be desirable).

To meet these requirements, the grant should be made to an organization whose staff includes professional social scientists interested in, and capable of, performing the key research planning and adapting tasks as required. Having a nucleus of skilled persons fully "read in" on the study is necessary to ensure the constant availability of professional staff to modify and direct the execution of the field study. The grantee should agree to have staff members available and to release these members from other duties to meet the needs previously described for a stand-by research planning capability. Estimates here are that a minimum of three professional social scientists would have to participate in any of the studies conducted by the project.

Preparatory Work. The grantee would prepare a research design and operational plan — oriented to selected, specifically predicted events and toward certain general hypotheses regarding reactions that might be tested against less well-anticipated events should they also occur. In advance of the occurrence of these project events, the grantee should carry through as much as would be practical of the following steps of the research:

1. The specification of hypotheses.

2. Design of a basic interview schedule and specification of procedures, along with schedules and plans for collecting other documentary and observational data.

3. The design and selection of panel samples.

4. The selection and training of interviewers and observers, and their organization for rapid performance of the several research and administrative steps required for *during* and *after* studies.

5. The pretesting and revising of schedules.

6. The development of base-line data from pre-event interviews and observations.

The grantee would also arrange for the incorporation of selected base-line items in national — and, if desired, international — public opinion polls. The organization would also review recently completed research and studies in progress that might provide additional base-line information.

Similar steps would also be taken with respect to a panel for a study of a participant public.

Field Associates. For a multinational comparative sample and for supplementary national panel studies, the project research organization would establish working arrangements with colleagues at approximately six domestic and six foreign universities or research centers. These field associates would be selected to provide a range of communities appropriate to the objectives of the research. They would be responsible for local planning and administrative arrangements for the studies, and for selecting and training pretest and stand-by research personnel for the desired studies in their localities. Each associate would also delegate and brief an alternate so that at all times there would be someone in the locality capable of directing an immediate field study on request. Each field associate would employ from three to five regular interviewer-observers.

Ideally, field associates would participate in a series of planning and training sessions to develop high uniformity of operational procedures, although this step could be undertaken by the preparation of detailed manuals and by subsequent correspondence.

The feasibility of conducting cross-national research on this basis, and the development of highly detailed specifications of survey research procedures for application in a multinational study are illustrated by a joint project of the Agency for International Development and a number of aid-recipient governments.[43]

These multinational stand-by capabilities would be available to conduct field research both on the occurrence of events for which specific pretest preparations had been made and for impromptu studies on the occurrence of unforeseen events. In either case, field work would be initiated on agreement of the grantee and grantor, with either party permitted to suggest the importance of undertaking a specific study. Flexibility would exist due to the fact that only some of the various cooperating associates might be asked to make observations using their panels on any given occasion. Furthermore, the sample sizes might be increased or decreased, depending on the scope of the particular event.

Cost Estimates.[44] An estimate of the cost of organizing the capability for research that has been discussed and for carrying out the

[43] See Bureau of Social Science Research, *Survey Guidelines: Evaluation of Participant Training Program* (Washington, D. C.: International Cooperation Administration, 1960).

[44] The original estimates made in 1962 were $45,000–$60,000. We have adjusted the figures to correspond to an increase in costs used by the Bureau of Social Science Research in 1965.

studies described through the administration and tabulation of pre-test data would be $55,000–$70,000. This would provide *before* data on approximately 800 domestic and 650 foreign cases, some basic national poll items, and a participant public *before* study including approximately 125 cases.

The stand-by field associates would have a presumed combined capability of conducting about 125 domestic and 125 foreign interviews per day on the initiation of a follow-up or impromptu field study. The panel designs would presume four-day studies as a minimum. For events requiring more rapid surveys, it would be necessary to sacrifice some of the quality obtainable from interviewers previously trained for the procedures of the specific survey, but the field associates would be capable of recruiting quickly an augmented interviewing staff. Costs of field studies of specific dramatic events would range from $5,000 to $25,000, depending on the scope of the questions and the detail of analysis that might be desired.

It is estimated that a total grant of approximately $75,000 would be a minimum cost requirement for an adequate pilot trial of the proposed stand-by research capability.

The Question

In addition to presenting in this chapter a general discussion of the need for, and nature of, stand-by research capabilities for the evaluation of a program such as space exploration, I have included an illustrative proposal for pilot research so that the reader might envisage more concretely what would be involved in terms of activity and expense.

I anticipate that the reader's reaction will be a function of his expectations. If he has been associated with research and development activities and puts a high value on the type of information that such stand-by facilities can supply, he will — almost by definition — regard the effort and cost of at least some pilot research as trivial. At the other end of the continuum, there are some persons whose reaction will be something along the lines of "A minimum of $75,000 is a pretty steep price to pay for a fishing expedition." It will be no surprise that my sympathies are more with the first reaction than with the second.

The thrust of my suggestion is that by greater exercise of such limited prevision as we do have, we may check the presumption of foreknowledge that is inherent in much systematic social observation at the present time. Our ability to guide the future of the society, I believe, will be dependent upon making our provisions for social observation more sensitive to the unfolding course of events. I have proposed a modest pilot application of this view in the context of charting the impact of space technology on society. The procedures I have outlined are not especially novel. In the main, the various steps suggested in this chapter have been tried, and many have been proved in other contexts. I have attempted to bring a number of these together in order to highlight the general need for anticipatory studies and stand-by research capabilities to evaluate the impact of programs, policies, and institutions on society.

Whether the candle is worth the cost in this instance is dependent upon how we answer the larger question posed by this book: How seriously do we want to understand the full consequences of what we are doing?

5

Problems of Organizational
Feedback Processes[1]

Robert A. Rosenthal and Robert S. Weiss

Introduction

Feedback refers to the total information process through which primary and second-order effects of organizational actions are fed back to the organization and compared with desired performance. In order to point up the importance of feedback systems to the survival, conservation, and effective functioning of organizations, let us examine an example of the origins and costs of an inadequate feedback system.

In a period of crisis, the top executives of a large automobile company try to pinpoint the source of their troubles within one of their plants. They are unwilling, however, to question the decision that created the original difficulties, a decision made by them, against the advice of their own staff men, to shift the plant precipitously to the production of a new type of eight-cylinder engine. Because of their strong commitment to this decision, made in the face of contrary advice, they reject information that suggests that problems in the plant are due to the confusion caused by the hasty switch, the ill-prepared introduction of automation, and the breaking up of well-established work teams through transfers within the plant. In short, some "other" explanation must be found. The executives decide the problem is an inefficient work force.

A new plant manager is called in to return the plant to efficient operation. The new manager, under considerable pressure from above to increase production quickly, misinterprets the usual expressions of discontent and wariness that follow a managerial shake-up. He becomes convinced, not without some justification, that his

[1] The authors of this chapter have drawn in part on an unpublished essay, "Feedback in the Bureaucratic Organization," by Victor A. Thompson, which represents one of the few extensive inquiries into this area.

staff and line employees resent the loss of their previous boss whom, as it happened, they had esteemed highly. He concludes further that they are malingering because of this resentment.

Subordinate executives who try to explain the situation to him are accused of being too sympathetic to the workers, unwilling to accept the need for increased production, and of being disloyal to the company. They are transferred to other plants, and new subordinates who share his viewpoint are brought in. Production continues to decrease, confirming his suspicion that there is collusion among line workers to interfere with the adoption of needed reforms.

To support his hunch, he establishes an intelligence network, which accurately feeds back to him expressions of discontent throughout the plant. He now has a great deal of feedback, but he uses it only to learn who is "for" him and who is "against" him. He now begins to transfer to other plants the workers he considers to be the ringleaders of the resistance. This disrupts further the positive interpersonal bonds necessary for work-group effectiveness.

At the end of a two-year period none of the original work groups remain intact, production has diminished further, employees at all levels fear demotion or transfer, and top executives are irked at the failure of a man they had considered to be one of their most promising young managers. Though the plant manager has been without a vacation for over a year and shows the effects of great physical strain, his doctor's request that he be permitted immediate leave is not granted since management feels that he has been lax in his administration. Consequently, the plant manager takes unauthorized leave, is hired by another company, and is soon doing superbly in a well-established plant.

The top management of his former company remains convinced, despite all indications to the contrary, that both staff and line employees in the plant are for unexplained reasons incorrigible.

At every stage in this unfortunate sequence of events, a failure properly to elicit and evaluate feedback information resulted in further worsening of the situation. To some extent the failure can be ascribed to a forward inertia that sometimes afflicts large organizations. This expresses itself in the maintenance of programs despite clear indication that revised goals are in order, because reputations in the company have been staked — or are thought to have been staked — on their correctness.

The commitment to a program led in turn to a distrust of any analyses of the plant's difficulties that questioned the program. The decision to appoint a new manager in a crisis atmosphere could only be supported by top management's rejection of the previous plant manager's analysis of the problem. This would not have been possible if top management had not also failed to respect the reactions of other plant personnel. In spite of the fact that feedback, sought and unsought, was plentiful, neither the corporate executives nor the new plant manager could break away from their preconceptions and role pressures long enough to treat a case of snowballing deafness.

Because this case contains many instances in which the information was available, in fact clamoring for attention, it illustrates not only the value of an adequate informational system but the organizational obstacles to its utilization. The example is atypical, fortunately, but its contours suggest some of the problems likely to be encountered as organizations — governmental, industrial, or social — try to evaluate their actions by reference to their effects.

In this chapter we shall deal with problems of feedback under these topic headings:

> Feedback and organizational survival
> Estimating feedback requirements
> Feedback from external sources
> Feedback from internal sources
> Feedback and its effects on policy
> Dangers of organizational feedback
> Research in maintaining feedback

Our major emphasis in this chapter will be to analyze the kinds of difficulties to which organizational feedback systems are prone, and to suggest an approach to their remedy. In the course of our discussion, we shall, when possible, apply our more general treatment of feedback to those problems that might be faced by NASA in implementing its concern with the secondary consequences of the space effort.

Feedback and Organizational Survival

The survival of an organization indicates a feedback process of at least minimal effectiveness. The feedback associated with bare survival has, however, a limited quality, involving as it does information gathering in relation to only the most essential of the organization's linkages to its environment.

Feedback for survival ordinarily reflects the reactions of only the organized and politically significant interests. Unorganized or politically insignificant interests are not represented, or else they are ignored. In addition, the organization tends to act on the immediate and apparent (nonrationalized and nonintegrated) responses of these interests to current organizational actions.

Thus it appears that the less obvious, more subtle, and far-reaching second-order effects are not incorporated in the survival feedback process, because they are neither "real" nor urgent. The survival process therefore gives an opportunistic quality to an organization. It also makes the organization appear as though it is easily intimidated by any strong outside force.

Given the nature of survival feedback, the interest of an organization, such as NASA, in a wide range of goals beyond survival, seems to require an independent effort to detect and report on second-order social effects. The whole NASA concern implies the recognition of other, nonprimary, nonpressure, nonaffective goals. Yet recognition and response to goals beyond that of mere survival may, in the short run, multiply survival problems.

Estimating Feedback Requirements

We may apply the term *feedback* equally well to the regular review of sales carried on in a commercial organization, to the monitoring of corporate image that seems to be good practice among the more imaginative of our industries,[2] to governmental subscription to foreign periodicals, and to the informal conversation of executives in social situations. Just as tracer bullets permit accurate aiming of rifles, so an organization requires its own form of feedback in order to direct its policy accurately. But organizations of different kinds at differing stages of development and strength will have vastly different feedback requirements.

Nonbeneficial Circumstances

Are there any rudimentary principles that can aid in the estimation of the amount and kind of feedback an organization may require, or the elaborateness of the feedback network that will serve this purpose? As indicated in the preceding example of the automotive plant, the sheer volume of feedback information useful to organizations (whether evaluated properly or not) is apt to be greatest when organizations are in flux. This generally occurs when

[2] See John W. Riley, Jr., ed., *The Corporation and its Publics* (New York: John Wiley & Sons, Inc., 1963).

1. They are newly established or function in nontraditional areas and ways.

2. They must constantly justify their operation to external groups.

3. They are in crisis (at any stage of development).

4. They have many options in the formulation of goals and the methods of achieving them.

The organization in flux discovers that previously proved measures of its success in fulfilling primary goals often turn out to be inadequate, misleading, and simplistic.

Ubiquitous Unpredictability. Under these conditions, unanticipated consequences are likely to be the rule, rather than the exception. It then becomes imperative that the organization, like the army in strange terrain, send out scouts to reconnoiter. Here we encounter another circumstance affecting the amount of feedback that is necessary: that is, the complexity and predictability of the environment. Consider the organization that not only lacks firm expectations as to the effect of its actions on its environment but cannot determine with any confidence the kinds and likely sources of information it should seek. Such an organization would have to search very widely to locate the information it requires.

Thus we see that, on the one hand, the more complex and unpredictable the environment, the greater the necessity for reconnaissance operations that involve wide scanning of the field. This will be the case for organizations, particularly government agencies such as NASA, which seek to assess the effects of their programs on American society as a whole. On the other hand, if the consequences of a given action are easily predictable, it will be unnecessary to devote much energy to the monitoring of responses to that action. Reactions will be known in advance.

Generally, the consequences of organizational action cannot be assumed to be predictable even when they might seem so. For example, NASA distributed free copies of a pamphlet on "Selected Welding Techniques." This is typical of the kind of organizational action that is described with the words, "It can't do any harm." However, it was entirely conceivable that recipients of the pamphlet had unrealistic expectations as to what they could learn from it. Such unfulfilled expectations have been known to produce disillusionment and negative feelings toward an organization.

In this instance, research conducted by the Committee on Space indicated that the over-all reaction was indeed favorable as intended. However, the fact that there was a small minority of recipients who said they felt less favorably toward the space program as a result of the pamphlet demonstrated that the decision to do the research was warranted. The possibility of unwanted effects did exist.

Illusory Immunity. There are situations in which an organization may appear to be immune to the consequences of its action, yet this appearance is illusory. An instance is the case of monopolies operated or protected by the state — such as utilities. Here the total absence of competition might make positive feedback seem of limited interest and value and thereby reduce the likelihood of its being gathered. However, governmental regulatory bodies would have to show some sensitivity to extensive negative reactions on the part of the public to failures of administration and function of the utility. Hence, information on "customer satisfaction," if not responded to directly, might result in a long-term shift in the relationship of the utility and the regulatory body.

Alternative Actions. Finally, the possibility of alternative lines of action will limit the amount of feedback required. If an organization *must* act, if only one line of action is possible, and if there is no latitude as to how or when the action takes place, then the information fed back concerning the consequences of that act is not likely to produce much, if any, change in organizational behavior.

However, suppose an organization has narrow goals, is absolutely committed to one line of action, occupies an unthreatened position, and possesses accurate knowledge of its environment. Even under such circumstances, it will still ordinarily have a great deal of flexibility regarding the *manner* in which it pursues organizational goals. It will often have to choose from among an alternative set of programs that one — or that combination — which seems to be the most effective program to achieve the desired result. The organization will almost always have the ability to control the pace at which a program is instituted — a range of choice that extends from a crash program introduced at breakneck speed to one slowly and carefully developed from modest beginnings. Realistically, therefore, while some organizations can make use of feedback less well than others, there can be extraordinarily few organizations that cannot make use of feedback at all.

Need for Restraint

While we have thus tried to explore the circumstances under which an organization might not benefit from feedback, these appear to be limiting conditions that do not occur in the real world.

To say that an organization the actions of which produce completely predictable consequences, which is completely immune, and which has no alternatives cannot benefit from feedback is not a discovery but a tautology.

However, there is very real merit in specifying that the further removed an organization's situation is from these ideal conditions, the more value it will derive from feedback. It is perhaps gratuitous to state that the NASA space program is quite far from the ideal circumstance of predictability, immunity, and lack of options. But, to state in quantitative terms that an organization, such as NASA, can benefit from a good deal of — or even complete — feedback still leaves unanswered many questions to which we shall address ourselves.

First, however, let us raise a small warning flag. When discussing feedback, there is a dangerous temptation to regard all blocks to, or failures of, feedback as dysfunctional. However, there are many actions necessary, either for individuals or organizations, that psychologically could not be taken under conditions of complete feedback. Preoccupation with all the potential, or even actual, consequences can paralyze one into inaction precisely when decisive action is most needed. Interdependent functional roles become structured to prevent complete feedback — to limit it to data relevant to specialized functions. In general, the impact of immediate, impulsive, affective-evaluative data must be dampened to enable long-range, integrated goals to be achieved. Within organizations, decision makers must often be protected from this kind of feedback if the primary goals of the organization are to be realized.

NASA's Special Problems

Now, turning our attention back to NASA, we shall look at some of the problems and unanswered questions that organization might face in its concern with the secondary consequences of the space effort.

We see two major problem areas concerning environmental feedback processes and the social-scientific interests of NASA:

1. The effects of feedback from external groups on NASA's functioning as an organization.

2. The difficulties involved in locating, developing, and utilizing social indicators of secondary consequences of the space program.

Both of these problem areas derive from the statement of goals of the study grant awarded to the American Academy of Arts and

Sciences. The areas are summarized in terms of the necessity to study "the relationships of society to efforts of massive technological innovation, with special reference to . . . this civilian space program,"[3] that is, to study the impact of NASA, an organization whose purpose it is to implement certain national goals, on our society in general and on specific groups who are affected by, or may have a special interest in, NASA's activities.

Although it is not our purpose to outline specific research projects, it must be realized that any serious and detailed proposals would have to be based on an analysis of the implicit and explicit goals of NASA in sponsoring such research, and on an estimation of the kind of support and energy that NASA could allocate to the exploration of the second-order consequences of the space program, without interfering with the pursuit of its primary goals.

Likewise, we should have to consider a number of other problems. How would the establishment of a novel research function affect NASA's existing organizational structure; it would, after all, give a previously "alien" group — social scientists — responsibility for formally gathering feedback relevant to secondary consequences. How might research be structured to determine under what conditions such feedback would interfere with the realization of primary goals? What kinds of relationships between researchers and other aspects of the NASA organization would best overcome some of the problems of recruitment, power, and responsibility that, as we shall discuss later, are frequently found arising from the development of marginal and innovative roles associated with an organization? Last, to what extent, and in what areas, is basic research feasible within NASA's governmental charge?

It is considerations of this sort that govern our thinking in the pages that follow.

Feedback from External Sources

The program of a large organization, whether intended or not, is a "broadcast" message; it affects a wide sector of the organization's environment, one much wider than the organization may understand to be its surrounds. Groups that are essential to an organization's continued functioning most likely make themselves

[3] Raymond A. Bauer, "Space Efforts and Society: A Statement of Mission and Work," photoprinted paper, a document of the Committee on Space Efforts and Society of the American Academy of Arts and Sciences (Boston, January 1963), 38 pp.

known. Potential suppliers agree or do not agree to contracts and then are contented or discontented; customers buy or refuse to buy; investors support or refuse to support the organization. Feedback information from groups whose support is essential may come too late, to be sure, if the organization does not make special efforts to get it, but it does come. This is not the case, however, with all affected groups.

Although many of the different parts of the organization's environment will be affected, only some of them will respond directly or spontaneously. Organizations that wish to deal responsibly with their social surrounds must be capable of eliciting and evaluating responses from those who realize they are affected but who are ordinarily silent, and from those who are affected but may not realize it. Referring to the most general, least audible audiences, "the public," Secretary of Labor W. Willard Wirtz describes this problem somewhat pessimistically:

Public opinion is unorganized and unidentified. It is also almost exclusively couched in terms of the settlement of a particular dispute and does not go substantially beyond this. Fifteen years ago, the nation was in an agony of concern about the problems of the coal industry. There was a strong feeling on the part of the coal industry. There was a strong feeling on the part of the public about these problems. But there has been almost no public expression of concern about the problems of labor relations in the coal industry since 1950, the date of the last strike. I do not suggest that there is a reason for concern, but the public does not know whether there is or not. It was concerned when there was the beginning and end of it. I think we fool ourselves when we seem to count on any effective expression of the public interest. . . .[4]

It might be said in passing that these remarks reflect the forces behind the ambivalence with which public opinion polls on controversial issues have been received. On the one hand, the polls might be regarded as a device for giving voice to an inarticulate, but large and important, segment of the public. On the other hand, they might be regarded as a device for bothering public officials with a statement of the interests of that segment of the public that is not likely to help or hinder a program, and that in the absence of poll information could conveniently be ignored.

Functionally Related Groups

We may differentiate groups from which feedback might be

[4] See Edward Reed, ed., *Challenges to Democracy: The Next Ten Years* (New York: Frederick A. Praeger, Inc., 1963), pp. 155–156.

necessary or desired on the basis of their functional relationship with the organization.

Groups that are actually or potentially involved in a direct functional relationship to the organization. These functional-relationship groups can be listed in four separate categories as follows:

1. Consumers, clients, or potential members of these groups: individuals who buy or use the services of the organization, whose response to the organization is a basis for evaluating the success of the service. In this sense, the American public is cast in the role of a client for the broad objectives of the space program. Similarly, the scientific community also is a client for some more specific findings.

2. Superordinate groups, including sponsors, regulatory bodies, and other agencies that have the power to force the organization to change those parts of its program that they consider undesirable. The Congress and the President are the obvious examples.

3. Coordinate groups that have the power to facilitate or inhibit the organization's operations. Real estate boards, professional associations, and citizens' groups might fall into this relevant category. For the space program, the other agencies of the Executive Branch and scientific and professional organizations are relevant.

4. The "supportive environment." An organization requires staff, funds, and sometimes friendly support in the right places in order to keep going. Depending on the nature of the organization, it may be dependent on the educational system to train its staff, on the financial community or the federal government for funds, on community support in acquiring land, and so on. In any event, the view of the organization and its program held by the supportive environment is of great importance to the organization. (The organization may also want broad general support from the public that facilitates the staffing, funding, and administration of its programs.)

Although groups with a direct functional relationship are almost invariably vocal and thus generally easy to identify, an adequate feedback system would not necessarily exaggerate the differences between responders or lump them together. Neither would it overreact to some and underreact to others. It is very easy for a small but determined group to overload an ordinarily "quiet" feedback channel so that the organization feels or fears it is hearing the voice of a multitude. Such has been the strategy of the special-interest group that has been successful in, of all things, keeping Polish hams and Yugoslav anchovies off the American supermarket shelves.

There are a few groups functionally important to the organization who will not make a great effort to communicate back to the organization their response to its programs. One such group, ironically, is the organization's friends. Criticism is more likely to be transmitted than is praise. The organization dependent on Congressional reaction, for example, ought to sound out its friends as well as listen to its enemies. Thus the public welfare agency that finds itself under attack by the press ought to consider how much support its policies have in important groups that are at the moment silent before trying to placate its critics with policy changes. This problem will receive further elaboration in the section on "Feedback from Internal Sources," which discusses feedback and its effects on organizational policies.

Nonfunctionally Related Groups

Groups that are not in a direct functional relationship to the organization. These groupings fall into the following three broad categories:

1. Innocent bystanders, individuals, or other groups not considered by the organization as its prime "target population," but who are, nevertheless, directly affected by it. Examples are the families that must move when a new highway is built; parking-lot attendants who lose their jobs when a new building goes up; and the townspeople whose livelihood is jeopardized when the military or defense industry personnel supporting their small businesses are removed in governmental cost-cutting attempts.

The organization can recognize these individuals, and each one of its personnel who deals with the outside world is likely to be in contact with some of them. Yet, it is difficult to expect a manager, who has been trained in the ideology of loyalty to his organization, to sacrifice organizational goals in any way for the sake of innocent bystanders. Often these groups are seen by the organization as barriers to effective organizational activity; the organization feels it has little or no responsibility for them.

A government organization is in a different situation from a private one in that it has its mandate from the public as a whole. Thus it often has the special and very difficult task of developing awareness of innocent bystanders even though its mandate for action may not make it possible to respond to all the needs embraced by its mandate for concern.

2. The second group of innocent bystanders is affected less directly but no less seriously. Within this group are teenagers whose

inhibitions against violence may be lowered as a result of the aggressive content of current TV programs; community-business elites whose power and status may be threatened by the influx of scientific and engineering personnel in a "space-oriented" community; skilled workers who are "subsidized" in meaningless positions even though their skills have become obsolescent as a result of technological innovations.

3. Finally, there are people who may not be in any way aware of the organization's actions but whose lives are, nevertheless, affected by it. When a university opens a new dormitory, landlords in the area find it harder to rent their rooms.

Indirectly Affected Groups

The examples just mentioned refer to direct effects on individuals who are not in a direct functional relationship to the organization. Additionally, incidental aspects of organizational programs may have effects on individuals and groups whether the affected persons are among the intended or unintended audiences of the organization, or, indeed, whether they are members of the organization itself.

For example, some corporations that revere their pioneer origins and pride themselves on being the last redoubt of individual initiative are, in fact, miniature welfare states wherein even the topmost executives are bound to their jobs by incentive raises, bonus plans, stock options, subsidized vacations, retirement pensions, and other inducements. Many of these people are no longer willing to risk the expression of individual initiative by proposing basic innovations that could conceivably fail.

Such effects that are not directly the consequence of programs may be termed the *second-order consequences* of organizational activity. They can be placed on a continuum ranging from greater or lesser inconveniences to innocent bystanders (sonic boom), to drastic modifications of men's lives (technological obsolescence), and, finally, to widespread societal changes (impact of the developments of railroads on many domains of American public and private life).[5]

Implicit in all these examples are a variety of reasons that make special effort necessary to elicit feedback from the groups that are

[5] See A. D. Chandler, Jr., "New Enterprise and the Evolution of Administrative Practices: The Impact of the Railroads, 1829–1860," in Bruce Mazlish, ed., *The Railroad and the Space Program: An Exploration in Historical Analogy* (Cambridge, Mass.: The M.I.T. Press, 1966), Chapter 5, pp. 127–143.

indirectly affected. Special effort is required partly because these groups are likely to lack power to represent themselves to the organization directly, and partly because they are most likely to be unconscious of the source of their difficulties. In addition they may be unorganized and, even if they recognize the role of the organization, will lack the knowledge to make themselves heard. Yet its inability to anticipate effects, and its ignorance of the environment, may make it difficult for the organization to believe in clear-cut or necessary relationships between effects on these groups and its own actions.

Consequently, some individuals within the organization will feel that the institutionalization of feedback channels for groups seen as only peripherally involved (if that) may serve to render the organization vulnerable to complaints, and to influence attempts of dubious urgency and untoward consequences. In short, to represent the interests of those who cannot represent themselves may just be asking for trouble. Even the proposal to investigate possible effects where they can be sensed only vaguely may evoke criticism and resistance. An example might be the investigation of the effects of space science fiction. Such investigations are characteristically reacted to as "far-fetched." Yet if one is concerned with the extent of traceable effects of organizational action, one can establish the limits only by going beyond them to demonstrate at some point that there is no traceable effect.

Adequate System Criteria

For any organization, then, whether it is or is not charged with the responsibility to assess second-order consequences, the establishment of an adequate feedback system depends initially on the following three conditions:

1. Its ability to distinguish among a multiplicity of audiences in its environment, vocal and silent, actual and potential.
2. Its capacity to assess the extent to which these audiences will be affected by its programs.
3. Its adroitness in obtaining feedback information within the time available for acting on it.

The organization must next consider the extent to which it wants and can afford to allocate resources to the formal representation of these otherwise unrepresented interests within its feedback network. The determination of the method of obtaining feedback — by continuous narrow or broad spectrum scanning, by periodical or one-shot research, or by the elevation of "trial balloons" — will have to depend on the magnitude and acuteness of anticipated consequences, and on the estimated or intuited probability that specific kinds of feedback information could affect decision making in the organization constructively.

Stating this in the more general terms of the preceding chapters, the decision must be made whether there will be reliance on continuing statistical series of the sort proposed by Gross or on research of the sort discussed by Biderman.

For an organization deeply committed to the exploration of secondary consequences there will obviously be less necessity to justify its search for effects. But the task will be no less formidable. That is because problems of coordinating diverse projects within the research function and of integrating a research department with other subgroups will be greater. These problems will be discussed briefly in succeeding sections of this chapter.

NASA's Salient Groups

To this point, we have been discussing organizational feedback from external sources in quite general terms. Now, let us look specifically at NASA's concern with feedback from the salient groups that are responsive to its space efforts. We can start by asking ourselves the following three questions:

1. Who are NASA's salient external groups?
2. In what sense can these groups influence the activities and policies of that organization?
3. What problems of feedback can arise from these groups?

An attempt to determine empirically such responsive groups, their compositions, and interrelationships, would be vital to any research that attempted to understand the operation of feedback from the environmental system into NASA. Obviously, we might be concerned with regulatory groups, such as Congressional committees; groups that may in some ways be in competition with NASA's activities, such as the military missile-weapons program and its research and development; groups that are working on similar problems in the private sector, such as business and professional associations; and groups that might perceive themselves to be in competition with NASA for technologists and scientists, such as the teaching professions, private industry, and other government agencies.

Two examples will indicate the kinds of feedback difficulties that

NASA has encountered and can expect to encounter in the foreseeable future in its attempts to assess the impact of its programs.

1. Researchers studying NASA-supported contracts — to determine "spin-off" of technical innovations and products that could possibly enrich areas unrelated to space — have discovered that some NASA contractors have been reluctant to communicate details of such spin-off back to NASA for fear that governmental regulatory agencies might get the wrong impression and think that contracts specifically granted for the development and manufacture of space-related "hardware" were being misapplied to private industrial ventures. Solution of this sort of problem, bland as it may seem, could require widespread innovations in communications between the involved groups.

2. The Space Committee's study of responses to NASA's pamphlet on welding techniques[6] indicated that often respondents could comment only in terms of familiar criteria of format, clarity of exposition, and so forth, as they had not had occasion to develop categories by which to evaluate concepts related to technological innovation.

In order to explore these areas in a more rigorous manner, it might be advisable first to make an intensive study of a particular group that works under a commission from NASA. One purpose of the study would be to determine the group's relationships with other outside organizations, and with individuals and departments within NASA itself. Another purpose would be to find out the processes by which such a group learns and determines the kind of information that is to be fed back to particular individuals within NASA, the way in which such information is actually fed back, and the way in which NASA itself feeds back such information to its internal subsystems.

Feedback from Internal Sources

An organization is a system of structured relations. But an organization also acts, and such actions imply intellectual, rational, decision-making processes. Both organization structure and the nature of the intellectual phase of organizational life (decision making) limit the modern organization's ability to absorb feedback

---

[6] John F. Archer and Stephen A. Greyser, "A Study of the Impact of 'Selected Welding Techniques,'" a document of the Committee on Space Efforts and Society of the American Academy of Arts and Sciences, 1964.

information, especially data regarding second-order social consequences. Learning how to perceive or detect these consequences is
difficult; it is even more difficult to make these perceptions effective
within the organization.

Channeling of Information

Thus the fact that information has reached the organization does
not necessarily mean that it has reached the decision-making groups
within the organization. An angry phone call may get no further
than the switchboard operator. A letter may get to an executive's
office only to be stopped by his secretary. Subordinates in an organization may sit on evidence of their own failures. Even if information should get through to decision-making groups, it may
be so watered down or deliberately distorted as to have very little
of its initial force; its intent may sometimes even be inverted. The
structure of interpersonal relationships that permits the organization
to coordinate the actions of its members often blocks, or at least
severely limits, communication of information between the feedback system and the rest of the organization.

Important in the disposition of feedback information are the
roles within the organization that may be characterized as *boundary
roles*. These are the roles that bring the organizational member into
contact with the organization's environment. Individuals in these
roles include purchasing agents; public relations, sales, and marketing personnel; secretaries (under some circumstances); research
people; and, of course, top officers who "represent" the organization
to many publics.

Individuals in boundary roles are in most cases the first recipients
of information about reactions to organizational programs. A University of Michigan study of role conflict[7] found that the occupant
of a boundary role usually lacked the formal authority to influence
and, if necessary, to coerce those outside his own department. He
could not force others to act in accordance with the demands of
his role without jeopardizing good will he might later need. He
certainly was unable to influence the behavior of those superior to
him in status, except in a most careful fashion.

Yet, despite these limitations of influence, the boundary-role
occupant may develop indirect power over policy through his
ability to control access to information fed back from outside

---

[7] See R. L. Kahn, D. M. Wolfe, R. P. Quinn, J. D. Snoek, and R. A. Rosenthal, *Organizational Stress: Studies in Role Conflict and Ambiguity* (New York:
John Wiley & Sons, Inc., 1964).

sources. In those situations where other feedback channels do not exist, it may be impossible to check on the accuracy of the information he relays. Thus he may be able to determine which respondent to the organization's program receives a hearing within the organization. He may also determine which sources within the organization will be contacted. For example, the secretary to an executive cannot control what he may say to a caller, but she can often influence greatly not only which caller will get to see him, but for how long and how soon.

Yet, because it is the occupant of the boundary role who acts as a "traffic officer" to incoming information, much criticism from outside the organization is apt to be directed toward him. Other individuals within the organization, on hearing complaints from outside sources about the boundary-role occupant, may not realize that such criticism may be the result of his performing his job correctly rather than the result of his own arbitrary behavior. Thus the occupant of the boundary role may find himself in a peculiarly vulnerable position. He is always open to criticism from within the organization for the way in which he deals with those outside. (Here we are assuming that those outside can, on occasion, get around the boundary-role occupant, if they so desire. (Given enough motivation on the part of those outside, this is generally possible.)

In many organizations — NASA is an excellent example — incoming feedback may be directed toward a boundary or liaison individual who is viewed by an outside group as being particularly sympathetic to the group's problems. Consequently, it may be the tacit responsibility of such an organizational person to "translate" the information into terms more familiar to policy makers; to tone down or recast complaints in such a way as to allow diplomatic presentation to organizational executives and thus to overcome resistances due to conflicts between organizational values and the values of the outside group, as well as to protect the outside group and the liaison individual himself.

The preceding refers, of course, only to feedback from external groups that would typically respond to NASA's programs. The problem of representing the effects of NASA's activities on ordinarily nonresponsive groups and "innocent bystanders" has been outlined in general terms earlier in this chapter.

Since it is the boundary-role occupants who often have the responsibility for launching feedback messages on their trips through an organization, it would seem that special attention should be paid to filling these roles. Too often, individuals are placed in boundary-role positions without full attention being paid to the fact that the prime function of those roles is the faithful transmission of vital information.

Authority System Pressures

An organization is not a homogeneous unit with a single interest, nor are all elements in identical contact with the environment. As an organization grows in size, it usually also grows in complexity through necessary differentiation in functions. The executive who previously prided himself on the extent and intensity of his personal contact with subordinates, suppliers, and consumers, discovers in the course of expansion that the demands of intraorganizational administration increasingly isolate him from outside contacts, forcing him to rely on what the staff reports to him concerning extraorganizational reactions to his acts.[8] He may or may not establish individual roles or departments charged with the elicitation and transmission of feedback. Whether he does or not, his view always tends to become constricted by the incompleteness of scope of particular subordinates due to the limitation of their contacts and responsibilities and to his own necessary reliance on their delayed presentation of summaries and reports rather than on his personal and immediate experiences. Often these subordinates are themselves dependent on other subordinates, so that the executive hears only echoes or reverberations of the original feedback messages.

Both the authority system and goal factoring in an organization stress subgoal and, hence, subgroup loyalty: the boss and his subordinates. Goal factoring, which is the organization's purpose or mission, is almost entirely in terms of primary consequences of actions. Authority roles in our society are structured in terms of certain basic rights with regard to subordinates, expressed in terms of "unity of command."

---

[8] However, in a given context this may be functional for the organization. Here is an observation from a previous study, involving a medium-sized company. The organization had been losing money for several years, and it was obvious that the operation had to be shut down. All of the staff executives, with the exception of the president, had personal contact with the line employees in the plant, and none of them could bear to issue the order that would result in the loss of jobs for men they knew, especially since the employees were older men with long seniority status (the younger men in the plant had already been let go) who would have difficulty in finding other employment. The president, however, after consulting with his board, was able to issue the shut-down order. One factor that permitted him to "give the word" was his lack of personal contact with the men who were affected, and his insulation from the human consequences of his decision.

The result of these two considerations, the kind of goal factoring and the nature of authority-role expectations, is pressure on all individuals for loyalty to primary subgoals and the authoritative groupings to which they are assigned. The means become the ends. Thus a never-ending problem is how to stimulate "efficient," as opposed to "effective," behaviors, that is, behaviors oriented to both primary *and* secondary consequences rather than to just primary actions.

Other Organizational Barriers

Status levels may also act as barriers inhibiting the upward and downward flow of feedback to the extent that executives may tend to withhold information among themselves. Similarly, not only may the upward flow of information be naturally diminished and distorted as it ascends level by level, but complaints regarding the behavior of executives are ordinarily confined to subordinate levels, both to ensure the security of the complainants and to maintain a free flow of information within that particular status level.

Boundaries between two departments may act as impedances to feedback, even though these departments are functionally dependent, because no two departments have identical interests. As a result, the departments may use different criteria of evaluation and different frames of reference. On the basis of recent research findings, we would expect that the degree of misunderstanding his organizational colleagues have of a given person's responsibilities (and thus his needs for information) increases with the magnitude of the barriers that exist between them. Barriers between different levels of departments may be so nearly impermeable that executives are virtually cut off from feedback to their organizational actions.

A social structure, or departmental structure that insulates the decision-making group from learning the results of its actions can develop for a number of reasons. Those who receive the feedback information may not know what elements of it are important, or to whom such data would be important, and so do not effectively relay the information.

Then again, the feedback information may be interpreted in a way that systematically supports already determined actions. It is said, in this connection, that research conducted by members of an organization's own staff is sometimes selectively developed for the sole purpose of supporting the predetermined decisions of highly placed executives. Consequently, one of the strongest arguments regularly invoked in favor of retaining consultants or outside researchers is to get the benefit of a "fresh, objective, and unbiased" point of view.

To the extent that intraorganizational units have overlapping or conflicting functions, the flow of feedback will be impeded under conditions of increased pressure, or in situations where the existences, missions, or interests of one of the units is perceived as being at stake. Typical examples of such conflict can probably be found in accounts of the relationships between such departments as credit and sales, production and quality control, and, of course, union and management. Feedback from one such group to another is often withheld because it might undermine the position of the unit in which it originated. For example, it is doubtful that a union steward would relish passing on to a time-study man the information that production line workers had innovated new methods of relaxing on the job while still maintaining production standards.

Whether chronic, recurring, or situational limitations of the time in which decisions must be made or limitations on the amount of money available to investigate a problem have more effect on the transmission and results of feedback information is difficult to say. Both the necessity to act within a limited time and the necessity to reduce costs make it impossible to canvass adequately the relevant external sources. Under these pressures, decisions must often be made on the basis of the expert advice of research workers who ordinarily would merely have transmitted the feedback. Whether or not the advice of research people is heeded depends on the urgency of the situation and the extent to which such advice represents a departure from the traditional functioning of the organization.

Fantasies, Constructive and Destructive

Over time an organization fabricates an idealized self-image, which becomes a sort of mythological basis for the organizational ideology that explains "what the hell we are doing." The elements of fantasy in the view of the organization involve, usually, some distortion of reality and, therefore, prejudice the evaluation of incoming information. For example, an organization easily develops the fantasy element of essential rectitude, which then leads its members to discount any information that would suggest otherwise. In some degree organizational myths are essential for continuity of purpose. If the myth of "what the hell we are doing" is overly responsive to signals from the environment, it cannot serve as an organizational balance wheel. Yet at some point there is an optimum balance between the benefits of continuity of purpose and the costs of biased information.

We cannot say, on the face of it, that misassessment of reality is necessarily maladaptive. Unjustified optimism, for example, has often given to supporters of minority political candidates, innovative groups, and underground organizations, to name a few, the energy and morale necessary to realize some of their goals against formidable odds. An important study with regard to feedback, therefore, would be to measure the gap between the idealized and the real version for several different kinds of organization, and the implications of discrepancy between the two.

In more frequent, but less noble instances, groups develop fictions that help them avoid cognizance of the less humane consequences of their activities. Consider:

1. Certain organizations — such as magazine subscription services, "benevolent" finance companies, funeral homes, and some insurance companies — need to maintain the belief that they are engaged in the adventuresome defense of the free enterprise system or in the promotion of the public welfare, in order to shield themselves from the possibility they may be exploiting some or all of their customers, if only inadvertently.

2. The personnel department, administering a company's early retirement program — which has as its purpose the removal of organizational "dead weight" by dropping older employees whether or not they want to leave — feels compelled to justify its actions by convincing itself that it is "rewarding" loyal employees with retirement while they are still young.

It seems probable that no organization actively seeks feedback information that contradicts such necessary organizational beliefs unless, of course, it is provoked to do so by some kind of crisis.

Along this line, an organization may erect barriers to information about the effects of its actions if these effects, in part, contradict some of the goals and values of the organization. Redevelopment authorities and urban renewal commissions are sometimes in this position, especially during the early stages of their programs. Although members of these organizations would like better and lower-cost housing for low-income and minority groups, they often have to implement policies that result in the dislocation of families in just these groups, who then have great difficulty finding accommodations they can afford. Recognition of these consequences not only threatens the humanistic self-image of the members of the organization, but is also perceived as giving aid and comfort to the opponents of any kind of urban redevelopment.

Suicidal Organizational Behavior

Until now we have been describing how individuals may defensively rationalize or deny knowledge of the adverse effects that they might inflict on others in pursuit of otherwise legitimate organizational goals. Few of these situations will actually jeopardize the organization's survival. However, in cases where the organization maintains rigid, basic ideological positions or programs antipathetic to the needs and welfare of affected groups (or of the organization itself), the resulting resistance to feedback may well threaten the very survival of the organization whose values are being preserved in the short run. Examples of such suicidal behavior are easily found in recent history:

1. The European nation that, ignoring the reactions and counsels of its allies and some of its own strategies, persisted in the debilitating pursuit of a doomed colonial policy in order to maintain nostalgic fantasies of an imperial identity.

2. The southern states that, in blind dedication to states' rights, disputed powerful, rational, and internal pressures for an end to racial discrimination, and thus failed to anticipate the certain consequences of resistance: the intervention of the federal government and the enactment of legislation forever limiting the power of the individual states.

On the industrial level, the more frequent, though obviously blander manifestations of the problem are instances where an organization persists in manufacturing a product, in spite of mounting losses and seriously diminishing demand, because that product is intimately linked with the organization's self-conception. An illustration of this can be seen in Chrysler Corporation's reluctance to give up production of its DeSoto line of cars in spite of steadily dwindling consumer acceptance and increasingly heavy financial losses.

Further consideration of the manner in which organizational values impair the proper evaluation of feedback in decision making will appear in the section that immediately follows. It should be recalled, however, that the thesis of this passage is that the preservation of some myth as to the character of the organization is desirable to the extent that it gives continuity to the organization's activities, but is undesirable when it causes decision makers and information gatherers to distort reality beyond a critical point.

Impedance by Individuals

In addition to organizationally based processes that limit or in some way distort the distribution of incoming information, there are many reasons why individual members of an organization might either consciously or unconsciously block a feedback system. Among these are fear of the consequences should a prior decision be known to have been a serious mistake, loyalty to others, inability to appreciate the importance of information, interdepartmental hostility or hostility to the organization, the desire to gain power or prestige and advancement in the organization through control of the information, and a sense of powerlessness to affect policy. These are but a few of the many individual motivations and orientations that can lead to the interruption of a feedback process.

There are also individual differences in personality characteristics associated with differential uses of organizational feedback channels, including tendencies to limit or increase communications selectively to colleagues of different status levels under some conditions.[9]

Feedback and Its Effects on Policy

Feedback regarding organizational efforts is of little value unless it eventuates in corrective action. What determines how much weight particular feedback information will have in the organizational decision process?

Let us begin with a cautionary tale. In the following example, an individual who was at the same time a consumer of an organization's methods and also one of its more distant, less salient members attempted to introduce a fundamental methodological innovation:

In 1900, information was received by the U.S. Navy that the system by which the Navy fired its guns at targets could be improved by a wide margin. The techniques in use at the time involved waiting until the roll of the ship brought the ship's guns on target, and then pressing the firing button that discharged the gun. The technological innovation, developed by a naval officer named Sims, was to alter the "gear ratio in the elevating gear to permit a

[9] See Robert K. Merton and Daniel Lerner, "Social Scientists and Research Policy," in *The Planning of Change*, W. G. Bennis, K. D. Benne, and Robert Chin, eds. (New York: Holt, Rinehart and Winston, Inc., rev. ed., 1964).

pointer to compensate for the roll of the vessel by rapidly elevating and depressing the gun." The result was an enormous increase in accuracy (as compared to a pathetic hitting average that had recently been scored in the Spanish-American War), as well as an increase in the number of shots that could be fired within a given period of time.

The reports of vastly improved firing records that were forwarded to the Naval Department elicited no reaction. Sims, on learning that his first reports lay neglected in the files of the offices to which he had sent them, sent additional reports and copies of the reports to other officers in the fleet, so that the Ordinance Bureau could not suppress them. The Ordinance Bureau then reacted by making three points: (a) there was no need to improve U.S. Naval fire power, as it had been adequate to win the Spanish-American War; (b) U.S. equipment was as good as the British with whom Sims had worked in developing his system, and, anyhow, the problem of U.S. accuracy lay with the men who were responsible for gunnery and not with the equipment; (c) continuous-aim firing was inherently impossible.

Only by circumventing usual lines of communication was Sims able to procure rational responses to his report.[10]

In attempting to explain why information that might have improved a basic practice of the organization was fought so fiercely, Morison notes the following four possibilities: (1) the suggestion came from a man who was at the time obscure and without status; (2) the information came from a source distant from the United States, and so it was more easily discounted; (3) the information was critical of techniques developed by the people to whom the information was sent; and (4) though the information suggested important improvements and presented evidence of their feasibility, the area was one where key figures in the organization felt improvements were not necessary. Thus, Morison notes, the first two possibilities permitted the organization members to discount the suggestions; the last two gave them the motivation for doing so.

Devalued Data Situations

We can hypothesize that feedback is apt to be discounted in two general types of situations.

1. If the response to an organizational action comes either (a)

---

[10] Summarized from E. E. Morison, "A Case History of Innovation," in *Engineering and Science Monthly*, 13 (April 1950).

from individuals who are not functionally related to the organization, who are not conceived of as intended targets of that action, or who are not regarded as legitimate critics of the organization; or (b) from individuals perceived as having little status and power, or as being geographically or socially distant (and, presumably, in either case seen as therefore irrelevant).

2. If the response represents severe criticism of an organizational program to which members of the organization are personally committed.

In a situation in which a devalued group within the organization's environment reacts critically to a valued program, we might expect the organization to justify its inattention to the source of opposition by portraying it as biased, irrational, or ignorant. Thus, Gamson has found that pro-fluoridation groups often stereotype their opposition as reactionary, and are therefore unable to appreciate arguments against fluoridation or to understand the basis of such arguments. Consequently, they may be virtually unable to modify their own approach toward another method that might more effectively allay the fears of the opposition.[11]

How can an organization counteract tendencies to ignore or discredit feedback coming from sources deemed unimportant or hostile and, at the same time, preserve the necessary screening functions that prevent decisions from being buried under a mass of incoming information. The concern here involves not only the maintenance of responsiveness to potentially relevant feedback but the development of rational rather than defensive criteria for the evaluation of feedback.

It was noted earlier that this problem is most complex in regard to the elicitation of feedback from audiences (usually unorganized) that respond to programs only indirectly if at all. As this is viewed primarily as a problem most likely to be solved through research, it will be discussed in the succeeding section on the use of research in maintaining feedback.

Dissident External Elements

The task of representing within the feedback system persons — either organized or unorganized — who are the unintended or incidental targets of organizational activities is obviously much easier when those individuals attempt to make themselves heard. Whether

---

11 W. A. Gamson, "On the Benefits of Faulty Communication," unpublished paper, 1962.

or not the organization is initially receptive to the respondents, it may legitimize their attempts at communication by inviting them to respond more formally, to file a complaint, or to contact a group representing similar interests. Sometimes the invitation is only a ploy designed to inhibit the flow of negative feedback by making the process unpalatably complicated. But more often it is an organization's fumbling attempt to assess the seriousness and articulateness of external concern.

If the respondents are culturally, professionally, or politically influential, the organization may request their presence at meetings, as with congressional committee hearings for example. Intentionally or unintentionally, this kind of legitimization can facilitate the coalescence of isolated respondents into organized interest groups, such as the formation of *ad hoc* stockholders' committees during annual meetings. The degree of organizational sympathy or hostility to the respondents does not necessarily imply that the organization will resist tendencies toward the formalization of such groups; even an antagonistic organization may wish to have its opposition out in the open in order to combat it more effectively.

Co-optative Internal Responses

When dissident environmental elements seriously threaten an organization's survival (particularly in the infancy of an innovative organization), it may attempt to incorporate those elements into its own structure. Selznick calls this maneuver "co-optation" — "the process of absorbing new elements into the leadership or policy-determining structure of an organization as a means of averting threats to its stability or existence."[12] The co-optative response may have as its aim the neutralization of the opposition by making it share responsibility for controversial actions,[13] or it may represent a genuine attempt at adaptation and flexibility through the introduction of new values and information into policy making. Regardless of its intention, co-optation often results in loss of some degree of organizational control to the elements that have been co-opted. That they should acquire power within the organization should not be surprising since the reason for their co-optation includes recognition of their power outside the organization.

[12] See Philip Selznick, "Foundations of the Theory of Organization," *American Sociological Review*, 13 (1948), 25–35.

[13] At political conventions the necessity for party unity dictates that opposition leaders second, and thus bless, the nominated candidates whom they had previously bitterly opposed.

However, as the organization matures and gains security it should become capable of interacting with other groups less defensively, and of incorporating feedback previously judged to be threatening into its decision processes without having to incorporate the sources of the feedback themselves.

Circumventing Internal Barriers

In extreme cases where those whom the organization affects cannot make themselves heard — due to organizational bias or structural incapacity to "hear" — there may be no other recourse than to inform or to influence other groups more powerful than their own, or to organize themselves into pressure groups and thereby develop incentives or sanctions that will force the organization to respond.

A fascinating case in point is provided by the Council for a Livable World, a unique kind of lobby organization composed mainly of academic and professional people, which seeks to influence governmental decision making on matters relevant to peace and war. To implement its program, the Council gives financial support to the campaigns of political candidates sympathetic to its views, attempts to inform candidates on topics in which its members may have some expertise (such as the nuclear arms race), prepares position papers, conducts seminars, and provides assistance in political speech writing. The Council promotes the views of individuals, who previously might have expressed their reaction to governmental policies only indirectly, through advertisements and professional meetings, and through restricted "expert testimony" on scientific matters. By having something to offer *besides* feedback, by actively backing political campaigns, and by presenting its members as persons who wish to aid congressmen in the performance of their duties and, of all things, in the *maintenance* of their prerogatives, the Council is able to circumvent many of the barriers that usually prevent private individuals from having a continuing voice in government.

Problems of Administrators

The identification of managers with organizational programs they have sponsored tends to be very strong. Our own personal observation and research have continually produced examples of resistance by managers to feedback data that calls into question decisions they have made. A manager's decisions constitute a demonstration of his competence that is witnessed and evaluated by his colleagues within the organization. Should his colleagues perceive him as having a low batting average, he will lose influence within the organization and will eventually be penalized by failure to gain the rewards given to the highly valued. To expect managers to deal dispassionately with evidence of their errors, then, is to mistake the nature of the managerial situation, in fact, to mistake the nature of human beings.

One somewhat questionable solution to this difficulty is to direct incoming information to levels in the organization superior to those levels on which the decisions are made. This means the group that evaluates the program is superior to the group that initiates it. This approach, however, seems likely to produce many other organizational problems in its wake. An immediate drawback is that the boundary-role individual who transmits evidence of error is in a position of great power vis-à-vis the initiator of action. Thus the whole system is productive of the high drama of continuing office politics.

Another possible solution, perhaps less sure in relation to a single organizational program but more likely to gain support from the managers, is for each decision maker to assume responsibility for evaluating feedback that relates to his own program. Here, however, still another problem arises. Take the case of a manager who is highly competent in initiation and administration of programs, but who is less competent in the evaluation of new information and the development of modifications of existing programs. This latter difficulty can perhaps be remedied by bringing managers who have decision-making responsibilities into association with staff individuals who can play evaluative and innovative roles.

Problems of Innovators

The studies in role conflict and ambiguity by Kahn *et al.*[14] paid some attention to individuals who are in such evaluative and innovative roles. As conceptualized in their studies, the innovative role is more sheltered from the day-by-day organizational pressures and so permits greater individual flexibility. The occupant of the role is more likely than most members of the organization to be responsive to new information and to develop appropriate programs of responses. The problem that individuals in such roles encounter is one of how to evaluate and innovate within the confines of the organizational *status quo*, without becoming identified too closely with, or completely disassociated from, the rest of the organization. Identification with professional reference groups is usually neces-

[14] R. L. Kahn *et al.*, *op. cit.*

sary for adequate functioning of such an individual. This identification provides necessary support in times of stress, even though it may, in some situations, suggest to managers (correctly) that the occupant of this role has loyalties outside the organization, and thus is not completely allied with it.

Individuals who play an innovative role sometimes find that they are developing a certain alienation from the value system of the organization, and that their influence depends on colleague respect for their expertise as well as their status position in the organization structure. The professional researcher — especially the individual who can both develop the findings and work out the applications of them — is very much in this sort of situation. His value to the organization depends on the acceptance of his findings and judgments. However, the value of his findings and judgments, in turn, depends to an extent on his being sheltered from routine task pressures, even while he is fully in touch with what is happening. A member of middle management who sees himself as someone concerned with a wide sector of organizational programs, rather than a narrowly defined task, also plays such a role. Sometimes such men function as interpreters of research, or as directors of research or planning groups.

Dangers of Organizational Feedback

Although it is important for an organization to be able to use information relating to its actions, immediate responsiveness to feedback is not always desirable. One image of organizational functioning currently in fashion portrays it as a dynamic organism that is constantly aware, infinitely responsive to subtle changes within its environment, adapting reflexively to all crises, and continuously blossoming with creative innovations. Yet, any organizational change involves a great many realignments in the interrelationships of personnel — changes of jobs and task responsibilities — and sometimes new definitions of the organization's basic purpose and objectives.

The more drastic the change, the more drastic will be the actual and necessary realignments. It is important to note the differentiation between "actual" and "necessary" realignments, for there is usually a gap between a change in organizational operations and the modification in structure that may be necessary to support that change. Our prejudice nowadays is to interpret the gap as the result of rigidity, but it may as easily arise from the sort of flexibility that masks panic in time of crisis and ambivalence of purpose in day-to-day functioning.

It is, therefore, necessary for those who manage an organization to be aware of the total picture of their commitments when evaluating the desirability of changes in the organization's operations and directions. A useful and rare quality in a top executive is the capacity to remain stolid in the face of a flurry of demands, and then to make a reasoned and sound judgment.

Overresponsive Reactions

An organization that is hyperresponsive to its environment is apt to sacrifice those parts of its program that are not of central importance, and that are most likely to come under some criticism, whether they are desirable elements or not. Certain kinds of research (with political implications) are unlikely to be sponsored by foundations, simply because such organizations are concerned about their vulnerability to criticism. Organizations are often more responsive to criticism than to reactions favorable to their programs. Thus an organization that is concerned with the intercession of regulatory bodies puts so much energy into forestalling or meeting criticism from such an outside agency that it often ends up regulating itself more severely than would otherwise have been the case. To illustrate: the reactions of the television audience to the first program of the Medic series were quite varied — 129 letters were received, of which 18 were critical. It was the minority of critical comments rather than the majority of favorable comments that concerned the staff of the "continuity acceptance" department of the television network. Every letter or phone call received by the television network was given a carefully phrased reply containing the network's reasons for presenting the program.[15]

Similarly, public utility organizations may be hyperresponsive to single complaining individuals for fear that a dispute may establish precedents against them, or that the Public Utilities Commission may view such complaints as a valid reason for opposing rate increases.

Criticism via the mass media is apt to receive great attention from any organization. Departments of social welfare are particularly responsive to newspaper attack. Although these departments

[15] Case material folder on "Business Administration and Government Policy," Report G-20, Business and Government 201, Harvard University Graduate School of Business Administration.

are relatively invulnerable, since they provide an absolutely essential community service, a demand for investigation of department practices by a newspaper will result in a serious reassessment of practice within the agency, often with the concomitant drop in morale and sometimes with functionally gratuitous shifts of personnel.

Feedback from competing or regulatory organizations may be more salient than feedback from consumers. For example, the average TV viewer may not be bothered by a dearth of news information and cultural programs on a particular channel, but the station may nonetheless increase its news coverage because it is concerned about the views of regulatory agencies.

Overresponsiveness is particularly likely to occur when an organization has developed a program that elicits a flood of responses from some public (a program of trade shows might be an example) and when this flood is directed toward members of the organization superordinate to those who initiated the program. Superiors receiving such criticisms are apt to be very sensitive to the external relations of the organization. Not having been directly involved in the execution of the program, they are not disposed to give adequate weight to the considerations that prompted it. The result is likely to be effective pressure for change.

Whether these are examples of overresponsiveness, or rather of appropriate caution, or of feelings of social responsibility is difficult to assess. Each case represents a sacrifice of program aims in deference to actual or anticipated criticism. Responsiveness as strong as this reinforces, in organizational personnel, feelings of vulnerability to outside appraisals and certainly heightens whatever tendency there is to play it safe in program development.

Oscillation and Flooding

Another indicator of overresponsiveness to feedback is a constant oscillation of organizational direction. Overresponsiveness resulting in oscillation of behavior often occurs in an organization that not only has difficulties in accomplishing its primary goals but has poor criteria for evaluating its methods. Thus a business organization that shows a poor earnings performance may respond by repeated shifts of its organizational policies, without waiting long enough to evaluate any one policy. This disposition to oscillate disastrously between contradictory policies is obviously not frequent or the rate of demise of organizations would be exceedingly high. However, moderate versions of this occur with sufficient frequency to challenge any platitudinous notion that "responsiveness" to feedback is at all times and in all ways beneficial.

Managers of an organization should be alert to still another danger: too much feedback. Since it is the nature of the organization both to over- and underreact, management efforts to dampen feedback should be an integral part of the feedback system. Thus the ideal organizational system is one that is geared to avoid the possibilities of oscillation in response, and overresponse, as well as of imperviousness to information.

The aim of decision makers should be to achieve balanced responsiveness to relevant parts of their environment, neither overresponding nor oscillating, nor permitting the pursuit of mistaken policies that are based either on too much or too little feedback from the environment.

Perhaps these warnings against oscillation and flooding may sound like an uncalled-for injunction to use common sense. The injunction may be justified, however, by the vast amount of writing on organizational practices that stresses flexibility of response and increased flow of information with no hint of the dangers involved in overresponsiveness or too much information.

Research in Maintaining Feedback

The development of appropriate research programs is one of the best ways available to the modern organization for maintaining feedback. In this connection, we shall take a brief look at two different kinds, broad continuing and limited *ad hoc* research programs.

Broad Continuing Research

What we have in mind is wide-spectrum research relevant to second-order consequences: research that is directed toward exploring ways in which the organization contributes to a developing society, and toward proposing ways in which the organization can contribute further. Traditional research techniques are unlikely to be useful here. More likely to be of use is a program of continuing research, which maintains close contact with those on the frontiers of action in many spheres of the national life and is directed toward learning how the organization's programs mesh with the actions of other groups.

Those responsible for this sort of wide-spectrum research should be perhaps a new breed of researcher quite different from those responsible for the current more narrowly focused research. These new researchers must be able to move in quickly on new ideas, grasp readily the thrust of a project in spite of the absence of proved indices, develop appropriate new methods, visualize new ways in which the organization might function, and be able to interpret the implications of all this for top-level management.

Obviously, one of the responsibilities of such continuing research would be to monitor continuing series of social statistics, such as those mentioned in the previous chapters in this volume. But, in addition, the men assigning this responsibility would build sensors into other relevant ongoing activities of the society.

Limited Ad Hoc Research

An organization often has a need for one-time studies to be undertaken by external research groups. Such studies are desirable when the issue is a hot one within the organization and an outside group's objectivity is desired, when the study to be done overtaxes the resources of the internal research group, and when the skills and experience required for the study are more likely to be found outside the organization. The commissioning of limited one-shot studies with outside groups requires that there be within the organization someone who can interpret the findings and make them organizationally meaningful, and also someone who can supervise the work of the outside group. Thus, even though the practice of the organization might be to contract out its research, it is probably of value to the organization to have as one of its members someone with sufficient expertise to interpret the findings.

We ought to recognize that there are a number of functions that can be served by limited research other than the rational gathering of information. Research can easily become an excuse for organizational inaction — "waiting until the returns are in" — or it can serve as a means of reducing conflict within the organization by suggesting that a quarrel on policy be settled by undertaking a study of fact. Research can also serve as a device for introducing criticism into an organization or for fending off criticism.

An executive once admitted that he always sponsors research when he can: if the report supports his position he uses it; if it does not, he buries it.[16] Here, too, research has a function, serving

---

[16] A particularly knotty problem occurs when an organization feels it must strengthen what is essentially a moral or ethical case through research findings in order to persuade an opposing faction that it is pragmatically desirable. This has been the situation with school integration discussions, where current re-

as a dispute settler rather than as information. Some organizations that encourage research are less interested in the possibility of achieving knowledge than in the secondary gains of research, such as the benefits of heavy financial support from government and private foundations or the ability to attract an illustrious staff. For the organization the level of competence of the research undertaken depends on the success of the organization in meriting future support; for the staff, on their own internalized standards. Biderman discussed at greater length in Chapter 4 the problem of setting a system for ongoing research.

Organizational Criteria Needs

However, if research is to be truly useful in the development and processing of feedback, the following four criteria should be met:

1. The problem focused on by the research should either be of a demonstrable functional relationship to the organization, or at least based on a thorough analysis of the organization's existing feedback structure, its goals, and operations — as well as any discrepancies within and between these — and a systematic, though possibly hypothetical, analysis of groups in its environment.

2. The data gathered should be cast in a form appropriate for use in decision making. Often research develops findings that give evaluations of programs without giving any indications of options for subsequent action or any criteria for selecting among these options.

3. Research functions should be formally integrated into the structure of the organization. Catch-as-catch-can research operations often obscure the problems that caused the research to be initiated. Also, the weakness of feedback channels permits the research either to be more easily disregarded by antagonists or to be inflated by protagonists, while offering little opportunity for correction by those most competent to do so. Often within an organization one department will conduct research that has bearing on another department's program, without any commitment from the latter group that the research will be used. In such cases, it would seem better to have the operating department subsidize some of the costs of the research or otherwise involve itself in some way. If it refuses, then it might be better in the long run to postpone the research until more integrated organizational commitments can be achieved.

---

search is inadequate to support either side, and where, at any rate, the constitutional aspects of the decision must be somewhat independent of the issue that the research seeks to prove.

4. Within the research program itself, there should be a rational coordination of continuing research with both narrow and wide commissions, and limited *ad hoc* research. Organizations that can neither coordinate nor distinguish these types of research often encounter difficulties. We have observed the far too frequently recurring situation where a one-shot research survey is given oracular significance, although only a series of longitudinal samplings could provide the necessary information.

Organizational Value Limitations

Special constraints must be noted, for both the researcher and the organization, when the research is used as a means of furnishing feedback. The most important constraint derives from the implicit or explicit value system of the contracting organization. Consider:

> If it is true that the policy maker always assumes certain features of his problem situation as *given*, as *constant*, as *modifying*, it at once limits the range and type of research that will be done with his support.[17]

The organization may direct the researcher to investigate one aspect of a problem, and to ignore other related aspects. For example, the task may be to find the best means of increasing production, without considering the effects of that method on employee morale. To the extent that the researcher accepts the value limitations of the contracting organization, he may be supporting the organization's institutionalized barriers against certain kinds of feedback, especially feedback that is at variance with organizational beliefs and values.

Researchers are often limited (legitimately) in the extent to which they are free to furnish feedback in the best of circumstances. It is generally felt that it is not within the bounds of the research individual's authority to communicate to the executive group in the organization all information that comes his way regarding the organization's actions. He may be bound to protect the confidential sources of his data in order to secure factual replies to his questions. He may become constrained not to communicate any information or impressions that might be construed as "meddling" in nonresearch areas of the organization. For example, if he should learn, incidental to his work, that in one department there is a great deal of discontent with some department head, he might not relay such information. Even if a situation should develop within the organiza-

---

[17] Robert K. Merton and Daniel Lerner, *op. cit.*, p. 63.

tional environment that presented a survival danger to the organization, the research individual — unless he were commissioned to study this particular type of situation — might believe it was not his responsibility to report it. Research mandates tend to be narrow in scope.

Another factor that may make research people hesitate to serve as general feedback channels derives from the very great value given to certain kinds of research findings in certain circumstances. The researcher may find his tentative pronouncements given the full weight of established facts, even though they represent the most mincing, cautious statements of probabilities. (When the domain being studied is unfamiliar to others in the organization, especially, the initiators of the research may be heavily dependent on the research person for the most rudimentary description of the phenomena.) In such situations the researcher may well be hesitant to pass on incomplete data or insecure inferences.

At other times, the researcher may be encouraged, and perhaps himself be eager, to accept the responsibility for critical studies in situations where it is not possible to base decisions purely on the basis of his findings. He may then find himself under pressure, especially in times of crisis, to generalize beyond the point permitted by his data and to defend his generalizations as research findings or, at least, as implications of research. It is only the extremely stable researcher who can always avoid these dangers, especially when under heavy pressure to produce information necessary for organizational decision making.

In addition, however much he may deny — or the organization may deny him — decision-making power, by reporting his findings and deciding on what is relevant and what is not, the social scientist creates an action for which he will always be, in some real though perhaps small sense, responsible. Furthermore, the mere process of choosing a language through which he strives to guard against the possible misinterpretation of his findings may in itself be regarded as an attempt, however niggling, to influence the policy makers to whom he reports.

Three Important Variables

Therefore, to understand the effects of entrusting to social scientists the task of gathering and interpreting feedback concerning the secondary consequences of the space age, it is necessary to explore those aspects of organizational structure that determine the relationship between researchers and other groups in the organization. This is particularly important in reference to the variables that determine the broadness or narrowness of the researcher's commission, the ways in which he may be considered to influence policy making, and the ways in which organizational values limit the responsiveness to and acceptance of specific kinds of research findings. Three important variables with which an exploration might well be concerned are as follows:

1. The nature and degree of the researcher's acceptance of, or alienation from, the organization's values.

2. The location of the research group within, on the boundaries of, or outside of the organization; and also its relation to the decision-making process within the organization.

3. The adequacy both of the organization's conception of the possibilities and limitations of social science and of the social scientist's presentation of his own role.

An understanding of these factors might yield principles by which an organization could design an "ideal" sort of relationship between researchers and other groups within the organization. This relationship would be one in which tendencies to perceive the research group as "alien" would be limited by a realistic understanding of the necessarily different frames of reference, and by attempts to clarify some of the problems of power and influence.

To this end, it might be possible to sample a number of organizations that differ in their structuring of relationships between researchers and the rest of the organization. It might be that under some conditions feedback from outside research groups would have a better chance of reaching policy makers undistorted, and of influencing policy, than a research group located within the organization.

Examining NASA's Requirements

Before the establishment of an integrated research activity on society's reactions to NASA's programs, it would first be necessary to analyze the nature of the messages that NASA's programs communicate implicitly or explicitly to the society. What are NASA's specific communications regarding, for example, its interest in the positive innovational "fallout" of civilian research contracts that it sponsors? What is its image among groups that may be able to influence the response of governmental, business, scientific, and technological groups, and within the general public? We might consider messages that are implicit, rather than explicit, such as the communication of the degree of responsibility, freedom, and restriction placed on the groups with which NASA contracts in order to do research in any particular area.

Another kind of message that may be regarded as more implicit, or as constructed by environmental groups from a variety of sources, refers to NASA's goal. Organizations such as NASA seek to implement a multiplicity of goals — such as the implementation of the manned space program, the support of basic research, the concern for social consequences, and the pursuit of political, quasi-military, and economic objectives — which may actually conflict at some points within the organization itself, particularly in regard to marginal groups, and which may be rightly or wrongly perceived by environmental groups as conflicting.[18]

The recent survey of the American Academy of Arts and Sciences on the reactions of their membership to NASA activities[19] heightens the impression that many individuals perceive some of NASA's goals as potentially conflicting with other national goals. For example: there is the view held among some academicians that a number of NASA's scientific activities are the result of a shotgun wedding between the interests of the peacetime space program and military-political competition with the Soviet Union. Whether or not this appraisal is factually true, it is reasonable to study its development. Certainly, it is an appraisal that can have effects on the organization. It could, for instance, affect the kind of cooperation that NASA needs from colleges and universities.

Social Receptor Roles[20]

Because existing informational feedback systems are interest-oriented, affective-evaluative, opportunistic, and overlook both unorganized interests and the more subtle and distant social secondary effects, they are not adequate to NASA's concern. New NASA-created "receptor organs" are needed. These new receptor organs become new points of what March and Simon[21] call "uncertainty absorption" — points at which the nature of the secondary social reality is finally determined for the rest of the organization.

---

[18] J. S. Goldsen, "Some Social Implications of the Space Program," *The American Behavioral Scientist*, VI (March 1963), 3–17.

[19] Geno Ballotti, ed., "An Analysis and Summary of Responses from Fellows of the American Academy of Arts and Sciences Concerning the Space Program as a Subject for Study and Thought," a photoprinted document of the Committee on Space Efforts and Society of the American Academy of Arts and Sciences, 16 pp.

[20] This section is paraphrased from Thompson, *op. cit.*

[21] See James G. March and Herbert A. Simon, *Organizations* (New York: John Wiley & Sons, Inc., 1958).

In addition to new social science receptor organs within NASA, it is necsssary for the organization to relate itself to many external receptors of this nature — in other government organizations and in the social environment at large. NASA has to take the initiative in encouraging the creation of such organs, and in identifying and establishing communication links with those already existing.

One problem that must be dealt with is that of securing consideration of, and response to, the feedback of secondary social consequences introduced into the organization by the new receptor organs. We suggest that NASA experiment with assigning missions or functions to units in the form of ordered systems of values or goals, rather than in the form of primary goals alone. We do not know whether this approach is possible, but it would be worth a try. It may be possible, and necessary, to create and organize "counterprograms" within NASA based on operationally defined secondary goals fed on operationally perceived secondary consequences, in order to give some effect to those perceptors. An example of a counterprogram is the federal Small Business Administration. Its mission is to modify the secondary consequences of other government programs.

It is highly likely that feedback of second-order consequences cannot become effective until we have well-established social receptor roles with a status of high acceptance so that they become fully integrated into powerful, secure, professionalized, group-decision processes in organizations. Furthermore, since a large part of the problem of giving effect to second-order consequences is interorganizational, structural changes may have to be encouraged in other, related, organizations. Thus a new type of organizational feedback system, which in its own way might match the rapidly expanding bodies of technology and scientific knowledge as a development of great value, would be one which through reliability, accuracy, appropriateness, and speed of transmission of information would reduce the wasteful incoherence of social action.

List of Contributors

Raymond A. Bauer is Professor of Business Administration at the Harvard Business School. He has published numerous scholarly studies of Soviet government and society, including *How the Soviet System Works* (1956), with Alex Inkeles and Clyde Kluckhohn; *The Soviet Citizen: Day-to-Day Life in a Totalitarian Society* (1959), with Alex Inkeles; and *Nine Soviet Portraits*. He is also the co-author, with Ithiel de Sola Pool and Lewis A. Dexter, of *American Business and Public Policy* (1963), which received the Woodrow Wilson Award of the American Political Science Association. He is a Fellow of the American Academy of Arts and Sciences and is currently serving as President of the American Association for Public Opinion Research. He was also a member of the American Academy's Committee on Space, which was responsible for the study on the effects of the space program on American society, and Chairman of the Committee's study group that planned and directed the research for the project.

Albert D. Biderman is a Senior Research Associate at the Bureau of Social Science Research, Inc., Washington, D. C. He is the author of *March to Calumny* (1963), and co-editor, with Elisabeth T. Crawford, of the *Social Role of the Social Sciences* (in press) and, with Herbert Zimmer, of *The Manipulation of Human Behavior* (1961).

Bertram M. Gross is Professor of Administration at the Maxwell Graduate School of Citizenship and Public Affairs, Syracuse University. He has served as Executive Secretary of the Council of Economic Advisers and as Leatherbee Lecturer at the Harvard Business School. He has numerous publications in the fields of administration, political science, and economics, including *The Legislative Struggle* (1953), *The Hard Money Crusade* (1954), with Will Lumer, and *The Managing of Organizations* (1964). In 1953 he was awarded the Woodrow Wilson Award of the American Political Science Association.

341

Robert A. Rosenthal is Lecturer and Research Associate at the Harvard Graduate School of Education and director of a project entitled "Pathways of Identity: A Study of Identification and the Development of Social Roles in Negro Youth" at the Center for Research and Development on Educational Differences at Harvard University. He is an author, with Robert L. Kahn, Donald M. Wolfe, Robert P. Quinn, and J. Diederick Snoek, of *Organizational Stress* (1964).

Robert S. Weiss is Associate Professor of Sociology at Brandeis University and Lecturer in Sociology at the Harvard Medical School Laboratory of Community Psychiatry. His publications include *Processes of Organization* (1956) and, with David Riesman, "Work in Automation: Problems and Prospects," published in *Contemporary Social Problems* (1966), edited by Robert K. Merton and Robert I. Nisbet. He has recently completed an article entitled "Alternate Methods for the Study of Complex Situations" to appear in *Human Organization* (Fall 1966).

Index

www.ingramcontent.com/pod-product-compliance
Lightning Source LLC
Chambersburg PA
CBHW060136280326
41932CB00012B/1536